# Studying Contemporary American Film

# Studying Contemporary American Film

## A Guide to Movie Analysis

**Thomas Elsaesser**

Department of Art and Culture, University of Amsterdam

**Warren Buckland**

School of Film and Television, Chapman University, California

A member of the Hodder Headline group
LONDON
Co-published in the United States of America by
Oxford University Press Inc., New York

First published in Great Britain in 2002 by
Arnold, a member of the Hodder Headline Group,
338 Euston Road, London NW1 3BH

http://www.arnoldpublishers.com

Co-published in the United States of America by
Oxford University Press Inc.,
198 Madison Avenue, New York, NY10016

*British Library Cataloguing in Publication Data*
A catalogue record for this book is available from the British Library

*Library of Congress Cataloging-in-Publication Data*
A catalog record for this book is available from the Library of Congress

ISBN 0 340 76205 5 (hb)
ISBN 0 340 76206 3 (pb)

1 2 3 4 5 6 7 8 9 10

Production Editor: Wendy Rooke
Production Controller: Bryan Eccleshall
Cover Design: Terry Griffiths

Typeset in 11 on 13 Minion by Phoenix Photosetting, Chatham, Kent
Printed and bound in Great Britain by MPG Books, Bodmin, Cornwall

What do you think about this book? Or any other Arnold title?
Please send your comments to feedback.arnold@hodder.co.uk

# Contents

Preface      vii

1      Film theory, methods, analysis      1

2      Classical/post-classical narrative (*Die Hard*)      26

3      *Mise-en-scène* criticism and statistical style analysis
(*The English Patient*)      80

4      From thematic criticism to deconstructive analysis
(*Chinatown*)      117

5      *S/Z*, the 'readerly' film, and video game logic
(*The Fifth Element*)      146

6      Cognitive theories of narration (*Lost Highway*)      168

7      Realism in the photographic and digital image (*Jurassic
Park* and *The Lost World*)      195

8      Oedipal narratives and the post-Oedipal (*Back to
the Future*)      220

9      Feminism, Foucault, and Deleuze (*The Silence of
the Lambs*)      249

Conclusion      284

References      294

Index      303

# Preface

Chuck Kleinhans recounts an anecdote about a society located in a tropical paradise that has never developed biological sciences. This society is surrounded by thousands of species of birds, and bird-watching is a favourite pastime amongst the locals, who enthusiastically watch, discuss, and write about birds. Then, one day,

> some people arrive from another society. They explain that they too want to watch the birds, discuss them, and even write about them, but they will be doing it differently. The newcomers seem as interested in recording data as appreciating the birds' beauty. They spend days studying the same bird and discussing questions such as how birds are able to fly, to migrate, to build the same kind of nest year after year. At first the natives try to laugh off the outsiders. But after a while, when the foreigners start dissecting and labelling birds and claiming that they know more about birds than the people who grew up watching them, it's gone too far. No longer does it seem adequate to dismiss it as a fad. The visitors are now discussing birds using a whole new vocabulary. Enough is enough!
>
> (Kleinhans 1976: 37)

This anecdote can apply to the academic study of film. Academic film studies has created a specialized vocabulary around films, mostly American films (and Hollywood in particular). But the specialized vocabulary is simply the tip of an iceberg: it represents a new way of seeing and thinking – that of 'the expert' – much like the biological sciences in the above story. The expert goes beyond the immediate, common-sense view of films (their consumption as entertainment, or their appreciation) and begins to ask a set of questions that common sense has no need for. Film scholars are experts who develop a passionate interest in 'unusual' theories, and ask 'strange' and 'obscure' questions about films. Where do these questions come from? Why are they important? What do you need to know to ask such a question, let alone answer it?

*Studying Contemporary American Film: A Guide to Movie Analysis* attempts to outline the various questions film scholars ask, to go beyond their obscurity and clarify their meaning and purpose, and to spell out why those questions are important. Furthermore, we do this in a unique way: in each chapter we outline, in as clear and as concise a manner as possible, the premises of a particular film theory, distil a method from it, and then analyse a particular film. In the same chapter we then analyse the same film again with a different method derived from another theory. We have structured and written each chapter in an identical way. We hope that our standardization of each chapter will render each theory and its method of analysis less opaque and more accessible, and make comparison easier. We want to demonstrate that film theories and methods are purposeful, or can be useful once their design is made explicit. The proof of the value of each theory and method is in the results achieved through the analysis of individual films. The critical reader may want to determine whether such results can be achieved without the assistance of the theories and methods outlined in each chapter.

Perhaps we can extend Chuck Kleinhans's anecdote and imagine that some of the natives, who have enthusiastically watched birds all their lives, took an interest in what the experts were saying and writing. This does not mean that they have to accept what the experts said, but it does mean that they critically engage with the experts' way of seeing and thinking by applying, correcting, and developing their ideas. The American philosopher W.V.O. Quine gives the hypothetical example of an anthropologist studying the language of a culture foreign to him. The anthropologist points to a rabbit; a native says 'gavagai', and the anthropologist writes down 'gavagai = rabbit'. However, it is only at meal time that he finds out that 'gavagai' means 'dinner'. The expert's knowledge is not necessarily better than the native's common-sense understanding. Both are asking different questions – the anthropologist in Quine's example is writing a dictionary; the native is thinking about his next meal.

In film studies, the film scholar is asking different questions to the 'native' film spectator. However, if that spectator wants to see films differently, he or she may turn to film studies. Yet many students are put off from film theory and methods largely because, we argue, they are not gradually introduced to the film scholar's way of thinking; students are simply presented with the *results* of that thinking. In this book we have not only published the results of our thinking about a group of important contemporary films. We have also tried to render our thinking processes accessible, to lay bare the procedures by which we achieved our analysis, in the hope that those procedures can be imitated, corrected, and extended. We do not apologize for presenting film theory as a specialized form of knowledge; we cannot and do not want to escape from this fundamental idea. But we do want to make that specialized knowledge accessible. Only after students have absorbed and internalized that specialized knowledge can they hope to go beyond it. Nietzsche argued that the atheist must become a priest before he or she can attack religion. The same applies to all world views, including film theories and their methods of analysis.

After working out the content and structure of each chapter, the authors divided up the writing as follows: Thomas Elsaesser wrote Chapters 2, 8, 9, and the Conclusion. Warren Buckland wrote Chapters 3, 5, 6, 7, and the Preface. Both authors collaborated on Chapter 1, and Warren Buckland wrote the first half of Chapter 4 and Thomas Elsaesser the second half. Both authors, of course, commented on and revised each other's chapters.

*Thomas Elsaesser's acknowledgments*: I want to thank Warren for his persistence in bringing this book about and his patience in managing the logistics of two authors working on a joint project in different physical locations. I also want to thank my colleagues at the University of Amsterdam for their comments on different chapters: Gerwin van der Pol and Patricia Pisters for Chapters 2 and 9, Charles Forceville for his acute remarks on Chapter 4, and Wim Staat for his generous and constructive comments on Chapter 8. My students at New York University in the spring semester 2001 were closer witnesses to the process of revision than they may have liked. I also much appreciated Ed Branigan's good humour and enthusiasm. Finally, it is to the post-viewing sessions of Hollywood movies at the Tuschinski and the Bellevue with Warren, Michael Wedel, and Peter Krämer that the book is dedicated.

*Warren Buckland's acknowledgments*: This book emerged from Thomas's frequent invitations to me to teach on the MA programme in film studies at the University of Amsterdam. As well as thanking Thomas for the numerous invitations, I also wish to thank the many students who listened to my reformulation of various film theories and methods.

My interest in film theory and its methods of analysis go back to the mid-eighties. I first encountered this new and 'exotic' way of seeing film while I was an undergraduate student of photography at Derby College of Higher Education (now the University of Derby). It was at Derby that John Fullerton introduced me to Bazin and Eisenstein and Metz, to *Citizen Kane* and *Apocalypse Now* and early Swedish cinema (there was a lot of early Swedish cinema). In 1999, now located at the University of Stockholm in Sweden, John invited me to teach a three-day workshop on film methodology. My preparation for that workshop enabled me to give shape to and refine many of my chapters in this book. And it was during that workshop that I began to feel nostalgic for those halcyon days in the mid-1980s when John devoted a great deal of his personal time and energy to my initiation into film studies. I hope my chapters in this book show that his efforts were worthwhile.

Additional friends and colleagues have read or listened to various drafts of my chapters, including: Sean Cubitt, Peter Krämer, Lydia Papadimitriou, Jay Stone, and Yannis Tzioumakis, but especially Alison McMahan, who saved me on numerous occasions from making errors in writing and argument. Geoffrey King also contributed his musical knowledge to the opening of *The Fifth Element*, and screenwriter John Leary generously located and provided videos, DVDs, and scripts.

I have presented various chapters at different conferences: the second part of Chapter 3 (on statistical style analysis) at the conference 'Style and Meaning: Textual Analysis, Interpretation, Mise-en-scène', at the University of Reading, 17–19 March 2000; the second part of Chapter 5 (video game logic in *The Fifth Element*) at the conference 'Consumption: Fantasy, Success, Desire', Liverpool John Moores University, 21–2 November, 1998 (published in *Moving Images*, ed. J. Fullerton and A. Söderbergh (London: John Libbey, 2000): 159–164); the second part of Chapter 6 (levels of narration in *Lost Highway*) at 'Wild at Heart and Weird on Top: The Films of David Lynch', University of Sheffield, 13 February 1999. Finally, I presented a version of the second half of Chapter 7 (possible worlds in *Jurassic Park* and *The Lost World*) at the Screen Studies Annual Conference at the University of Glasgow, June 1997, and, in revised form, at 'Technologies of Moving Images', University of Stockholm, 6–9 December 1998. It was subsequently published in *Screen*, 40, 2 (1999): 177–92). I wish to thank John Libbey publishers and Oxford University Press for permission to reprint material.

# 1 Film theory, methods, analysis

## Introduction

What is cinema and what is a film? A mere hundred years old, the cinema has – in its different manifestations – become at once so obvious and so ubiquitous that one hardly appreciates just how strange a phenomenon it actually is. Not only an extraordinary entertainment medium, a superb story-telling machine, it also imparts a kind of presence and immediacy to the world unparalleled elsewhere, and undreamt of before the cinema was 'invented'. Nothing else seems to give such intense feelings; nothing involves people so directly and tangibly in the world 'out there' and in the lives of others. The combination of image, movement, and sound is obviously something quite mysterious in its effects on human beings, almost magical, often described as a kind of doubling of life itself, a form of immortality, a permanent and permanently fascinating mirror. At the same time, it also presents a danger to life, threatening to be its substitute, a replacement, a diversion and a distraction, a virtual world, a permanent fantasy under the weight of which the real – or, at any rate, another reality – seems to disappear, to be destroyed or wither away: the cinema, a man-made world between total truthfulness and total falsehood.

For anyone wanting to study the cinema, its familiarity and immediacy create a problem. Christian Metz wrote that 'a film is difficult to explain because it is easy to understand'. We all have an intuitive sense of what a film is, and what it means. *What*, then, is there to study in film studies? And *why* study it? If we get beyond these fundamental questions we are then faced with another: *How* do we study film? We shall approach each question in turn. A summary is to be found at the end of the chapter.

## 1.1. What do film scholars study?

As with all forms of inquiry, film scholars need to choose 'objects of inquiry' (the domains to which they direct their investigation), and then select problematic aspects of those objects to solve. The film projected in the cinema or consumed on TV is simply the end product of economic, technological, sociological, psychic, and semiotic processes. The film is unproblematic only if we ignore all these processes and position ourselves as consumers. Film scholars are critical consumers because they also reflect upon the processes that lead to the film's existence.

We can identify three broad areas of inquiry in film studies: film history, film theory, and film analysis. The problem with old, or traditional, film histories is that they are informally written by amateur historians. Their histories are governed by at least two underlying assumptions: a teleological assumption that focuses the historian's attention only on films that display technical innovations, and an essentialist assumption proposing that these technical achievements are important because they exploit cinema's essence, or inherent capabilities. Traditional film histories therefore consist of lists of films organized linearly, from primitive films displaying little technical achievement or innovation (which are not perceived to exploit cinema's essence) to more sophisticated (more 'cinematic') films. Furthermore, these histories are usually global and general, based on the writer's selective memory of films or on faulty secondary sources, resulting in a vague and patchy history of film. The 'New Film History', which emerged in the 1970s as film studies became institutionalized in the university, developed specific, delimited (rather than global) areas of film history to research, and carried out this research using rigorous, systematic, and explicit methods, including the extensive citation of primary archival evidence, all of which has resulted in the complete revision and rewriting of traditional film histories.

Film theorists do not study film as an unproblematic, pre-given entity, but as a complex and little-understood medium with it own properties and cultural and social effects. Film theorists therefore challenge and go beyond the common-sense ideological understanding of film as a mere form of harmless entertainment, and instead maintain that it is an intrinsically significant medium integral to twentieth-century modern and postmodern society.

The problem when carrying out film analysis is to make the process manageable. Analysts study film as an abstract and idealized object, extracted from its context of production and reception. Although this may sound like a limitation (as reception studies scholars argue), this process of abstraction and idealization is in fact the necessary first step in making analysis possible. To make the analysis of film manageable involves, initially, delimiting the boundaries of the object of inquiry, which requires the film scholar to judge at least some of the elements which come under the heading of 'film' to be irrelevant and insignificant. Only at a later stage can the discarded elements be studied. This accounts for the progression from structuralism to post-structuralism; the progression in psychoanalytic film theory from the study of unconscious mechanisms (such as voyeurism and fetishism) that fix the film spectator in place, to theories of fantasy that conceive the spectator's relation to the film as fluid and heterogeneous; the shift from the analysis of films to reception studies, which focuses on texts and discourse surrounding a film; and, in cognitive film theory, the progress from the study of the spectator's rational mental activities to the spectator's emotional activities.

Film analysis has traditionally privileged narrative. And one of the many problems narrative raises is to understand its centrality to cinema, which in turn may mean to understand the centrality of narrative in our culture, and by extension, in Western systems of representation. It is in this context that another object of inquiry stands out: what has variously been called 'New', 'post-classical', or 'contemporary' American cinema (with a continued emphasis on Hollywood). Two of the many problems to be addressed include: What is the role of narrative in contemporary American cinema? And: What is the relation between classical and contemporary American cinema? These problems require us to interrogate American cinema both as a formal system and also as an ideological discourse, in order to assess why classical American cinema in particular turned so massively to narrative, and to determine if contemporary cinema is post-narrative, or whether the classical/contemporary distinction is made on other criteria (which presupposes that contemporary cinema continues the narrative tradition of classical cinema). While addressing these two problems throughout *Studying Contemporary American Film*, we examine them in detail in Chapter 2.

How does theory relate to methods and to their application in analysis? The common assumption is that theory functions as a frame of reference for methods, as a conceptual scheme that enables the film scholar to analyse and formulate problems (for example, is post-classical Hollywood cinema dominated by narrative logic?), thereby providing the analyst with guidance on what to look for when analysing a film, and how best to analyse it. In a now celebrated statement in his book *Making Meaning*, David Bordwell questions the determinate link many film scholars assume exists between film theory, methods, and analysis. Bordwell argues that film analysis is not directly influenced by film theory. Instead, he argues that film analysis follows general human cognitive and inferential abilities – the same ones used when making a quilt or constructing furniture (Bordwell 1989: xii). In this book we argue for the common assumption that a determinate link exists between theory, methods, and analysis; that is, that theory plays a key role in developing methods and in conducting analyses of films.

# 1.2. Why study films?

This question should be reformulated to read: Why study classical and contemporary American films? First, we need to understand the role of narrative in contemporary cinema, because we may have come to a historical watershed, a transformation of the mode of representation, of the logic of the visible we associate with narrative cinema. Second, without classical and contemporary American films one probably would not be studying the cinema. Hollywood film in particular is the American art par excellence, like tragedy is the art of the Greeks, the pyramids are associated with the civilization of Egypt, and the great cathedrals with the Holy Roman Empire. In this respect, the twentieth century was the American century, and its cinema – its film genres, stars, and stories – most consistently enchanted a public, an international public. This is a great historical achievement: a cultural form has been created. American film's dominance has also stifled, repressed, and marginalized many other forms of cinema; its sheer economic power has 'colonized' the rest of the world, its images, its fantasies, its lifestyles, its dreams and aspirations, its idea of reality.

For Hollywood cinema is a world industry, just as much as it is a world language, a powerful, stable, perfected system of visual communication. As such it represents real power, not just in and through the cinema: the coding of images on TV, the imaging of politics, advertising, lifestyle, etc. goes via the encoding of messages and meaning in and through images, and the image–word combination.

# 1.3. How to study film?

We have addressed what to study and why study it. But now we come to the big question: How do we study contemporary American films? In the remainder of this chapter we shall endeavour to answer this question by outlining the form of inquiry in film studies. The following chapters will add substance to this form by focusing on practice. The form of inquiry in film studies involves a threefold distinction between (i) theory, (ii) methods, and (iii) analysis.

## 1.3.1. Theory

Films are analysable on the basis of their inherent form and structure. However, this structure is not immediately visible in itself. Instead, certain aspects of it become visible from within a certain theoretical perspective (and other aspects become visible from other theoretical perspectives). Moreover, theoretical perspectives may overlap in incommensurate ways. In general, the aim of theory is to make visible the invisible structure that orders and confers intelligibility upon films. The invisible structure is unknown and cannot, therefore, be discovered by means of inductive procedures such as taxonomies. At the same time, the structure is not unknowable, for it can be represented as a system of theoretical hypotheses, concepts, or propositions, which only have a tentative or speculative status. Theories therefore offer explanatory depth rather than mere empirical generalizations. A particular theory enables the analyst to identify specific aspects of a film's structure, and to look at and listen to the film from the perspective of its own values. There is no value-free perspective from which we can directly 'see' and 'hear' a film; we can only 'look at' and 'listen to' a film with a particular set of values. The aim of theory is to construct different conceptual perspectives on a film, each informed by a specific set of values. A biased or value-laden theory not only is inescapable, but is also the condition of knowledge, and of applying methods that guide analysis. Reflective deliberation on the values inherent in a theory and its methods of analysis is the starting point for choosing a theory and applying its methods in an appropriate way.

The values inherent in all film theories have directed theorists' attention to particular aspects of film's general nature or 'essential' properties. For example:

- Classical film theorists tried to define film as an art by focusing on its 'essence', which they located either in cinema's photographic recording capacity (e.g. André Bazin), or its unique formal techniques that offer a new way of seeing (e.g. Rudolf Arnheim).
- Film semioticians attempted to define film's specificity in terms of a specific combination of codes.
- Cognitive and psychoanalytic film theorists focus on the specific nature of the interface between film and spectator: either the way a film addresses unconscious desires and fantasies, or the knowledge and competence spectators employ to comprehend films.

Each theory formulates hypotheses about the general nature of film, leading to the formation of declarative knowledge – in the terminology of the philosopher Gilbert Ryle, 'knowing-that' (Ryle 1949: 28–32). Theory's system of interrelated, tentative hypotheses need to be justified – that is, grounded and tested. In principle, this is achieved by means of analysis guided by methods extracted from theories.

## 1.3.2. Methods

Every discipline establishes standards of professional competence – or, negatively, pressure to conform to professional standards. To gain competence in film studies involves, to a significant extent, the mastery of methods, since the methods of film studies constitute the 'acceptable' (the profession's preferred) ways of carrying out film analysis. The term 'method' is used here simply to refer to procedural knowledge, rather than declarative knowledge. In Ryle's terminology, it is 'knowing-how': using a set of skills or procedures to achieve a goal (Ryle 1949: 28–32; 40–41). Procedural knowledge, or method, provides tools for the analysis of films. Methods turn film analysis into an explicit, systematic, and repeatable discipline based on reliable procedures; it avoids relying on intuition, introspection, and hidden assumptions. Of course, this can be perceived as a hindrance rather than a benefit, stifling creative thinking and turning students into drones all producing the same routine analyses of films. Abraham Kaplan calls this 'trained incapacity' – 'the more we know how to do something, the harder it is to learn to do it differently' (Kaplan 1964: 29). However, we can overcome this 'incapacity' by learning several incompatible methods, rather than dogmatically adhering to one or two. Film analysts therefore have three choices:

- to base their analyses on unqualified assertions – instantaneous judgments and spontaneous opinions of a film;
- to adhere dogmatically to one theory and its method of analysis, resulting in 'trained incapacity';
- or to learn several theories, so that they can apply specific theories in appropriate contexts, rather than use the same theory in all contexts.

In *Studying Contemporary American Film* we adopt the third option.

Our approach to teaching several theories and methods of analysis is to make explicit the procedures in conducting any analysis. To achieve this aim we shall borrow from ancient rhetoric, particularly Aristotle's *The Art of Rhetoric*. For Aristotle, rhetoric is a general activity that produces knowledge. It is not tied to a particular subject matter, nor does it simply consist of the study and use of artificial, inessential ornaments of discourse that function to persuade listeners or readers of an argument that is not in their best interest. As a discipline that produces knowledge, rhetoric identifies the discursive aspect of any subject matter, the stages involved in an entire course of reasoning, from start to finish. By promoting rhetoric to the level of knowledge, Aristotle equated it with the study of grammar and logic.

In *The Art of Rhetoric* Aristotle divided up rhetoric, now understood as a general discipline, into the stages in which arguments are produced, arranged, and expressed in discourse – namely, invention, composition, and style. Rhetoricians who came after Aristotle added two minor stages, resulting in the following five areas of rhetoric:

- *inventio* (invention, or discovery)
- *dispositio* (disposition, composition, or arrangement)
- *elocutio* (elocution, or style)
- *actio* (verbal delivery, oration)
- *memoria* (committing to memory)

In *Making Meaning* Bordwell (1989) also uses the first three areas of ancient rhetoric to identify the conventions and routines of film analysis and interpretation. The following discussion is indebted to Bordwell's book, as well as to Corbett and Connors' *Classical Rhetoric for the Modern Student* (1999), which discusses *inventio, dispositio*, and *elocutio* in great detail.

**Inventio**    Writers are faced at the starting point of each assignment with a blank piece of paper, or an empty computer screen with a flashing cursor waiting for input. Such writers are not alone. In ancient Greece the speakers at the popular assemblies were required to speak on a variety of subjects. Rather than wait for inspiration, they devised a procedure by which to generate – or invent – arguments. *Inventio* is the first stage of discourse on any subject matter. It answers the question: How are arguments invented? Corbett and Connors (1999: 17) write that invention is 'a system or method for finding arguments', which guides the speaker or writer on 'how to "discover" something to say on some given subject' (p. 19). The importance of *inventio* is reflected in the fact that most of Aristotle's *The Art of Rhetoric* (as well as his book *The Topics*) is devoted to argument invention.

For Aristotle, one of the primary ways to invent an argument is by means of 'the topics'. The topics name a grid for generating arguments, a system that classical rhetoricians devised to help find something to say. Topics enable the writer or speaker to conduct a logical analysis of the subject under discussion. Common topics for conducting logical analysis of any subject matter include: 'definition', 'comparison', 'relationship', 'circumstance', and 'testimony', which add up to a pattern for organizing thoughts that enables the speaker or writer to define the essence of a subject, to differentiate between subjects, or find similarities, establish relationships, and so on.

Definition involves two stages: putting the subject matter to be defined into a general class, and then indicating the specific differences that distinguish this subject from other subjects in the same class. For example, 'man' is defined as a 'rational animal', in which 'animal' designates the general class and 'rational' the specific difference between man and other subjects in the same general class of 'animal'. Similarly, any subject matter can be defined in this way. We have already mentioned how classical film theorists attempted to define film as an art by focusing on what they thought is its essence – indeed, Bazin's famous collection of essays is called *What is Cinema?* which is a question seeking a definition. The general class in the classical film theorists' definitions of film is 'art', and the specific difference is the essence of film that distinguishes film from the other arts (this is the disputed part of the definition – namely, 'photographic recording capacity' for Bazin, 'form' for Arnheim). Furthermore, the topic of definition can be used to criticize the arguments of others, particularly arguments that contain vague definitions, or that use the same term with different meanings. Definitions can be controversial and can constitute the main part of an essay. Classical film theorists agreed that film should be defined as an art. But such a definition is open to dispute and clarification. The meaning of 'film' is delimited by being put into the general class of 'art' (does this definition include documentaries, medical films, and so on?). Furthermore, the classical film theorists disputed amongst themselves about film's specific difference from other arts. This long-running dispute within classical film theory is basically a dispute over definition. Film semioticians attempted to surmount the classical film theorists' difficulties over definition by defining the specific difference of film, from the general class 'art', in terms of codes. Definition is therefore one fundamental way in which arguments are invented. However, students should go beyond the superficial activity of simply quoting a definition from a dictionary (or simply indicating the etymology of a word) without carefully integrating that definition into the overall argument of an essay. Isolated definitions serve no purpose; when used properly, however, they can strengthen and clarify an argument.

Another way to invent an argument is to compare the subject matter with another subject. Comparison involves bringing two or more subjects together and then looking for similarities and differences, and ranking these similarities and differences in terms of degree (e.g., 'more or less', 'better or worse'), all of which enable the writer to invent arguments about his or her subject matter. The debate focusing on the relation between classical and post-classical Hollywood films is conducted using the topic of comparison. One can argue that there are essential similarities between classical and post-classical Hollywood films, and only superficial differences, or that the differences outweigh the similarities (see Chapter 2). The values embedded in the *auteur* approach to film use the topic of comparison to focus the *auteur* critic's attention to the similarities across a director's films. Occasionally the *auteur* critic will also point out the differences in a director's films, and then use the sub-topic of degree to distinguish the better films from the worst ones. Of course, such judgements are subjective, and require additional justification.

We can also use the topic of comparison to identify the similarities and differences between various film theories, and the sub-topic of degree to determine which is better or worse for our purposes. For example, if we focus on our experience of a film, our analysis is 'subject-focused' – that is, focused on what happens 'in here' (in us, the subject). But if we focus on the film itself beyond our experience of it, then our analysis is 'object-focused' – that is, focused on what happens 'out there'. The introduction of structuralism to film studies led to an object-focused approach to film, which regarded the film as a text to be examined and analysed above and beyond any individual's experience of it. And the structuralists used the topic of comparison to emphasize the fundamental differences between their object-focused approach and earlier subject-focused approaches to film to argue that their own approach is better than earlier approaches. Post-structural and cognitive theories combine subject and object-focused studies by concentrating on inter-subjective, unconscious (or subconscious in the case of cognitive film theory) responses to films. Whether cognitive or psychoanalytic, these film analysts begin from the spectator's experience of the film, but then rapidly go beyond the boundaries of experience towards abstract thinking and speculation (indicating one way in which theory relates to analysis).[1]

Although there are several sub-topics to the topic of 'relationship', we shall consider only one, cause and effect. One can generate an argument by starting with a cause and indicating what effects it will have, or begin with effects and trace their cause(s). Film analysts frequently adopt the latter approach, which involves explaining the effects of a film in terms of a number of probable causes. For example, why and how does *Lost Highway* (1997) disorient spectators? One answer is because of its unusual narrative structure, which we analyse in Chapter 6. How does *Jurassic Park* (1993) create the credible effect of dinosaurs interacting with a photographic background? Through the digital simulation of photographic effects, as we argue in Chapter 7.

The topic of circumstance includes the sub-topics 'the possible and the impossible' and 'past facts and future facts'. At times the writer needs to convince the reader that the subject matter under discussion is possible and that other subjects are impossible, or that some events have taken place and others will take place. The subject-focused approach to film analysis combines both these sub-topics of circumstance. We invent arguments in a subject-focused approach by writing as a hypothetical spectator. It is as if the analyst is writing a commentary on the thoughts and impressions of an ideal spectator. In effect, the analyst is writing about what he or she experienced when watching the film (past facts), and then generalizes from those impressions, and assumes that everyone who sees the film in the future will react to and understand the film in the same way. In addition, the analyst who sets up a hypothetical spectator is writing about possible reactions to the film – predicting that past and future spectators have reacted or will probably react in the same way as the hypothetical or ideal spectator. An influential incarnation of the ideal spectator appears in feminist film theory, particularly its notion that narrative films construct a masculine 'subject position' (one based on voyeurism and fetishism) that all spectators adopt when watching narrative films. In recent times, however, the hypothetical spectator has been severely criticized. First, by reception studies, which analyses a broad range of possible reactions to a film. It presents more varied accounts of the way present and future spectators react to films, and the way past spectators reacted to films (historical reception studies; see Staiger 1992). Similarly, in his review of essays written on *Psycho*, Leland Poague writes:

> The problems with [standard readings of] *Psycho* are many – chief among them the contention that audience response to *Psycho* is so completely under Hitchcock's control that an idealized viewer is in fact the film's 'central character.' The methodological problem is obvious. Upon what grounds can one claim to know how all members of a given audience, much less all members of all possible audiences, will respond to a particular film?
>
> (Poague 1986: 340–41).

Whereas the previous topics involve logical analysis of the subject matter under discussion, the topic of testimony invents arguments by referring to external sources, particularly authority (informed opinion) and examples. It has become commonplace in film studies to generate an argument by appealing to authorities – either to the personnel involved in the making of the film (director, cinematographer, producer, etc.), to other film scholars, or, more typically, to theories imported from outside film studies (feminism, psychoanalysis, Marxism, etc.). Another way to generate an argument is to refer to the film – to cite examples. (Here we are deviating from the rhetorical understanding of 'example' – which is close to 'precedent' in the judicial meaning of the term[2] – and instead are using the term in the sense of 'citation', which is also a form of testimony.) When conducting an analysis, we need to consider carefully the examples we use from the film, how we use them, and how many times we use examples. Of course, it is impossible and undesirable to cite every shot, but we need to consider why one shot (or scene) has been selected over another, since our choice needs to be justified. In general, although examples increase the probability of theoretical arguments, they do not prove or disprove them. They have persuasive value but do not offer logical proof.

Arguments can be invented in other ways as well, such as by formulating a question that addresses a problem. One of the main justifications for writing about a film is not 'I like this film', but that the film genuinely adds something new to the cinema, something that has not been done before. The problem to be addressed here is general – a lack of knowledge. The digital effects in *Jurassic Park* – particularly their conformity to codes of photo-realism – is an exemplary instance (discussed in Chapter 7). Or the film may raise general problems that need to be addressed: for example, how are women represented? How is the narrative structured? Many of these questions arise from theoretical perspectives (e.g. feminism, narrative theory), which then guide the analysis.

Finally, arguments can also be invented by pointing out the limitations of previous researchers, and by making finer distinctions than they do. This is usually carried out in a literature review, which surveys recent research on the subject matter under discussion. By reading through and summarizing this literature, the researcher is placing his or her study in a larger context. A literature review not only frames one's research but justifies it as well, by highlighting the limitations in the research of others.

'Definition', 'comparison', 'relationship', 'circumstance', and 'testimony', together with their sub-topics, constitute the common topics, which can be applied to any subject matter in order to invent an argument. Specific subjects, including film theory and film analysis, have their own special topics. In *Making Meaning* Bordwell (1989: 211) lists a number of the special topics that film analysts use to discuss films, including: 'a critically significant film is ambiguous, or polysemous, or dialogical'; 'the film's style is so exaggerated that it must be ironic or parodic'; 'putting characters in the same frame unites them; cutting stresses opposition' (this is a formulation of the 'same-frame heuristic', which we apply in some detail to *The English Patient* in Chapter 3).

**Dispositio**    The second stage in the formulation of arguments is called disposition, which refers to the arrangement of an argument. Corbett and Connors write that disposition is 'concerned with the effective and orderly arrangement of the parts of a written or spoken discourse. Once the ideas or arguments are discovered there remains the problem of selecting, marshalling, and organizing them with a view to effecting the end of the discourse' (1999: 20). After inventing arguments, we need to decide how they are going to be arranged. Do we simply put them down on paper in any order? If not, how do we decide to organize our argument? The question is one of disposition, or arrangement. In *The Art of Rhetoric* Aristotle divides disposition into four stages: introduction, presentation, proof, and epilogue. He compares the introduction to a musical prelude, for both should establish the keynote of what is to follow. The presentation consists of a recounting of the facts and events (for film analysts, the presentation of the analysis). The proof consists of the writer establishing his or her case and refuting that of others (a presentation of the results of the analysis and the inadequacies of the analyses of others). Finally, the epilogue should aim not only to summarize the research but also to dispose the audience favourably towards the speaker and to amplify one's own arguments.

In terms of presentation, some film analysts simply follow the unfolding film – in other words, they retell the story as it unfolds. The disposition of the essay is therefore governed by the disposition of the film. This is popular with subject-focused criticism, because the subject (the spectator) experiences the film in a linear manner (at least at the cinema). Other critics may focus on one scene only, or pick a series of scenes they find fundamental to the film. Such critics go beyond subject-focused criticism and treat the film as an object or text. It may be relevant to present two or more readings of the same film. For example, a contemporary film can first be read as a classical narrative film (in which the values embedded in the theoretical perspective focus the analyst's attention on moments where the film confirms to classical narrative), and then reread as a post-classical film. All these decisions are informed by theoretical concepts.

*Elocutio*    The third stage in the formulation of arguments, and usually the last one discussed in any depth, is style. For classical rhetoricians, style is not a mere ornament, but is an integral part of discourse. Corbett and Connors write that 'all rhetorical considerations of style involved some discussion of *choice of words*, usually under such heads as correctness, purity (for instance, the choice of native words rather than foreign words), simplicity, clearness, appropriateness, ornateness' (1999: 21). Word choice, of course, involves enlarging one's vocabulary so that specific words can be used in appropriate contexts, which is preferable to using the same general words in all contexts. To enlarge one's vocabulary is not, therefore, simply a matter of acquiring the specialized vocabulary of a particular discipline. In addition to word choice, style covers word order, selection and use of different sentence structures to form a coherent paragraph, figures of speech, and the avoidance of stock phrases and clichés.

The language one uses aims to persuade the reader that one's arguments are correct and worth listening to. At one extreme of the stylistic scale are the figures of speech, which Corbett and Connors define as 'artful deviations from the ordinary mode of speaking or writing' (1999: 379). Such figures apply equally to deviation from the ordinary patterns or arrangement of words (schemes) and deviation from the ordinary and principal signification of a word (tropes) (Corbett and Connors 1999: 379). The overuse of figures of speech should be avoided in academic writing. At the other extreme of the stylistic scale are stock phrases and clichés. Film analysts need to be aware of clichéd phrases in their own writing as well as the writing of others. An analyst may write 'of course', suggesting that the point they are making is obvious, whereas in fact they are trying to make it obvious by using the phrase 'of course'. Or they may write 'it is necessary' – as in 'it is necessary to consider the relation between the opening and closing of a classical Hollywood film'. Is it necessary? Maybe it is; maybe the analyst is right after all. The point is that such stock phrases should not be accepted at face value. Linear, causal phrases also need to be examined carefully, particularly sentences beginning with words such as 'Therefore', which signify, using the topic of relationship, a causal conclusion to an argument. But is the link between argument and conclusion really causal?

**Actio and Memoria**    Rarely mentioned are *actio* and *memoria*, for they involve the delivery of arguments rather than their formulation. *Actio* designates skills used in the pronunciation of a speech, as well as other forms of delivery such as visual aids, including hand gestures and body posture. *Memoria* is concerned with the skills in memorizing speeches. Both are neglected because the invention of the printing press in the fifteenth century shifted emphasis to written discourse rather than speech. But in an academic setting, the verbal delivery of arguments, in the form of lectures, seminar presentations, and conference papers, is still important, and many professors and students alike would benefit greatly from lessons in delivery. These skills can also enable speakers to decide how to illustrate their talk (or books and articles), and to decide whether to read out a conference paper or offer a summary of its ideas.

## 1.3.3. Analysis

After theory and methods, the third and final part of the answer to the question 'How to study film?' involves analysis. One major objective of close textual reading is to address the problem of cinematic signification: of how a film creates meaning. The question could be phrased in the form of a series of paradoxes. Is there not a contradiction between, on the one hand, the perception of a film as a continuous experience, with the action often starting *in medias res* (without a narrator setting the scene or introducing the characters, and the story developing its own momentum, as it follows a more or less linear trajectory right to the end) and, on the other hand, the fact that when we look at the strip of celluloid, or even when we slow it down on the video player, a film is made up of wholly discontinuous, discrete and separate entities (individual scenes, which themselves consist of segments)? Each segment is furthermore a series of individual shots, and the shots themselves – at least in the photographic mode – consist of tens or hundreds of individual frames.

As an industrial, technological product, film is a commodity, produced to make money and created on the basis of a complex and sophisticated division of labour and tasks, with a high degree of specialization in each of its branches of production. Its textual basis is the shooting script, itself a historically evolved practice, at one end comparable to a blueprint for an engineering project, on the basis of which tasks are allocated, schedules distributed, and budgets worked out; and at the other end, comparable to a poem in which strictly conventionalized forms, such as length, rhyme-scheme, and metre, nonetheless allow for the most extraordinary versatility and ingenuity.

This tension between heterogeneity and homogeneity applies not only to the image but to the sound as well: it, too, gives the illusion of continuity while in actual fact, sound fragments are normally spliced together to produce the impression of a persistent and always present sound ambience. Sound is separately recorded, in order to be matched, mixed, and dubbed. It undergoes a considerable amount of work and processing, because it serves a complex set of functions in respect of narrative and image. In order to make either sound or image into material for filmic signification one needs first of all to separate and break down the various elements, before they can be combined.

The essential discontinuity of the image and the discontinuity of the sound therefore combine, in both classical and contemporary American film, in various ways. The most basic functions are to serve as spatial markers, either synchronous to indicate co-presence of sound source and representation, or in counterpoint to indicate off-screen space. As a temporal marker, synchronicity signifies simultaneity, but sound can often structure the future of the narrative (anticipating events through musical motifs, for instance), or it can act as narrative memory (an echo or reminder). There is always a kind of dialogue going on between sound and image: the sound asks 'Where?', and the image replies 'Here' (see Altman 1980). This question-and-answer game (or this 'dialogue' which Noël Carroll calls the 'erotetic' principle (1996a: chs 5 and 6)) serves to establish an illusion of presence, of a time–space continuum, and thereby generates the impression of realism. Realism in this sense, too, relies on separation and division. The relation of sound to image could be called the double confirmation of a double illusion: two falsehoods in this instance make one truth.

The film analyst tries to explain the functioning of the film as a coherent and continuous experience. But this raises two problems: (1) How is it that a film suggests a world that is seamless, always already there, continuous beyond the film's frame and the film's time, while at the same time it tells a story, builds up a narrative, develops an intrigue, a drama with beginning, complication, climaxes, and resolution? The second problem is even more difficult to come to terms with: (2) How does a film create the impression of a world 'out there' (of which we are merely the invisible witnesses) when all the while the film itself only exists for our benefit, 'in here', thereby cunningly disguising that it only aims at and addresses us? One could say that the first problem involves two kinds of logic: the logic of the actions in a film, and the logic of the spectator's position vis-à-vis the action. So strong is this impression of unity and coherence that Hollywood films in particular seem to obey some principle of regularity, maybe even some sort of 'law'. Traditionally, therefore, the logic of the actions has been discussed by asking whether film possesses a language or a grammar. In which case, the object of inquiry for analysis might be to define this film grammar, this language of cinema. The result of this move was a reorientation of film studies, its transformation into a semiotics of film. Largely owing to the work of Christian Metz, the question of whether film is organized according to the same principles as is language – for instance, with a vocabulary or a semantics, and a grammar or syntax – has been given the answer 'yes and no'. While this seems a pretty unsatisfactory answer to most people, film theorists have actually learnt a lot about film this way, especially for analysis.

Nonetheless, some scholars have concluded that linguistics may have been a dead end for film studies, perhaps even the wrong way altogether to look at the problem. Others merely criticized the kind of language model used (i.e. that of Ferdinand de Saussure) and that other ways of thinking about language (e.g., Charles Sanders Peirce, Noam Chomsky, George Lakoff) might turn out to be more productive. The extensive involvement of film analysis with semiotics, structural linguistics, transformational grammar, and the study of metaphor has been complemented by an equally extensive discussion of narratology, theories of narrative, narration, and focalization, in order to understand how a filmic text obtains its cohesion, how it constitutes a 'signifying system'. Already during the heyday of semiotics, Metz attempted to classify, correlate, and order narrative sequences in fiction films (see 'Problems of Denotation in the Fiction Film' (Metz 1974: 108–46)).

For the second problem, of how the film addresses and positions the spectator, narratology has proved one of several entry points. In order to describe what is sometimes called the 'enunciative' level as distinct from the narrative level, scholars have, again, borrowed from both structural linguistics (Émile Benveniste) and Freudian psychoanalysis to explain the reality effect that this classical narrative system attains and the phenomenon of identification which puts the spectator, as it were, inside the action. The psychoanalytic approach has proceeded from the assumption that a film necessarily positions us as voyeurs (which turns the film into an exhibitionist), but also that it involves a particular form of suspension of disbelief, or 'disavowal', characterized as typical of fetishism (Octave Mannoni's 'I know, but nonetheless . . .'). This approach has been thematized by feminist film criticism and film theory, and is associated with the names of Laura Mulvey, Teresa de Lauretis, Kaja Silverman, Tania Modleski, and Linda Williams, among many others.

Other scholars, most notably the 'cognitivists', represented by David Bordwell and Edward Branigan, are not convinced by psycho-semiotics.

They have instead preferred to examine theories of 'narration', and – borrowing from Gérard Genette – have tried to elaborate a model of filmic narration which dispenses with the notions of enunciation/identification, or voyeurism/fetishism, as well as with the distinction between 'narrative structure' and 'identification', replacing both by the concept of 'narration'. Narration can deal with all these processes, once it is seen as an act of structuration, hierarchizing, and prioritizing, the result of which is both an impression of structure (of the form, the patterns inherent in the work) *and* an effect of comprehension and identification (subject-effect, whether gender-specific or not). Hence the greater emphasis placed by such scholars on levels of narration and instances or modes of narration (see Chapter 6).

In a more common-sense usage, narration might be seen as the process by which the relationships between the impression of 'out there' and 'in here' are being negotiated, manipulated, and controlled. One could add that analysis tends to assume – for methodological, and therefore more or less purely pragmatic or procedural reasons – that meaning is located 'out there' in the text. Calling a film a 'text', however, is at first sight a fairly counter-intuitive and arbitrary procedure, because a text is something composed of language, something one reads, while a film is viewed by the eye or experienced by the ear, i.e. it is above all a sensory-perceptual environment.

Whether intentional or not, text and analysis refer us to the study of literature, and it is a reminder that what we do in Film Studies is actually historically and methodologically related to the study of literature, and in particular to that tendency within literature which used to be called 'practical criticism' or 'close reading': it regards novels, plays, and poems as free-standing, self-contained works, as objects. In the famous phrase of Cleanth Brooks, citing the English Romantic writer John Keats, a poem is like a 'well-wrought urn' – a self-sufficient object of beauty which you can handle, pick up, turn around and inspect from all sides. That's how analysis sometimes treats a film – cut loose from its conditions of production, cut loose from its creator(s), and also cut loose from its condition and history of reception (i.e. its spectators and audiences). In which case it is probably quite fitting that an urn is the sort of receptacle in which you keep the ashes of your dear departed after you have cremated them – and that's probably what some readers new to film studies may think: analysis is a way of turning a living film into a corpse, and not only a corpse, but a heap of ashes.

But analysis is different from interpretation (understood here as a 'hermeneutics of suspicion' – the search for hidden and repressed meanings). The object of close analysis in this sense is not necessarily to arrive at a new or startling interpretation of a film or a sequence of a film, but rather the opposite: to explain what David Bordwell has called the 'excessive 'obviousness' of a Hollywood film based on a classically constructed film scenario, and what Raymond Bellour has called the interplay of 'the obvious and the code', in a famous essay on a scene from *The Big Sleep* (Bellour 2000: 69–76). What both writers allude to is the fact that we can all understand a Hollywood film, we can all react to it, we are all experts in judging it. And we can learn how it is put together: we can study its building blocks and structural principles. Indeed, a Hollywood film usually gives us its instructions for use: it comes with its own manual (see Chapter 2).

What is of interest is the functioning of film as a system of relations and interdependencies, complex in its means, obvious in its effects. We therefore need to focus attention on the formal, symbolic, narrative, and figurative processes typical of and standardized in the American cinema: a system that, historically speaking, remained extraordinarily stable from about 1920 to at least the 1970s, i.e. for about 50 years, if not much longer. Bordwell, Staiger, and Thompson (Thompson 1999; Bordwell et al. 1985: 367–77), for instance, have frequently affirmed that they think the classical cinema is still intact and in use today, and there is a lot of evidence to prove their point, when one thinks of the extraordinary success of the films by a thoroughly classical contemporary film-maker such as Steven Spielberg. But there are many counter-examples to indicate that contemporary American cinema is post-classical and post-narrative. Rather than conceive of classical cinema as an absolute norm, we need to relativize it, to demonstrate that it exists now as just one film practice among many.

## 1.4. Chapter contents and alternative films

Chapters 2–9 have an identical structure, or disposition. We identify the main premises behind a traditional film theory, distil a method from it, and then analyse a film. We then identify the main premises behind a more recent film theory, distil a method from it, and then analyse the same film again. Chapters 2–9 are therefore structured in the following way:

> Section 1: Traditional film theory
> Section 2: Method
> Section 3: Analysis
> Section 4: Recent film theory
> Section 5: Method
> Section 6: Analysis

We therefore systematically split up the process of film analysis into its component parts. This makes comprehension and comparison easier. That is, we try to demystify the process of film analysis by breaking it up into stages and by spelling out the procedure by which each theory can be applied to a film. Furthermore, by presenting each theory in the same way, comparison becomes a straightforward matter, since like can be compared with like. In sum, this identical disposition makes the teaching, learning, and application of theories in film analysis more manageable.

The chapter titles also take the same form. They indicate the traditional theory, the more recent theory, and the film(s) under analysis. The traditional theories are (in which 'theories' encompasses schools of criticism): *mise-en-scène* criticism; thematic criticism and auteurism; post-structuralism (Roland Barthes's *S/Z*); David Bordwell's cognitive theory of film narration; theories of realism; Freudian and Lacanian psychoanalysis; and feminism. The more recent theories are: computational statistical style analysis; deconstruction; new media theory (video game design); Edward Branigan's cognitive theory of film narration; theories of digital realism and modal logic (possible world theory); New Lacanian psychoanalysis (especially Slavoj Žižek); and Foucault's and Deleuze's theories of subjectivity and gender.

The contemporary American films (plus two imitations) we analyse include: *Die Hard* (John McTiernan, 1988); *The English Patient* (Anthony Minghella, 1997); *Chinatown* (Roman Polanski, 1974); *The Fifth Element* (Luc Besson, 1997); *Lost Highway* (David Lynch, 1997); *Jurassic Park* and *The Lost World* (Steven Spielberg, 1993, 1997); *Back to the Future* (Robert Zemeckis, 1985), and *The Silence of the Lambs* (Jonathan Demme, 1991).

In Chapter 2 we take issue with critics who establish the distinction between classical and post-classical Hollywood on the basis of binary oppositions such as spectacle vs narrative, and other 'either/or' constructions of difference. We suggest that critics may define the post-classical as an 'excessive classicism', rather than as a rejection or absence of classicism, or as moments in a classical film when our own theory or methods appear in the film itself, looking us in the face. Any contemporary Hollywood film can be analysed (at least) twice, giving preference first to its conformity to the principles of classical aesthetics, and second to its conformity to post-classical aesthetics (such as mannerism). In Chapter 2 we subject *Die Hard* to a double (classical/post-classical) analysis.

In Chapter 3 we present a *mise-en-scène* analysis of *The English Patient*. We identify a number of the 'heuristics' that *mise-en-scène* critics developed in the 1950s and 1960s to analyse classical Hollywood films (including foreground–background, foreshadowing, same frame, cutting vs the long-take heuristics), and then apply them to *The English Patient*. We could have selected other relevant and similar films, many of which are produced, or co-produced, in Britain, and many of which are based on literary classics or contemporary literature, including 'Merchant Ivory' films such as *The Bostonians* (1984),

*Room with a View* (1987), *Maurice* (1987), *Howards End* (1992), *The Remains of the Day* (1993), *Surviving Picasso* (1996), and *The Golden Bowl* (2000). David Lean's last film, *Passage to India* (1984) – which he also edited – falls into this category (although Ernest Day's cinematography is far less restrained than John Seale's in *The English Patient*). Another ideal candidate for *mise en scène* analysis is, of course, *The Talented Mr Ripley* (1999), in which Anthony Minghella teams up again with John Seale and Walter Murch. The statistical style analysis developed in the second half of the chapter quantifies film style, particularly the parameters of the shot (shot scale, shot length, camera movement, camera angle, strength of the cut), and then performs statistical tests on those parameters using computer technology. This type of analysis can be applied to any narrative film, although its results are more reliable in the analysis of full-length feature films.

The first half of Chapter 4 outlines thematic and *auteur* film criticism, both of which share the focus on the central ideas behind a film, particularly those ideas that unify a film (or a director's œuvre). Both thematic and *auteur* criticism are general forms of criticism in a dual sense – they can be applied to any film or group of films, and they aim to generalize, i.e. determine a film's underlying, abstract meanings. These abstract meanings, relating to fundamental human experiences such as suffering, alienation, freedom, and creativity, bring the process of criticism to a close, for they seem to offer a 'natural' end point, for once the thematic or *auteur* critics finds these fundamental human experiences in a film, they feel the film's ultimate meaning has been identified, and that no further analysis is required. We explore thematic and *auteur* criticism in relation to Roman Polanski's film-making, focusing in particular on *Chinatown*. Thematic and *auteur* criticism have been criticized for reading films from a reductive and totalizing perspective. Chief among the critics are deconstructionists, for whom discrepant and disruptive details in a text are significant to the extent that they undermine the dominant thematic meaning. In the second half of Chapter 4 we read *Chinatown* again, this time focusing on the rich web of discrepant details that go far beyond the film's standard thematic meanings.

In Chapter 5 we outline the post-structural theory and method of Roland Barthes's *S/Z* (Barthes 1974), and then apply it to *The Fifth Element*, a French imitation of the Hollywood blockbuster. The five codes central to Barthes's analysis (the hermeneutic, the proairetic, the semic, the symbolic, and the referential) are aimed particularly at mainstream rather than avant-garde texts. Many contemporary films can therefore be taken apart in terms of the five codes. However, we argue that the five codes do not identify all the dominant codes in *The Fifth Element*. In particular, we argue that the film's narrative is structured along the lines of a video game. In the second half of Chapter 5 we outline the main rules of video game logic (serialized repetition of actions, multiple levels of adventure, space–time warps, magical transformations and disguises, immediate rewards and punishment, pace, and interactivity) and then seek them out in *The Fifth Element*. Alternative films that respond well to a 'video game' analysis include *The Matrix* (Larry and Andy Wachowski, 1999) and *eXistenZ* (David Cronenberg, 1999) – not because of the *content* of both films (they represent computer game simulations in their narratives), but primarily because they adopt the *structure* of computer games (the primary focus of the analysis of *The Fifth Element* in the second half of Chapter 5).

The cognitive theories of narrative and narration developed by David Bordwell and Edward Branigan focus on the way spectators comprehend narratives. While the process of comprehending an uncomplicated narrative (linear, causal narratives focused around and motivated by a few clearly identifiable central characters) is far from straightforward, the value of a cognitive analysis of narrative processing comes into its own when films with complicated narratives are analysed. In Chapter 6 we subject David Lynch's *Lost Highway* to two cognitive analyses, because it presents complications in terms of how it is comprehended (or not comprehended). Cognitive theories of narration can pinpoint those moments when comprehension breaks down, and can identify the reasons why a shot or sequence becomes incomprehensible, or difficult to understand. Alternative films we could have analysed include *Total Recall* (Paul Verhoeven, 1990), which is almost as challenging as *Lost Highway*, because it presents three alternative levels of reality for the main protagonist, Doug Quaid, to inhabit, and at key points in the film, both Doug Quaid and the spectator are confused about which level of reality is operative. Is Quaid simply a lowly construction worker on Earth? Or is he strapped into a chair at Rekall being fed memories of a trip to Mars, pretending to live the life of a secret agent? Or is he really a secret agent on Mars, working in collusion with Cohaagen to kill the leader of the Mars resistance? A cognitive reading of *Total Recall* may not solve these inherently ambiguous moments in the film, but it will certainly bring them into sharper focus. *eXistenZ* also presents three levels of reality, and creates ambiguity concerning what level the characters are living in. But by the end of the film, it is evident that the film began on level two (in a computer game), progressed to level three (a computer game within a computer game), and then ended on level one (the characters' real life) – although a throwaway ending 'challenges' this reading. The confusion of levels is simply caused by the fact that each level imitates the others, and the film begins on level two, not level one. Finally, *Memento* (Christopher Nolan, 2000) offers similar challenges in comprehension, because the narrative events are presented backwards. Or, more accurately, within each scene, events unfold normally (except the opening sequence). But following scenes represent events that took place before. From scene to scene, the film therefore gradually works it way backwards through the narrative events. To complicate matters, between each scene is a fragment, in black and white, from a long sequence in which the main character, Lenny, talks to someone (later identified as Teddy, a policeman) on the telephone. In addition, the film contains flashbacks to other events. The film therefore has three temporal structures: the present, presented backwards; the telephone call (which becomes part of the present towards the end of the film); and flashbacks to the 'murder' of Lenny's wife.

One of the main aims of Chapter 7 (as well as Chapter 3, on *mise en scène*, and Chapter 4, on *auteurism* and thematic criticism) is to demonstrate that classical theories are also applicable to contemporary films. In Chapter 7, Bazin's theory of perceptual realism is shown to be relevant to analysing Spielberg's *Jurassic Park* and *The Lost World*. We hope that this chapter will encourage readers to test out the relevance of these 'old' theories to new films. Nonetheless, Bazin's work cannot articulate the specificity of Spielberg's dinosaur films: that digital effects are deliberately 'constrained' in these films to imitate 'optical' reality; that is, the digital effects are invisible (as digital effects) and try to create the impression that the images were produced optically. Such invisible special effects can save money by creating effects that cost a lot of money to produce. But in the case of Spielberg's dinosaur films, digital special effects are used to create photo-realistic images of objects that do not exist: dinosaurs (or no longer exist, and therefore cannot be photographed). In Chapter 7 modal logic is introduced to discuss the status of these photo-realistic but nonexistent dinosaurs. An alternative film to discuss in these terms is *The Matrix*, in which a digital reality is presented as if it were 'optical' reality (the premise of the film is that the world as we know it is simply a computer simulation). However, on occasions the digital status of this optical reality becomes noticeable, particularly when it is distorted, for the main characters are able to manipulate the laws of gravity and time. For example, we see them freeze in mid-air (while the camera moves around them), a technique visualized on screen by the Manex Visual Effects company by means of 'bullet-time' special effects technology.

Chapter 8 uses Freudian, Lacanian, and New Lacanian concepts in an interpretation and close analysis of *Back to the Future*, in which the time travel narrative is combined with an Oedipal narrative. The film therefore conforms to an Oedipal interpretation, but with the terms reversed: Marty (the film's protagonist) travels back in time and encounters his future parents – in which his future mother falls in love with him (her future son) and his future father is depicted as a weak, non-authoritarian character. A New Lacanian reading, however (which is based on the work of Slavoj Žižek) focuses on the film's post-Oedipal, post-patriarchal meanings through concepts such as shame, humiliation (centring on the very idea of paternity and masculinity in relation to race politics), the regime of the brothers replacing the totemic father, and redefining the function of the superego. Other films that could well have been chosen include *Total Recall, Brazil, Pulp Fiction,* and *Twelve Monkeys.*

Chapter 9 reviews the transformations in psychoanalytic film theory, particularly its move away from Freudian and Lacanian inspired feminist film theory and towards Michel Foucault and Gilles Deleuze, from sex (biology) to gender. Gender belongs to the register of the discursive and the performative, necessitating a different kind of 'sexual politics'. The importance of gender explains why this chapter focuses on Foucault and queer theory, and ends up with Deleuze, to determine the value of their work in the analysis of the way film as a discourse performs gender roles. The film under analysis in this chapter, *The Silence of the Lambs,* shows the unworkable patriarchal order from the perspective of the young professional female. When analysed from a classical feminist perspective, which privileges the way film perpetuates sexual inequalities, *The Silence of the Lambs* is shown to centre on Clarice Starling and her 'problem': how to make it in a man's world, when the markers of sexual difference and gender identity have come under pressure though the pathology of figures like Buffalo Bill, and socially, by the improved career opportunities open to young women. In addition, the film privileges its Oedipal initiation story, though this time centred on a female, occupying the structural position of the male. The film in fact brings us to the limit of the relation between sexual difference and representation, of the representation of sexual difference in the cinema. To go beyond these limits requires a search for another type of interpretation, based on a set of new concepts: no longer the psychoanalytic concepts of absence, fetishism, or voyeurism, but institution as discourse, power and discipline, planes of vision, scopic regimes, enfolding gazes, madness and pathology, persecution, sensory, tactile, sonorous surface (Foucault), plus the crisis of the action image, deterritorialization, body without organs, becoming, and the fold (Deleuze). Other films that we could have analysed include *Se7en* and, of course, *Hannibal.*

## 1.5. Summary

### 1.5.1. What do film scholars study?

There are three broad areas of film study:

- film history
- film theory
- film analysis

'Old' film history is based on two assumptions: a *teleological* assumption that focuses the historian's attention on films that display technical innovations, and an *essentialist* assumption proposing that these technical achievements are important because they exploit cinema's essence. The 'New Film History' (1970s onwards) develops specific, delimited (rather than global) areas of film history to research, and carries out this research using rigorous, systematic, and explicit methods, plus the extensive citation of primary archival evidence.

## 1.5.2. Why study (classical and contemporary American) films?

(1) To understand the role of narrative in contemporary films. (2) Without classical and contemporary American films one probably would not be studying the cinema.

## 1.5.3. How to study films?

The form of inquiry in film studies involves a distinction between theory, methods, and analysis.

*Theory.* The aim of theory is to make visible the invisible structure that orders and confers intelligibility upon films. The values inherent in all film theories direct theorists' attention to particular aspects of film's general nature or essential properties. Each theory formulates hypotheses about the general nature of film, leading to the formation of declarative knowledge (or 'knowing-that', Gilbert Ryle).

*Methods.* The term 'method' simply refers to procedural knowledge ('Ryle: knowing-how'). Rhetoric identifies the stages involved in an entire course of reasoning, from start to finish. These stages involve invention, composition, and style, or:

- *inventio* (invention, discovery)
- *dispositio* (disposition, composition, arrangement)
- *elocutio* (elocution, style)

***Inventio*** For Aristotle, the primary way to invent arguments is by means of 'the topics': definition, comparison, relationship, circumstance, testimony.

Definition: put the subject matter to be defined into a general class; and then indicate the specific differences that distinguish this subject matter from other subjects.

Definition of 'man' = 'rational animal'; 'animal' is the general class; 'rational' is the specificity that distinguishes man from other animals.

Classical film theory: 'film' = 'art' (the general class).

Bazin: photographic recording capacity is the specificity that distinguishes film from other arts.

Arnheim: film's unique form is the specificity that distinguishes film from other arts.

Comparison: involves bringing two or more subjects together and then comparing and contrasting them, and sometimes ranking the two subjects in terms of the sub-topic of degree ('better or worse', 'more or less').

The debate focusing on the relation between classical and post-classical Hollywood cinema is conducted using the topic of comparison.

The values embedded in the *auteur* approach to film uses the topic of comparison to focus the critic's attention on the similarities across a director's entire output.

Relationship: cause and effect. With this topic, film analysts can explain the effects a film has on spectators by looking for probable causes.

Circumstance: 'the possible and the impossible'; 'past facts and future facts'. The analyst may set up a hypothetical or ideal spectator, and then write about what s/he experienced when watching a film (past fact) and then generalizes from these impressions, assuming that everyone who sees the film will react in the same way (future facts). Moreover, the analyst who sets up a hypothetical spectator is writing about possible reactions to the film.

Testimony: reference to external sources, either authorities (informed opinion) or examples from the film. We need to consider carefully the examples we use from a film, how we use them, and how many times we use examples, and why we choose one scene rather than another.

Arguments can also be invented by formulating a question that addresses a problem, or by carrying out a literature review and identifying the weaknesses and limitations of previous research.

**Dispositio**    Aristotle: introduction, presentation, proof, epilogue. For film analysts, the key is 'presentation'. The disposition of some analysts is determined by the disposition of the film, while others select specific shots and scenes.

**Elocutio**    Correctness, purity, simplicity, clearness, appropriateness, ornateness of language; avoidance of clichés.

**Analysis** One major aim of analysis is how a film creates meaning. Is there not a contradiction between the perception and reception of a film as a continuous experience and the fact that, at the material level, when we look at the strip of celluloid and even when we slow it down on the video player, a film is made up of wholly discontinuous, discrete entities: individual scenes, which themselves consist of segments? The analyst addresses this contradiction by focusing on the film itself, its fundamental units and how they are put together, or on the relation between the film and spectator (from the perspective either of psychoanalysis or of cognitive science).

## Endnotes

1 Cognitive film theorists would no doubt object to our strategy here of using the topic of comparison to identify the similarities between their theory and psychoanalytic film theory. They prefer to use the same topic to identify the differences between their approach and psychoanalytic film theory, and then use the sub-topic of degree to argue that these differences characterize the cognitive approach as superior to the psychoanalytic approach.

2 Precedent: 'a judicial decision in the past that can be used as a standard in making judgments about subsequent similar cases' (Corbett and Connors 1999: 119).

# 2 Classical/post-classical narrative (*Die Hard*)

## Introduction

This chapter sets itself the task of defining what is at stake in making a distinction between so-called classical and post-classical Hollywood cinema. After setting out the currently available range of definitions for this distinction (economic-institutional, period-based and historiographic, stylistic, cultural-political, technological and demographic), the chapter will focus on the stylistic one, and examine the often heard but not always convincing opposition between narrative and spectacle as one of the key features dividing 'old' from 'new' Hollywood. In the course of clarifying these terms, it will be necessary to recall some basic principles of cinematic story-telling. This we shall do by briefly outlining the premises and procedures of two types of narrative analysis that have dominated academic film studies: the Aristotelian, poetological one of the well-made (screen)play, and the structuralist one, originally derived from Claude Lévi-Strauss's analysis of myths and Vladimir Propp's morphology of the folk tale, sometimes transformed into a diagrammatic representation known as A.J. Greimas' 'semiotic square'.

As to spectacle, we shall be asking whether it can or should be construed in opposition to narrative at all. Thus, we are not comparing the two approaches to narrative directly with recent theories of spectacle, as developed, for instance, by feminist film theory's gendering of the opposition of active male scopophilia/epistemophilia (narrative: 'sadism demands a story') and passive female self-display (spectacle: 'to-be-looked-at-ness'); by historians of early cinema (the 'cinema of attractions' vs the 'cinema of narrative integration'); by proponents of special-effects movies ('roller coaster rides'); or by theorists of the media event ('spectacle, ceremony, festival'). Instead, we shall proceed in a more inductive manner, developing some of the relevant terms out of the analysis of the blockbuster *Die Hard* (produced by Joel Silver, directed by John McTiernan, screenplay by J. Stuart/ S.E. de Souza, 1988, starring Bruce Willis, Bonnie Bedelia, and Alan Rickman).

Our working thesis will be that the film is both 'classical' and 'post-classical'. We shall argue that the difference depends at least as much on one's critical agenda as on the 'objective' formal or technological properties of the film. For instance, we shall be citing some of the original reviews of *Die Hard* which tend to agree that the film stresses spectacle and neglects plot, though they are ambivalent as to whether they welcome or regret this shift. These newspaper reviews will be contrasted with a more academic textual analysis that highlights features of *Die Hard* usually associated with classical rather than post-classical Hollywood, in order then to propose another reading that stresses elements that could be called post-classical, but now grounding the latter in a slightly different set of criteria from those underlying the opposition spectacle vs narrative and the claim that post-classical Hollywood invests in special effects *at the expense* of plot. The chapter will conclude by suggesting that among film scholars, too, the boundary between classical and post-classical cinema tends to shift according to the domain a critic chooses to privilege, so that a jagged rather than a clean line separates the two terms, leading some to question the usefulness of the term 'classical' altogether. In this way, the distinction made in Chapter 1 between analysis and interpretation, as a change of focus rather than of object (briefly, a change from perceiving difference 'out there' to seeing it generated 'in here'), will have been put to use, notably by offering several – classical and post-classical, formalist and culturalist – readings, without making them compete for pre-eminence or exclusivity. It also foreshadows our approach in the subsequent chapters, where the different textual analyses justify themselves not so much because of a natural fit between the method and the film itself, nor because we feel that certain products of contemporary Hollywood cinema finally deserve an analysis backed by a challenging or prestigious theory. The aim is rather to show how different assumptions (e.g. those underlying a cultural studies approach with a gender perspective, or those taking on psychoanalytic and post-structuralist perspectives) can bring out different facets of the film text and the film experience, without thereby invalidating more tightly focused formal or narratological readings.

We have chosen *Die Hard* for a number of reasons. As indicated, it had mixed reviews when it was first released, but was immensely successful at the box office and went on to become a classic of its genre. In fact, it can be taken as paradigmatic of the new action film whose emphasis is supposed to be on spectacle and special effects rather than on story-telling and narrative. *Die Hard* also re-launched its leading actor Bruce Willis as a megastar, after a career mostly in television. As we shall see, his action-hero persona is unusual in that it engages in unexpected ways with gender, class, and race issues. Among aficionados of the genre, *Die Hard* was praised for its unusual soundtrack, a feature often cited when discussing the use of innovative film technology in post-classical Hollywood. Finally, it was popular enough to spawn several sequels (*Die Hard 2*, *Die Hard with a Vengeance*), each almost equally profitable for its producer–screenwriter–actor team, which suggests several layers of film industry self-reference, another feature of the post-classical mode.

In *Die Hard*, New York policeman John McClane (Bruce Willis) returns to Los Angeles on Christmas Eve, hoping to be reconciled with his wife, Holly (Bonnie Bedelia), now working as a senior executive for a Japanese multinational company. Straight from the airport, McClane joins her at the Nakatomi Christmas party, held at the Corporation's brand-new all-glass high-rise tower. Just as he and Holly are beginning to make up, a group of thirteen bank robber-terrorists, led by the formidable German Hans Gruber (Alan Rickman), burst in on the executive floor, demanding convertible bonds from the chairman, but eventually taking the entire staff as hostages. Having used the bathroom at the time of the attack, McClane is the only one who remains undetected, but he is trapped on some half-finished floors of the tower. A battle of wits and weaponry ensues between the high-tech terrorists and the barefooted cop-on-leave in his undershirt. With some help from a black LA policeman on the outside with whom he establishes radio contact and a buddy relation, McClane foils and eventually decimates the robbers/terrorists, killing their leader, freeing the hostages, and winning back his wife.

## 2.1. Theory: classical Hollywood cinema

The debate around the distinction between classical and post-classical Hollywood is often conducted polemically. The question is usually put as: is it still 'business as usual' in post-classical cinema, or do we need to change our vocabulary in order to 'do justice' to the movies made in Hollywood since the mid- to late 1970s? One faction (represented, for instance, by David Bordwell and Kristin Thompson) argues that there is no need to change one's approach, insofar as even the contemporary Hollywood blockbuster is in many salient respects faithful to the stylistic and narratological principles that have informed mainstream cinema from the 1920s to the 1960s. Another faction (one might cite Thomas Schatz, Tim Corrigan, Scott Bukatman) would argue that what we need to explain is not the elements that have stayed the same, but what is different, in order to account for the major revival of the fortunes of Hollywood picture-making. For instance, if we make questions of studio ownership, the package deal, new marketing techniques and global distribution networks the key factors that have transformed Hollywood since the mid-1970s, then we can conclude that this 'new' Hollywood is defined by its different spectator appeal and a shift in demographic profile to younger, more mobile and global audiences. If we focus on narrative, then we can still detect changes, though perhaps more gradual and contradictory: there is first the influence of the European art cinema of the 1950s and 1960s, introducing a looser chain of cause and effect actions, a less purposive hero, with more open-ended story outcomes; and as if to counter these changes, there is a parallel development where Hollywood narrative began to return to archetypal myths and stereotypes, but now filtered through the genre formulas of an earlier era's television series.

Advocates of a 'post-classical' break would add that it is special effects, new sound design, and the bodily sensations of the theme park and roller coaster ride which most clearly typify the aesthetics of New Hollywood, and that horror, violent death and explicit sex have migrated from the B-movie (and pornography) margin to the mainstream centre. Together, these sensory stimuli and thematic preoccupations have changed the way films are designed and visualized, with the result that they are differently interpreted (or used) by audiences. 'Spectacle' in this context would connote that such movies are 'experienced' rather than watched, that they offer a fantasy space to 'inhabit', rather than opening a window onto reality. The emphasis on sense impact and emotional contact makes it easy to think that story-telling no longer mattered in the way it used to during the period of the so-called classical style. But what exactly is or was the classical style?

## 2.1.1. Classical Hollywood narrative: two possible models

When outlining some of the possible prototypes of the classical Hollywood narrative, two groups or families come to mind, both of them literary in inspiration: one is derived from classical drama and the novel (Aristotle's poetics, Russian formalism, Gérard Genette); the other from oral narratives such as myths, fairy tales, and the early (picaresque) novel (Lévi-Strauss, Propp, Bakhtin). In film studies, the first is associated with the canonical story structure as taught in screenwriters' manuals, and refined in David Bordwell's neo-formalist poetics (Bordwell 1985); the second either adapted Vladimir Propp's *Morphology of the Folk Tale* (1973) (e.g. Wollen 1982) or evolved via Claude Lévi-Strauss's *Structural Anthropology* (1972) (as modified by, for instance, Raymond Bellour or Fredric Jameson) a standard structuralist reading of classical Hollywood that was widely debated thanks to exemplary analyses, such as *Cahiers du Cinéma*'s collective essay on John Ford's *Young Mr Lincoln* (in Nichols 1976: 493-529); structuralist studies of certain genres (the Western, the gangster film), or Colin MacCabe's ideological reading of the 'classical realist text' in literature and film (1985; 1986); finally, some scholars derived a method for the analysis of (mainly non-Hollywood) films from Mikhail Bakhtin's theory of the 'dialogical' or 'heteroglossic' text (e.g. Stam 1992). To these one could add the narratological model developed by Roland Barthes's *S/Z*, which will be laid out in more detail in Chapter 5.

Generally speaking, these models make a distinction between the macro-analytical level, which all narratives share, regardless of the medium and the material support (i.e. oral, written, film narratives, strip cartoons, allegorical painting), and the micro-analytical level, where one would be looking for the medium-specific stylistic devices and formal elements most pertinent to the analysis – in this case – of the cinematic discourse (the scale of the shot, camera movement and camera perspective, composition of the image, the transitions from shot to shot, the possible relations between sound and image).

For the macro-analysis, Lévi-Strauss has provided some of the more familiar categories, such as the notion of binary pairs as the building blocks of most known narratives. His method proved influential not because it represents some 'truth' about the world or even about the human mind, but because his key text in this respect, the 'structural study of myth' (1972: 206–31), adheres to a rigorous formalism and highlights central theoretical concerns of all narrative analysis, such as the question of segmentation, categorization, and classification, with (perceptible) 'difference' as the minimal condition for the production of meaning. Lévi-Strauss also drew some inferences as to the socio-cultural function of narratives: how narratives construct a culture's idea of nature and the supernatural, how they articulate kinship relations (and thus address the question of sexual difference), how they deal with contradictions (what logical categories are involved in narratives), and finally, how important they are for symbolizing a society's economic relations (their implicit systems of exchange and equivalence). He also provided a handy soundbite for the overall relation of narratives to the non-narrative world of brute facts and the social conditions of existence: myths are, he says 'the imaginary resolution of real contradictions' and therefore help human beings make sense of their lives.

The Aristotelian model by comparison seems to stress overall unity (of time, place, and action), rather than segmentation. It also centres on characters as initiating agents rather than on interpersonal transactions (functions) as the core elements of a narrative. But this type of analysis still distinguishes discrete units, such as act division (as in Greek tragedy, or the 'well-made' boulevard play), while also specifying the relation between acts (according to Aristotle, the 'complication' is followed by the 'reversal of fortune' which leads to the 'unravelling', coming after the 'moment of recognition'). Aristotle also noted that dramatic narratives are generally centred on a single protagonist. Accordingly, commentators agree that much of classical Hollywood narrative conforms to such a pattern:

> What is narrative ('a sequence of action ordered in time and space'), and what is Hollywood narrative? The scriptwriters' manuals borrow their models from drama, the Aristotelian division, or from the short story. Three or four act division, development of character, transformation, the initial situation, the complication, the resolution, the consequences of the resolution.
>
> (Hauge 1988: 83)

This contrasts with the Russian formalist model, which either follows Vladimir Propp, who simply chained together a series of narrative functions, or takes its lead from Victor Shklovsky and distinguishes between the underlying narrative material (story: the time–space continuum) and its compositional arrangement (plot: the discontinuous distribution of information). Shklovsky's distinction of *fabula* (story) and *syuzhet* (plot) has been reworked by David Bordwell, in his influential books *The Classical Hollywood Cinema* (co-authored with Janet Staiger and Kristin Thompson, 1985) and *Narration in the Fiction Film* (1985), where he theorizes the macrostructures and micro-levels of the canonical story-telling format by a blend of Aristotelian and Russian formalist principles. (In the first part of Chapter 6 we use *Narration in the Fiction Film* to analyse *Lost Highway*.) Thus from Aristotle Bordwell takes the 'character-centred' causal nexus driving the action forward, adding to it the double plot-line in the classical Hollywood film, the adventure and the romance plot, with the terms of narrative closure depending on the way these two plot-lines are intertwined, cross each other, and become the conditions for each other's resolution. From the Russian formalists he takes the idea of narration as the variable distribution of cues which the spectator has mentally to reassemble into a linear time–space continuum.

The double plot structure usefully directs attention to another way of describing the Hollywood film, which would combine the Proppian model with the Lévi-Straussian one. Instead of a double plot-line, one could speak of two levels, each of which is organized in specific ways. For instance, the adventure plot could be said to provide a film's 'surface structure', while the romance plot traces out a 'deep structure': one supplying the overt logic, the other a covert one. Simplifying perhaps, one might say that a particular kind of interaction links surface structure to deep structure, where 'realism' (verisimilitude) competes with 'fantasy' (a complex of desire and prohibition) and 'intelligibility' with 'real contradiction'. If we wanted to give this interaction a psychoanalytic turn, we could distinguish between the 'rational agent logic' and the 'logic of desire'. The former is unilinear, sequential, and causally connected; the latter is attached to the past, typified by repetition, and therefore often circular. These two levels can stand in a marked tension to each other, but this need not be noticed by an audience. In fact, it may be in the nature of the logic of desire to be invisible because in order to be effective emotionally as well as ideologically, it has to remain 'unconscious'.

To anticipate one point of our analysis of *Die Hard*: as a rational agent, McClane is trying to reclaim his wife, and he can do so only by rescuing the hostages and defeating the terrorists. But parallel, or 'underneath' this rational agent motivation, there is the logic of desire – or anxiety – which centres on McClane's desire not so much to retain his family as to maintain his identity as a working-class male, whose position in life is threatened both by the ascendancy of women in the world of (middle-class) management and by the devaluation of manufacture through the rise of (multinational) companies and their ability to shift production to low-wage countries. Thus, while at the rational agent level, McClane has to act purposively by calculating means and ends, at the level of desire he stubbornly sticks to his guns, an American male who asserts himself through macho values, brute force, and physical bravery. The skill of the film (or its 'ideological work') is to balance these two kinds of logic by melding them into a single, emotionally acceptable, and narratively plausible story. What appears as natural and self-evident to an audience focused on action and suspense could also be seen as a dubious ideological manoeuvre to reassert the values of patriarchy and (white) supremacy during a period of acute economic and multicultural transformation. At the surface structure, the film invents an external threat – the foreign terrorists – who are made to 'stand in' for the internal threat in the hero's deep structure, namely the contradiction between patriarchal masculinity (in the film encapsulated by the hero's wish never to have to say sorry) and corporate capitalism (its need for women in middle management jobs, dealing with personnel, communication and services, at the expense of semi-skilled males in the manufacturing sector). A substitution of one set of problems ('terrorists' or gangsters) for another (gender, race, and class identity) allows the film's narrative to engineer a trade-off between rational action logic and the logic of desire/anxiety whose exact working remains hidden and unconscious to both the hero and the audience.

## 2.1.2. Narrative as syllogism: the semiotic square

This psychic dilemma (of the hero) or ideological operation (of the narrative) can be described also in terms of formal logic or rhetorical strategy. Rather than presenting it as a simple opposition (surface structure vs deep structure), of binary pairs (male/female; white/non-white; American/foreign), we could see John McClane's rational action/ unconscious desire in terms of a more three-dimensional, dynamic process, of which the narrative is the linear, sequential articulation, at the same time as it is layered, differently textured, and contradictory. Lévi-Strauss assumed that a society starts telling itself myths when, as a culture, it is faced with contradictory experiences which it cannot make conscious to itself. The myth preserves the contradiction at the same time as it 'resolves' it in another medium and through another modality – e.g. that of 'art' or 'narrative' – which is why he argued that myths are 'the imaginary resolution to real contradictions'. Using the Oedipus myth as his example, Lévi-Strauss established a set of successive equations with multiple variables (A:B = C:D), in order to show how a family of mythic narratives transforms initially contradictory statements into apparently unproblematic equivalences (see Lévi-Strauss 1972). In our example, it would be 'terrorists taking women hostages' = 'working-class male identity taken hostage by middle-class female values', with the result that 'male identity' is allowed to rescue 'women hostages'. A.J. Greimas (1983) recognized in such representations of unconscious societal contradiction a traditional tool of logic, similar to Aristotle's syllogism which establishes the rules of deductive reasoning (see Corbett and Connors, 1999: 38–9). In order to deduce valid conclusions from a given premise, logicians distinguish between universal and particular propositions (quantity) and between affirmative and negative assertions (quality). Once these premises are fitted into the so-called 'square of oppositions', propositions can be tested as to their validity by diagrammatically placing the terms involved into the different corners of the square, according to whether they are positive or negative terms (e.g. human/not human), and whether they make universal or particular claims (all humans/some humans). The diagonals, top and bottom, left and right will then be readable as establishing pertinent relationships. From this example, Greimas developed his so-called semiotic square, in order to provide a structural model for the conditions of possibility of narratives. Made up of contradictions (mutually exclusive terms), contraries (a double negative generating a positive term), and implications (terms generated by complementary relations), the semiotic square is intended to identify the 'elementary structure of signification' by specifying the 'semiotic constraints' underlying culturally meaningful narratives.

For instance, seeing the repetitions, redundancies and relationships of mutual implication in Propp's morphology of the Russian folk tale, Greimas sought to reduce Propp's linear succession of narrative events to a closed system, where the semiotic constraints of the syllogistic square could account for the permutation of functions, after Propp had already successfully demonstrated how the multiplicity of characters in folk tales can be reduced to a relatively limited repertoire of functions, and particular actions can be understood as general 'moves'. If in a tale someone pronounces a prohibition, this will inevitably be followed by a transgression, so that prohibition and transgression imply each other and only amount to a single move. Greimas put forward the notion of semes (minimal semantic units) and arranged them in a four-term homology:

These four semes establish logical relations to one another. Seme S1 is the positive term. S2 establishes a relation of opposition to S1; –S1 is the contrary of S1; and –S2 is implied by S1. For example, if we invest S1 with the semantic content /human/, S2 = /anti-human/, –S1 = /not-human/, and –S2 = /not-antihuman/. James Kavanaugh finds these semes to be the dominant values in Ridley Scott's *Alien* (Kavanaugh 1980: 98):

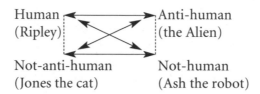

Greimas therefore shows how a narrative generates a sense of coherence and closure by a structure which contains negation, equivalence, opposition, and contradiction, as the logical types of relation elaborated to accommodate ideologically or culturally contradictory material. As Fredric Jameson sums up the advantages of the semiotic square:

> The first merit of Greimas' mechanism is to enjoin upon us the obligation to articulate any apparently static free-standing concept or term into the binary opposition . . . which forms the very basis for its intelligibility. [This] might take the form of the invention of some mediatory concept which bridged the gap [of the contradiction.] Or [the mechanism may function as] a value-system, in which raw materials coming in from the outside are at once given their place in the rectangular structure and transformed into symbolically signifying elements within the system.
>
> (Jameson 1972: 164)

Jameson has himself drawn a number of such semiotic squares for Hollywood feature films, including *Dog Day Afternoon* and *The Shining* (in Jameson 1990: 35–54, 82–98), in each case gathering up the socio-political 'material' that the film in question is said to transform.

Treating *Die Hard* as such an accumulation of culturally problematic 'material' from the outside, we can see how it is converted into binary pairs, and what sort of functions and relations are highlighted when we devise for these pairs the 'rectangular structure' of a semiotic square: male and female, working class and middle class, foreign and domestic, the police and the criminals could all be the binary pairs necessary for supplying the contradictory, contrary, and complementary relations, across which the imaginary resolution can be generated. There is even a 'mediatory concept bridging the gap', in the figure of the black patrolman Al Powell: we shall see how crucial not only he but 'race' is for the logic of the film's overall action and the plot's successive moves.

## 2.2. Classical Hollywood narrative: method

In terms of method, both the screenwriters' manual and the structuralist model can be used for the purposes of segmentation. Both name principles of division and difference, define what constitutes discrete units, and apply the processes that join the individual parts, in order to impart the impression of wholeness and completion to a narrative. But they also identify general characteristics, which we shall here divide between cultural definitions and formal definitions.

### 2.2.1. The 'classical cinema': some cultural definitions

While Aristotle argued that the cultural function of drama is to 'purge' the emotions by evoking 'fear and pity', the Russian formalists did not specify the purpose of narratives in this way. By contrast, Lévi-Strauss and his followers, as we saw, offer a number of explanations why story-telling and dramatic narratives are such universal features of human societies. In film studies since the 1970s, these explanations have tended to be narrowed down to those indicated above, namely ideology and gender (to which have been added race, ethnicity, religion, and colonialism). The broad underlying assumption of structuralist, post-structuralist, deconstructivist, postmodernist, and post-colonial analysis has thus been that the purpose of Hollywood story-telling is to disguise the ideological contradictions of contemporary capitalist society and to enforce patriarchal values in the form of normative heterosexuality. There is, nonetheless, a certain broad consensus, from Aristotle's 'catharsis' to structuralist 'semiotic work', from cultural studies' 'ideological work' to post-structuralist 'textual work' and cognitivist 'problem-solving' routines as to the cultural purpose and use of narratives. Even where they do not agree about the 'culturalist' assumptions, the 'political interventions' or the precise 'identity politics' agenda, the competing models here introduced nevertheless provide, at the macro-level of analysis, a number of common features. If we take David Bordwell as representing one of our models and Raymond Bellour the other, we can, for instance, note that:

- They agree on the effect of (ideological) self-evidence and the means by which it is achieved: David Bordwell calls classical Hollywood an *excessively obvious cinema*: 'classical cinema has an underlying logic which is not apparent from our common-sense reflection upon the films or from Hollywood's own discourse about them. Armed with [concepts like norm, paradigm, stylistic alternatives, levels of systemic function] we can go on to examine how that style [called the classical] organises causality, time, and space, [so distinctly that] like Poe's purloined letter, it 'escapes observation by dint of being excessively obvious' (Bordwell *et al.* 1985: 11). Raymond Bellour, for his part, speaks of *the obvious and the code*: 'According to Rivette's famous formula, "obviousness is the mark of Howard Hawks's genius." No doubt – provided we recognize the extent to which that obviousness only comes to the fore insofar as it is coded' (Bellour 2000: 72).
- They agree on the structural importance of normative heterosexuality: Bordwell's insistence on the romance plot echoes Bellour on 'the formation of the (heterosexual) couple'.
- They are also in agreement that the classical Hollywood cinema has been a remarkably homogeneous cultural phenomenon, having remained stable over a relatively long period of time: what Bordwell *et al.* call the 'classical mode of representation' is given a time frame from roughly 1917 to 1960. Similarly, Bellour would date classical cinema from D.W. Griffith's *The Lonedale Operator* (1911) to Hitchcock's *Marnie* (1964) (see Bellour 2000).

## 2.2.2. The 'classical cinema': some formal definitions

Implied in the cultural definitions above is the recognition that the Hollywood cinema's 'impression of reality', i.e. to pass off as natural something which is historical or ideological, is actually not so much a matter of how real that is which is being filmed (the documentary value or veridical status of what is before the camera) but how formally elaborated and how culturally ingrained the codes, norms, or conventions are that govern cinematic representation. It is not 'reality' that makes things appear real on the screen, but a rhetoric, a formal system which also transports a cultural logic. Among some of the indices are:

- Character-centred causality, based on psychological traits. Non-psychological forces are discounted as causal agents unless they can become metaphors of the protagonist's psychological conflicts, e.g. wars, revolutions, natural disasters, alien intrusions are made to mirror inner dilemmas, as we saw above in the case of John McClane's dilemma in *Die*

*Hard*. 'The classical Hollywood film presents psychologically defined individuals who struggle to solve a clear-cut problem or to attain specific goals. ... The principal causal agent is thus the character, a distinctive individual endowed with an evident, consistent batch of traits, qualities and behaviors.' (Bordwell, in Rosen 1986: 18). This contrasts, as indicated, with the functionalist and relations-based, essentially a-causal and instead more complexly 'logical' and 'semantic' structuralist and post-structuralist model of character and causality.

- Repetition/resolution (underlying the formation of the couple): 'a ... fundamental effect, proper to many American classical films, [is that] the textual volume multiplies and closes off doubly the field of its own expansion. The systematic accumulation of symmetries and dissymmetries throughout the filmic chain, decomposed by the work of a generalized segmentation, constantly mimics and reproduces (because the one produces the other) the schema of family relations which founds the narrative space' [... and] which makes of the segmental the textual condition for a happy slide from the familial to the conjugal' (Bellour, 2000: 205–6). What Bellour here indicates is that the sophisticated formal system of classical Hollywood is in the service of category shifts and logical transformation, which in turn is necessary for the ideological 'work' that makes Hollywood an important institution of ideological reproduction in the US, and increasingly so also in the rest of the world.

- Continuity editing (which creates a spatially consistent visual field and single diegesis by means of the following editing conventions: the 180 degree rule, the shot/reverse shot pattern, staging in depth, eyeline matches, cutting only within a 180/30 degree radius, match on action cuts) prevails over montage editing (multiple diegesis, discontinuity of shots in time and space, juxtaposition of shots). In the classical film, the fictional world is homogeneous: discontinuity and juxtaposition can always be reintegrated by the viewer at another level of coherence which does not violate the (generically defined) standards of verisimilitude and plausibility, with regards to either action, character motivation, or coherence of place/space. What this means in practice, as we shall see, is that everything in a classical film is motivated and serves a purpose, while the 'rules' of continuity editing ensure smooth, invisible (because either expected or retrospectively explicable) transitions from shot to shot and from segment to segment.

- Narration (variable distribution of knowledge among characters and between characters and audience). Narration is not primarily a matter of style or mode (melodramatic vs realistic or serious vs comic) but a question of how information reaches the audience and is mentally or emotionally processed. It is thus a key factor in how a film addresses, involves, implicates, activates, and manipulates the spectator. The function of filmic narration is to guide the eye and cue the mind, which might involve either an optical or cognitive centring of the spectator, drawing him or her into the picture, or a manipulation of the spectator's position of knowledge, playing either with his/her desire to see and observe (voyeurism, visual pleasure, scopophilia) or on his/her desire to know and to infer (exploiting ignorance, anticipation, or superior knowledge vis-à-vis the characters).

## 2.2.3. The logic of the actions: macro-analysis

Thus, one way of tying these features together and understanding their concerted effect in creating (the impression of) unity and coherence within a classical narrative film is to study the logic of the actions: what a character does, why s/he does it, what goals or aims are being pursued, what obstacles are encountered. Classical narrative in this sense is the name for a particular kind of logic – notably a temporal, a spatial, and a causal logic, held together by an overall trust in the efficacy of problem-solving procedures. At the same time it is a sort of semiotic operator, which uses the relation of parts to the whole, the hierarchy of characters, and the arrangement of their functions as elements for another kind of procedure – that of making meaning out of actions and moves rather than out of words and statements, in order to accomplish certain ideological tasks, such as presenting specific cultural values or social relations as natural, self-evident, and inevitable.

This already belongs to the category of (textual, psychic, political) work, and alludes to the second kind of logic, which we called the 'logic of desire' and which is also a logic of the actions, often identified with the Oedipus complex, by which Freud specified the model of (male) identity formation, but also a contradictory relationship between knowledge and belief, between the motives for action and their conscious rationalization. The particular interplay of surface and depth structure, linear movement, and obsessive repetition at the formal level has thus been called the 'Oedipal trajectory' of classical narrative. What this implies is that, irrespective of what a protagonist thinks his goal, problem, or ambition is at the practical, everyday level, he is also engaged at the symbolic or cultural level, usually in a crisis of identity, worrying about what it means to be or to become a man, anxious about his masculinity or ethnic identity, his place in the world, and in the process of finding out who he is, defending himself against castration anxiety and the threat of sexual difference. This Oedipal logic is particularly evident in the action-adventure genres, as well as the Western, the thriller, and the *film noir*. A differently gendered variant would be the logic of melodrama, where the main protagonist is generally a woman, and where the film charts the formation of female identity, or rather, its impossibility (what Mary Ann Doane (1987) has called 'the desire to desire').

An Aristotelian or Proppian analysis generally does not seek to describe this Oedipal trajectory. When clarifying what drives a narrative forward, what gets the protagonist going and keeps him/her going, the neo-formalist model does not problematize, for instance, the relation between the adventure plot and the romance plot. It is satisfied with noting the conflict between the hero wanting something and the world (often embodied in a clearly defined antagonist), putting obstacles in the way of the hero's object of desire. In Propp's morphological model, the motor is a lack, a missing object or person that the protagonist has to restore to its rightful place, like returning the princess to the king (her father) or getting the magic ring back from the evil dragon. In either case, however, positing an Oedipal trajectory does not invalidate or contradict the logic of the actions, and instead supplements and deepens it. For instance, identifying 'lack' with 'castration anxiety' is in one sense merely to link the object of desire or the missing object to a transgression: if in Aristotelian tragedy the hero has knowingly or unknowingly broken a law, which produces consequences that the hero has to address and his actions are called upon to redress, then in a more psychoanalytic language we could say that his actions are designed to defend himself against the anxiety of (sexual) difference, through adopting fetish objects and a narcissistic investment in his own bodily identity. A film like *Die Hard* is an outstanding example of this kind of logic: McClane assembles a number of fetish objects, and he has a particularly striking obsession with his physical body. So much so that we may even have to consider these features once more under the rubric of the post-classical, if we concede that the post-classical is not the non-classical or the anti-classical, but the excessively classical, the 'classical-plus'.

On the other hand, invoking the most abstract and general level of classical narrative, we could also summarize the logic of the actions as revolving around a disturbance/transgression, followed by the closing of a gap, and the return to a revised *status quo ante*. An even more basic schema would be to say that any narrative structure is complete when it consists of a triple structure: a state of equilibrium, followed by a disequilibrium, which is worked upon until a new equilibrium is established. This, too, would fit the situation of *Die Hard*: the equilibrium is the nuclear family (and the traditional roles of male/female within the family), disturbed by Holly leaving for Los Angeles (and taking on the male role of provider), which is being 'worked upon' (Holly exposed to mortal danger, John coming to her rescue), until the equilibrium is re-established (at the end, John is once more in control and presumably Holly is ready to have him resume his role as head of the family).

Thus, one of the tasks of textual analysis – one of the hypotheses when analysing a film – is to ask: what is the nature of the goal, the missing object or lack, or the disturbance/transgression in this particular film? If one follows Lévi-Strauss, the question would be: what is the 'real contradiction' for which the film narrative provides the imaginary resolution? And if one adopts Greimas's semiotic square: what are the relations of contrariness, contradiction, and implication that hold the contending forces in balance and at the same time move them towards the generation of a new, mediating term?

In all these cases, the greatest formal resource of the classical film would seem to be the extraordinary number of different kinds of symmetry, asymmetry, and repetition it generates, whether in the form of mirroring and doubling, or of splitting and reversal, echoes and parallels. Bellour has made this feature central to his type of textual analysis (in his essays on *The Birds, Gigi,* and *The Lonedale Operator,* in Bellour 2000). Analysing a sequence from Hitchcock's *The Birds,* for instance (Melanie crossing Bodega Bay to deliver the pair of love birds), Bellour can demonstrate how different kinds of symmetry, asymmetry, and alternation manage to structure the scene into a coherent statement, merely by exploiting three types of binary pairs: moving camera/static camera, Melanie looking/Melanie being looked at, and close shot/long shot. In Minnelli's *Gigi,* Bellour takes a whole film and meticulously demonstrates how its individual sequences are organized into an exactly symmetrical shape, so that the whole film folds into itself, like an intricate origami figure, but also folds outward from relatively simple units, which are like themes and variations in music, to build up a complete, seemingly linear narrative. Not only is the film structured like a poem, in that each sequence rhymes with another sequence, but individual sequences often turn out to have the same structure as the film overall, in other words, repeating itself at different levels, like the morphology of a plant, or like the fractals of the Mandelbrot set that computers generate out of very simple forms and programmes.

In the case of Griffith's *The Lonedale Operator,* Bellour argues that the Hollywood narrative film progresses and comes to a closure by what he calls the 'repetition-resolution' effect, which is his micro-analytical adaptation of Lévi-Strauss's equation with multiple variables. In other words, the excessive and insistent symmetries of the classical film are in fact no mere ornament or 'formal play', but the essential semantic/syntactic elements which the narrative puts to 'textual work', in order to accomplish an aesthetic effect (coherence, homogeneity, natural or organic unity) that doubles as ideological work (the naturalization of different kinds of cultural contradiction). This work one can describe in two ways. First, it is this repetition-resolution which reconciles or makes imperceptible the two different levels we mentioned earlier, the surface level and the depth level. While on the surface a Hollywood film impresses with its relentless forward drive, it cause-and-effect logic, its blow and counterblow, its question-and-answer progression, at the other level nothing really moves, and the narrative simply repeats the same configuration over and over again, as if the film – or its central character – was coming up against the proverbial brick wall.

Bellour has a name for this effect, too. He calls it the 'symbolic blockage' (see his analysis of Hitchcock's *North by Northwest*, or the final remarks in his essay on *Gigi*, in Bellour 2000), and also ties it firmly to the Oedipus complex, according to which both men and women have to learn to live within the patriarchal law, and the gender imbalance it implies. Rational agent logic and the logic of desire are therefore the recto and verso of each other, two sides of the same coin, put in circulation to help us cope with the contradictions of our culture or the conditions of human subjectivity/identity. The advantage of Bellour's formula is that it combines a micro-analysis of classical Hollywood's stylistic devices and formal features with a macro-analysis of Hollywood's cultural significance and 'civilizing ' achievement. These he ranks as highly as Greek mythology and the realist novel, insofar as they all represent aesthetically satisfying, self-contained, and self-regulating 'universes' that not only perfectly express the world-view of the periods or nations that brought them forth but also retain a validity and truth even for those who do not (or no longer) subscribe to their value systems or ideology.

To some extent, the neo-formalist analysis of classical narrative would be able to go along with Bellour's evaluation, maybe even extending it by arguing that there is a natural convergence between the formal characteristics of classical narrative and the organization of the mind: that the principles of Hollywood story-telling are closely modelled on the human mind's perceptual and cognitive organization, which explains both the longevity of the form and the universality of its appeal.

However, there are many who would dissent from this view, considering it ahistorical and ideologically blind, unacceptably ethnocentric, and biased in favour of the United States, its economy and its ideology, its patriarchal capitalist values, and its hegemonic role in the world. Thus, there is a second manner of looking at the 'work' done by classical narrative, with its formal semantics that relies so heavily on symmetry and repetition, using them to disguise and naturalize the very fact that it is a semantics and a rhetoric – which is to say that these images of fictional characters, their actions, reactions, contests, and victories, also spell out messages, addressed to someone, with the expectation of persuading and the effect of exacting assent. These sharply ideological critiques of classical Hollywood narrative, as an instrument of capitalism and the bourgeois value system, predominated in the 1970s. They were followed by a further radicalization of the argument in the 1980s, when feminist critics deconstructed this anti-bourgeois critique, in order to add to the charge-sheet patriarchy and sexual difference: classical narrative perpetuated gender stereotypes and reinforced gender imbalance not only by its emphasis on heterosexual romance but in the very stylistic devices that guarantee continuity editing, notably the shot/reverse shot and the eyeline match which split the visual field into the gendered opposition of 'seeing' and 'being seen'. In the 1990s, this reading of classical narrative once more gave way to a broader historical and cultural critique that added 'race' to the previous critical paradigms of the ideological and the feminist critique, now referred to as 'class' and 'gender'. We shall come back to the co-presence of three such critical concerns or 'discourses' in the analysis of classical Hollywood, making them part of our hypothesis about the possible definitions of the post-classical, and of our case for seeing the label fulfil a valid critical function, beyond or apart from its uses as a distinct stylistic or formal category.

## 2.2.4. The logic of the actions: micro-analysis

To conduct a complete analysis of *Die Hard* in the spirit of either Bellour or Bordwell would take up more space than we can give it here. Therefore we shall switch between macro- and micro-analysis, first by picking for commentary only one, albeit extended, passage (the opening), and second, by choosing a form of segmentation that varies between noting specifically filmic elements (the treatment of sound and image, of space, camera movement, and visual composition) and non film-specific ones, i.e. cognitive body schema and spatial categories, such as inside/outside, arrival/departure, or culturally (over)determined roles (such as 'husband/wife', 'mother/ father', 'superior/ subordinate') and character attributes ('violent'/'vulnerable', 'nurturing'/ 'macho'). We shall leave out the more fine-grained analysis of a single sequence or shot, of the kind Bellour has done in his analysis of *The Big Sleep* (2000: 69–76), where he minutely breaks down and segments no more than twelve shots to demonstrate their inner cohesion. Nor shall we conduct an analysis that hierarchizes shots of different type and specifies the order of their combination (as Christian Metz has tried with his *grande syntagmatique* (1974: 108–46)).

Some of the most influential extended application of this type of micro-analysis to classical Hollywood films can be found, besides the work of Bellour, in essays by Stephen Heath, who has conducted readings of entire films in an effort to provide exemplary and generalizable models of textual analysis (see his analysis of Welles's *Touch of Evil* (Heath 1975). Both Bellour and Heath have come to rather similar conclusions, which beyond individual authorship may either confirm the homogeneity of the Hollywood classical system or indicate common positions (or problems!) in their methodological assumptions. Especially with regard to the latter, Heath's work has received sustained criticism by scholars such as David Bordwell, Noël Carroll, and Edward Branigan, who in their turn have also provided close textual analyses of particular films and sequences, using cognitivist rather than psychosemiotic models (cf. Bordwell's analysis of *Rear Window* (1985: 40–47), and Branigan's analysis of *Hangover Square* (1992: 125–40)). Bordwell has also provided close stylistic analysis of shots and sequences, often on a comparative basis, by trying to describe the larger systems behind compositional choices, such as background/foreground, figure placement, and the staging and blocking of the action (following, e.g., in his *On the History of Film Style* (1997) the analyses of early cinema conducted by Barry Salt, Kristin Thompson, or Yuri Tsivian).

In our 'classical' analysis of *Die Hard*, we shall begin with a brief overview of the vocabulary recurring in the newspaper reviews, before moving to a more scholarly defined set of terms, used predominantly in structuralist analyses, such as the one by Thierry Kuntzel. His textual analysis of *The Most Dangerous Game*, a non-*auteur* Hollywood film from the early 1930s, is in some sense exemplary for our purposes because it is a sort of theoretical summary of the formal phase of analysing classical narrative, while also touching on broadly ideological motifs insofar as he subscribes to the assumption that the cinema when telling stories also does 'work', in the sense discussed above (Kuntzel 1980). Besides having internalized the methodological debates around Propp, Lévi-Strauss, and Greimas, followed the narratological developments around Barthes and Genette, and attended to the film-specific codes identified by Metz and Bellour, Kuntzel has also looked once more at Sigmund Freud's model of dream-work, in order to make some of its key concepts, such as condensation and displacement, useful for film analysis.

## 2.3. Classical analysis

### 2.3.1. The reviews

As mentioned, *Die Hard* is generally regarded as paradigmatic of the new Hollywood action-adventure picture, and has been compared to the Rambo films (e.g. *First Blood*), to Arnold Schwarzenegger vigilante films (e.g. *Predator*), and to the bi-race buddy films (e.g. the *Lethal Weapon* series). This genre or sub-genre (sometimes also known as the 'male rampage film') is judged by journalists to be a high-velocity, shoot-'em-up piece of mindless fun, a general opinion reflected in the specific reviews of *Die Hard* that appeared on 15 July 1988, in the week of the initial release:

[The film's] strategy . . . involves the deployment of a great many stunts and special effects, such as when Willis swings through a plate glass window on the end of a fire rope or when he drops plastics explosives down the elevator shaft.

(Roger Ebert, *Chicago Sun-Times*)

The new Bruce Willis picture *Die Hard* is a logistical wonder, a marvel of engineering, and relentlessly, mercilessly thrilling. It has masterfully executed effects, a pile-driver steady pace and a sleek, nonporous design. Add a percussive, big-star performance to the state-of-the-art mechanics, turn up all the knobs, and you've got a sure-fire, big-bucks, major-studio-style summer attraction. All that's left is to light the fuse.

(Hal Hinson, *Washington Post*)

[Due to weaknesses in the script, *Die Hard*] is a mess, and that's a shame, because the film does contain superior special effects, impressive stunt work and good performances, especially by Rickman as the terrorist.

(Roger Ebert, *Chicago Sun-Times*)

Willis has found the perfect vehicle to career wildly onto the crowded L.A. freeway of *Lethal Weapon* and *Beverly Hills Cops*. And he keeps a respectable grip on the wheel, his only acting requirements being to shift that *Moonlighting* glibspeak into R-rated high-drive and fire his Baretta 92 [*sic*] to heart's content. Never mind that the script is a monument to illogic. Led by a Mr. Hans Gruber (Alan Rickman), a stereotypical German elitist, the invaders have come to this high-rise, not to take hostages, not to issue demands, but to get at Nakatomi's moola – more than $600 million in a formidable safe. (So why bother invading the party to take hostages? Why not just rob the place at night, trouble-free? And why does it have to be Christmas Eve? And – oh, forget it.)

(Desson Howe, *Washington Post*)

As nearly as I can tell, the deputy chief is in the movie for only one purpose: to be consistently wrong at every step of the way and to provide a phoney counterpoint to Willis' progress. The character is so wilfully useless, so dumb, so much a product of the Idiot Plot Syndrome, that all by himself he successfully undermines the last half of the movie.

(Roger Ebert, *Chicago Sun-Times*)

McClane is in a bedroom suite when the gunmen burst in. So he hides out in air ducts, above elevators, on the roof, in an attempt to pick them off. And this cat-and-mouse is where director John (*Predator*) McTiernan earns his money. McClane takes the bad guys on one by one, the biggest fight being with gunman Karl (Alexander Godunov), a flaxen-haired tough cookie who's real mad at McClane for killing his brother and fellow thug. By the time all is said and gunned, the building's aflame, an FBI helicopter is downed, and the subplots are piled higher than the ubiquitous debris, the various *Die Hard* characters literally line up before the camera to complete their respective story lines.

(Desson Howe, *Washington Post*)

The film's early scenes, before the burglars arrive and the shooting starts, are tentative and unfocused. ... *Die Hard* is designed to present Willis as an action hero in the Schwarzenegger–Stallone mode, and he has the grace and physical bravado for the job. He can also be engagingly funny, an Olympian wiseacre. But there isn't much opportunity here for him to flash his wits. For most of the film we watch Willis, barefoot and stripped down to a T-shirt, work himself into precarious jams, then, through a combination of cleverness, chutzpah and superhuman athleticism, work himself out again. ... every detail in the film has been calculated purely for audience effect. The director, John McTiernan ... is unapologetic about his manipulations.

(Hal Hinson, *Washington Post*)

When describing the action of *Die Hard*, the newspaper reviews resort, quite stereotypically and consistently, to metaphors of speed, machine energy, violence (physical and pyrotechnic): 'stunts', 'special effects', 'pile-driver pace', 'logistical wonder, 'marvel of engineering', with Willis keeping a firm 'grip on the wheel', or ready to 'light the fuse'. These action set pieces are contrasted with 'the script [which] is a monument to illogic', 'tentative and unfocused' opening scenes, while certain characters are the 'product of the Idiot Plot Syndrome' who in the end 'literally line up before the camera to complete their respective story lines'. The underlying opposition of (impressive) spectacle and (incompetent) plotting is reinforced by reference to unashamedly commercial calculation with no pretensions to anything else: 'the director ... is unapologetic about his manipulations, giving the studio what it wants, a "sure-fire, big-bucks summer attraction"'. Although these reviewers seem to speak the (Aristotelian) language of the screenwriter, their mode of argumentation fits well into a structuralist model, since the contrasts they deploy are almost all organized into binary pairs (spectacle/narrative, commerce/art, glibspeak/flashes of wit, 'good performances'/'minimal acting requirements'). One (polemical) way of defining the shift from the classical cinema to the post-classical is here encapsulated. It unfavourably contrasts the supposed absence of (narrative) substance with the fireworks of special effects, a roller coaster ride, which the critics nevertheless confess to being impressed by.

One simple way to move beyond the polemical divide between spectacle and narrative is to ask whether *Die Hard* can still be discussed in the categories itemized above for analysing classical narrative cinema. Does it make sense as a psychologically motivated narrative, following a cause-and-effect logic, adhering to the three unities? Is it narrated coherently, so that the 'distribution of knowledge' (who knows what, when, and how) is in the service of comprehensibility and the regulated deferral of expectation known as 'suspense'? Or can we account for it according to the structuralist model, follow its Oedipal logic, articulate the binary pairs of oppositions that could be plotted as a system of semiotic constraints, and see whether they undergo the sort of transformations implied by the repetition–resolution effects?

The answer, as has already been hinted at, is yes, both of our models make good sense of the film. *Die Hard* has a very classically constructed three-act scenario; its script is professionally written, with the moves, character motivations, and plot-points carefully worked out. Its narration is consistent, focused mostly on the central protagonist (in Bordwell's terminology, 'restricted'), and the story keeps to an impressively intricate unity of action, place, and time, taking up roughly twelve hours from dusk to dawn on Christmas Eve in a single LA location. Furthermore, a detailed segmentation would show how the film adheres to both Bordwell's and Bellour's rules that govern the relation between the transparency and 'obviousness' of the dramatic scenes, and the coded, elaborated, stylized manner of their representation. We have already noted the film's Oedipal trajectory and the formation of the couple, along with the character-centred causality and the double plot structure. What the plot may lack in verisimilitude and plausibility (but by which standards are these to be measured in the action-adventure genre?) it more than makes up in its semantic texture, its obsessive concern with male white identity and sexual difference at the symbolic level, and its many references to the topical cultural studies themes of 'race–class–gender–nation'. Yet it is precisely because some of the 'excessiveness' elaborated around the 'obviousness' is so foregrounded (not only in the action scenes), and because the film at times flaunts a special knowingness about its own generic conventions (it jokes about being a remake of *High Noon*, for instance, and exposes Gruber as an ignorant snob: he thinks that John Wayne rather than Gary Cooper played the lead), that one has to conclude that its 'ideological work' on the fashionable themes of 'identity politics' is not so much unconscious and displaced as self-consciously displayed. These, then, are more reasons for considering *Die Hard* also as an example of 'post-classical' cinema, a thesis whose implications we shall be probing in the second part of the analysis.

## 2.3.2. Classical analysis: the opening

In keeping with the points listed under 'Method', we shall concentrate on the logic of the actions, trying to combine elements of the Aristotelian model with those of the structuralist one. For many of the considerations just mentioned, the openings of films take on a privileged role, being in a sense that part which sets up the terms of the system. They pose the enigma, the dilemma, the paradox, to which the film as a whole will appear to give the answer, the resolution. Openings of classical films are somewhat like manuals. The manual is what one finds when unpacking the box of a new appliance. It belongs to the package, but it is also at one remove from the package: a meta-text, to use a word one would not normally employ for a manual. Similarly, the opening of a film could be regarded as a special case of a meta-text. It is separate from and yet part of the narrative, in that it usually establishes setting, place, and time, as well as introducing the main protagonist(s). But it is also a kind of meta-text in the sense that by introducing us to the rules of the game, it shows us how a film wants to be read and how it needs to be understood. In this regard, the opening is also different from a manual, which is usually a text about an object, while the opening of a film is made of the same 'material' as the object itself. In fact it is, for most viewers, indistinguishable from (the rest of) the film. To mark the special textual/meta-textual status of the opening of a classical film, critics have had recourse to a number of metaphors. For instance, the opening has been considered as a 'compression' or 'condensation' of the film. Another term is that of *mise-en-abîme* – literally, a plumbing of depths. Originally derived from medieval heraldry and baroque picture puzzles, the term hints at a particular type of self-reference, a 'drawing attention to itself'. Applied to an opening sequence, it designates the economy of mean(ing)s with which a Hollywood opening prepares the stage and often presents (in a different form or code) the whole film in a nutshell.

It is this effect of compression or enfolding of a larger unit in the opening which made Thierry Kuntzel turn to Freud's analysis of dreams in his essay on *The Most Dangerous Game* (1932, dir. Schoedsack and Cooper) (Kuntzel 1980) and a similar one on *M* (1932, dir: Fritz Lang) (Kuntzel 1978), which he collectively called 'The Work of Film' (*Le Travail du film*). If we think of a dream as a text, its typical feature is that it can seem a very ordinary story, visually coherent and even logical, except that the very ordinariness serves to disguise another level of meaning, where unconscious fantasy material is being negotiated. On the other hand, a dream may consists of very vivid scenes or violent set pieces but make no overall sense at all. These tensions between the overt and the covert meaning of the dream led Freud to posit a number of transformational moves brought about by the unconscious activity he called dream-work. The main moves Freud described under such headings as 'condensation' and 'displacement', 'screen memory' and 'wish-fulfilling fantasy', 'representability' and 'secondary elaboration'. Taking our cue from Kuntzel's use of Freud for the overall framework, but combining the terminology of Propp, Lévi-Strauss, and Bellour as well as Freud, we shall be looking at the film's opening. Not least in light of the opinion of one reviewer that the opening scenes were 'tentative and unfocused', it will be instructive to put his judgement to the test.

### 2.3.3. Entry (into the film, entry into the fiction, entry into the characters)

The opening of *Die Hard* lasts from the moment John McClane lands in LA, walks through the lobby, and witnesses another passenger being welcomed by his wife or girlfriend to the time he collects his baggage and is picked up by the Nakatomi chauffeur, Argyle (with whom he has a discussion about his family, Christmas music, and the size of Argyle's expected tip), before being dropped at the entrance of the Corporation headquarters. The sequence is thus bracketed by two arrivals (at the airport and at the Nakatomi Tower), but these two visual rhymes are prepared and punctuated by a whole series of 'brief encounters': with the passenger on the plane, the stewardess on the way out, the blonde woman in white hot pants who for a moment he thinks is smiling at him, the black chauffeur Argyle, the security guard, the Nakatomi CEO, and finally, Holly.

Not only do these encounters between two arrivals structure the sequence into smaller units of action, charting a sort of narrative path for McClane, they are also designed to give us a lot of information about McClane as a character: even though travelling on a plane, he carries a gun, he has the roving eye for the ladies (and they for him), he is disappointed that Holly thought herself too busy to meet him in person (hence the mistaken welcome from the blonde), and that – compared to his status as a New York cop – she is clearly an important person in the corporation if she can send a chauffeur. In the conversation with Argyle, McClane gives us the gist of his central problem (he is separated from his wife and does not like it) and the way he intends to resolve it (by joining his wife and little daughter for Christmas, the ideal family occasion in a season of peace and reconciliation). McClane's most bulky item of luggage is a giant teddy bear, which foreshadows a 'Father Christmas' theme that is to become important subsequently (see below). In order to close off the opening scene even more, and mark it as a self-contained unit, a kind of complete mini-narrative, Argyle, who has been discussing McClane's marital situation and the chances of a successful reunion, says to McClane as he drops him: 'and now we get the music playing and they live happily ever after – but just in case they don't, here's my telephone number. I'll be waiting for you in the car-park.'

### 2.3.4. Repetition, alternation, and reversal

Already in the opening we note a number of formal repetitions, such as the series of encounters with secondary or even apparently irrelevant characters, expendable in that some are one-offs and seem to contribute little to the plot, and yet indispensable in other respects. For apart from telling us something about the main protagonist or giving him an occasion to tell us about his motivation and goals, they also exist in order to alert us to the principle of repetition itself. In one case, as we shall see below, McClane's encounter with the passenger next to him, his utterance spells out – albeit in riddling or highly coded fashion – the terms of the narrative's resolution. The principle of repetition as alternation and reversal is rehearsed twice more in this opening. Once when the passenger, in response to McClane's puzzled look after receiving his advice about what to do in order to avoid jet lag, answers: 'Trust me, I've been doing it for nine years', a phrase which McClane repeats – with a slight, but significant variation – immediately after, in response to the Asian-American's puzzled look, upon seeing McClane's gun on his shoulder-holster, as he stretches to get his jacket from the overhead luggage hold: 'Trust me, I've been a cop for eleven years'. The second verbal exchange of the opening is built exactly like the first. When Argyle, nearly missing him, greets McClane by apologetically saying to him: 'It's my first time *driving* a limo (as chauffeur)', McClane repeats the sentence, reassuring Argyle that it also is his first time *riding* a limo (as passenger)'. Again, beyond signalling McClane as a wiseacre and smarty-pants (who is heading for a comeuppance), the verbal repartee 'draws attention to' (acts as a *mise-en-abîme* of) the principle of repetition.

## 2.3.5. Characters and functions: transfer and substitute

The question of expendable characters brings us to the issue of who and what the spectator identifies with, and what, in a classical narrative, is the function of secondary characters. One way to describe them is in Proppian or Greimasian terms: instead of centres of autonomy or agency, they are relays, vehicles of transfer. They can signal a displacement, or they can be initiating a chain of substitutions. In this function they are supported by the *mise-en-scène* and narration, i.e. the formal elements of composition, camera placement, and attention guidance. In *Die Hard*'s opening, the camera is noticeable by being so clearly in the service of the narrative (underlining plot-points) and narration (manipulating the distribution of knowledge). After an initial shotcountershot scene of the exchange with the passenger, edited in classical continuity style with eyeline matches, the camera seems to take on a movement of its own, independent of McClane for part of the time, and then again lending itself to his point of view (for instance, in order to trick us into making the same mistake as he), while also cleverly shifting to Argyle's point of view, the cut made imperceptible by a near-collision between Argyle and the baggage trolleys. By a threefold mimetic process of equivalence (or doubling, as Raymond Bellour would say), the camera associates itself successively with different points of view, while nonetheless keeping the movement from one place to the next extremely smooth, and managing to establish the main protagonist as focus of attention as he moves through this space. Narratively, this movement is determined by the logic of events and their code of verisimilitude: what one does when deplaning and arriving inside an airport. Figuratively, the camera movement draws attention to particular objects (such as McClane picking up the teddy bear from the luggage conveyor belt). Symbolically, it elaborates the characters' function as substitutes: the woman in white substitutes for the absent Holly, and Argyle out of his depth as chauffeur substitutes for McClane out of his depth in the world of company executives.

Twice, the camera's point of view is delegated to the main character via a close-up: once of an object, in the form of a POV shot (of the oversized teddy bear), and once of a face (of the smiling woman, itself a repetition of the stewardess's smile, who had not only seen McClane's come-on look but decided to ignore it). The second close-up connotes a situation of collusion and participation in which the spectator is implicated by way of inference: once we know more than McClane (we see what the stewardess sees), and once we know as little as McClane (we too think that the woman in the white pants is smiling at him). The shots thus give us access not only to the field of vision of the character, which may be deceptive, as in the point of view (POV) shot of McClane looking at the blonde woman, but also to the character's intention, secret plans and thoughts, which we infer via the object brought to our attention. The transfer is from camera to object, but the meaning of the shot has little to do with the object as such, because the object is itself a stand-in, a substitute: for the characters' motivation, inner thoughts, and response.

More generally, in a classical Hollywood narrative such as this one, the action progresses by involving us with the protagonists, successively and by transfer, using the film's objects as much as the dialogue, to foreshadow its future action spaces, and using its secondary characters to mirror the main ones via substitution and equivalence. One sub-category of this mode of transfer is what has been called the 'erotetic' principle of question and answer, where one scene implicitly 'answers' the previous one. For instance, at one point, Holly slams down the photo of McClane on her desk, as if to answer the blonde woman leaping into the arms of her man at the airport. Later on there are several more such ironic links, especially in the breakdown of communication between McClane and Argyle (his self-appointed, useless helper) and the intuitive communication between McClane and Al Powell (his initially reluctant helper).

## 2.3.6. The emblematic cluster

In an opening scene or sequence, we often find a privileged image or composition which in a sense gathers together diverse and heterogeneous elements in a single configuration, whose meaning will only become fully apparent in retrospect, and which thus functions rather like an emblematic picture, or a condensation of the various narrative motifs, as well as implying a temporal structure of anticipation and foreshadowing. In *Die Hard*'s opening there are a number of such constellations, chief among them the verbal exchange between McClane and the passenger sitting next to him on the plane as they land in LA. The passenger, noticing how tense McClane is before and during touchdown, gives him a piece of advice: 'When you get home, take off your socks, and curl your toes into a fist.' The phrase represents, in figurative form, three central oppositions (or enigmas) which the narrative sets itself the task to resolve: the culturally difficult relationship between masculinity and the exposed body, the anxiety-producing relationship between vulnerability and violence, and finally, the counter-intuitive relationship between common sense and a winning strategy.

The opposition toe/fist, as well as the suggestion to take off his socks, will, as we shall see, feature prominently – and unexpectedly – in the subsequent narrative. The figure of the passenger is also important in another respect: he is an Asian-American, and thus introduces the semantic cluster of race and ethnicity, used in the film both as a semantic category (it gives rise to a number of pertinent oppositions with which the narrative can play to advance its resolution) and as a cultural-historical category, in that it hints at the antagonistic constellation of Americans, Japanese, and Germans, which the film exploits also for an (anti-?) globalization argument.

## 2.3.7. The enigma

Narratives, according to Tzvetan Todorov, can be characterizsed, at their most basic, as structures which begin with a steady state, an equilibrium, a balance. This balance is disrupted by an intervention, an irruption (in *Die Hard*, the breakup of John and Holly McClane's marriage, the sudden burst of the terrorists' entry into the office Christmas party) which it is the task of the narrative to neutralize and to eliminate, so that finally an equilibrium can be re-established which resembles the initial one, but with significant differences.

As we saw above, the narrative's necessary interruption can also be presented as a lack, a desired object that is lost or, as in this case, an enigma, a puzzle. On the surface of *Die Hard*, the lack or lost object is the family unit which McClane has come to restore. At the deep-structure level, however, we are now arguing, it is the Asian-American's piece of advice which is the enigma, except that neither we nor McClane know that it is actually a riddle.

In the terms of our analysis, therefore, it belongs to the logic of desire rather than to rational-agent logic.

The opening scene by itself does not reveal the riddling nature of the advice. Instead, it lets us see the constellation also from the other point of view – that of Holly and, by extension, the Nakatomi Corporation. As McClane lands and leaves the airport, we cross-cut to the Christmas party at the Corporation headquarters, the speech of the CEO, and Holly telephoning her maid at home and speaking to her daughter. From this combined perspective of Holly and the people at the Nakatomi Tower, McClane constitutes the interruption and intrusion, drawing a powerful parallel between McClane and the terrorists. On the face of it, the terrorists only appear in the subsequent segment, taking over the lobby, and then bursting into the building and violently crashing the party. But covertly, the terrorists do appear in the opening sequence, and this twice over. After Argyle's limousine has entered Nakatomi Plaza, the camera cuts to a big, sinister-looking truck also heading in the same direction. This, as it turns out, is the delivery truck the terrorists use to gain entry into the underground parking of the corporate tower, which they do at about the same time McClane is told by Argyle that he'll wait for him in the parking lot. In this way, the film establishes a parallel between McClane's arrival and the terrorists' arrival: both are outsiders, both are disruptive forces in the lives of Holly and the Nakatomi Corporation.

The first time the terrorists appear, however, is even earlier, on the plane, when the Asian-American passenger notices McClane's gun. A gun on a plane usually means only one thing, terrorists plotting a hijack, and this is the inference which McClane's answer acknowledges: 'Don't worry, I've been a cop for eleven years.' This scene, too, draws a parallel between the terrorist and McClane, but now on the basis of his being a policeman – a parallel that the narrative takes up several times later when the police inadvertently help the terrorists, instead of McClane.

## 2.3.8. A system of semiotic constraints

Openings, then, are also an opportunity to identify surface and deep structure, and their interrelatedness. Here, the formal-textual operations play through the different repertoire of making continuity out of discontinuity while at the same time 'thickening it' by way of figuration and verbal texture. The Hollywood text is 'closed' but also 'open': there are different entry points for an audience, many of the cues are ambiguous, but it is a planned ambiguity, multi-layered and multi-levelled. But the opening can also be read as quite unambiguous, formally closed, semantically and syntactically complete – in which case it does serve as a *mise-en-abîme* of the whole and as a miniature version of the overall design. *Die Hard*'s opening scene, although not detachable, is nonetheless an entire story, in that the meeting of John and Holly at the Christmas party could already be the reunion and reconciliation that both partners are obviously hoping for. But if this was the ending of the story, it obviously would not be worth a movie, and on the other hand, it would not give us the 'cultural' message: that for a relation like this to come together again, both partners have to work for it. In this sense the intrusion of the terrorists is, from the point of view of the story of John and Holly McClane, only the external motivation to render inescapable the necessity for them to 'work' on their relationship. The action-adventure movie becomes the place for family–couple therapy.

The point we are trying to make is threefold. One: the examples give an idea of how the signifying economy functions in classical Hollywood narrative – a relatively limited number of elements or pro-filmic events are subjected to several permutations and combinations, in order to yield complex structures, whose logic can be quite abstract. The nature of the narrative intrigue of a Hollywood film is such that in terms of motivation of the protagonists, and in terms of information about them (what is visually, verbally, or aurally introduced), the conflict and the psychology are kept simple, in order for the overall design and effect to become complex and intricate. And in the process, everything is made to count, everything is put to use. Nothing is wasted: as with a good butcher or housewife, there are few leftovers at the end of the day, or like a modern car production line, where profitability means a minimum of components, arriving just in time and capable of being assembled into several models. What the craft that goes into a Hollywood screenplay is in the service of – and justifies the many individuals who sometimes work on it – is not only the neat act division, the complication and reversals, or the tying up of loose ends, but what David Thomson, in a review of Howard Hawks's *The Big Sleep*, once called 'the obliging servitude of the arranged world'. Everything is constructed, created, but then seems just sufficiently dense and opaque to be experienced as 'real', seems just sufficiently 'there' to become part of a rhythm of rupture and resistance, difference and separation, in order for there to be the impression of a fit between story and 'world', and their successful narrative integration.

Second: when decomposing/recombining the image material, in order to draw from it its full narrative and semiotic potential, classical cinema relies very heavily on relations of similarity and difference, by employing the rhetorical possibilities inherent in the similarity/difference axis represented by metaphor and metonymy. Some of these similarities are visual and verbal, i.e. echoes and rhymes, but others require a fair amount of abstraction in order to register. It would therefore seem that there is a kind of continuum from the perceptual to the cognitive, from the sensory to the conceptual. One cannot neatly separate what is 'out there' in the image from what goes on 'in here', the mind of the spectator.

At the same time, it is always surprising to realize how much 'work' of very different kinds (textual work of scripting and *mise en scène*, professional expertise in staging, production values) goes into the simplest Hollywood scene. To take a moment of the textual (micro-) level: there is an apparently merely functional scene, when the cop car with Al Powell, the patrolman, is driving up to Nakatomi Plaza after the emergency call, but fails to find anything suspicious (i.e. he is 'blind' to the real goings-on). On the soundtrack there is a reference to a blind singer, 'not Ray Charles but Stevie Wonder' – and the car's headlights are on/off depending from whose point of view they are seen, the unsuspecting Al's or the anxious McClane's. The narrative perspective, the way the scene is seen, in other words, crucially differs in each shot, and the *mise en scène* underscores this difference in the moral (as opposed to optical) point of view of the two characters, by introducing what to some sharp-eyed commentators, appeared to be a continuity error (the on/off headlights). But the continuity has not 'goofed', as the blooper sheet has it (see http://us.imdb.com/Goofs?0095016 listing the continuity errors in *Die Hard*). Rather, the director seems to have taken – perhaps surprisingly for a mainstream Hollywood film, but these moments in the past were the delight of *mise en scène* or auteurist critics – some liberties with plausibility, for the sake of added psychological depth and narrational involvement.

Third: this 'work' on the surface texture and the narrative-thematic context of a film is, however, not quite the 'work' we alluded to earlier on, whether we call it 'dream-work' after Freud or 'ideological', 'textual' work and 'problem-solving' after culturalist, post-structuralist, and cognitivist critics. What we identified as the level of abstraction produced in the opening scene of *Die Hard* is the 'work' of repetition, with specific gestures or actions repeating themselves to generate a concept, which is to say, a relation imbued with meaning. It is at this point that the 'work' we are trying to identify goes beyond a purely binary structure of oppositions and can be cast in the form of a syllogism of the kind identified above with Greimas's semiotic square.

For the genre of action-adventure films called 'male rampage films' and which, besides *Die Hard*, includes *Lethal Weapon I and II*, Fred Pfeil has worked out what could be called a 'system of ideological constraints'. Seeing the films as fables of 'masculinity in crisis', he distinguishes between male and not-male, phallic and non-phallic, state (police) and business (the multinational corporation), wilderness and domesticity, with the heroes and the villains symmetrically positioned as opposites, but each one also ambiguously poised as an outsider 'in between' (in the case of John McClane, between the non-phallic wilderness of bi-racial male bonding and the feminine world of sexual difference and the family, while Hans Gruber is in between the phallic world of authority/the law and the 'neutered' world of the multinational corporation). In Pfeil's scheme, *Die Hard* features as an example of an ideological narrative which tries to mediate between Fordist and post-Fordist values, but does so by a complex *combinatoire*, made up of quite basic anthropological units:

> [Position (S1)] is the nameable yet never represented space of 'the Wild' – the place the white protagonist has come from before he lands in LA, be it Viet Nam (in *Lethal Weapon*) or, in *Die Hard*, that other well-known symbol of multiracial rot and riot, New York. The Other, or [S2] of this space would then clearly be 'Domesticity,' the site of (heterosexual) life and family life. The Opposite [–S1] in these films must be the place of Business or professional-technical work. And finally, filling the place of [–S2], functioning as the inverse of the nurturant realm of hearth and home, we find the official space of law, authority, and order, i.e., the State.
>
> (Pfeil 1993: 127)

Around this Greimasian analysis, we could also establish for *Die Hard* a slightly different system of semiotic constraints, constructed as the (cultural, ideological) incompatibilities of home and office, subtended by the (natural, cultural) difference between male and female. Although it broadly comes to the same conclusions, it would help us grasp one of the turning points of the story, namely the moment where McClane is closest to giving up, thinking he is about to die, while asking Al to tell Holly that he is sorry for how he behaved. The significance of this scene at the level of cultural contradiction is that McClane's situation here most exactly promises the structural resolution to the initial problem, namely that of Holly as a 'working mother'. He has become a 'feminized male', whose body bears the marks of femininity (connoted by his bleeding feet, to which the film has given a gender connotation – see below), whose interpersonal situation is emotional dependence (on Al, the cuddly desk cop, coded as a non-phallic male) and whose subjective state is his readiness to apologize (again, culturally coded as unmasculine). At the level of the Oedipal deep structure, it is the moment where he 'accepts castration', but at the ideological level, it would be the end of patriarchal disavowal of castration, while on the level of the action/rational agent logic it is the moment of greatest danger and imminent death. Thus, the narrative has to invent an escape for McClane, thereby also initiating a gradual climb back to phallic masculinity and a reclaiming of patriarchal values, towards the finally reassertion of an apparently unreconstructed macho identity. The Greimasian model thus allows us to trace more precisely the semantic/logical operations that make the ideological work possible and – an important point – pleasurable to that part of the audience that unconsciously identifies with McClane's anxiety and consciously wants to emulate his cocky masculinity.

## 2.3.9. Repetition/resolution

Part of this work, as we have stressed several times, is a certain excessiveness. This makes *Die Hard* also an example of what Colin MacCabe or Stephen Heath have analysed as a necessary instability of the classical system, its constant breakup of the configurations and their reassemblage. Heath, in his essay 'Narrative Space' (1981: 19-75), traces the different kinds of excess and instability in Hitchcock's 'geometry of representation', as they can be seen, for instance, in the different function of two paintings in *Suspicion*. This necessary instability, it might be argued, manifests itself in *Die Hard* as an emphasis on special effects, on the pyrotechnics of violent assault on bodies and buildings, typical of an action film but here staged in such a flamboyantly self-confident way that one suspects an underlying panic to be part of its violent urgency. For this kind of excess only serves to displace and cover up others kind of instability: the skewed 'relations' between male and female protagonist, the non-congruence between what John wants/needs and what Holly wants/needs for their gendered identity, and the asymmetry that locks executive female and working-class male into conflict and contradiction. A Bellour-type reading would identify the 'symbolic blockage' around the impossibility of McClane accepting his second, social 'castration' (in the new world of globalization), and therefore starting the pyrotechnical mayhem, a sort of fetish action by which he hopes to escape the acceptance of his first, originary castration under the law of patriarchy. This would identify his actions as motivated by guilt feelings about 'unfinished business' (in relation to his wife, but also to his profession as a New York cop), and it would confirm that while this classical narrative is apparently 'about' the male hero's psycho-sexual identity, 'woman trouble' is also at its heart. *Die Hard* can indeed be shown to be a film where the woman's unstable position in the world of men appears as the 'real' trouble in the system, not post-Fordism. But at the surface level, it is the trouble with a certain type of masculinity that actually propels the film. Such an emphasis on male desire and male anxiety means that masculinity becomes the motor of a perfectly functioning narrato-logical machine, where there can be no interruption or pause, and where even minor details and detours are relentlessly reintegrated, or retrospectively re-motivated as contributing to the central dilemma, by providing either possible solutions (the roads not taken by the hero) or impossible solutions (the pitfalls avoided by the hero).

One of the impossible solutions avoided by the hero is that provided by the subplot around Ellis, Holly's colleague and McClane's sexual rival. While Ellis may be more respectful of Holly's professional identity, both his predatory sexuality and his subservience and betrayal are severely punished by the film. His bad character's uncompromising stance towards McClane and Holly retrospectively confirms the hero in having been right in his uncompromising stance, also vis-à-vis his wife. As to a possible solution not taken by the hero, there is a scene of the sex-mad couple at the party, who burst into the room where John and Holly are trying to make up, looking for a safe place to copulate. It is a shot that is repeated when the terrorists burst in, and its importance is indeed twofold: it demonstrates in a jokingly graphic way one option for John and Holly to get together again very fast indeed. But it also sets up expectations – false as it turns out – that the second time will also be an irruption of unbridled libido, when in fact it is an entirely different danger to the Christmas festivities. Here the repetition does not provide a resolution, but points to a dead end (for the couple), in the sense that their 'work' on the relationship encompasses more than sexual desire, which is shown (as so often in classical American cinema, with its puritan streak) to have destructive consequences: the wild sex drive of the couple is directly associated with the criminal drives of Gruber and his gang.

Another road not taken for McClane is the fate of Al Powell, the black patrolman. On the one hand, we see how his goals chime in with those of the main characters, especially McClane, both as a cop (to do his duty) and as a man (to have a family to go home to). He gets caught up in the action, on his way home to his pregant wife, to whom he wants to bring the hostess cakes she has a craving for. In this respect he is a McClane without the macho-chip, but we see what a terrible price he has to pay: he is traumatised from having once shot and killed a youngster by mistake, a desk-bound cop (shorthand for emasculation in many Hollywood films, witness the Robert Duvall character in *Falling Down*), who needs to redeem himself as a policeman and a professional. He thus presents the (unacceptable) solution to McClane's dilemma, since the nurturing male for this genre is inevitably a traumatised or 'castrated' male.

## 2.3.10. Summary of the classical reading

The classical reading has highlighted a (macro-) structure that consists of three acts plus opening and coda. The opening ends with McClane arriving at the Nakatomi Plaza, while the terrorists are closing in as well. The first act ends with McClane talking to his wife in the bathroom. He is vulnerable (no shirt, shoes, or socks), but not repentant enough to respond to Holly's double invitation: to stay in the spare bedroom (rather than share her bed) and to pick up her admission that she misses him, by saying how sorry he was for not backing her career. The second act ends with McClane wounded, on the rooftop of the building, talking to Al Powell via the two-way radio about his possible death, eventually asking Al to tell his wife Holly that he is sorry. The third act ends with Hans Gruber falling to his death and Holly (as well as the hostages) safe. The coda ties up the loose ends, including the restitution of Al Powell to full professional manhood. After nearly killing the hapless Argyle – and thus almost repeating his traumatic mistake – he successfully eliminates the oddly indestructible Karl. There follows the bi-racial embrace/male bonding of McClane and Al, and the 'masculine' gesture of Holly socking the TV journalist.

We have also established, thanks to the criteria of the well-made (screen)play, as itemized, for instance, by Bordwell, Straiger, and Thompson (1985; see also Thompson 1999), that the film has a goal-oriented hero who wants his wife back and to repair his marriage, preferably at no cost to his macho values. This hero is embedded in a psychologically motivated, character-centred plot, whose purpose is to allow each of the characters to pursue their objectives in a linear, resolute, and resourceful manner. Also conforming to the rules, the film has a double-plot structure, each plot strand braided together with the other: the romance plot and the terrorist plot, with the hero having to defeat the terrorists and the police, in order to resolve the romance plot. The ending finds a satisfactory closure with the death of all the villains, the formation of the heterosexual couple, and the rehabilitation of Al.

Had we conducted our analysis with the help of Propp and his 'morphological' approach, it would have yielded a slightly different segmentation, but the film's canonical format and overall structure would nonetheless have been confirmed. For instance, we might have rephrased the question of the enigma slightly differently, so that the constitutive lack/absence would have been more explicitly expressed in the terms of a fairy tale: Holly as the princess, who has been abducted (first by the Nakatomi Corporation, who made her an offer she could not refuse, and then by Gruber and the terrorists who keep her as a special hostage when they learn she is the wife of McClane, their antagonist). It is, of course, the job of McClane to rescue her and return her to her rightful place: the family home. In order for McClane to do so, he has to be recognizable as the hero, and we do indeed witness the creation of a hero: first of all, as in a fairy tale, there are several tests, with magic objects (for instance, the contents of the tote bag of the terrorist he manages to kill), helpers (like Argyle or Al Powell), and the eventual confirmation of the male protagonist as 'hero' by his confrontation with and recognition of the villain (despite his disguise as a helper). McClane becomes worthy of being the hero via the three stages or steps of 'contest, conquest, and coronation'. More complicated – but in line with Propp's model – is the question of the helpers, several of whom are ambiguous, obstructive, and deceiving: in fact, in *Die Hard* the hero, as in many Hitchcock films, has both the villains and the police against him. Some of the baddies turn out to be good helpers (especially when dead) and vice versa. The film skilfully plays with these ambiguities, especially around the police, whom

McClane expects to be helpers but who inadvertently help Gruber instead; Argyle, the driver who wants to be a helper but is for the most part useless; or the television crew that also inadvertently helps Gruber by revealing the identity of 'Ms Genaro' as Mrs McClane.

In view of the relatively straightforward linear, goal-oriented action-line, we have perhaps concentrated too much on the deep-structural story-line, grouped around contradiction and propelled by the logic of desire. Where both storylines come together is in the interaction between the characters, an interaction that presented itself as a kind of battleground of cross-purposes, made up of their incompatible goals, but also of the many parallel relations joining them together, across apparently inexhaustible resources of repetition. Different kinds of incompatibility were seen to mirror each other. For instance, McClane's goals turn out to be incompatible: he wants his wife back (and to function in the domestic sphere as father and head of family), but he also needs to be a good cop (to maintain and retain his professional self-esteem). This turns out to involve a contradiction that is resolved by seeing his conflict mirrored or paralleled in other characters. Thus, Holly McClane (Genaro) wants to be a professional (and make a career as executive in the Nakatomi corporation), but she also needs to be a good mother and wife. Here, too, two perfectly reasonable ambitions or goals are made to appear incompatible and contradictory: on the surface, because she is married to a macho cop with a chip on his shoulder, but also at the deep-structural level, because these are symptomatic tensions, either on the psychic battleground of sexual difference and human subjectivity or on the ideological battleground of the 'culture wars' in Reagan's America of the 1980s, on the verge of experiencing the social and domestic impact of its globalized, globalizing economy.

We also established that the secondary characters in crucial respects 'mirror' the central ones, and thus play through alternative version of or variations on the central dilemma. As we saw, Al Powell and Ellis 'mirror' John McClane's double dilemma, in one case that arising from his being a cop and thus committed to the 'macho' values of law and authority, and in the other case that of being a husband and lover, where his problem is to accept Holly as an equal partner in the marriage. On the other hand, a character like Ellis also mirrors Holly's dilemma, and he is in some sense her alter ego, even though he turns out to embody the unacceptable solution. He is like Holly, in that he takes her professional ambitions for granted and even accepts her professional status, to the point of being envious of her Rolex watch. He also suggests how she could solve her other problem (as a single mother without a male companion) by wanting to date her, the problem there being that he sees her only as a sexual object/partner, and is not prepared to recognize or respect her obligations as a mother. Ellis, like Holly, wants to be boss, but the way he goes about it – ingratiating himself with anyone who is in charge – is a negative example to her, and he promptly (and, for the audience, deservedly) is killed by Gruber.

Similar analyses could be made for several other, minor characters, such as Holly's Spanish maid (who wants to bring the family together, but needs to go undetected for being an illegal immigrant), the journalist (who badly needs a scoop), and Karl (who wants to avenge his brother's death but because of his private vendetta becomes a liability to Gruber): each has his own reasons, and each echoes the basic structure of mutual exclusiveness or contradictory goals powering the narrative. A special case are the 'black helpers' on either side: among the terrorists, the black safe-cracker wants a money share of the profits, and on McClane's 'team', Argyle the limousine driver also wants money – a fat tip: a parallel in the sub-plot across the difference of their respective allegiances. Similarly doubled and divided is the function of the Police. The LAPD wants to play it by the book and is always wrong; the FBI wants to defeat the LAPD even more than the terrorists, which is why the FBI men end up helping the terrorists (by shutting off the electricity in the building which inadvertently opens the safe).

The role of these characters is thus not only to generate complications and obstacles for the hero, but also to be at cross-purposes with each other; they are functions more than rounded characters, grouping themselves around the incompatibility of the goals of John and Holly, i.e. the apparent irreconcilability of domesticity and career, of being private and professional, of being 'man' and 'woman' at home and at work. In this sense, each character has his or her double somewhere, and all are linked to each other by a system of parallels and binaries that is woven around contradiction, contrariness, and complementariness, with every localized contest a version/variant of the other (or main) characters' dilemmas. Overall coherence in the classical narrative is thus the effect of macro-conflicts and micro-contradictions mirroring each other: repetition (and difference) as resolution (and unity).

## 2.4 The post-classical reading: theory

Given that the narrative of *Die Hard* seems so perfectly readable in terms of the classical model, is there even a need to move to another level and invoke the contested distinction classical/post-classical? What is it in the film that demands additional explanation? The questions bring us back to one of the terms we started with, namely spectacle (which we initially excluded in favour of a discussion of narrative) in order to consider the implicit polemical charge that spectacle and narrative exclude each other. What we hope to have established – and maybe even excessively so – is that if one defines the post-classical as the priority of spectacle over narrative, then either the label as such is unconvincing or this particular definition of it will not hold. On the basis of our analysis, whether Aristotelian (the linear logic of the screenplay) or structuralist (the Oedipal logic of the narrative), we can conclude that the opposition drawn by the reviews is false: even assuming there is a new kind of emphasis on spectacle in contemporary Hollywood, then judging from *Die Hard*, it does not seem to be at the expense of the screenplay, the craftsmanship of the plotting, or indeed to the detriment of the deep-structural 'work' which classical narrative is said to accomplish on behalf of the dominant ideology.

Thus, the difference between classical and post-classical cannot be established on the basis of a binary opposition such as spectacle vs narrative, nor, we suspect, any other 'either/or' construction of difference. One suggestion was that we may have to look for a definition of the post-classical more along the lines of an excessive classicism, rather than as a rejection or absence of classicism. Applied to *Die Hard*, this would involve, on the one hand, a reconsideration of the (narrative, deep-structural) function of the spectacular scenes, as already hinted at several times above, and on the other, a deconstruction of both 'narrative' and 'spectacle', and with it a reconsideration of those elements that we have, up to now, so confidently assigned to the binary pairs of our respective semiotic squares.

Before doing so, however, let us briefly review once more the other definitions on offer for identifying the post-classical as a distinct mode: not only of representation and style, but also of production and reception.

### 2.4.1. Post-classical Hollywood: production and reception criteria

There is now a fairly broad consensus among film scholars how to understand the transformations of Hollywood picture-making that took place between the 1960s and the 1980s, which have led to the unexpected revitalization of the American cinema as both an economic and a cultural force. Among the key features are the gradual undoing of the consequences of the Paramount decree of 1947/48, which obliged the studios to divest themselves of their theatre chains and to break up the vertical integration that had sustained the film industry as a trust or cartel for the previous 25 years. Several waves of mergers and acquisitions within the audio-visual, televisual, and telecommunication sectors in the US during the 1970s and 1980s (favoured by a lax governmental anti-trust policy and accompanied by radical changes in management and business practices) did ensure that by the mid-1980s something rather similar to vertical integration had been re-established.

However, the engine of the revival and the symbol of the new clout of

Hollywood was the blockbuster, a heavily marketed, high-concept, multi-functional audio-visual entertainment product, which also served as showcase for new technologies in sound (Dolby) and image (special effects, computer-generated images). Able to attract new audiences and benefiting from saturation media exposure and global distribution, a blockbuster could reap huge revenues in a relatively short period. These encouraged sequels, hybrid genres, or formulas, as well as favouring the 'package deal', where either a star or a team around a producer could corner the market in a particular sub-genre or 'concept movie', which often combined a tested literary property, a particular visual style, and a marketing gimmick (known also as 'the book, the look, and the hook'). *Die Hard* fits this 'high concept' package deal approach to movie-making very well, seeing that it does form part of a sub-genre, the bi-racial buddy film, a niche market successfully colonized by a creative team assembled around the Gordon/Silver producer partnership, working as a semi-independent unit, but distributing via a major studio, in this case Twentieth Century Fox: 'It's good, dumb fun brought to you by producers Lawrence Gordon, Joel Silver and scriptwriters Jeb Stuart and Steven E. de Souza, who among them have already churned out *48 Hours*, *Predator*, *Commando* and *Lethal Weapon*' (Desson Howe, *Washington Post*, 15 July 1988). *Die Hard* also established a certain look of 'gritty glamour' as fashionable, and it had a punchline ('Yippi-ky-aye, motherfucker') that, like other famous movie one-liners ('Make my day, punk', 'Are you looking at me?!'), took on a life of its own in the culture at large.

Third, blockbusters, but also other Hollywood productions, fitted themselves around the entertainment expectations and trends of the 'youth culture' which in the 1980s had mutated from identifying with the 'counter-culture' to aggressively participating in the event and experience culture of shopping malls, theme parks, video arcades, hip-hop, raves, and music television. To this extent, mainstream movies had to learn to address this more diverse but also more volatile audience, differently segmented from the family audience of both cinema and television in the 1950s and 1960s. Hollywood's new audiences, male and female, domestic and international, expected the much-hyped sound and image technologies to deliver intense bodily, sensory, and emotional involvement.

## 2.4.2. Post-classical Hollywood: formal and cultural criteria

It is this high-impact, technologically sophisticated involvement on the part of the primary target audience that Hollywood needed to appeal to which has found in the notion of 'spectacle' a shorthand common denominator. Technological advances in very different fields of popular entertainment (from animatronics in theme parks to computer games on play stations) and at all levels of picture-making and sound reproduction (from IMAX screens to digital sound, from morphing to virtual reality environment) have indeed made inroads in such a traditional mass entertainment form as the cinema, and they have affected its staple product, the full-length feature film. One way, therefore, of interpreting the opposition spectacle/narrative – and with it, the division classical/post-classical – is to say that, just as in previous periods of cinema history it was new technologies that were putting pressure on the mode of production as well as transforming reception, so it has always been the task of story construction, *mise en scène*, and narration to absorb these changes, by adapting narrative structure and genre formats. Contemporary Hollywood gives every indication that it too has transformed and adjusted itself to recent technological changes, while in important respects retaining the features that have secured its success in the past. It is in this sense that one can say that the classical cinema is merely refigured within the post-classical, neither abandoned nor opposed – or, as we phrased it earlier, the post-classical is also the excessively classical cinema, a sort of 'classical-plus'. What this 'plus' in each case amounts to (including whether some see it in fact as 'minus') remains to be specified. Thus, one could think of the post-classical as a pastiche of the classical, or its meta-discursive and self-referential citation, but one could also picture a more two-way process of absorption, exchange, and modification, where technology is only one factor among many in the general realignment of Hollywood, its mode of production, story-telling skills, and audience/user expectations. For instance, one can imagine that the binary opposition classical/post-classical might disappear altogether, if Hollywood – as some predict and as we consider in subsequent chapters – were to concentrate more and more on developing narratives that are the blueprints or pilots for interactive computer games. Whether this is likely to happen or not, for the theorist the possibility alone is enough to suggest that such an interactive narrative might come to be looked at as the more general category, of which what we now call classical and post-classical would merely be the limited, transitional, or specialized instances.

This leads us back to the cultural aspect of the classical/post-classical interchange, notably the factor we have been calling 'work', the meaning-making processes whereby internal (formal, stylistic, rhetorical) procedures are transforming external (social, ideological, referential) materials into narrative. In the cinema, this conversion of sounds and images *of* the world into assertions and feelings *about* the world makes narrative, in its widest sense, a remarkable vehicle of cultural communication and social reproduction. What, therefore, happens to this 'work' in the 'post-classical' cinema, which we might consider as a mere phase in a continuous process of adaptation or realignment? At first glance, and given our analysis of the textual and ideological work in *Die Hard*, it does look as if it is 'business as usual' too in this respect. But then, we also noted how often the film puts on show its own rhetoric, as well as the ideological material it is supposed to transport and transform.

In a somewhat different vocabulary, and arguing within the framework of 'postmodernism' rather than post-classical cinema, these thoughts preoccupy Fred Pfeil, who introduces his discussion of 'male rampage' films as follows:

> Thanks in no small part to the *Lethal Weapon* and *Die Hard* films I have come to see ... postmodernist cultural practices migrate, drift or [be] exchanged, like designer-label knock-offs or smallpox-infested blankets, across the porous frontiers separating hip from straight-out mass culture. In fact, one of the first things that struck me about these four films ... was precisely their unsettling affinities to previous, canonically hip postmodern works. True, their straightforward plots have little in common with the loopy surprises and multiple thematics of a *Brazil* or *My Beautiful Laundrette* .... But on the more formal level of cinematic style, narrative structure, and constitutive space-time, our fast-paced smash-'em-ups have a lot more in common with certified pomo art films like, say *Diva*, than you might think.
>
> (Pfeil 1993: 124)

Pfeil then lists what he sees as the chief crossover features: the 'urban look' in the colour schemes ('washed-out pastels and dark metallic blues and greys'); the Bakhtinian chronotope of two sharply contrasted spaces within one diegetic temporal realm (in *Die Hard*, 'the spanking new high-rise office building ... and the functioning viscera [of] ventilation ducts and elevator shafts') where the space–time relations only seem to know one time (*now*) and one space ('the action is simply taking place *here* – and *here* – and *here* – in spaces whose distances from one another are not mappable as distances so much as they are measurable in differences of attitude and intensity'). As to the films' narrative structure, Pfeil adopts the view we have been arguing against, when we came across it in the reviews: 'an older model of plot development, moving from a state of stasis ... to a new and more fully resolved stasis, is largely superseded ... by the amnesiac succession of self-contained bits and spectacular bursts' (Pfeil 1993: 124-5).

However, as we saw from his Greimasian square, what concerns Pfeil about these films more than a close textual analysis of *Die Hard*'s surprisingly intricate plotting and careful *mise en scène*, both dedicated to the virtues of classical narration, is their handling of the large cultural formations of race, class, and gender, which he holds up against the political realities of the Reagan era, with its Iran–Contra cover-ups and Ollie Norths, and the economic realities of globalization with its shake-out of the labour market, squeezing the (manufacturing) middle while the (managerial) top, as Pfeil says, gets multinational and the (unskilled) bottom multiracial:

> Our films ... depict a very specifically white/male/hetero/American capitalist dreamscape, inter- and/or multi-national at the top and multiracial at the bottom, in which the interracial is eroticised even as a sharp power-line is reasserted between masculine and feminine: in which, indeed, all the old lines of force between races, classes, and genders are both transgressed and redrawn. If the results of all these constructions and operations are scarcely to be extolled as examples of radical or liberatory cultural production ..., they nonetheless suggest a new and vertiginous psycho-social mobility, a moment of flux.
>
> (Pfeil 1993: 147)

Thus, despite his qualification of the plot as 'amnesiac', Pfeil still expects the narrative of *Die Hard* to be doing its customary work of ideological 'constructions and operations', though no longer unambiguously in the service of the hegemonic value system, producing instead mobility and flux within the categories of race, class, and gender. 'New mobility' and 'a moment of flux' are, of course, terms which themselves belong to the (positive) vocabulary of postmodernist discourse, so that at this point the ideological work of the film and the critical work of the theorist miraculously mirror each other.

Yet, as Pfeil is only too aware, this effect is due to the fact that what is at stake in postmodern thinking is the very dissolution of binary oppositions, including those basic ones that for nearly three decades have informed much of textual analysis itself, such as radical/conservative, progressive/reactionary, critical/hegemonic, left/right. The consequence is that the mode of engagement with the object of analysis is also no longer the same, for instead of keeping its critical distance, the analyst's tactic now turns around notions such as 'appropriation', 'cooption', and 'deconstruction', where it is understood that even conservatives and hegemonic ideologues are now deconstructivists, adept at reading the mobile signs of hybridity and bricolage around the formerly radical or critical discursive formations of race, class, gender, and nation.

## 2.5. Post-classical reading: method

More or less the same dilemma confronts us in our definitions of the 'post-classical', and especially when we try to turn the economic-technological analysis of contemporary Hollywood's mode of production, and Pfeil's formal-cultural definitions of postmodern cinema, into a 'method' for the stylistic analysis of post-classical films: post-classical, we now want to propose, are above all those moments in a classical film when our own theory or methodology suddenly turns up in the film itself, looking us in the face: either gravely nodding assent, or winking. In subsequent chapters – especially those on *Chinatown* (Chapter 4), *Back to the Future* (Chapter 8), and *Silence of the Lambs* (Chapter 9) – we shall encounter a similar phenomenon, and each time we will try to make it productive as the moment where a different method or paradigm can make its entrance. In the present chapter, in which we try to describe these déjà vu's and uncanny encounters in some detail, it will not lead to a different paradigm, but to a sort of action replay of our own classical analysis, to see how we can recapture these moments of nodding or winking.

- We shall begin by once more looking at the *narrative structure*, probing it to see what else it might reveal.
- We shall also reconsider our heuristic distinction between *surface* and *depth*, to find that the film takes it more literally than we would want it to be taken, especially with respect to its *Oedipal logic*.
- This will allow us to comment on *race, gender*, and the *male body*, arguing that certain areas of taboo, censorship, and indirection in the classical mode of representation (of bodies, genders, and races) have been 'opened up', although possibly with the result that 'transgression' itself has become a mere 'surface effect'.
- In the section on the *transnational/post-colonial/globalization theme* we shall be arguing that a double perspective envelops the film's socio-political themes: while the story is clearly *about* certain aspects of transnational capitalism from an American point of view, the film knows that it is itself also very much *part of* this globalization, a situation it seems to address by becoming a sort of two-way mirror of national clichés in a multicultural setting.
- What holds the mirror in place and the spectator in the picture, we shall be concluding, is the film's penchant for punning: from the star's trademark wisecracking to visual jokes and structural ironies, elaborated around tag-lines or riddling phrases, *Die Hard* keeps us on our toes without giving us a firm foothold, thanks to what we are calling its *sliding signifiers*.

# 2.6. Post-classical analysis

## 2.6.1. Narrative structure

Perhaps the case for *Die Hard* as a post-classical film, Pfeil's remarks notwithstanding, is at its weakest when argued on the basis of its plot development, which follows quite straightforwardly the canonical three-act structure, centred on a male protagonist. However, as one goes through the act division once more, two features invite further comment: one is the spacing and pacing of the violent action scenes that intersperse the unfolding of the drama, and the other is the fact that the three-act division can also be 'turned', so as to be centred not on John McClane, but on Holly Genaro or Hans Gruber. Although the overall momentum of the action seems to favour McClane, each act offers parallel nodal points of development for the other characters. For instance, Act 1 ends with Holly admitting that she still loves John; Act 2 ends with her being taken hostage by Hans Gruber, after he recognizes her as the wife of John McClane; Act 3 ends with her having to part with the Rolex watch, symbol of her social status as a career woman, in order to save her life. The coda ends with her socking the journalist who had pried into her family life.

Similarly, it is possible to chart the rise and fall of Hans Gruber around the same three-part act division: his successful surprise entry, the discovery of a 'rogue' occupant in the building, the internal unravelling/decimation of the gang, and his fatal fall clutching a Rolex watch. Thus, the story makes sense from the perspective of each of the three principal characters, with the spectacular set pieces dividing the initiative almost evenly between McClane and Gruber – the action with the fire hose or the elevator shaft being all McClane's, while Gruber calls the shots (with McClane a mere spectator) in one of the most chilling scenes, the assassination of Tagaki, Holly's boss. The case for a post-classical reading, therefore, does not depend on the absence/presence of the canonical story format per se, but would build on the evidence of a 'layering' of the traditional screenplay, which opens it up to several players or avatars, allowing the film to migrate quite comfortably from big screen to the video arcade or the gameboy console. Unusual for a classical film, but again relevant to an interactive scenario is the motive-shifting of the villain: Gruber seems to change his mind as to why he is occupying the building at least three times, morphing from international terrorist to thief and back again to a man with a grievance and the brains and the firepower to act on it.

## 2.6.2. Surface structure and deep structure

Much has been made in our classical analysis of the distinction between surface structure and deep structure. Yet these terms are merely spatial metaphors to direct attention to a disparity of dramatic movement, to a cognitive tension, or a difference in emotional patterning or intensity. In some ways, however, *Die Hard* behaves as if it knew about this purely heuristic distinction. For instance, it constantly alludes to its surface texture, by staging a quite extraordinary play on 'glass'. In fact, one way to define 'spectacle' in *Die Hard* would be to say that it draws some of its most memorable effects from the splattering and shattering of glass – the big plate-glass windows that McClane has to smash to push out the body in order to draw the patrolman's attention to the fact that not all is what it seems at Nakatomi Plaza; Gruber ordering one of his men (in faulty German) to fire on the glass in order to make of it a carpet of splinters which will cut McClane's feet to bleeding shreds; the blood and brains of Tagaki clouding the glass partition and blocking McClane's view. Glass also provides some intense sound effects throughout, and there is even a Roy Lichtenstein-inspired pop art picture of a shattering pane of glass on the wall in Holly's office, shown twice – the second time accompanied by the crackling sound of machine-gun fire.

Similarly, with respect to the narrative's deep structure, our argument has been that it is there that the story's Oedipal logic unfolds. 'Ho-ho-ho,' the film says, not only to Oedipus, but to patriarchy, and gives us Father Christmas instead. The fact that one of the reviewers should ask, 'Why Christmas?' suggests that he cannot have watched the film all that carefully. In fact, Christmas is crucial in at least two distinct ways. It is, as indicated, the season for family reunion and reconciliation, motivating McClane's return to Holly. It is also a culturally overdetermined holiday season (white, first world, Christian), and there is something distinctly off-key in the Nakatomi Corporation having an elaborate Christmas party (a fact which the film acknowledges musically when it cross-cuts between Bach and Handel at the Nakatomi reception and rap music in the limo). Christmas in sun-baked LA always carries a surrealist touch, with snow-powdered Christmas trees, an incongruity verbalized in the opening scene mostly by Argyle, whose limo's in-car entertainment consists of hip-hop and rap, and who is suitably facetious about 'white' Christmas music: when asked by McClane: 'Don't you have some Christmas music?', he answers 'This *is* Christmas music.'

But Christmas is even more pervasively embedded in the visual, verbal, and thematic texture of the film, functioning as a semantic resource in several distinct registers. An explicit reference, for instance, is Gruber's delight that the FBI is making him a Christmas present by shutting down the electricity, which 'lights up his tree': Gruber expects a miracle, and it occurs when the lights go out and the last door of the safe opens, like an Advent calendar on Christmas Eve. More oblique, but hardly to be missed, is McClane's practical joke on one of the villains, the intellectual Fritz. McClane helps himself from Fritz's bag to cigarettes, lighter, a machine gun, and a walkie-talkie, then dresses the dead body up as Father Christmas, having first emblazoned his teeshirt with the words 'ho-ho-ho', before sending him down the elevator as if it was a chimney ('Father Christmas coming down the chimney'), a visual pun that is once more activated when McClane plunges the explosives down the ventilation shaft and it lights up at the bottom like a fire in the hearth. One additional element of the (Anglo-American) Christmas ritual is worked into the narrative: it seems as if by taking off his socks, McClane had 'invited' Father Christmas to fill his stockings, so that the magic objects he needs for his fight against the robbers/terrorists are in fact *his* Christmas presents.

In other words, the signifier 'Christmas' is both a 'sliding signifier' (see below) and at the centre of a culturally, visually, and cognitively rich seam of meaning, which the film (in terms of script and *mise en scène*) exploits in order to give a special texture and resonance to the actions. In the family reunion drama, Christmas acts as a element of verisimilitude; in the LA setting, it provides an atmosphere of dissonance, alerting us to the ethnic theme; in relation to Gruber and McClane, it adds dramatic irony to the fairy-tale motif of donors and helpers; for McClane it is the occasion for practical jokes at his enemies' expense, and for the *mise en scène* it motivates one of the metaphoric uses of the spatial configuration unfinished building/unfinished business (elevator shafts and ventilation ducts/terrorists to be dispatched); finally, the socks/stocking allusion contains an irony directed at McClane's emotional immaturity, while the Father Christmas references sarcastically comment on the patriarchal quest of the hero, in search of a new foundation for his fatherhood and masculine identity.

## 2.6.3. Race, gender, and the male body

Also alerting us to 'surface structures' is another element that did not escape the critics, often said to belong to the arsenal of the post-classical cinema, namely the emphasis on the body, and in particular on the display of the male body:

> Bruce Willis in another one of those Hollywood action roles where the hero's shirt is ripped off in the first reel so you can see how much time he has been spending at the gym.
>
> (Roger Ebert, *Chicago Sun-Times*, 15 July 1988)

As Ebert implies, the film reflects a preoccupation of popular culture and especially media culture since the 1980s with the eroticized male body, as we know it from body-building, *Baywatch* and jogging, leading another reviewer to speak of *Die Hard* as 'a body-intensive, cardiovascular workout movie' (Hal Hinson, *Washington Post*, 15 July 1988).

Not least because of television, and its ability to invest sports performers via close-up with a special kind of physical glamour, representations of the male body have changed dramatically in the past two decades. Slow motion and action replays have turned televised football (or soccer) into one of the most lucrative forms of entertainment ever known, helping to make this traditionally uniquely male spectator sport also pleasurable to women audiences. The male body has become big business visual spectacle, in contrast to the classical male body, usually seen as the bastion of abstraction from its physical manifestations (except in pornography), neither eroticised nor 'marked' (for fear, it is said, of yielding to the homoerotic subtext that has always been present in Hollywood). Although there have been exceptions in certain genres (such as the boxing film or the war film), certain stars (Clark Gable's string vest), and certain directors, notably in Anthony Mann's Westerns, and almost all of Robert Aldrich's films, classical cinema has mostly shown its men fully clad and physically unimpaired: their Oedipal wounds have remained symbolic, the bodily envelope largely unaffected. But not so in *Die Hard*, where Bruce Willis's body is exposed and put on display. Physically wounded and relentlessly punished, McClane's vulnerability is graphically shown; indeed, his body is 'somatized' and so are we as spectators: we 'feel' how painful it is to walk over broken glass and have the tender skin of our soles torn open and bleeding.

This attention to male skin as a surface – tender in both senses of the word – has not escaped commentary, when film scholars theorize the shifting relations of gender, and in particular, the representation of gays. Whether as pin-ups presented for visual pleasure to male and female viewers, or in scenes of same-sex physical contact between males of different race, Hollywood has not hesitated to follow trends in fashion, advertising, and other areas of popular (sub)culture, in order to make what once was called 'deviance' or even 'miscegenation' consumable. We have already quoted Fred Pfeil, who links the slippage of the classically tabooed race boundaries in the representation of males to the problematically 'multiracial community' of unskilled workers gathering as a reserve pool in low-paid service industries. Yet it is again remarkable how *Die Hard* looks as if its makers had read all the relevant cultural studies literature, so as to provide 'something for everybody'. With the bi-race buddy theme between McClane and Al Powell (and their tearful final embrace), with the 'Johnson and Johnson' joke of the two FBI agents ('no relation'), and the Spanish maid occupying structurally the same nurturing role in respect of Holly as Al does in respect of McClane (aligning 'people of colour' as unthreateningly neutral in the caring positions/ professions), *Die Hard* has ensured that the interpretive community of 'race–class–gender' studies can have a field day, by catering to hoary clichés and stereotypes, while sufficiently mixing the categories and boundaries to mildly impress even radical activists like Pfeil.

Sharon Willis is less impressed. In her essay on the genre (Willis 1997), covering much the same ground as Pfeil, she is nonetheless careful to make a distinction between the formations of gender and race, arguing that it is race which, precisely because it is so excessively foregrounded, remains the unacknowledged pivot of the film's ideological construction. Rather than the film translating racially coded issues into gender-coded ones, she sees a constant slippage and reversal, indicative of what she calls the 'trade-offs' between race and gender, from the point of view of masculinity in crisis, which then release different 'erotic economies' that entail the consequence that 'black' and 'female' emerge as incompatible with each other, unable to exist within the same discursive space. For Willis, it is therefore race that remains the bi-racial buddy films' actual trauma, which they cover up by jocular homoeroticism, spectacularized bodies, and a liberal presentation of interracial communication around the upholding of the law. This strategy disavows the very real impossibility of the white United States to come to grips with its racism, especially seeing that blacks in America do not so much represent the law as have the law inscribed on their bodies in the penal institutions they so disproportionately populate. The liberalism or 'licence' of representation in the films, along with the permanent sexual innuendo and the physical bravado, are the mask that a deeply reactionary genre gives itself, in order to reassert the narrowest of social spaces and the most clichéd of discursive places reserved for non-whites, and to redraw more firmly the lines of sexual and racial difference.

## 2.6.4. The transnational/post-colonial/globalization theme

Sharon Willis's remarks, along with Pfeil's point about the untranscendable horizon of post-classical (or, in his terminology, postmodern) cinema being that of transnational capitalism are well taken. If we are to look for a historical framework within which to place the tectonic plates and shifting surfaces of *Die Hard*'s identity politics, the information economy of services, and the 'outsourcing' of manufacture to low-cost labour countries by multinational corporations on the one hand and the plight of American urban blacks on the other are as persuasive as any. And yet in at least two respects these political reflections, too, only plunge us deeper into the self-referential double-binds that seem so typical of the post-classical mode.

First of all, *Die Hard* plays a joke on the conditions of its own possibility. Standing in for the Nakatomi Corporation's headquarters as the film's principal location was the then brand-new Century Plaza office tower, home of Twentieth Century Fox, the production/distribution company for which Gordon and Silver made this film and the others in the series. The joke is double-edged: by offering its own real estate as location, the Fox company made a shrewd investment, but it also hints at the irony that a blockbuster's budget in the 1980s was beginning to exceed the construction cost of a high-rise office tower. The fact that the producers make use of the tower in its half-finished state, only then to let it go up in flames and bring it down as debris, is itself a nice touch, an ironic thank-you note addressed to the host and client.

The other level of self-reference relates to the film's extensive deployment of the signifiers of nation: national identity and international business, against the backdrop of transnational history since the Second World War. If we can assume that the plot does indeed engage with the anxieties of America's working class about the future of its jobs and, more generally, the US economy's competitive position vis-à-vis Japan and Europe (in the days before the 'new economy' had taken off, which in the 1990s put America again in the lead), then the choice of nationalities and foreign nationals in the film is very knowing indeed:

> The terrorists, too, are a multinational group, led by a German named Hans Gruber (Alan Rickman) who is well-dressed and has a neatly trimmed beard and talks like an intellectual and thinks he is superior to the riffraff he has to associate with. He has a plan that has been devised with clockwork precision.
>
> (Roger Ebert, *Chicago Sun-Times*, 15 July 1988)

Ebert's review, once again, mimetically tries to render the film's flavour, faithfully reproducing the national clichés in circulation, down to the 'clockwork precision' still inevitably evoking (Nazi-) Germany. Thus we could, without much difficulty, devise for the national/transnational axis another semiotic square. The villains are Germans, the bosses Japanese: from the point of view of America, these two nations have much in common. In the past, during the Second World War, they had been the USA's most formidable enemies, but they are now among its closest political allies. Yet even at the time of *Die Hard*'s release both Japan and Germany were still an economic threat, notably to the US auto industry, and thus to the very emblem of blue-collar jobs that individuals like McClane are likely to lose. This history/present-day binary pair is overlaid by another pair, differently split but equally pertinent, because situated in an intermediary historical period, insofar as the terrorists are identified with the German Red Army Faction of the 1970s – notoriously anti-American and pro-Vietnam in their bombings and assassinations of US military targets in West Germany – while those called upon to defeat them, the FBI and LAPD, are too young to remember, traumatized by or once more gung-ho for another Vietnam. If the film freely indulges in anti-German resentment, it does not spare the Japanese either, even though they appear as the 'good guys'. What underlies the latent hostility – not least on the part of Hollywood itself – is the fear of Japanese takeovers, when we recall the aggressive moves made in the 1980s by companies like Sony and Matsushita to buy up studios like Columbia Pictures and Universal. The in-joke here would be that the Nakatomi Corporation is housed in the headquarters of another Hollywood studio, Twentieth Century Fox, itself owned by a 'Far-Easterner', the naturalized American but originally Australian Rupert Murdoch.

A more subdued but also overdetermined US/UK rivalry makes itself felt as well: it is present via the actor Alan Rickman, who plays the suave Hans Gruber, swapping – James Bond fashion – name and address of his tailor with Nakatomi's CEO, before brutally and casually dispatching him. Truly formidable and treacherous villains in Hollywood are always best played by Englishmen (apart from Rickman, one thinks of Laurence Olivier in *Sleuth* and *The Marathon Man*, or more recently, of Anthony Hopkins's *Hannibal Lecter* as well as the ubiquitous, versatile, but always fiendish Gary Oldman). The melting pot/salad bowl coalition of ethnicities, since the 1980s obligatory for the US film and TV industry, is also present, with the Celtic contingent (McClane), the Italians (Holly), Blacks (Al Powell), and Hispanics (the maid) all represented.

A special place in the intercultural and transnational semiotics of *Die Hard* is reserved for Hans Gruber: international terrorist, avenging angel, common criminal. At one level, he wants to teach Japan and the US a (political) lesson; at another level, he wants to steal $600 million in bearer bonds (fancy monetary instruments of new economy globalization?). Yet, as we know from his gentlemanly manners and sharp clothes, he is also at home in the executive suits of international business. Thus he seems to be an international terrorist turned international banker, but turns out to be a common, if rather resourceful thief. At yet another (symbolic) level, he is a creature from a different kind of movie, because a master of disguises. Terrorist, businessman, bank robber, employee, and victim: his capacity for disguise makes him not just a villain but a monster, as in fairy tales or a horror movie. It is as if Gruber (and Karl) are Dracula-like 'drive creatures' (as opposed to 'desire creatures'), who apparently cannot be defeated by ordinary means because they have supernatural powers: even the LA police and FBI help Gruber, as does television and the media. Finally, when considering him structurally in relation to McClane's dilemma of class and status, Gruber is a mediator/alter ego: he has the brute force and manual skills of McClane, but he also belongs to the world of executives and global capital to which Holly aspires.

## 2.6.5. The sliding signifers

> On a technical level, there's a lot to be said for *Die Hard*. It's when we get to some of the unnecessary adornments of the script that the movie shoots itself in the foot.
>
> (Roger Ebert, *Chicago Sun-Times*, 15 July 1988)

In all likelihood Ebert intended to make a pun, but one wonders whether he did not speak truer than he knew. The film in any event seems to know, since it certainly fetishizes McClane's feet more intensely than almost any other part of his body, including his bare chest. Starting with the Asian-American fellow passenger on the plane, who advised McClane to clench his toes into a fist – Chinese-style, one supposes – the foot references are never far away in this film, with close-ups of bare feet, bleeding soles, bandaged feet dragged across the floor so often focusing the action on McClane's delicate but damaged extremities. But encouraged by Ebert's pat phrase, how can one not think of the name of the mythic hero, and the impediment to which he owed his name: Oedipus, the club-footed?

This sort of slippery punning – in and out of the text – may itself be an indicator of the post-classical: not as a style, and more as frame of mind, on the part of aficionados and analysts alike. There is certainly no shortage of this kind of bad and ingenious, profound, and facetious wordplay in the film, underscoring also Bruce Willis' star image as an irrepressible wisecracker in many of his roles before and since *Die Hard*. The trend is helped, as indicated, by the inroads that marketing experts have made on blockbuster productions, invariably launched with tag-lines and soundbites ('the hook'). But instead of calling them hooks or bylines, we have opted for the suspiciously semiotic term 'sliding signifier' to indicate a pun's variable relation between signifier and signified, where language exploits plurality on the side of the signifier (verbal or visual doublets) and the film exploits plurality on the side of the contexts (ambiguity, irony, and reversal allowing the signifieds to float). Although this is merely an extension of classical cinema's structural use of symmetry and repetition, such puns in the post-classical mode are at once staged and compressed, drawing attention to the device and to the reversibility of the relations and situations to which it points. By calling these moments of condensation sliding signifiers, we also want to note their 'mobility' and 'drift', since they not only slip and slide between different referents, as puns are meant to do, but also migrate from inside the film to its promotion and packaging, at times entering, as with McClane's war cry, the common parlance of popular culture. Finally, we also want to allude to (and salute) another widely held view about the post-classical, namely that surface extension, recto and verso are the principles that organize meaning, rather than depth and interiority. However, we emphatically wish to resist the prevailing notion that attention to surface must mean being intellectually or emotionally 'shallow'.

A good example of the cinema working the verbal surface of a text are the names and the title. This is not specific to cinema, and even less so an exclusive mark of the post-classical. We only need to think of Charles Dickens's novels, where names such as Mr Gradgrind, Mrs Sparsit, Mr Bounderby, Mr Harthouse, and Mrs M'Choakumchild (from *Hard Times*) all by themselves define the moral atmosphere of a fictionally complete world. In the classical cinema, too, we could cite any number of instances, from the male chauvinistically named Mrs Ruttland in *The Big Sleep* to the middle initial 'O' in *North By Northwest*'s Roger Thornhill. Kuntzel, in his essay on *The Most Dangerous Game*, pointed out the triple pun in the title, but he hardly needed to have bothered, since in the film the villain himself, Count Zaroff, takes time out to gloss the double entendre of 'game'.

Again, while the post-classical does not break with this staple of popular fiction in any medium since times immemorial, it vigorously pushes the envelope. It is no accident that John [McClane] should have as his rival Hans [Gruber], when their Christian names are identical in their respective languages. McClane's name is associated with the Scottish word 'clan', i.e. 'family', which is close to the root meaning of his wife's maiden name, 'Genaro'. 'Holly', her first name, inevitably makes (Anglo-Americans) think of Christmas, while 'Tagaki', the name of her boss, apparently means 'tall tree' or *paterfamilias* in Japanese. Johnson and Johnson, the two FBI agents, certainly do not evoke baby powder, but possibly the name of the largest publisher of black American magazines, while Al Powell turns out to have real 'pal power' for John McClane. He also *buys* his sweets ('hostess cakes'), while one of the 'terrorists' (in between guarding the hostages) cannot resist the temptation to *steal* his sweets.

In *Die Hard* ambiguity, polysemy, and irony also cluster around the title: ambiguous, in that a diehard is someone who does not give up easily, thus referring to McClane, but it can also mean someone who just refuses to die, which in the film applies to Gruber's out-of-control associate Karl, absurdly indestructible. Polysemic insofar as the word 'hard' refers to Bruce Willis's macho hard-body image as an action hero, to McClane being a hard man (by not saying sorry to his wife until it's almost too late), as well as to the role played by class in *Die Hard* (hard-hat – working class masculinity). Ironic, finally, in that – as Pfeil points out, by quoting Webster's Dictionary – 'diehard' also means 'an extreme conservative', as if the film was cocking an ideological snook at its progressive critics.

The puns do not have to be only verbal, though even the visual ones often require an implicit linguistic reference point: it being Christmas, the idea of snow is in the air, however incongruous this might be in Southern California, despite Bing Crosby's song or Argyle's scoffing. But in one of the first scenes inside the Nakatomi building, we see Ellis snorting coke ('snow'), and at the very end, the towering ruin of the Nakatomi building becomes itself something of a Christmas tree, from which thousands of sheets of paper, like flakes, are gently falling to the ground, giving John and Holly a white Christmas after all.

The fact that such wordplay and visual punning permeate even the most seemingly insignificant features says much for the professionalism that goes into the making of Hollywood's 'dumb fun'. As a permanent meta-commentary in a minor key, it also reminds the audience of the film's particular rhetoric of generating meaning out of difference and similarity, metaphor and metonymy, preparing spectators for the introduction, for instance, of a special object, multiply motivated and radiating signifying power at different points and in different contexts. Such a symbolic – or totemic – object is Holly's Rolex watch. It condenses a whole range of motifs, from her rapid rise in the Corporation and her status as a professional woman to her ambivalent relations with Ellis, who keeps pushing her to show it off to McClane, half-proud of her, half-envious. But the Rolex moment of glory is when Holly has to part with it in order to save her life. When McClane finally sees it, it is only to release it from her wrist: symbolically charged icon of her independence, the watch enters the drama as a Hitchcock handcuff, in a situation where the choice is made easy: it's life or death. But the fact that Gruber clings to it is also like a displacement of Holly's desire to cling to it as a precious representation of her 'working mother' identity, so that it becomes doubly ironic that McClane is the one who snaps the Rolex off. These repeated appearances of the Rolex at different junctures in the plot make it function like a semantic battery, plugged into the narrative current, in order to be charged and recharged with meaning. In its way it, too, is a sliding signifier: never more so than when, along with Gruber, it slides off Holly's wrist.

But let us pick a pun that at first does not seem to be one, and therefore needs special unpacking, because it is both a riddle and a mantra, the traditional ways of using enigmatic language for 'serious' (dramatic) purposes, and therefore once more not something unique to the post-classical. We are thinking of the piece of advice McClane receives on the plane: 'Curl your toes into a fist.' Well-meaning though it is, the mantra turns out to be disastrous as well as providential in a quite different context than that intended. Disastrous because, by following it, McClane is caught in the bathroom, not (like Vincent Vega in *Pulp Fiction*) with his pants down, but nonetheless with his socks down. Providential, in that his retreat to the bathroom means he escapes the roundup and the hostage taking. As argued in the classical analysis above, the phrase, however, also functions figuratively in a wider context, that of the central contradiction of the film between male and female, for which it already predicts and spells out the terms of its possible resolution. How so? By making use of the cultural connotations of the body parts which happen to be gender-specific. 'Fist', it is easy to see, suggests masculinity and violence, but what about 'toes'? 'Curl your toes' alludes to bound feet, with distinct female connotations. These are underlined when we think of the bandages McClane will have to wear later on, to stop the bleeding. The metonymies of toes/feet/soles/bleeding/bandages reinforce these associations of femininity, giving us a key as to the metaphoric significance of McClane's bleeding feet: they are part of his 'feminization', his painful journey to being able to say sorry, his having to learn to become vulnerable, to realize the in- and underside of his diehard obstinacy and hard-body masculine carapace. 'Curl your toes into a fist' has to be read inside out, back to front, in order to spell out the healing formula for McClane's dilemma as a macho: 'make toes out of your first', i.e. admit the female side of your masculinity, open up your violence to your vulnerability. In order to be a proper father/husband, the old macho has to become the new man – before he can become the new old macho again: these are the stages McClane emulates, and they follow the classic narrative triad of 'state of stasis/destabilization/more fully resolved stasis' which Pfeil found lacking in *Die Hard*. Read prospectively, the advice predicts McClane's drama; read retrospectively (and in reverse, as a coded discourse around gender), the Asian-American's message, like the riddle of the Sphinx to Oedipus, like the Wise Man from the East (inscrutable being the appropriate cliché association), names his dilemma and gives him the terms of his possible redemption.

A parallel regendering trajectory is undergone by Holly. She has to be stripped of all her (traditionally male) professional attributes: she starts off in control, and (like a man) takes over when her boss is shot. But when directly confronting Gruber, she 'reverts' to female demands: a sofa for her pregnant colleague and for the women to be allowed to go to the bathroom. She is then taken hostage not as the boss of her firm, but as wife of John McClane, once more becoming the stereotypical object of exchange between males. Then in another scene, she is shown sitting with the pregnant woman, acting as her maid or midwife. In the end, she gets John back, but is properly reduced to the role of mother and nurturer, with only one consolation: she does curl her 'toes' into a fist, when she socks the journalist on the jaw, just before walking away with McClane, the classical 'formation of the couple' having become a post-classical *re-formation* of the couple.

In its bold associations, its 'trangressiveness', and yet also its thematic economy and power of compression, the toe/fist sliding signifier does indeed, we think, qualify as post-classical, at least in the way we have here been discussing it. Yet once again, it suggests that this 'post' is the same, but different, where 'different' may have to be understood in the (deconstructionist) sense of 'deferred', as a delay, which is, after all, one of the meanings of the word 'post', marking a shift in temporality, rather than in substance or quality.

# Conclusion

Have we, by thus deferring the elements of a classical reading from those of a post-classical reading, been able to answer either the question of spectacle vs narrative or to resolve the polemical opposition 'classical/post-classical'? We started from the assertion that film scholars draw the boundary between classical and post-classical cinema as a function of their critical agendas, while the film itself as artefact and object does not, on the whole, predicate or demand a particular decision one way or another. Once we have clarified the meaning of narrative and spectacle, perhaps we can begin to perceive the boundary between classical and post-classical in the context of the overall status of the film: not only a logically and narrato-logically readable 'text', but (in light of the pressures brought by technology, consumerism, and audience expectations to mainstream cinema) also as a coherently orchestrated 'experience'. Our argument has been that we have to regard the category of spectacle less in the sense of visual excess, or as indexed by physical violence and spectacular display of technology, and maybe not even as the moments where 'showing' overpowers the (narrative) reasons to show. Rather, in the broader context beyond the binary divide, it connotes a different kind of self-display or 'knowingness', a special sort of awareness of the codes that govern classical representation and its genre conventions, along with a willingness to display this knowingness and make the audience share it, by letting it in on the game. This type of spectacle manifests itself, among other things, in the deployment of what we called the sliding signifier, an excess of signification and meaning-making that attaches itself to the visual, verbal and sonic material and makes it available for semantic play (puns) and surface display (glossy look), as well as for special (sound) effects and special (pictorial) effects. As we saw, the signifier 'glass' plays such a role in *Die Hard*: semantic feature, material object, pictorial subject matter, and sound-effect, it is also narratively integrated as an efficient dramatic resource, thereby giving a many-layered, multimedia, polysemic 'texture' to *Die Hard*, performing its narrative, in order to make it part of the somatic–bodily experience of the film.

For it is this knowingness about itself as self-display, as well as about its role in the marketplace of popular culture and cultural politics, that gives the film its multiple entry points for diverse audiences. This includes servicing the needs of fans, of technical aficionados, of radical intellectuals, and of definition-hungry scholars, but also of a new kind of commodification of the Hollywood product via interactive video games: indicating that the post-classical film knows that it has to reach not only the supposedly homogeneous audience of middle America but the by now highly specialized, culturally and ethnically segmented audiences of global reach, of which women, for instance, make up a high proportion, even for action movies.

In other words, what finally matters about post-classical cinema and at once defines the category and defies it, is that certain films seem to 'know' that they are post-classical. From the perspective of production, post-classical films stand in a tradition: they have mastered the codes of the classical, and they are not afraid to display this mastery as 'play', in the way they are able to absorb, transform, and appropriate also that which initially opposed the classical – be it other film-making traditions, such as European art cinema, Asian cinema, television advertising, or even video installation art, or be it oppositional theories and political practices, such as the critical discourses around the formations of race, class, gender, and nation. From the perspective of reception, it is this knowingness – which may, as we have suggested, be no more than the reflection of the critics' theoretical or political agenda, as it bounces off the film's polished, smooth, chrome-plated surface 'look' – that gives, with its several reflexive turns, the label 'post-classical' its most defensible validity and, perhaps more problematically, its only stable application. The 'work' of classical narrative – dream-work, textual work, or ideological work – is becoming, it seems, the 'play'-station of the post-post-classical. This, if true, would indeed demand the shift to a different paradigm.

# 3  *Mise-en-scène* criticism and statistical style analysis (*The English Patient*)

## Introduction

A cursory glance at the literature on *mise-en-scène* criticism reveals a broad consensus on what *mise en scène* is: generally, it is understood as a study of the relation between subject matter and style (the relation between *what* and *how*). For example, a *mise-en-scène* critic may focus on the relation between how the cuts from shot to shot relate to the action and dialogue. More specifically, *mise-en-scène* criticism studies the relation between actors and decor, or foreground and background. Jacques Joly asks: 'What is *mise en scène*, if not precisely the confrontation of a character and a setting?' (Joly, quoted in Hillier 1986: 22). On a more abstract level, the *mise-en-scène* critic may focus on bodies and gestures in space (or abstracted from space), and the movement of actors and objects within a moving or still frame. Michel Mourlet understands *mise en scène* in a yet more abstract way, as the interplay of light and shadow, surfaces and lines in a moving or still frame: 'The mysterious energy which sustains with varying felicities the swirl of shadow and light and their foam of sounds is called *mise en scène*. It is on *mise en scène* that our attention is set, organizing a universe, covering the screen – *mise en scène*, and nothing else.' He adds that *mise en scène* consists of 'an incantation of gestures, looks, tiny movements of the face and body, vocal inflections, in the bosom of a universe of sparkling objects' (Mourlet, quoted in Hillier 1986: 117).

In contrast to this broad consensus is disagreement. In a narrow theatrical sense, *mise en scène* refers only to *what* appears in front of the camera – to the pro-filmic events, not to the procedures which transpose those events onto film. But for most critics *mise en scène* refers both to what is filmed and to how it is filmed. To avoid conflating the *what* and the *how*, Sergei Eisenstein invented the term *mise en shot*: 'For the designation of the particularities pertaining to cinematographic *mise en scène* . . . I wish to introduce a special term that has been non-existent in film practice hitherto. If *mise en scène* means staging on a stage, the arrangement of the stage, then staging in the shot let us henceforth call *mise en shot*' (Eisenstein, quoted in Nizhny 1962: 139). However, film scholars have not adopted Eisenstein's new term, with the exception of Vlada Petric (see Petric 1982). In this chapter we shall use the term *mise en scène* in its broader definition, to designate both subject matter and film style – or, more importantly, their interrelationship.

*Mise-en-scène* criticism is the first approach to be outlined in this chapter. We shall outline several key strategies employed by *mise-en-scène* critics to analyse a film, and then apply one of these strategies (the 'same-frame heuristic') to *The English Patient* (Anthony Minghella, 1997). The second method to be presented in this chapter is statistical style analysis (also known as 'stylometry'). The function of statistics is to quantify data, and then represent its underlying pattern of regularity. In the analysis of literary and film texts, statistics is used to analyse – or, more accurately, quantify – style. Statistics has little presence or support in the humanities, for it is seen as a dehumanizing process that reduces experience to a set of numbers, bar charts, or tables. Yet film style is readily open to statistical analysis, once we identify the relevant data to quantify – 'relevant' in that they are good discriminators of a film's style. Following on from Eisenstein's comments on *mise en shot*, it becomes evident that style can be identified and quantified from the parameters of the shot, particularly those parameters directly under the director's control. One of the few film scholars to quantify style is Barry Salt (1974; 1992), whose work we shall review in section 3.5 and then apply to *The English Patient* in section 3.6. But we shall go further than Salt by using computer software to quantify film style and represent the results both numerically and visually. The outcome, as we hope to show, is a clear, systematic, and rigorous analysis of style that goes beyond the *mise-en-scène* critics' tendency to be selective and subjective. Some readers may find this statistical analysis too reductive and too abstract – too abstracted from the experience of the film. But such an analysis yields unexpected information that cannot be gained by simply watching the film. Furthermore, and to repeat the main theme behind this book, the statistical analysis of style is just one of many theories that can be applied to film. Like other theories, it consists of its own methods that yield unique information on the film being analysed.

## 3.1. *Mise-en-scène* theory

In the early days of *mise-en-scène* criticism (the early 1950s), *mise en scène* was defined in terms of film's immediate perceptual presence, its physical and concrete rendition of space and bodies on screen. These critics (Jean-Luc Godard, Claude Chabrol, Jacques Rivette, François Truffaut) valorized immediacy and presence because, they believed, it relates to film's specificity, its visual and aural tactility, and, most importantly, its adherence to the truth of surface appearances (for a selection of their work, see Hillier 1985).

During the same period (the early 1950s), a number of the above critics mystified the concept of *mise en scène* by making it intangible, linking it to the notions of spirituality and to pure creativity. In effect, they reduced *mise en scène* to a director's individual vision or world-view, their unique inspiration that cannot be generalized. In opposition to this Romantic or existential view, we can develop a non-mystifying understanding of *mise en scène* by thinking of it in terms of a series of compositional norms from which directors choose how to construct their shots, scenes, and whole films. Individuality re-enters the 'non-mystificatory' critic's vocabulary when he or she focuses on how, in an individual film, its subject matter is translated into the specifics of *mise en scène* (rather than being translated by the director's 'unexplainable' vision). The *mise-en-scène* critic ideally focuses on an individual film's stylistic and thematic development, that is, the film's moment-by-moment progression as it concretely manifests or realizes its themes through its *mise en scène*. Fred Camper mediates between this spiritual and 'secular' view of *mise en scène* by focusing on the way inner spirituality is manifest and made visual and concrete – or tangible – in a film's visual style, as we shall see in his analysis of *Disputed Passage*.

*Mise en scène* names what is there on the screen and emanating through the loud speakers, before the spectator's eyes and ears. It is what the spectator looks at and listens to, but not necessarily what they see and hear. *Mise-en-scène* criticism is a form of connoisseurship that directs the spectator's awareness to the significance of certain elements of *mise en scène*. Victor Perkins notes: 'My standard for good criticism is not that I agree with it but that it tells me something I haven't noticed about a film, even if I've seen it a number of times.' He goes on to emphasize the position of the *Movie* critics: 'We are helping people not to know which are the right and wrong films, but to see what's in a film. . . . We're not concerned with the education of taste, but with the education of awareness' (Perkins *et al.* 1963: 34).

*Mise-en-scène* critics point out the significance of certain visual and aural elements of a film. The critic draws attention to the design of the *mise-en-scène*, highlighting the significance and importance of what the non-connoisseur spectator takes for granted. For example, one fundamental assumption of *mise-en-scène* criticism is that foreground–background relations are significant; these relations are not pre-given – that is, 'natural' or purely denotational – but have to be designed by the director, and the choices he or she makes signify different meanings (connotations).

More generally, a fundamental assumption of *mise-en-scène* critics is that the relation between what and how, between style and theme or subject matter, is not arbitrary. *Mise-en-scène* critics dismiss the common-sense assumption that all a director needs to do is simply place the camera where the action can be seen best. Filming involves a productive relation between film style and subject matter, of style transforming the subject matter. This is where *mise-en-scène* criticism becomes evaluative, because its adherents evaluate films according to the skill and artistry in which subject matter is creatively transformed by the specifics of the film medium. *Mise-en-scène* critics valorize classical Hollywood films (particularly those directed by *auteurs*) on the basis of their successful (economical and significant) transformation of subject matter into film. But with the decline of the studio system and the ageing of the Hollywood *auteurs* in the 1960s, a number of the most prominent *mise-en-scène* critics (primarily the original writers for *Cahiers du cinéma* in the 1950s – Godard, Chabrol, Rivette, Truffaut, but also Victor Perkins in *Movie*) detected in New Hollywood directors a decline in the creative use of *mise en scène*.

To place this shift in *mise en scène* in historical context, we shall use Adrian Martin's essay (1992) which establishes three basic categories of *mise-en-scène*, of the relation between style and theme: classical, expressionist, and mannerist *mise-en-scène*.

In Martin's definition, films that adopt a classical *mise en scène* 'are all works in which there is a definite stylistic restraint at work, and in which the modulations of stylistic devices across the film are keyed closely to its dramatic shifts and thematic developments' (1992: 90). In classical *mise en scène* the film style is unobtrusive, for it is motivated by the film's themes and dramatic developments. These films maintain a balance between showing and narrating, since style is linked to function, rather than being autonomous: 'stylistic effects and decisions *serve* the creation of a coherent fictional world. ... what is crucial is that the fictional world be an *embodiment* and *dramatization* of a thematic particular to each film' (p. 100). Classical *mise en scène* results in a coherent film 'in which, under continued scrutiny, more and more of [a film's] elements can be seen to function as integral parts of the whole, reflecting (by comparison or contrast) aspects of the over-arching thematic' (p. 100).

Marc A. Le Sueur notes that classical *mise en scène* is based on what he calls the classical synthesis principle: 'There is an implication [in the classical synthesis principle] that the content should necessitate the techniques used, and that, as Aristotle has maintained, none of these technical components could be reduced or changed except at the expense of the aesthetic whole. Form and theme are then meshed and synthesized in a unitary web' (1975: 326). The celebration of classical *mise en scène* parallels the work of art critics who celebrate High Renaissance art. Classicism in both film and painting is valorized because it does not distort the truth of appearances, but renders those appearances faithfully.

Victor Perkins is also an exponent of classical *mise en scène*, which he defines in terms of a film's credibility and coherence. Noël Carroll notes that, for Perkins, 'a narrative fiction film must *first* satisfy the realist requirement of credibility, *after which* it may go on to be as creative in terms of shaping meaning and significance as it can, while abiding by the basic restraint of credibility' (Carroll 1988a: 181). But what does Perkins mean by credibility? 'A narrative fiction film will be credible or not according to whether its images are consistently derived from the fictional world it depicts' (Carroll 1988a: 181). The concept of credibility therefore refers to a film's adherence to the truth of a fictional world. As Carroll points out, within the fictional world of Hitchcock's film *The Birds*, it is perfectly credible for birds to attack humans. We can refer to a more recent example: within the fictional world of Spielberg's *Jurassic Park*, it is perfectly credible to see dinosaurs walking about. However, is it credible to see them opening doors? It is at this point that the film's credibility begins to break down.

Although credibility is a necessary condition for analysing a film's *mise en scène*, it is not sufficient in itself. For Perkins, the second condition is coherence: the more coherent a film, the better it is. He identifies coherence with a film's heightened significance, derived from the creative transformation of the events onto film (what he calls 'cinematic elaboration'). Heightened significance is created by means of symbolism added to the events by the *mise en scène*. However, these attempts to create coherence by means of symbolism must not compromise credibility. The symbolism must therefore be implicit and unobtrusive: 'What happens on the screen must not emerge as a directorial "touch" detached from the dramatic situation; otherwise the spectator's belief in the action will decrease or disappear. The director's guiding hand is obvious only when it is too heavy' (Perkins 1972: 77). When symbolically enhancing a dramatic situation a director must not impose meaning on it. Instead, he or she needs to ensure that the additional meaning emerges from the drama. Perkins examines a scene from *Johnny Guitar*, where a group of mourners set out to capture the killers of the man who has just been buried. The sister of the dead man, Emma, leads the posse. As she advances, the wind blows off her black-veiled hat, and the camera follows it as in lands in the dust:

The 'action' of the hat amplifies our view of the character: grief for the loss of her brother is not the motive guiding Emma's actions, and her sorrow has been forgotten in the exhilaration of the chase.

Nothing in the story or dialogue obliged the director to include this action in the sequence. It was invented to convey a particular view of Emma's character and motives. But we can respond to it simply as information; within the film's world it happened because Emma was in such a hurry, not because it was significant.

(Perkins 1972: 78)

The scene remains intelligible whether or not the spectator is aware of the symbolism, since the credibility of the scene remains more important than the symbolism. But symbolism that can work within the boundaries of credibility becomes a valuable addition to the film.

Expressionist *mise en scène*, Adrian Martin's second category, is found in films 'whose textual economy is pitched more at the level of a broad fit between elements of style and elements of subject. . . . general strategies of colour coding, camera viewpoint, sound design and so on enhance or reinforce the general "feel" or meaning of the subject matter' (Martin 1992: 90). Martin mentions the films of Robert Altman, Michael Mann, Abel Ferrara, the Coen brothers, and Alan Rudolph as representative examples of expressionist *mise en scène*, for they use film style to enhance particular meanings in the subject matter.

Finally, in mannerist *mise en scène*, 'style performs out of its own trajectories, no longer working unobtrusively at the behest of the fiction and its demands of meaningfulness' (Martin 1992: 91). Style is autonomous, for it is not linked to function, but draws attention to itself. In other words, style is not motivated or justified by the subject matter, but is its own justification. It is in such (predominantly post-classical Hollywood) films that the original critics of *Cahiers du cinéma*, as well as Perkins, see the concept of *mise en scène* being inoperative, precisely because the style does not serve the subject matter. Martin seems to be in partial agreement with these critics when he writes that, if post-classical Hollywood film 'gains something interesting and novel, it seems to also lose a great deal that has been associated with the lofty concept of *mise en scène*. In particular, it loses the capacity for a more subtle kind of "point-making" – the kind we associate with a certain critical distance installed between the director and the events that he or she shows' (Martin 1992: 90). However, Martin, Perkins, and the *Cahiers du cinéma* critics are simply lamenting the demise of classical *mise en scène* in mannerist films, not *mise en scène* itself.

Le Sueur also calls this type of filmmaking mannerist (1975). He finds a parallel between mannerist films and mannerist paintings of the sixteenth century, which disregard the classical synthesis principle of Renaissance painting. Instead, mannerist painters worked to create a disjunction between form and theme, an unmotivated form that does not lead to coherence, but to disharmony.

The critics who valorize classical *mise en scène* do so because style productively conveys themes. And they criticize mannerism because style and techniques stand out as techniques, creating a dislocation between style and theme. In other words, mannerism replaces truth of appearances with artifice. But critics who valorize mannerism in the cinema argue that *mise en scène* becomes interesting once it is freed from theme and subject matter, from the need slavishly to represent subject matter accurately. One result is that *mise en scène* may start working against the subject matter, offering alternative information and subverting the film's dominant theme.

Le Sueur makes the now obvious point that such forms of classification are not absolute and watertight. This suggests that we can find moments of mannerism in films otherwise dominated by classical *mise en scène*, amongst which he includes the films of Josef von Sternberg, King Vidor, Vincente Minnelli, and Orson Welles, together with the mannerist aesthetic of musicals.

Another key dimension of *mise-en-scène* criticism is the opposition between the script and the activity of filming. François Truffaut clearly articulated this opposition in 'A Certain Tendency of the French Cinema' (Truffaut 1976), where he criticizes the dominant tendency in French cinema during the 1940s and 1950s – the 'tradition of quality'. This cinema is a contrived and wooden cinema that projects a bourgeois image of good taste and high culture. For Truffaut, the tradition of quality offers little more than the practice of filming scripts, of mechanically transferring scripts to the screen. The success or failure of these films depends entirely on the quality of their scripts. The privileging of the script in the tradition of quality deflected attention away from both the film-making process and the director. Truffaut (together with the other *Cahiers du cinéma* critics and the New Wave filmmakers) defined himself against literature, against the literary script, and against the tradition of quality, and instead promoted 'the cinema' as such.

From this opposition of script and filming emerges the opposition between the director as *auteur* and the director as a mere *metteur en scène*. An *auteur* is a director who does not mechanically transpose a script onto film, but transcends the script by imposing on it his or her own style and vision. The script is the mere pretext for the activity of film-making, and an *auteur* film is about the film-making practices involved in filming a script, rather than being about the script itself. An *auteur* works out his or her own vision by establishing a consistent style of *mise-en-scène*, a style that usually works over and above the demands of the script. By contrast, a *metteur en scène* is a director whose films depend on the quality of their scripts – they make good films from good scripts, and bad films from bad scripts. *Auteurs* consistently make good films because they transcend the script, whether it is good or not.

## 3.2. *Mise-en-scène* method

From the above 'theory' of *mise en scène*, we can begin to extract a method of analysis. David Bordwell has already begun to formalize the strategies of *mise-en-scène* criticism (1989, Ch. 8), although here we shall go much further. Bordwell identifies in *mise-en-scène* criticism an implicit use of the 'bull's-eye schema' and two 'heuristics': the expressivist heuristic and the commentative heuristic. (The term 'heuristic' refers to an informal strategy of reasoning that assists us in discovering ideas. It is therefore similar to Aristotle's topics, outlined in Chapter 1. A *mise-en-scène* heuristic enables the film critic to identify patterns of coherence in a film.) When critics draw correlations between different layers of a film – specifically, characters, settings, and elements of film discourse (such as camera movement and editing) – they are using the bull's-eye schema. Bordwell calls this a bull's-eye schema because, for *mise-en-scène* critics, characters are central to narrative films (the centre or bull's-eye of a 'target'), followed by the setting (the second ring of a target), and then film discourse (the outer ring of a target). There is a hierarchy between the all-important centre (the characters) and the less important periphery (film discourse), although the periphery is more encompassing than the setting, which is in turn more encompassing than the characters.

The primary purpose of the bull's-eye schema is to enable critics to ascribe coherence to a film by linking up these three levels. Bordwell identifies two ways critics have used this schema: the levels of a film are linked either from the core to the periphery, or from the periphery to the core. Critics who begin from the core and link it to the periphery are using the expressivist heuristic, while those who work in the other direction are using the commentative heuristic.

In the expressivist heuristic, 'Meaning is taken to flow from the core to the periphery, from the characters to manifestations in the diegetic world or the nondiegetic representation' (Bordwell 1989: 181). In other words, the setting or filmic discourse should carry the meaning the critic locates in characters' actions. The significance of the settings and of film discourse are justified by referring them to character traits. Bordwell quotes John Russell Taylor's claim that, in Fellini's films, the mental and spiritual state of characters is manifest and reflected in his films' landscapes.

The term 'commentative heuristic' 'suggests that something – narration, presentation, narrator, camera, author, filmmaker, or whatever – stands "outside" the diegetic realm and produces meaning in relation to it' (Bordwell

1989: 183). The critic who uses the commentative heuristic begins with film discourse (or sometimes the setting) and notes how it qualifies or frames the characters' actions. A clichéd example includes unbalanced framing, in which the skewed positioning of the frame in relation to a character suggests that the character is unbalanced. Framing and composition therefore comment on the character's state of mind. In an early essay on Hitchcock's *Notorious*, Bordwell uses the commentative heuristic to show how the setting comments on the relationship between Devlin and Alicia: 'The romantic balloon is deflated in a fine scene in their hotel. Alicia has burned the roast for their dinner; on the terrace, as the tension between them grows, they become more and more distant, until Alicia, saying , "It's cold out here," goes in to desperately down a drink; the transition from hot to cold mirrors the movement of their relationship' (Bordwell 1969: 7). The transition from hot to cold in the film's diegesis not only functions of a literal level, but on a symbolic level as well – as a symbol that comments on the relationship between the two characters.

A more general sign of commentary in the cinema is to be found in the way film discourse foreshadows future events, as when the camera is placed so as to capture the future unfolding of events. The camera (or other agent external to the events) 'knows' in advance how the events are going to unfold. Of course, such a technique can be overplayed, as Ian Cameron argues: 'In *The Wolf Trap*, a highly respected movie, the camera is placed more or less behind a character so that it will produce a "dramatic" effect when she turns away from the table and faces the camera. On the other hand the only reason for her to turn away from the table at the big moment is so that she can face the camera and produce the effect. Because it has all been rigged so that the action has been falsified, the effect is pointless' (Cameron, in Perkins *et al.* 1963: 34). In this example, style dictates the content rather than serving it. Other forms of commentary critics try to identify include irony and distancing.

The expressivist heuristic is suitable for making sense of films dominated by classical *mise en scène*, in which characters' actions and the settings motivate film discourse. Meaning arises from within the film's action, rather than being imposed from the outside by the director. By contrast, films dominated by a mannerist *mise en scène* are more suited for the commentative heuristic, because the work of an external agent such as a director is more evident in mannerist films, in which film discourse is not motivated by characters or settings, but is motivated from outside the film.

Referring back to the previous discussion, we shall now identify additional *mise en scène* heuristics, and then examine examples of *mise-en-scène* criticism that employ these heuristics.

1.  Critics implicitly or, more rarely, explicitly, identify the type of *mise en scène* by which the film has been constructed. Adrian Martin's threefold

distinction between classical, expressionist, and mannerist *mise en scène* has heuristic value:

    1a. In classical *mise en scène* the film style is unobtrusive, for it is motivated by the film's themes and dramatic developments. These films maintain a balance between showing and narrating, since style is linked to function rather than being autonomous; the *mise en scène* functions as unobtrusive symbolism that confers upon the film heightened significance. The expressivist heuristic is used to praise classical *mise en scène*. Perkins uses the concepts of credibility and coherence to praise classical *mise en scène*.

    1b. In expressionist *mise en scène* (not to be confused with the expressivist heuristic), there is a broad fit between style and theme.

    1c. In mannerist *mise en scène*, style is autonomous, for it is not linked to function but draws attention to itself. In other words, style is not motivated or justified by the subject matter, but is its own justification. The commentative heuristic is typically used to praise mannerist *mise en scène*.

2. Script/filming: *mise-en-scène* critics privilege the filming over the script. An integral part of *mise-en-scène* criticism is therefore to downplay the film's plot and instead focus on the process by which the script has been translated onto the screen.

3. *Auteur/metteur en scène*: this heuristic directly follows on from (2). If the film has merit beyond its script – if it transcends the script – then it is said to be the work of an *auteur* (who therefore demonstrates mastery over *mise en scène*). If the quality of the film is dependent on the quality of the script (where filming is subordinate to the script, to translating the script to film), then its director is downgraded to a *metteur en scène*.

4. Foreground–background: using this heuristic, the critic determines if there is any significant relation between a film's foreground and background. One privileged example of this heuristic is the analysis of deep-focus cinematography in the work of Renoir, Welles, and Wyler, where several planes of action remain in play and in focus in the same frame. This heuristic is based on the bull's-eye schema, for it focuses on the relation between characters (usually in the foreground) and the setting (the background).

5. Foreshadowing heuristic: does the film discourse presage upcoming events? (Foreshadowing is part of the commentative heuristic.)

6. Same-frame heuristic: although we have not discussed it up to this point, this widely used heuristic posits that, if characters appear in the same

frame (either a static frame or linked by camera movement), they are united; but if they are separated by cutting, then they are in conflict, or isolated from each other. Bordwell (who named this heuristic) quotes the following example: 'Where the cutting is used to isolate the individual and his responses, the camera movement, as it reintegrates space, reunites the individual with his group to establish a sense of wholeness' (William Paul, in Bordwell 1989: 179).

7.  Cutting or the long take: another very common heuristic to be found throughout the history of film criticism. Film makers have a choice of shooting a scene in one continuous take, where the camera is left rolling while the whole of the action takes place, and shooting the same scene with several shots. The first option involves the film-maker filming the action as it unfolds, uninterrupted. The second option involves breaking the action down into individual shots. Each new shot will include a change in camera position, camera angle, shot scale, and so on. Film makers have to weigh up the advantages and disadvantages in choosing one technique over another for each scene, since the choice of technique will influence the way spectators respond to the film.

## 3.2.1. Examples

Perkins has nothing positive to say about the British 'New Wave' directors of the 1960s – Tony Richardson, Karel Reisz, John Schlesinger, and Jack Clayton. He uses the foreground–background heuristic to criticize them: 'Richardson, Reisz, Schlesinger and Clayton are weakest exactly where their ambitions most demand strength: in the integration of character with background. Because of this weakness they are constantly obliged to "establish" place with inserted shots which serve only to strengthen our conviction that the setting, though "real," has no organic connection with the characters' (Perkins 1962: 5).

As an example, Perkins cites the following from Schlesinger's *A Kind of Loving*:

> the first 'love' scene in *A Kind of Loving* is filmed mainly in a medium shot which shows us the boy and girl necking in a park shelter. On the walls behind and to the side of them we see the usual graffiti of names and hearts. The setting makes, in this way, a fairly obvious but relevant comment on the action. But Schlesinger has no appreciation of the power of his décor; he destroys the whole effect by moving his camera to take the actors out of the shot and isolate the inscriptions in a meaningless close-up. As if he hadn't done enough damage he continues the movement until we come to rest on a totally gratuitous detail: a poster forbidding mutilation of the shelter.
>
> (Perkins 1962: 5)

In this example, Perkins argues that the director begins by making an obvious but coherent commentary on the action by placing the couple against the park shelter wall covered in graffiti. But when the camera moves away from the couple and focuses only on the wall, then the commentary becomes obtrusive and destroys the film's credibility.

Perkins employs the heuristic of opposing script to filming, and implicitly opposes *auteur* to *metteur en scène*, in his discussion of Seth Holt's film *Taste of Fear*: 'Excellent films have been made from mediocre scenarios – *Party Girl* is perhaps the *locus classicus* but there are plenty of other examples. *Taste of Fear* is a useful reminder that there is a level below which a scenario becomes untranscendable' (Perkins 1962: 7). Perkins recognizes the quality of Holt's film despite the poor quality of the script: 'What sets [*Taste of Fear*] apart from other British pictures? Simply that it reveals time and again a director who can create cinematically, where other directors are content with illustrating their scripts' (Perkins 1962: 7). Perkins then employs two additional and interrelated *mise-en-scène* heuristics to back up his claim – namely, praise for classical *mise en scène*, and the expressivist heuristic: 'The distinction [between *auteurs* and *metteur en scène*] is as easy to see as it is difficult to explain: it has, of course, nothing to do with those collections of cute tricks that currently pass for style. We must be able to respond to the rhythm of the film' (Perkins 1962: 7). Here we see Perkins praise classical *mise en scène* and critique mannerism, which he reduces to 'cute tricks' of style. One successful moment in *Taste of Fear* where the classical *mise en scène* works is 'the tracking shot where the camera accompanies [Ronald] Lewis down the cliff-path to the salvaged car and communicates, in its movement, the character's growing uneasiness' (Perkins 1962: 7). Here we see Perkins use the expressivist heuristic, in which the camera movement is not only motivated by character movement but, in addition, expresses that character's state of mind.

Fred Camper (1976) implicitly uses the distinction between *auteur* and *metteur en scène* in his analysis of Frank Borzage's *Disputed Passage* (1939). He begins by summarizing the film's plot, focusing on the main characters' relation to spirituality, of the transformations a number of them undergo towards spirituality. Such a summary, Camper argues, could just as well relate to the script, or to Lloyd C. Douglas's novel upon which it is based. Camper argues that the film has interest because Borzage successfully transcends the script: 'it is the profound visual beauty of Borzage's style that is the deepest expression of these [spiritual] ideas; and it is the style that makes him a true romantic artist rather than simply a translator or *metteur en scène*. His style is not simply representative of spiritual transcendence, but rather seeks ways of visually representing the world which in themselves might lead to transcendence' (Camper 1976: 340-41). Camper does not, therefore, reduce Borzage's *mise en scène* to ineffable and intangible concepts such as spiritual transcendence, but analyses it in terms of concrete elements of film. The heuristics Camper uses are foreground–background relations, foreshadowing, and the same-frame heuristic. Camper argues that, to study how the film visually represents the spiritual transformation of characters, 'One might first direct one's attention to the visual position that the characters occupy in Borzage's conception of things' (p. 341). Camper argues that the characters in *Disputed Passage* are not firmly fixed in space, since they do not exert their physical presence in relation to their surroundings. He gives the example of Dr Forster lecturing to students: 'The shot of [Dr Forster] with students in the background lack the kind of depth which would give him, by separating him from the students he is lecturing, physical force. The extreme high shots in the scene hardly add to his presence. All the characters have presence only in two dimensions; as real beings they seem almost weightless, floating in abstracted surroundings' (p. 341). The significance of this *mise en scène* is that it foreshadows the characters' conversion to the spiritual world, renders this conversion inevitable, because the characters' weightless presence means they do not belong to the physical world.

Closely associated with characters' lack of presence is their lack of fixed location in the frame. In a scene depicting Dr Forster and Dr Cunningham, Camper writes:

> In the graduation scene, while Cunningham is making a speech, we see Forster seated at the right of the frame. One could say it is logical to show Forster there because his beliefs are so at odds with Cunningham's. But due to shallow depth of field his face is a little out of focus, we do not see him reacting specifically to the speech; most importantly, Borzage then cuts to close-ups of Forster's face during the speech, then back to shots of Cunningham with him in the background.
>
> (p. 342)

Camper notes how this scene could have been filmed otherwise (i.e. more conventionally): the scene would contain an establishing shot showing Forster and Cunningham in the same space, but would then proceed to show the two characters separately. But on this occasion (and many other occasions in the film) Borzage keeps the two characters in the same shot, but films them from different angles and distances, creating the effect that their position in space is not fixed, which again illustrates their spirituality. But an additional effect of this cutting which keeps characters in the frame but alters their position is that it links them together, or creates connections between them. For Camper, cutting is therefore used to unite characters, not to oppose or isolate them. While employing the same-frame heuristic, Camper has nonetheless reversed its meaning – or at least the meaning Bordwell imposes on it. Walter Murch offers one solution to these contradictory readings of the same frame heuristic: 'In the States, film is "cut," which puts the emphasis on *separation*. In Australia (and in Great Britain), film is "joined," with the emphasis on *bringing together*' (Murch 1995: 5).

Richard Jameson implicitly defines Mamoulian as a mere *metteur en scène*, for his direction cannot transcend the script: 'Mamoulian keeps faith with the triviality of his ostensible subjects; he dresses them to advantage but he does not transcend them; he can be bright and clever, but when his material is turgid (*Blood and Sand*) or intractable (*We Live Again*), so will his film be' (Jameson 1980: 10). By contrast, in *All Quiet on the Western Front*, Lewis Milestone focuses on an important subject, and attempts to employ the important techniques of *mise en scène* to realize this subject on screen, including 'key cinematic principles' such as 'visual unity of foreground and background planes (*All Quiet*'s soldiers-to-be in their classroom while troops drill outside the window), linking camera energy to character energy (admiringly tracing Adolphe Menjou's Walter Burns through the roaring print shop), the possibilities for syncopation in camera movement and montage (countless troops tracked laterally as they march into all-embracing battle)' (Jameson 1980: 10). Jameson goes on to highlight two moments in the same sequence, one exemplifying Milestone's direction, the other exposing its limitations:

> When enemy troops charge the German trenches, a lateral track along a barbed-wire barrier is synchronized with the collapse of charging men as they come into camera-range; it is as though the camera itself were a machine gun (the previous shot was of a machine-gun crew opening fire), and when the Germans' counter-attack is photographed in the same manner a few moments later, a lucid statement is made about war as a machine indifferently chewing up lives.
>
> But midway between these shots comes a spate of hand-to-hand combat. Milestone again tracks, this time from a slightly raised camera position looking down into the trenches. As his camera arrives at each defender's position, an enemy soldier likewise arrives to leap in on his opposite number. Unlike the camera-as-machine-gun ploy, this shot lacks organic, intrinsic logic; or, more accurately, it is based on a logic at variance with that controlling the rest of the sequence. The careful synchronization of camera's-arrival is entirely a function of the desire for distinctive spectacle. The moralist behind the camera has been displaced by an obscene choreographer. Technical bravura has outrun stylistic sense. And style is conscience – even conscience in default.
>
> (Jameson 1980: 10).

Jameson is therefore another apologist for classical *mise en scène*.

## 3.3. *Mise en Scène* analysis: *The English Patient*

*The English Patient* is a highbrow mega-movie that combines technical virtuosity with a large-scale story. The technical credits include veterans such as cinematographer John Seale ASC, ACS, whose credits include *Witness* (1985), *The Mosquito Coast* (1986), *Gorillas in the Mist* (1988), *Rain Man* (1988), *Beyond Rangoon* (1995), *City of Angels* (1998), and *The Talented Mr Ripley* (1999); and editor Walter Murch, ACE, who edited *The Conversation* (1974), *Apocalypse Now* (1979), *Ghost* (1990), *The Godfather, Part III* (1990), and *The Talented Mr Ripley* (1999) (he also worked as sound editor on many of these films). In the following analysis we shall focus on Seale's (and, to some extent Murch's) input to the creation of a classical *mise en scène* in *The English Patient*, plus the applicability to his work of a number of the *mise-en-scène* heuristics listed above. What emerged as the analysis progressed was the pertinence of applying the same-frame heuristic to this film, and the need to refine it to include the function of selective focus and pull focus (where the selective focus changes as the shot progresses).

In the introduction to an interview with John Seale after the release of *The English Patient*, Mary Colbert wrote:

> Seale maximised his brilliant use of natural landscape metaphors of emotional and psychological states, in the juxtaposition of the dual narrative strands: warm glowing tones for the pre-war African passion-filled sequences, and the more sombre, bleaker look and lighting in the Italian end-of-war scenes when Count de Almásy (Ralph Fiennes), close to death, and cared for by the Canadian nurse, Hana (Juliette Binoche), in an old Tuscan monastery, reflects on past passion and political intrigue.
>
> (Colbert 1997: 7)

The colour of the *mise en scène* therefore functions on a connotative level, for the warm, glowing oranges and yellows in the pre-war desert sequences 'express' desire and passion, while the bleak, cold greens and browns of the Italian sequences 'express' the death of desire, hope, and love. Colbert uses the foreground–background and expressivist heuristics to establish a relation between landscape and characters, to indicate how the landscape carries the meaning of the characters' psychological states. Furthermore, the transition between these two landscapes is also coded as psychological: as Almásy in the Tuscan monastery remembers the past, slow dissolves to the desert landscape mark the transfer. The slow dissolves therefore function as Almásy's change of consciousness, from his present surroundings to his memories of his past.

In the interview with Colbert, John Seale indicated the need to establish a balance between foreground and background:

Anthony [Minghella] and I discussed the fact that the desert, ultimately, is not a performer in this picture. It is the proper – and colourful – stage for the characters. We deliberately avoided the temptation to lapse into travelogue or picture-postcard photography. It's not my rôle to be overpowering with these visuals. I never panned the landscape unless it continued the storyline. Each image was always connected to the story. Compositions kept the people up front. . . . This was a film about people in the desert, not the desert with people.

(Colbert 1997: 8)

In an interview in *American Cinematographer*, Seale explained how the choice of lens kept the people up front: 'We wanted to feature the characters in the foreground, so we tended to use medium to long lenses. This helped to reduce distortion on the actors and "pull up" the background. In this way we were able to surround the characters with the environment, keeping it a "presence" rather than featuring it as another character or subject' (quoted in Oppenheimer 1997: 31). This balance between foreground and background, in order to allow characters to dominate the frame, is one indication of Seale's (and Minghella's) adherence to classical *mise en scène*. (Seale also mentioned that filming the landscape for its own sake – in autonomous shots not related to the story – would simply have increased the length of an already long film. It may have also tipped the *mise en scène* into mannerism.)

In another indication of his adherence to classical *mise en scène*, Seale said, responding to a question about his dislike for obvious camera movement: 'I prefer to think the camera is moving to enhance the physical positioning of actors within the scene or set, and is being used to heighten some movement by the actor or machinery, not just to track around somebody for the sake of creating visual energy because maybe the words aren't good enough. . . . if you're cutting correctly in your mind, and the performance is right, the audience will be transfixed. Moving the camera can distract both audiences and actors' (Colbert 1997: 8–9). Here we see Seale's clear adherence to classical *mise en scène*, which he further clarified when he criticized Michael Ballhaus's cinematography in Scorsese's *The Color of Money* (particularly the 360 degree shots around actors, which function simply to create visual energy) (Colbert 1997: 9).

Finally, Seale's adherence to classical *mise en scène* is evident in his practice of '[using] the zoom as much as possible as a "fixed" lens. I try to hide the movement of the zoom in a pan, dolly or track so that the audience is never aware of the movement' (quoted in Oppenheimer 1997: 36).

In the following analysis of *The English Patient* we will first focus on the opening credit sequence and determine how it relates to the rest of the film; identify key moments in the film where the *ménage à trois* between Almásy, Katharine, and her husband, Geoffrey, is articulated in the *mise en scène* (with particular emphasis on the same-frame heuristic); and briefly employ other heuristics to analyse key moments of the film's *mise en scène*.

### 3.3.1. The credit sequence

The credit sequence consists of a close-up of a piece of paper, upon which a figure is gradually painted. As the credits finish, the image of the painted figure slowly dissolves into an aerial view of the desert landscape. The two-dimensional brown painted figure changes to a grey colour, and then begins to interact with the undulating sandscape. When the figure finally disappears, the shadow of a biplane takes its place. The camera moves back to reveal the biplane flying over the sandscape. It has two passengers, whom we later find out are Almásy and Katharine.

The soundtrack of the film's opening is equally complex. Before the credits even begin, we hear a percussive sound, which we can later locate in the film as the clatter of small vials of medicinal oils. In addition, we hear male voices chanting, a Hungarian folk song, non-diegetic orchestral music, and the diegetic sound of an aeroplane engine. These opening shots and sounds contain a wealth of associations, which we shall attempt to unravel.

We could argue that the rest of *The English Patient* simply elaborates and extends the elements of the *mise-en-scène* condensed in the credit sequence and opening shot. The painted figure is the same as the figures Katharine paints in the Cave of Swimmers. We can therefore suggest that this image derives from the scene in the Cave of Swimmers, and that Katharine is painting the figure. The Cave of Swimmers is important to Katharine because it is her tomb, the place where she dies at the end of the film.

The sand dunes and the painted figure momentarily superimposed over them are similar in shape. The similarity in shape creates the metaphor that the sands take on a human form. Heightened significance or implicit symbolism is therefore created through the superimposition (through cinematic elaboration, in Perkins's terms). This metaphor is relevant to Almásy's first flashback scene. In the foreground of the shot, we see him sitting talking to a desert tribesman about how to locate the Cave of Swimmers. Almásy is seen drawing the cave, and translates the tribesman's words – 'It is shaped like a woman's back'. But just before the tribesman gives this metaphorical description of the cave, a biplane lands in the background. The tribesman pauses, sees the plane, and then offers his description, which Almásy then translates. A few shots later, we realize that Katharine and her husband are in the plane. The associations established in the film's opening, between Katharine and the Cave of Swimmers, is therefore strengthened at this moment in the film.

Furthermore, we can use the foreground–background heuristic to identify the significance of the play between foreground and background. The superimposition in the film's opening links the figure being painted by Katharine to the desert (more specifically, to the Cave of Swimmers, which can be identified because it resembles a woman's back) to the shadow of the biplane carrying Almásy and Katharine. By the end of the film we realize that this image shows Almásy flying away from the Cave of Swimmers after retrieving Katharine's body. Moments later the plane is shot down and Almásy is badly burnt. Katharine is further linked to the painted figure and the Cave of Swimmers when Geoffrey describes her as being like a fish in that she loves water and can swim for hours.

The painted figure is significant in a further respect: Katharine's paintings mark the initiation of Almásy and Katharine's love affair. When the two of them are stranded in the desert, Katharine offers Almásy several of her paintings, to put in his copy of Herodotus' *History*, which serves as a scrapbook of his life. At first Almásy politely refuses them. But by the next morning, he changes his mind and says he will be honoured to put them in his book.

The sounds in the credit sequence are equally significant, although not so straightforward to explain. The sound of the bottles of medicinal oils is located in the film at the moment when a tribesman attends to Almásy's burns. He uses some of the oil to cover Almásy's face. The Hungarian folk song is located in the moment when Katharine stays the night with Almásy in his hotel room. In the morning he plays on a gramophone the folk song which, he says, was sung to him when he was a young boy.

### 3.3.2. *Ménage à trois* and the same-frame heuristic

When Geoffrey and Katharine's plane arrives at the desert base camp of the Royal Geographical Society's team of map-makers (who call themselves 'the International Sand Club'), the whole team travel in a truck to greet them. However, Almásy remains behind with the truck and watches from afar. The same frame heuristic is relevant in describing this moment, as the whole team plus Katharine and Geoffrey are portrayed in one shot, and Almásy is shown alone in another shot. Because he remains aloof, he is introduced to Geoffrey, and then Katharine, in the following scene. The scene consists of 17 shots and lasts 60 seconds. Almásy appears in eight shots, including the opening establishing shot, and Katharine appears in seven (she does not appear in the opening shot). Other people appear in the first five shots featuring Almásy (1, 2, 4, 6, 8), which means he is isolated in his own shots as the scene progresses (shots 10, 12, and 16). Katharine is never isolated in her shots, for she appears in the frame with other members of the team, and with her husband (in shots 15 and 17). Towards the end of the scene, the discussion centres on different

types of love. In shot 15 Geoffrey mentions his favourite type of love –
'excessive love for one's wife', and then kisses Katharine. In shot 16, Almásy
turns away and says, 'There you have me.' This could have been a justified end
to the scene. But shot 17 is added, almost an extra shot that lingers on
Geoffrey and Katharine. Geoffrey simply smiles after his comment, while
Katharine turns her head away with a bemused, or perhaps embarrassed,
smile. This extra, lingering shot emphasizes in purely visual terms possible
differences between Geoffrey and Katharine on the subject of love. Although
they are depicted in the same frame, Katharine's gestures indicate possible
discord between her and Geoffrey. But perhaps another heuristic takes
precedence over the same frame heuristic.

The editor of *The English Patient*, Walter Murch, has written: 'by cutting
away from a character *before* he finishes speaking, I might encourage the
audience to think only about the face value of what he said. On the other
hand, if I linger on the character *after* he finishes speaking, I allow the
audience to see, from the expression in his eyes, that he is probably not telling
the truth, and they will think differently about him and what he said' (Murch
1995: 67). In the scene under discussion, shot 17 represents the lingering
moment after the talking is over. The scene could well end on shot 16, cutting
immediately after Almásy's admission that he is unmarried. Shot 17 can be
understand it in terms of the commentative heuristic of foreshadowing, for it
consists of a moment of cinematic elaboration that foreshadows the future
ménage à trois.

In the following scene of Geoffrey and Katharine flying in one plane, and
Almásy and Madox in the other, there is a significant exchange of looks
between Katharine and Almásy. Katharine looks up toward Almásy, who
looks and waves back. However, Katharine simply looks at him for a moment
before turning away, refusing to acknowledge his wave.

The next exchange between Katharine and Almásy takes place around the
camp fire. Each character entertains the others in various ways. Katharine
recites the story of Gyres, from Herodotus' *History*. The story in effect is about
a *ménage à trois* involving the husband's murder and the lover taking his
place. As Katharine recites the story, a slow tracking shot gradually unites her
and Almásy in the same frame, with Almásy in the foreground and Katharine
in the background. However, the shot is constructed using selective focus,
with Katharine initially in focus and Almásy out of focus. But as Katharine
recites '. . . and she [the Queen] was more lovely than he [Gyres] could have
imagined' she looks towards Almásy, and the focus is pulled so that Almásy is
now in focus, and Katharine out of focus. The focus is reversed a few moments
later, when Katharine recites the part of the story where the Queen realizes
Gyres is watching her: '. . . although she said nothing, she shuddered.'
Katharine then pauses as she exchanges a gaze with Almásy, depicted in a

quick shot/reverse shot pattern. The shot of Katharine in focus in the background, and Almásy out of focus in the foreground, is repeated a few moments later, as Katharine recites that Gyres must kill the king and take his place. The shots, selective focus, and editing do not simply depict the events, but offer commentary. They function to relate the events being recounted to the as yet unspoken events currently unfolding between Almásy, Katharine, and Geoffrey. The same-frame heuristic can be used to explain how pull focus works to separate Almásy and Katharine in the same frame (they are not in focus at the same time, and the quick shot/reverse shot separates them further). And the commentative heuristic can be used to explain how the action and film discourse are united, or how the film discourse transfers the meaning of the recounted story to the current events.

The next significant shot depicting the *ménage à trois* occurs in the hotel, where the Sand Club meet up and toast the absent wives of the other members. Katharine proposes a toast to Almásy. Looking at him, she toasts future wives. As she does so, there is a cut to Almásy in the background of the shot, but in the centre of the frame and in focus, with Geoffrey and Katharine in the foreground at the edge of the left and right frame, and out of focus. Geoffrey turns to Katharine and raises his glass, while Katharine's expression remains hidden, and Almásy looks off-frame, clearly uncomfortable with Katharine's comment. Geoffrey's expression suggests that he is still ignorant of the sexual attraction between Almásy and Katharine. Furthermore, the *mise en scène* adds more foreshadowing: Almásy is literally (i.e. spatially) depicted coming between Katharine and Geoffrey in the same shot. The framing, camera position, and selective focus position the three characters in the same frame, but does not unite them. Instead, these elements of the film discourse signify the future dramatic conflicts that are to unfold. Again, the same-frame heuristic and the commentative heuristic are relevant to an analysis of this film.

In the following scene, however, a number of the Sand Club members take turns to dance with Katharine. The shots of Almásy and Katharine dancing are briefly interrupted by an insert of Geoffrey, who occupies the foreground, while Katharine and Almásy occupy the background with other dancers. Again pull focus is used (this time very quickly) to shift focus from the background to the foreground. Geoffrey's expression, as he turns away from the dance floor, shows signs that he is uncomfortable with Almásy dancing with Katharine. But there is no dialogue to suggest his unease. Instead, his feelings are conveyed simply by inserting the shot of him into the scene at the right moment.

In the scene where Geoffrey temporarily leaves to take aerial photographs, an additional exchange of looks between Almásy and Katharine is depicted. As Geoffrey leaves, Almásy advises him not to leave Katharine behind in the desert environment. Geoffrey simply asks him why 'you type of people are threatened by a woman', and walks away. The scene ends with an exchange of looks between Almásy and Katharine. We cut from behind Almásy's shoulder to behind Katharine's shoulder. However, they are at least 200 feet apart. Each in turn appears in the foreground and extreme background. Such an unusual spatial disposition (reminiscent of the extreme shot/reverse shots in *Citizen Kane*) is ambiguous: using the expressivist heuristic, we can argue that the huge space covered by the shot/reverse shot can signify either that the two of them are still far apart emotionally, or that they are fated to come together with the temporary absence of Geoffrey.

One of the most significant scenes where the same-frame heuristic can be used to analyse the *ménage à trois* is the International Sand Club's farewell dinner scene. By this time, Katharine has attempted to end her affair with Almásy. Furthermore, everyone around the table appears to know that the affair took place. Almásy turns up late to the dinner, and is very drunk. The main characters (Almásy, Katharine, Geoffrey, Madox) are primarily isolated in single shots. But on three occasions Katharine is filmed in profile with Geoffrey in the background. Selective focus is used, and Katharine is kept in focus on all three occasions, while Geoffrey is out of focus in the background. On two occasions Geoffrey is filmed in profile in the foreground, with Katharine in the background. Selective focus is again used to construct these shots. However, Geoffrey is in focus in the first shot but out of focus in the second.

The first of these 'profile' shots occurs when Almásy directs a question to Madox, who is sitting between Katharine and Geoffrey. The shot consists of Katharine in the foreground, Madox in the middle ground, and Geoffrey in the background. However, even though the question is directed to Madox, he does not dominate the frame, and is out of focus (only Katharine is in focus). A conventional way to film Madox would be to continue filming him in isolation in his own shot. But Seale's deviation from this standard is conveying, via cinematic elaboration, the distance between Katharine and Geoffrey, plus Madox's attempt to mediate.

The second 'profile' shot is the reverse of the first, with Geoffrey occupying the foreground, with Katharine in the background. Madox has left the table to try and control Almásy. Although Geoffrey is in the foreground, he is out of focus; only Katharine, in the background, is in focus.

The third profile shot repeats the first, except that Madox is still absent. But the focus remains on Katharine. The fourth shot repeats the second, with Geoffrey in the foreground and Katharine in the background. Madox is shown sitting down, occupying the middle ground. However, the focus has now switched from Katharine to Geoffrey. The fifth and final profile shot repeats shot 1 with Katharine in the foreground in focus, Madox in the middle ground, and Geoffrey in the background. In keeping with his dislike for unnecessary camera movement, Seale has decided to use a still camera and selective focus rather than, say, a panning movement from Katharine to Geoffrey (or vice versa). In the interview in *American Cinematographer*, he indicates why he used framing and focus in these profile shots: 'We never related the two [Katharine and Geoffrey] by pulling focus. In fact, we *isolated* them by *not* pulling focus. I love that. It visually tells the story of these two – the infidelity between them' (quoted in Oppenheimer 1997: 37).

This is the first scene where we see Almásy and Katharine together after she has attempted to end the affair. The camera focuses on Geoffrey's and Katharine's individual reaction to Almásy's presence and comments. In the previous moments mentioned above, we have detected a discrepancy between Katharine's and Geoffrey's reactions to Almásy, from the first meeting in the desert to the scene where Geoffrey flies off, leaving Katharine in the desert with Almásy. Only the inserted shot of Geoffrey reacting to Katharine and Almásy dancing has previously indicated any discomfort he may feel, but the shot is ambiguous and brief. In the five profile shots, both Katharine's and Geoffrey's disapproval of Almásy is clearly evident, although their disapproval is not united (we only experience their disapproval separately, even though they appear in the same shot five times), and Katharine's disapproval is privileged over Geoffrey (Katharine is in focus for four of the five shots). The sequence is in keeping with the previous scenes mentioned in this section because it continues to emphasize the emotional conflict and tensions the main characters feel – particularly Katharine, who is in love with two men at the same time. Furthermore, these two men are sitting around the same table with her, and the scene is focusing on her unspoken reactions and conflicts.

### 3.3.3. Additional heuristics

At the exact moment Hana learns about the death of her fiancé, the army hospital tent where she is located is suddenly bombed. The bombing is not part of some larger offensive, nor are any consequences indicated in the film. On a literal level, the bombing functions as an element of verisimilitude (it is an event that happens in war). But beyond this, its primary aim is to express Hana's extreme state of mind at hearing the news. In Perkins's terminology, the bombing is first and foremost a credible element within the film, and can function on this level only. Beyond this literal meaning, however, the bombing serves to express a character's state of mind. We can use the expressivist heuristic to read the bombing as an event in the film that expresses character psychology.

Another element of cinematic elaboration that takes place in the film are the transitions effected from the present in Tuscany to the pre-war past in the desert. We have already noted that these transitions can be understood psychologically, as representing Almásy's change of consciousness. In addition, many of Almásy's memories are triggered, in Proustian style, by small cues. The first flashback is triggered by Almásy knocking over his copy of Herodotus, and the contents spilling out on the floor. Slow dissolve to Almásy holding the open book and drawing the Cave of Swimmers. The transition back to the present is marked by a visual analogy, not a memory. As the two biplanes fly over the desert, the camera focuses on the rugged landscape. This slowly dissolves into a shot of Almásy's crumpled sheets as he lies in the monastery bed. The dissolve is 'motivated' by the visual similarity between the landscape and the sheets. The second transition is effected via sound. Hana is outside the monastery playing hopscotch. The sounds she creates, which are heard by Almásy, motivate his flashback to the desert campsite, which begins with a drumming sound similar to the sound Hana creates. (Sounds trigger several additional flashbacks.) The third flashback is triggered by Caravaggio, who asks Almásy if the name Katharine Clifton means anything to him. The transition back to the present takes place as Almásy and Katharine are dancing. The close body contact brings Almásy back to the present, where Hana has fallen asleep on him.

As one final example of the foreground–background and same-frame heuristics, we shall simply quote Seale's description of a shot in the monastery with Hana and Caravaggio (played by Willem Dafoe):

> In another scene set in the Italian monastery, Hana, with lantern in hand, walks into the monastery's kitchen to wash herself, only to collapse in tears of stress and emotion. 'In the background, Willem Dafoe comes through the door,' Seale says. 'Juliette throws her head on the table, and even though we only had focus on the top of her head, we still didn't throw it [the focus] back to Willem. Because it's *her* scene, *her* emotion, *her* moment, and he's intruding upon it. If you pull [focus] to him, you include him in her moment. By not pulling, you keep him back and force him to come forward, which he does. He walks forward and leans down, and just his face and hands are sharp.'
>
> (quoted in Oppenheimer 1997: 37)

# 3.4. Statistical style analysis: theory

The statistical style analysis of motion pictures is primarily a systematic version of *mise-en-scène* criticism – or, more accurately, *mise-en-shot* criticism. We have already seen that Eisenstein invented the term *mise en shot* to focus attention on the way shots are staged – that is, the way the parameters of the shot translate the actions and events into film. The advantage of statistical style analysis over *mise-en-scène/shot* criticism is that it offers a more detached, systematic, and explicit mode of analysis. Statistical style analysis characterizes style in a numerical, systematic manner – that is, it analyses style by measuring and quantifying it. At its simplest, the process of measuring involves counting elements, or variables, that reflect a film's style, and then performing statistical tests on those variables.

More specifically, there are three standard aims of statistical style analysis: (1) to offer a quantitative analysis of style, usually for the purpose of recognizing patterns, a task now made feasible with the use of computer technology. In language texts, the quantitative analysis of style and pattern recognition is usually conducted in the numerical analysis of the following variables: word length, or syllables per word, sentence length, the distribution of parts of speech (the different percentage of nouns, pronouns, verbs, adjectives, and so on in a text), calculating the ratio of parts of speech (for example, the ratio of verbs to adjectives), or by analysing word order, syntax, rhythm, or metre; (2) for the purposes of authorship attribution, in cases of disputed authorship of anonymous or pseudonymous texts (see Foster 2001); and (3) for purposes of identifying the chronology of works, when the sequence of composition is unknown or disputed (e.g. Plato, Shakespeare's plays).

The first aim, the quantitative analysis of style, involves descriptive statistics, and the second and third (authorship attribution and chronology) involve both descriptive and inferential statistics. As its name implies, descriptive statistics simply describes a text as it is, by measuring and quantifying it in terms of its numerical characteristics. The result is a detailed, internal, molecular description of the formal variables of a text (or group of texts). Inferential statistics then employs this formal description to make predictions. That is, it uses this data as an index, primarily an index of an author's style, or to put the author's work into chronological order on the basis of measured changes in style of their work over time. Whereas descriptive statistics produces data with complete certainty, inferential statistics is based on assumptions made by the statistician on the basis of the descriptive data. These assumptions only have degrees of probability rather than certainty.

## 3.4.1. The quantitative analysis of style

One of the few film scholars to apply statistical style analysis to film is Barry Salt. In his essay 'Statistical Style Analysis of Motion Pictures' (1974), and later in his book *Film Style and Technology* (1992), he describes the individual style of directors by systematically collecting data on the formal parameters of their films. Salt then represents the quantity and frequency of these formal parameters in bar graphs, percentages, and average shot lengths (there will be more on these methods in section 3.5). When he compares and contrasts the form of the films of different directors, he moves into the realm of stylistic analysis. Style in this sense designates a set of measurable patterns that significantly deviate from contextual norms. As just one example, Barry Salt calculated that the average shot length of a film in the 1940s is around nine to ten seconds. A 1940s film with an average shot length of 30 seconds therefore significantly deviates from the norm, and is thus a significant indicator of style.

## 3.4.2. Authorship attribution

Authorship attribution is a long-standing, traditional subject in New Testament scholarship, study of the classics, and literary scholarship as well as in the legal context (for inferring whether the defendant wrote his or her confession, or whether it was 'co-authored' with the police, for example). Statistical style analysis has contributed its computerized statistical methods to these areas with controversial results.

One of the principles behind authorship attribution of written texts is that the stylometrist should not focus on a few unusual stylistic traits of a text, but on the frequency of common words an author uses – particularly minor or function words, the use of which is independent of the subject matter or context. These include words such as prepositions (*of, to, in*) as well as synonymous function words such as *kind* vs *sort*, or *on* vs *upon*. One author may be prone to use *on* instead of *upon*, or *kind* rather than *sort*. (Stylometric analysts usually look for dozens of synonymous pairs in an author's work.)

At first it may seem odd to distinguish writing style by analysing an author's consistent use of frequent function words, which he or she is not conscious of using. But as A.Q. Morton argues, these words offer the stylometrist a common point of comparison between authors: 'A test of authorship is some habit which is shared by all writers and is used by each at a personal rate, enabling his work to be distinguished from the works of other writers' (Farringdon 1996: 274). So it is the quantity, or personal rate, of common words that is important, rather than their absence or presence in an author's writing. Furthermore, we can argue that a stylometric analysis is analogous to fingerprinting or to DNA testing. Humans share an enormous amount of DNA with other animals. It is only the minute details that distinguish humans from animals. Furthermore, human beings can be distinguished from each other on the basis of DNA testing or, more conventionally, on the basis of other small details – particularly fingerprints. One of the most common metaphors of stylometric authorship attribution is that it 'fingerprints' authors. Anthony Kenny writes: 'What would a stylistic fingerprint be? It would be a feature of an author's style – a combination perhaps of very humble features such as the frequency of *such as* – no less unique to him [or her] than a bodily fingerprint is. Being a trivial and humble feature of style would be no objection to its use for identification purposes: the whorls and loops at the ends of our fingers are not valuable or striking parts of our bodily appearance' (1982: 12–13).

A writer's style can therefore be measured in terms of a constant use of language features, or a combination of features. Just one example, on Raymond Chandler:

> Chandler's style, like that of any author, consists of the *conjunction* of its constituent elements . . . . Much of the action and color in Chandler's stories is conveyed by dialogue, which comprises, on average, 44% of all the words in a story; for every thousand words of text, there are, on average, approximately 30 verbal exchanges, which last approximately 15 words apiece. For every thousand words of text, Chandler's stories also contain approximately one argot word, three similes, one vulgarity, no obscenities at all, and 38 coordinating injunctions.
>
> (Sigelman and Jacoby 1996: 19)

This information identifies Chandler's style – at least from a quantitative perspective – and can be used as the norm by which to attribute an anonymous story to Chandler.

If we think of the descriptive possibilities of stylometric authorship studies for film analysis, we note that, as with *mise-en-scène* criticism, statistics can be used to make *auteur* criticism more rigorous – that is, detached, systematic, and explicit. The *auteur* critic should then focus on the frequency of the common stylistic parameters a director uses – the use of which is independent of the subject matter or context – rather than on a few unusual stylistic traits of a film. In other words, it is possible to use the descriptive dimension of authorship attribution to identify the series of invariant stylistic traits in a director's work (again, the traits linked to the parameters of the shot, in the first instance). It is imperative to think of a director's unique style in terms of the combination of all the parameters related to the shot (what statisticians call multivariate analysis).

The inferential dimension of authorship attribution has a more limited application to film, but some films such as *Poltergeist* have disputed authorship (was it directed by Tobe Hooper or Steven Spielberg?). By systematically analysing the parameters of the shots in *Poltergeist*, and then comparing the results to samples from Hooper's and Spielberg's other films, it may be possible to identify the film's authorship (defined in terms of *mise en shot*, i.e. the parameters of the shot). Of course, because we move from descriptive to inferential statistics, then the result can never be certain, but only predicted with a degree of probability. Only the descriptive aspect of the analysis remains beyond doubt.

On a cautionary note, the variables chosen to determine a director's style need to be valid (Salt has covered this problem by collecting data on the variables under a director's control). And the results need to be statistically significant, rather than due to chance occurrence. Many statistical tests are in fact tests for significance.

### 3.4.3. Chronology

The third area of statistical style analysis is chronology. Here again the statistics used can be either descriptive or inferential. A description quantifies and measures the changes in a body of work, usually of a single author. The point here is that an author's work changes in a predictable manner. An inferential study uses these descriptions of change to place an author's work into chronological order where that chronology is unknown or disputed. By identifying a pattern of change, and by measuring and quantifying that change, the author's work can then be put in chronological order. An assumption underlying inferential chronological studies is that an author's work is rectilinear, in other words, there is a linear progression in the change in an author's style. Furthermore, the idea of change needs to be reconciled with the idea of the author's style remaining constant in author attribution studies.

In film, chronology studies can be used descriptively to identify a change in style across a director's work. The most obvious example is charting the change of any shot parameter across a director's career, such as average shot length, distribution of shot scales, or use of camera movement.

## 3.5. Statistical style analysis: method

In his *Film Quarterly* essay 'Statistical Style Analysis of Motion Pictures' (1974), Barry Salt aimed to identify the individual style of a director by systematically collecting data on the formal parameters of films, particularly those formal parameters that are most directly under the director's control, including:

- duration of the shot (including the calculation of average shot length, or ASL);
- shot scale;
- camera movement;
- angle of shot;
- strength of the cut (measured in terms of the spatio-temporal displacement from one shot to the next).

Salt collected data from these parameters by laboriously going through the film shot by shot. For most of his analyses, he in fact collected data on all the shots that appear in the first 30 minutes of each film, because this is a representative sample from the film. We shall employ (and test the viability of) this practice in our statistical style analysis of *The English Patient* in section 3.6. Salt is also interested in combining the results of each parameter. For example, he argues that it would be useful to combine 'duration of the shot' with 'shot scale' for each film (or indeed, a director's entire output), in order to determine 'the relative total times spent in each type of shot' (Salt 1974: 15), 'giving an indication of the director's preference for the use of that type of shot' (p. 15). So, a director may use close-ups for a total of 20 minutes during a film, long shots for 30 minutes, and so on.

After analysing a sample of films from four directors, Salt finds that both shot scale and ASL are significant and defining characteristics of a director's style. (Calculating the ASL involves dividing the duration of the film by the number of shots.) However, the distribution of shot scale is similar for the four directors he analyses.

In a statistical style analysis of the films of Max Ophuls (Salt 1992: ch. 22), Salt uses standard stylometric tests to analyse the distribution of stylistic parameters in each film. First, histograms, or bar charts, represent the number of each shot type in each film (the number of close-ups, long shots, etc.). Second, he takes equal lengths of film, calculates the expected number of shots and shot types in each section, and then counts the actual number of shots and shot types in that section, to determine whether they conform to the average (the mean) or deviate from it. There are several ways to select the equal section intervals:

1. Salt recommends intervals of one minute (i.e. 100-ft intervals on 35mm film).
2. If calculating shot types one can define the intervals in terms of number of shots (e.g. 50) and calculate the expected number of shot types, and the actual number of shot types.
3. Take the ASL of the whole film, and then analyse it scene by scene (each scene is defined in terms of spatio-temporal unity and in terms of events). Work out the expected number of shots and shot types for each scene, and count the actual number of shots. If the ASL is ten seconds, and the scene lasts two minutes, the expected number of shots for that scene is 12.

In his analysis of *Letter from an Unknown Woman*, Salt notes:

> For instance, in scene 1 five shots would be expected if the cutting were even throughout every part of the film, but in fact there are only three shots. Contrariwise, in scene no. 5, while only seven shots would be expected, there are actually fourteen.
>
> (Salt 1992: 309)

This type of analysis can also be applied to the expected number and the actual number of shot types in each scene and the number of shot types. Salt's analysis of Ophuls' film *Caught* shows how this information can be useful in analysing a film's style:

> *Caught* is the first Max Ophuls film in which there is a very definite reduction in the amount of variation in Scale of Shot and cutting rate from scene to scene, and this becomes very apparent if a breakdown into 100ft sections is made on a 35mm. print. After the point in the film at which Leonora has married Smith-Ohlrig and been left alone in his mansion, we have for the next half hour of screen time very little departure from the average Scale of Shot distribution, and the cutting rate is also very steady for lengths of several minutes at a time, despite the occurrence of scenes of quite varied dramatic nature. It is only in the last 12 minutes of the film, when the most dramatic twitches of the plot take place, that there are any strong deviations from the norms.
>
> (Salt 1992: 310)

Salt is able to determine not only how the shot lengths and scales are distributed across the whole film, but also how this film compares to Ophuls' other films ('*Caught* is the first Max Ophuls film in which there is a very definite reduction in the amount of variation in Scale of Shot and cutting rate from scene to scene'). Salt develops this historical analysis by considering Ophuls' later films, and notes that Ophuls pares down variation in shot scale even more (relying more and more on the medium long shot), and using longer and longer takes, often combined with extensive camera movements.

For example, in *La Ronde*,

> with the scene between The Young man and The Chambermaid we get, after the first 11 shots, long strings of up to 10 shots each with the same camera distance in every shot. Most of these are also in the Medium or medium Long Shot scale, and the film continues in the same manner after this scene. At one point there is a string of 15 consecutive close ups, which is the sort of thing that just did not happen in other people's films in the same period, as a little checking will show.
>
> (Salt 1992: 311)

In summary, statistical style analysis is a very precise tool for determining both the stability and the change in style that takes place across a film-maker's career. Statistical style analysis focuses the research on how films are put together, rather than how they are perceived or comprehended.

Barry Salt carried out his statistical analysis by hand, which limited the types of test he could perform on the data he collected. With the exponential growth in computer technology and software over the last decade, statistical style analysis can now be carried out using computer technology and powerful software programs. In the following analysis of *The English Patient*, data was still collected by hand, but it was then entered into the software program SPSS for Windows (Statistical Package for Social Scientists). SPSS is a spreadsheet program, with rows and columns. In film analysis, each row (which is automatically numbered) represents a shot, and each column represents a parameter of that shot. The parameters recorded include: shot scale, shot length, camera movement, direction of moving camera, and camera angle. Once the data has been entered, it can be represented both numerically and visually, and numerous statistical tests can then be performed on it.

The following analysis of *The English Patient* will consist of both the visual and numerical representation of data (particularly bar graphs and frequency and percentage tables). Then a few simple statistical tests will be applied: measure of the mean or average shot length; measure of the standard deviation of shot length; and the skewness of the values for shot length and shot scale. (The results will also be compared to a similar analysis of *Jurassic Park*.) The mean is a measure of central tendency, of the average value of a range of values. Standard deviation is the reverse of measuring the mean, for it is a measure of dispersion, or distribution spread of values, around the mean; if the value of the standard deviation is large, this means that the values are widely distributed. Skewness measures the degree of non-symmetrical distribution of values around the mean. If the values are perfectly distributed, then the skewness value will be zero. If more of the values are clustered to the left of the mean (i.e. if their value is less than the mean), then the distribution is positively skewed. If the values are clustered to the right of the mean, the distribution is negatively skewed.

These tests properly apply only to ratio data (where zero is an absolute value – zero weight, zero time, etc.). Only shot length is, strictly speaking, ratio data. In the shot scale, numbers have been assigned to the categories, which means that they constitute a nominal scale (Very Long Shot is 7, but there is not reason why it couldn't be 1). However, by using the nominal scale consistently (1 = big close up, 2 = close up, 3 = medium close up, etc.) the norm, standard deviation, and skewness do at least have some heuristic value.

Other stylistic issues that can be raised (but won't be for this exercise) is to enter the number of scenes in the SPSS program, and then calculate the average number of shots per scene, and therefore calculate the expected number of shots per scene, and the actual number. Other useful data can be collected on positional reference (for example, what position do close ups typically take in a film? – the first, second, third shot?) or contextual reference (do close ups usually follow long shots?). Percentiles are also a useful tool. They measure the number of variables at regular intervals of a text. For example, at every 5 per cent, count the number of variables (e.g. close-ups) in the film. This will reveal whether the variables are evenly distributed throughout the film, or concentrated in a particular part of it. One of the most interesting tests, however, is to determine the correlation between variables. For example, what is the correlation between shot length and shot scale? We would expect some correlation, because close-ups usually appear on screen only for a short time, whereas a very long shot usually has a long duration on screen. But we can determine if there is a correlation between any of the variables – camera movement and shot length, or camera movement and shot scale, for example.

## 3.6. Statistical style analysis: *The English Patient*

Data was recorded from the following five parameters of the shot over the first 30 minutes of *The English Patient*: shot length, shot scale, camera movement, camera direction, and camera angle. For comparative purposes, the same data were recorded from the first 30 minutes of *Jurassic Park*. Barry Salt has already argued that 30 minutes is a representative sample to analyse. To test this hypothesis, we shall compare the results of the statistical style analysis of the first 30 minutes of *Jurassic Park* with the statistical style analysis of the whole film.

The statistical tests applied in this section to the collected data are the simplest ones available on SPSS: calculating the frequency of variables (i.e. counting them), representing those frequencies as percentages, calculating the mean, the standard deviation, and the skewness of the results.

The first 30 minutes of *The English Patient* (up to the moment where Caravaggio introduces himself to Hana, and they go into the kitchen of the monastery) comprise 356 shots. In terms of shot length, the main values are to be found in Table 3.1 (on p. 113).

The first column indicates shot length values (1 second, 2 seconds, and so on); the second column the number of times this shot length appears in the first 30 minutes of *The English Patient* (1-second shots appear 41 times, 2-second shots 84 times); and the third column indicates the percentage of shots with each value (1-second shots constitute 11.5 per cent of all the shots in the sample, while 2-second shots represent 23.6 per cent of all the shots in the sample).

Table 3.1 only represents shots of length 1–10 seconds. There are additional values, up to 129 seconds (the opening credit sequence shot), but the frequency of shot lengths above 10 seconds is usually very small – one or two examples. Shots of length 1–10 seconds constitute 92 per cent of all the shots in the sample.

Table 3.2 shows that the mean (the average) value of shot length of this sample is 5.1. In other words, the average shot length (ASL) of the film is 5 seconds (there is, on average, a cut every 5 seconds). The standard deviation of shot length is 8, indicating a wide dispersion of values around the mean, while the skewness of values is 10.97, indicating a very strong postive skewedness of values, favouring those values below the mean. What this means is that there are a large number of shots in the range 1–4 seconds. All of this information can also be represented visually (Fig. 3.1, on p. 112).

The value of this information may not be readily apparent. One of the best ways to make sense of it is to conduct a comparative analysis. The first 30 minutes of *Jurassic Park* (up to the end of the scene where Grant, Sattler, Malcolm, and Gennaro see a dinosaur egg hatch in the lab) consists of 252 shots, in comparison to *The English Patient*'s 356, a difference of 104 shots. This indicates that *The English Patient* has 40 per cent more shots than *Jurassic Park*, a surprising result considering that *The English Patient* is a highbrow mega-movie imitating art cinema aesthetics, while *Jurassic Park* is a blockbuster full of fast action.

We can make many other comparisons. *Jurassic Park*'s values for shot length can be found in Tables 3.3 and 3.4 (on p. 113). The shot lengths in the range 1–10 seconds only constitute 80 per cent of all the shots in the sample, suggesting that Spielberg's film has a wider variety of shot lengths. This is reflected in a skewness value of 2.68 (the mean value is 7 seconds and standard deviation is 6.69). Whereas the skew value of *The English Patient* is 10.97, in *Jurassic Park* it is only 2.68. This shows that the shot length values are more evenly distributed around the mean of 7. There is still a bias towards lower values (lower than the mean), but the bias is far smaller than in *The English Patient*. This information can also be represented visually (see Fig. 3.2).

We can explore further this difference in shot length values. In *The English Patient*, 52 per cent of the shots fall in the range 1–3 seconds. In *Jurassic Park*, only 35 per cent of the shots fall within this range. We have to include the values up to 5 seconds before *Jurassic Park* reaches the same percentage (in fact shots falling in the range 1–5 seconds constitute 54 per cent of the film's total). However, by looking at the bar graphs we can detect a similar pattern: a low value for 1 second, rising steeply for 2 seconds, and then falling gradually for the values 3 and 4 seconds. Furthermore, no shot length above 4 seconds in *The English Patient* and no shot length above 6 seconds in *Jurassic Park* constitute more than 10 per cent of the total values. Whether these results only represent patterns common to *The English Patient* and *Jurassic Park*, are common in film-making, or are an anomaly will require further research.

With the above tests we are simply scratching the surface of what can be achieved with statistical style analysis. It is also possible to apply the same tests to the results obtained from the other four parameters of the shot. But because this would make this chapter even longer, we shall instead consider camera movement and shot scale. With the data collected on camera movement, we

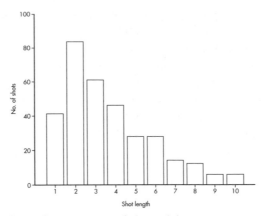

**Fig. 3.1.** Shot length for the first 30 minutes of *The English Patient*

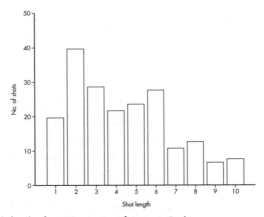

**Fig. 3.2.** Shot length for the first 30 minutes of *Jurassic Park*

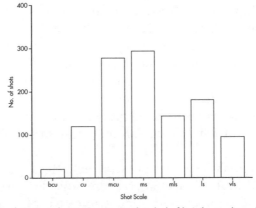

**Fig. 3.3.** Distribution of shot scale in *Jurassic Park* (whole film) (bcu = big close-up; cu = close-up; mcs = medium close shot; ms = medium shot; mls = medium long shot; ls = long shot; vls = very long shot)

**Table 3.1. Frequency and percentage of shots in the first 30 minutes of**
***The English Patient***

| Shot length (seconds) | Frequency | % |
|---|---|---|
| 1 | 41 | 11.5 |
| 2 | 84 | 23.6 |
| 3 | 61 | 17.1 |
| 4 | 46 | 12.9 |
| 5 | 28 | 7.9 |
| 6 | 28 | 7.9 |
| 7 | 14 | 3.9 |
| 8 | 12 | 3.4 |
| 9 | 6 | 1.7 |
| 10 | 6 | 1.7 |

**Table 3.2. Mean, standard deviation, and skewness of shot length in the
first 30 minutes of *The English Patient***

| | |
|---|---|
| No. of shots | 356 |
| Mean | 5.1 |
| Standard deviation | 8 |
| Skewness | 10.9 |
| Standard error of skewness | 0.129 |

**Table 3.3. Frequency and percentage of shots in the first 30 minutes of
*Jurassic Park***

| Shot length (seconds) | Frequency | % |
|---|---|---|
| 1 | 20 | 7.9 |
| 2 | 40 | 15.9 |
| 3 | 29 | 11.5 |
| 4 | 22 | 8.7 |
| 5 | 24 | 9.5 |
| 6 | 28 | 11.1 |
| 7 | 11 | 4.4 |
| 8 | 13 | 5.2 |
| 9 | 7 | 2.8 |
| 10 | 8 | 3.2 |

**Table 3.4. Mean, standard deviation, and skewness of shot length in the
first 30 minutes of *Jurassic Park***

| | |
|---|---|
| No. of shots | 252 |
| Mean | 7 |
| Standard deviation | 6.69 |
| Skewness | 2.68 |
| Standard error of skewness | 0.153 |

can test John Seale's claim that he avoids moving the camera unless absolutely necessary (see Table 3.5).

**Table 3.5. Camera movement values in the first 30 minutes of *The English Patient***

|  | Frequency | % |
|---|---|---|
| Still camera | 302 | 84.8 |
| Pan | 31 | 8.7 |
| Track | 22 | 6.2 |
| Crane | 1 | 0.3 |

The still camera is by far the most common value (85 per cent of all shots), with only 15 per cent of the shots containing camera movement. This seems to confirm John Seale's claim that he likes to keep the camera still.

In comparison, *Jurassic Park* contains the values shown in Table 3.6. These results may surprise some readers, especially the high percentage of still shots in an action blockbuster. But the percentages are significantly different to *The English Patient*, since *Jurassic Park* has 11 per cent more moving shots than *The English Patient*.

**Table 3.6. Camera movement values in the first 30 minutes of *Jurassic Park***

|  | Frequency | % |
|---|---|---|
| Still camera | 187 | 74.2 |
| Pan | 33 | 13.1 |
| Track | 26 | 10.3 |
| Crane | 4 | 1.6 |
| Pan and track | 2 | 0.8 |

Finally, in terms of shot scale, the distribution in both films conforms to what statisticians call a 'normal distribution', with high values in the middle (the mean) and progressively lower values on either side (see Fig. 3.3, p. 112). The result of these normal distributions is that the standard deviation and skewness values are low. Both directors favour medium close-ups (28 per cent in *Jurassic Park*, and 33 per cent in *The English Patient*) and medium shots (21 per cent in *Jurassic Park*, and 20 per cent in *The English Patient*), although *Jurassic Park* only contains half as many close-ups as *The English Patient* (9 per cent in *Jurassic Park*, 18 per cent in *The English Patient*). *Jurassic Park* compensates with almost three times as many long shots as *The English Patient*.

In summary, *The English Patient* contains a short range of shot lengths averaging out at 5 seconds, heavily biased towards shots of 1–3 seconds, with a very high percentage of still shots. *Jurassic Park* has a much wider distribution of shot lengths, which average out at 7 seconds, with a bias (but not as much as in *The English Patient*) towards shots below this value, with a slightly higher percentage of camera movement. Seventy-one per cent of shots in *The English Patient* are at eye level, compared to 81 per cent in *Jurassic Park*. Furthermore, 7 per cent of shots in *The English Patient* are from a low angle, compared to 11.5 per cent in *Jurassic Park*. This similarity is surprising, for Spielberg is well known for using low camera angles. The values for shot scale are more 'stable' in both films, and conform to the normal distribution of values.

One final task needs to be carried out to check the viability of the above results – the representative nature of the first 30 minutes of a film. Here we shall simply note major similarities and differences between a statistical style analysis of the first 30 minutes of *Jurassic Park* and an analysis of the whole film. (When two figures are quoted, the first one always refers to the 30-minute sample and the second to the whole film.) First, shot length. The mean for the first 30 minutes is 7 seconds (252 shots divided by 1,800 seconds), whereas for the whole film it is 6 seconds (1,145 shots divided by 6,870 seconds), suggesting that the cutting rate increases as the film progresses. This increase in cutting is not surprising for an action film with its usual climatic ending, but what is surprising is that the increase is small. Standard deviation remains stable between the two samples, whereas skewness increases from 2.68 to 3.58, suggesting a increase in bias towards shots of shorter length in the whole film. And indeed, when we look at the percentage of 1- second shots, we note that, in the 30 minute sample, they constitute 8 per cent of shots, whereas in the whole film, they constitute 14.5 per cent. The other low values of shot length also increase slightly in the whole film. Whereas, as reported above, 54 per cent of shots in the 30-minute sample fall between 1 and 5 seconds, in the whole film 54 per cent of shots fall between 1 and 4 seconds. Put another way, shots between 1 and 5 seconds in the whole film constitute 63 per cent of shots (as opposed to 54 per cent in the 30-minute sample). Shot scale remains almost identical in both samples, as does camera movement (surprisingly, the number of still shots only falls 1 per cent to 73 per cent in the whole film, despite the increase in action). Significantly, the percentage of low camera angles almost doubles when we take into consideration the whole film – from 11.5 per cent to 21 per cent.

The information that the SPSS software has yielded is simply the raw material for writing about the style of *The English Patient*, and for comparing its style to that of other films. The above analysis only presents a small sample of data and even fewer tests on the stylistic patterns to be found in the film. The primary difference between this analysis and more conventional *mise-en-*

*scène* analysis is that statistical style analysis is more systematic and rigorous, and is more narrowly focused, for it exclusively analyses shot parameters. When reading the results of a statistical style analysis, we need to keep in mind that both the computer and statistics are merely tools, means to an end to analysing data on style, a way of quantifying style and making easier the recognition of underlying patterns.

# 4 From thematic criticism to deconstructive analysis (*Chinatown*)

## Introduction

Common questions film spectators ask themselves (and each other) after watching a film include: What does this film mean? What is it trying to tell us? Does this film have any significance, or is it simply a form of harmless entertainment, containing as much substance as the popcorn and carbonated drinks consumed while watching the film? All these questions are trying to identify on an informal level the film's 'theme', a term originating from literary criticism. Whatever type of text we are referring to – a novel, poem, or film – the theme refers to that text's substance, its principal idea, what it is about. However, themes are usually implicit or indirect, which makes for lively discussions after a screening, for each spectator attempts to make the film's implicit theme explicit and direct. Disagreements arise when some spectators link up particular elements in the film and unify them under a general idea, while others, although privileging the same elements, may try to unify them under a different general idea. Different spectators may then disagree over the selection of elements to privilege, and come up with their own list. Such an activity is also characteristic of thematic criticism, to be outlined in the first half of this chapter. We shall explore thematic criticism by summarizing two thematic analyses of Roman Polanski's films, and then analysing the themes in *Chinatown* (1974).

In the second half of the chapter we shall return to *Chinatown*, but this time from the perspective of deconstructive analysis. On the way, we shall review the main premises of the *auteur* theory, which has many similarities to thematic criticism, particularly its privileging of a coherent, unified text. By contrast, deconstruction privileges excess, deferral, dispersal, dissemination, contradiction, undecidability, unlimited semiosis, and supplementation, the elements of a text that escape unification. As with all theories, thematics and auteurism are partial, in this instance because they focus on a text's unifying features at the expense of those elements that escape unification.

# 4.1. Thematic criticism: theory

There are three basic elements to a thematic analysis of film: (1) the identification of a general theme in a particular film; (2) the rules that govern the relation between the general and the particular; and (3) the nature of the general categories.

## 4.1.1. Identification of a general theme

To read a film thematically involves determining its significance, identifying a general level of meaning that links the film's various elements into a unified structure. Roland Barthes argued that: 'The force of meaning depends on its degree of systematisation: the most powerful meaning is that whose system takes in the greatest number of elements, to the point where it seems to encompass everything notable in the semantic universe' (Culler 1975: 227). This involves relating a particular film to a set of general categories of understanding. A thematic analysis therefore 'reduces' a film to a set of abstract meanings. The internal validity of such a process depends on the 'rules' the critic uses to move from the particular to the general, and whether the general, abstract categories and meanings are relevant to understanding the film's significance. When a critic argues that he or she has identified a film's significance, he or she is therefore claiming to have identified and made explicit the film's themes, or implicit meanings.

Thematic criticism begins from the particular nature of a film, and then relates it to a set of general, fundamental categories. It is therefore similar to a symbolic analysis of a film, in which the film is read, not in its own terms, but in the context of general human values.

## 4.1.2. Rules governing the relation between the particular and the general

How do thematic critics move legitimately from the particular to the general? That is, how can they make general values *adhere* to particular films? One of the main problems with thematic meanings is their implicit status: themes are not immediately 'visible' or self-evident, but must be *inferred* or *generated* from a film. In other words, a theme is a 'pragmatic' rather than a 'semantic' feature of a film. Whereas semanticists argue that meanings are embedded in messages, pragmatists argue that meanings must be inferred or generated by the receiver of messages, since the message does not contain meanings, but simply clues on how to construct the relevant meanings. If receivers of a message do not have the capacity (the 'competence') to infer its meanings, then the message will remain meaningless to them. This process of inferring or generating meaning is more complex than outlined here, and involves multiple levels of meaning. Whereas film spectators quite easily comprehend the events in a film such as *Invasion of the Body Snatchers* (Don Siegel, 1956), they may not be able to infer that it is trying to tell them something indirectly about Western society in the 1950s. The less obvious the meaning, the more capacity or competence required to generate it.

The thematic critic looks at films obliquely, in an attempt to determine what they are saying indirectly. But because indirect meanings are not self-evident, they are open to dispute. This is apparent in the way the theme of *Invasion of the Body Snatchers* has been read by various critics. The film depicts the inhabitants of a small town in California being gradually replaced by pod people, who grow out of pods and look exactly like the people they replace, but with one crucial difference: they lack emotions and empathy. The theme of this film indirectly tells spectators something about the politics of the Cold War society in which it was made. It seems to 'say' that communists may look just like anyone else, but they lack a crucial human trait. The film indirectly represents the result of a communist invasion and takeover of American minds by means of communist ideology. In effect, the film is depicting the result of communist brainwashing: one will become an emotionless robot passively conforming to the totalitarian state.

However, the film can also be read in the opposite way: as a criticism of placid conformity to American Cold War ideology. The ideology perpetuated by the American government about the threat of communism to the American way of life instilled fear in the American public. The American government's ideology (as with all ideology) imposed a restriction on the way the public thought about and lived their everyday lives. This ideology established hysteria about an imminent invasion of America by Soviet communists, who would be aided by members of the Communist Party in America. This ideology encouraged the American public to root out the communists (the 'aliens') living amongst them, because they were seen to pose a threat to national security.

Another example of a conflicting thematic analysis took place in the pages of *Sight and Sound* in 1955 around the final sequence of *On the Waterfront* (Elia Kazan, 1955). The film focuses on the moral transformation of its main character Terry Mallory (Marlon Brando), a dock worker who also works for the mob that controls the dock workers' union. However, by the end of the film Terry has turned his back on the mob, with the result that he can no longer get a job at the docks. Furthermore, the dock workers are hostile towards him. In the film's final sequence, Terry confronts and defeats the corrupt union official, Johnny Friendly, wins the support of the other dock workers, and gets his job back. However, he is badly beaten in the incident. On the basis of actions in the final sequence, Lindsay Anderson attempted to identify Terry Mallory's intentions and motives, plus the principles he is fighting for (Anderson 1955). As with most film characters, Terry's actions are self-evident and manifest in the film. But his motives and intentions remain implicit, and Anderson concludes that, in the film's final sequence, it is difficult to identify them. Anderson attempts to identify the theme of the last sequence by focusing on the actions of other characters – particularly Father Barry, Edie, and the dock workers. Anderson reads the actions of Father Barry and Edie in symbolic terms (Father Barry's actions are not those of an individual, but represent the Catholic Church, while Edie's actions represent 'a Spartan mother'). Anderson interprets the dock workers' words and actions as indicating that they are weak and incapable of self-government, and in need of a strong leader. Anderson infers that Terry will become their new leader now that he has banished Friendly, the corrupt union official. Anderson concludes: 'The conception of this sequence seems to me implicitly (if unconsciously) Fascist' (1955: 128), for the ending cannot be read in any sense as a liberation for the dock workers. Instead, Anderson argues, the ending can only be taken as expressing the theme of hopelessness, or as implicitly expressing contempt for its subject matter.

In his defence of the film, Robert Hughes (1955) argued that its final sequence manifests different themes than those proposed by Anderson. By the end of the film, Terry exists in a no-man's-land between the mob and the dock workers. For the film to achieve resolution, his position needs to be fixed and specified. The last scene depicts the final and decisive stages of Terry's moral transformation and the dock workers' perception of that transformation. Far from signifying their weakness, the dock workers' support for Terry signifies their assertiveness and realization that Friendly no longer has power over them, for one of their own has defeated him. Both Anderson and Hughes are commenting on the same scene, with the same characters, the same actions, and the same dialogue, but they identify different themes or implicit meanings at work in that scene.

In a review of *Rosemary's Baby* (Roman Polanski, 1968), Andrew Sarris discussed the implicit nature of themes. He argued that '[t]he qualities of a good plot are simplicity, directness, and an oblique treatment of essentials. *Rosemary's Baby* can be synopsised in one sentence as the adventures of an actor's wife, delivered to the devil and his worshippers by her ambitious husband so that she might bear the devil's baby, which she does. The beauty of the plot is that it virtually conceals its real subject. On the surface *Rosemary's Baby* seems merely the reversal of Mary's baby' (1970: 374). Sarris goes beyond the surface and identifies two themes in the film: 'two universal fears run through *Rosemary's Baby*, the fear of pregnancy, particularly as it consumes personality, and the fear of a deformed offspring, with all the attendant moral and emotional complications' (p. 375). Sarris argues that a film which directly portrayed these fears would be unbearable to watch. It is only by dealing with them obliquely that the film becomes watchable and powerful at the same time, for the audience's fears are depicted indirectly, yet the film still addresses those fears. Similarly, many of the themes in films and novels address general human values.

## 4.1.3. The nature of general categories

Thematic criticism is not an arbitrary activity that involves analysing a film in terms of the critic's idiosyncratic set of values. Instead, it relates films and other forms of human communication to a small, basic set of values universally shared by all humans. For Jonathan Culler, thematic criticism involves analysing a text 'as expressing a significant attitude to some problem concerning man and/or his relation to the universe' (Culler 1975: 115). Universal humanist values therefore offer a motivated point of closure in thematic criticism: 'primary human experiences serve as conventional stopping points for the process of symbolic or thematic interpretation' (p. 228). Barbara Smith similarly argues that 'allusions to any of the "natural" stopping places of our lives and experiences – sleep, death, winter, and so forth – tend to give closural force' (in Culler 1975: 228). Barthes makes the body the centre of symbolic meaning (which he discusses under the 'symbolic code' in *S/Z*; see Chapter 5 below), while Todorov speaks of the individual's relation to the world, or to himself (see Culler 1975: 228). In his critique of thematic criticism, David Bordwell offers a list of the main values it adheres to: 'the meaning of a film [for thematic critics] will often revolve around individual problems (suffering, identity, alienation, the ambiguity of perception, the mystery of behavior) or values (freedom, religious doctrines, enlightenment, creativity, the imagination)' (1989: 108).

Thematic criticism is anything but arbitrary and unrestrained. Indeed, it is often criticized for reducing remarkably different texts to the same small set of general abstract meanings. At the same time, the thematic critic would argue that the general abstract humanist meanings they attribute to texts are relevant because they encompass a wide range of experience and affect all forms of human communication. This is one of the strongest arguments for thematic criticism, since it begins to explain why films are made (beyond the profit motive) and why millions of spectators have the competence to comprehend and enjoy them, often across significant differences of religious, cultural, and political values.

## 4.2. Thematic criticism: method

- The starting point of thematic criticism is to look at a film obliquely, to determine what human values it is indirectly communicating.
- A useful way to begin identifying themes in a film is to keep in mind at the outset the common themes found in all forms of human communication, such as those listed by Bordwell above (suffering, identity, alienation, the ambiguity of perception, the mystery of behaviour, freedom, religious doctrines, enlightenment, creativity, the imagination, etc.).
- Then determine which themes are manifest in the film under analysis. One useful strategy is to analyse the film scene by scene, in order to determine what each scene contributes to the film's overall meaning. In particular, ask yourself: What themes are the characters manifesting through their actions?
- Focus on the themes that cohere across the film. Unity of theme is an important aspect of thematic criticism.
- A perennial problem with thematic criticism is that it is too reductive, to the point of reducing the film to a set of meanings that are so abstract that the criticism becomes banal (a comment such as 'this film is about life' won't win any prizes). One way to avoid this is to identify the basic themes in a film or director's work, and then attempt to establish precisely how they relate to one another, which will reintroduce an element of specificity to the analysis.
- Some thematic critics also attempt to outline the director's attitude or stance toward the themes in his or her films, and to assess whether a director is able to be both 'inside' his characters and 'comment on' them at the same time. When discussing the relation between thematic criticism, genre, and *auteur* studies, film scholars have often invoked such a double perspective in order to highlight the 'critical' dimension that auteurs are said to impart to 'conformist' genres such as family melodrama (Douglas Sirk and the 'unhappy happy ending') or the women's film (Max Ophuls in films like *Caught* or *Letter from an Unknown Woman*). A similar case can be made with respect to degrees of 'knowingness' (see below) or the double inscription of a 'naïve' and a 'sophisticated' spectator when arguing the merits of distinguishing between 'classical' and 'postclassical' Hollywood.

## 4.3. Thematic criticism: analysis (Roman Polanski)

One thematic analysis of Roman Polanski's films claims: 'Polanski's work might be seen as an attempt to map out the precise relationship between the contemporary world's instability and tendency to violence and the individual's increasing inability to overcome his isolation and locate some realm of meaning or value beyond himself' (Telotte and McCarty 1998: 388). This analysis, although general, is nonetheless quite precise in its delineation of Polanski's themes. It does not simply state that Polanski's films contain a conflict between 'the contemporary world' and 'the individual' (which is not very informative). Instead, it adds detail to each category of the opposition – a *violent, unstable* contemporary world; an *isolated* individual with *no faith or conviction*, who finds it increasingly difficult to overcome his isolation or adopt beliefs.

Telotte and McCarty's characterization then outlines the themes of instability and isolation in more detail. First, isolation. Many of Polanski's films focus on a character or small group of characters isolated from society. Examples include (we have added to Telotte and McCarty's list): characters confined to boats in *Knife in the Water, Bitter Moon*, and *Pirates*; a small group of characters occupying an isolated castle in *Cul-de-Sac*; characters isolated in their own apartments in *Rosemary's Baby* and *The Tenant*; three characters cut off from the rest of civilization in an isolated house in *Death and the Maiden*; an American doctor lost and isolated in France as he tries to find his kidnapped wife (*Frantic*). In addition, Telotte and McCarty argue: 'All [Polanski's] characters try continually, however clumsily, to connect with other human beings, to break out of their isolation and to free themselves of their alienation' (p. 390). As is common in thematic criticism, Telotte and McCarty focus their analysis on characters, particularly their actions and psychological states. They even use the 'commentative heuristic' (see Chapter 3 above) to map the desolate landscape characters occupy onto the characters' psychology: the 'geography of isolation [in Polanski's films] is often symbolically transformed into a geography of the mind, haunted by doubts, fears, desires, or even madness' (p. 389).

In terms of Polanski's second main theme, that of a violent contemporary world, Telotte and McCarty do not only relate it to the theme of isolation, but also outline Polanski's attitude towards it: '[Polanski] is able to assume an ironic, even highly comic attitude towards the ultimate and, as he sees it, inevitable human problem – an abiding violence and evil nurtured even as we individually struggle against these forces' (p. 390). The isolated individuals struggle against the violence and evil of the contemporary world, but at the same time they nurture what they struggle against. This complex theme is epitomized in one of Polanski's most famous films – *Rosemary's Baby*: 'The basic event of *Rosemary's Baby* – Rosemary's bearing the offspring of the devil, a baby whom she fears yet, because of the natural love of a mother for her own child, nurtures – might be seen as a paradigm of Polanski's vision of evil and its operation in our world' (pp. 389–90).

Virginia Wright Wexman analyses Polanski's themes from a different perspective, by identifying the influence of the Theatre of the Absurd and Surrealism on his films (Wexman 1979). Polanski's focus on man isolated in a meaningless universe is a theme that derives from the Theatre of the Absurd. Wexman then argues that Polanski develops this theme by focusing 'on shifting power relationships, usually precipitated by the arrival of an outsider into a group, which forces a reshuffling of status and privilege' (Wexman 1979: 8). Additional consequences of the influence of the Theatre of the Absurd include these: Polanski's films are full of pessimism, of callous exploiters and willing victims, and circular plots, which 'leave the characters no better off at the end than they were at the beginning' (Wexman 1979: 10). One of the clear influences of Surrealism is to be found in his films' focus on deviant behaviour, persecution, and paranoid delusion. Finally, Wexman does not argue that Polanski assumes an ironic or comic attitude towards his themes, but argues instead that he refuses 'to permit audiences to feel for his characters what the characters are unable to feel for one another' (p. 12).

## 4.3.1. Thematic analysis of *Chinatown*

In this section we shall focus on how *Chinatown* establishes the values of its main character Jake Gittes (Jack Nicholson), and then explore two of the film's general themes.

In the opening scene Jake Gittes, a private investigator who specializes in matrimonial issues, has handed over to Curly, a working-class male client, a set of photos of his wife having an affair with another man. As Curly gets more and more upset, trying to express his anger, Jake is shown to be laid back. He is in control of the situation: he offers Curly a stiff drink, smokes in his presence, and tells him he need not pay the whole bill.

In scene 2 Jake talks formally and politely to a new client who calls herself 'Mrs Evelyn Mulwray', the wife of Hollis Mulwray, a high-level official in the Water department. (In fact, it is the character Ida Sessions, pretending to be Evelyn Mulwray.) 'Evelyn Mulwray' is the opposite of Jake's previous client: she is a confident, calculating, rich upper-class woman who expresses herself clearly. But despite her difference from Curly, her needs are the same: she suspects her spouse of cheating, and wants him investigated. Jake is able to treat his new client on her own level, and raises the same issues with her, especially money (except that he emphasizes to her the expense an investigation may cost). The main difference between scenes 1 and 2 is that, whereas Jake smokes in scene 1, 'Evelyn Mulwray' smokes in scene 2. Unlike many private investigators in classical *films noirs*, in this neo-*noir* detective film Jake is a well-off, upwardly mobile private investigator who feels at ease with all his clients (as well as most of the other people he comes into contact with).

In scene 3 Jake is shown attending a public meeting where Hollis Mulwray is to speak. Jake is depicted as being uninterested in the political issues discussed in the meeting (Los Angeles' precarious position between a desert and the sea, its lack of drinking water, and a proposal to build a dam). During the debate, he is shown reading a sports paper. He only looks up when Hollis Mulwray speaks, and only reacts to the events when a farmer unleashes his sheep into the meeting (and also accuses Mulwray of corruption). This scene establishes Jake's self-imposed isolation from contemporary political debates. He simply wants to do his job and solve his clients' matrimonial problems.

Jake continues to follow and photograph Mulwray in scenes 4–7. In scene 8, in a barber-shop, he gets into an argument with a mortgage broker, who criticizes Jake for the dishonest nature of his job. Jake strenuously defends his job as an honest business, which seems to be the main purpose of this scene, beyond the revelation that Hollis Mulwray's affair has made it into the papers. Jake also describes his job (to the real Mrs Mulwray) as a business in scene 11 when he goes to visit Hollis Mulwray at home. Jake's pride and business have been tarnished, and he wants to find out who set up both him and the Mulwrays (that is, he wants to discover why someone would want to set up Mrs Mulwray by impersonating her, and why this imposter would come to him). His motivation for investigating further is therefore primarily personal.

From the few scenes mentioned, we can already identify the film's main themes. The opening two scenes emphasize the theme of illicit relationships, of spouses having extramarital affairs. By the end of the film we realize that this is one of the film's dominant themes articulated across the whole film, but that it ultimately involves incest between Evelyn Mulwray and her father, Noah Cross, as well as an affair of some kind between Hollis Mulwray and his stepdaughter Catherine. If we ask what *Chinatown* is 'about', what its 'substance' or 'principal idea' is, one answer is that it is about breaking a fundamental law of society, the incest taboo, a law that creates stable identity boundaries and societies. Familial relationships define identity, and so the film's emphasis on relationships is also an emphasis on the fundamental theme of identity, and the suffering caused by illicit relationships.

This first theme is related to the film's second primary theme: political corruption. This theme is first raised at the end of scene 3, when a farmer accuses Hollis Mulwray of political corruption. Jake ignores this cue, however, and, furthermore, it is a false cue, since Hollis tries to expose the corruption. After Hollis is killed, the corruption theme is put into sharper focus, as Jake proposes to Evelyn that her husband was murdered because he tried to expose corruption. Jake continues the investigation to find out who set him up, and to find out what Evelyn is hiding. At first he suspects her of the murder, but later finds out that her 'secret' is that her daughter was fathered by her father, Noah Cross. Furthermore, Evelyn proposes to Jake that her father may be behind the political corruption (and behind her husband's death). It is only towards the end of the film that Jake is able to link together the first theme, illicit relationships and identity, and the second theme, political corruption, and realize that Noah Cross is behind both. Perhaps, therefore, we can link these two themes, and argue that *Chinatown*'s overall theme is 'patriarchal corruption', of the father's corruption of both family and politics.

*Chinatown* includes many of the themes common to Polanski's films. The hero is isolated from society by the nature of his job (a private investigator who handles matrimonial cases), although he is far from being a completely alienated investigator as found in classical *films noirs*. However, Jake is unable to establish any beliefs or values beyond his own work ethic, since he explains that his motivation to investigate Mulwray's death is primarily personal, and he is shown to be uninterested in politics. The contemporary world is shown to be violent, as Jake's life is threatened on several occasions and his nose is badly cut. Furthermore, Cross in particular is depicted as a callous exploiter, indulging in transgressive behaviour; the film's plot does not lead to resolution or a happy ending (Polanski rewrote Robert Towne's original happy ending), but is circular, because the characters are no better off at the end than they were at the beginning – indeed many are worse off, as Evelyn is killed, Jake is injured, may lose his licence, and has lost a woman he loved, and Catherine is handed over to Noah Cross, who seems to escape prosecution. Because of the ending in particular, the film moves from sharp wit to sombre pessimism, as the central character slides from cocky assurance and self-confident cynicism to moral confusion and professional ineptitude.

## 4.3.2. Thematic criticism and auteurism

One of the most prototypical instances of thematic criticism is auteurism, the attribution of a single source of a film's intentionality, value, and meaning to the director. It was, as the name suggests, initially formulated in Paris, around the influential journal *Cahiers du cinéma*. Subsequently, auteurism was taken up by *Movie* magazine in London (see Chapter 3) and by Andrew Sarris in New York, who for a brief period edited *Cahiers du cinéma in English* and in 1968 published *The American Cinema: Directors and Directions* (Sarris 1996), the auteurists' bible in the English-speaking world.

What made auteurism a radical doctrine (a 'politics') during the 1950s in France and the early 1960s in Britain and the United States was that it took the commercial mainstream cinema (and thus a vital aspect of popular culture) seriously. *Auteur* critics challenged the traditional division between the arts into high and low media, but the real provocation lay in actively maintaining the criteria and classifications of traditional aesthetics: the belief in the artist as a controlling creative identity behind a work, the idea of the consistency of themes, and the notion of the coherence of an entire body of work over a lifetime of artistic production. Setting themselves off against film appreciation as much as against film reviewing in the daily press, the *auteur* critics elevated the genre films and studio products directed by Alfred Hitchcock, Howard Hawks, John Ford, Vincente Minnelli, and others to the status of art, and claimed for these directors (*auteurs*) the rank of major artists. Commenting on François Truffaut's influence in developing the polemical understanding of the film director as auteur, Andrew Sarris notes: 'Truffaut's greatest heresy [in the eyes of traditional film critics] was not in his ennobling direction as a form of creation, but in his ascribing authorship to Hollywood directors hitherto tagged with the deadly epithets of commercialism. This was Truffaut's major contribution to the anti-Establishment ferment in England and America' (Sarris 1996: 28).

More specifically, the *auteur* critics elevated a select group of Hollywood directors to the status of classical artists – that is, artists who work within institutions (in this instance, Hollywood studios), but who expressed themselves through adhering to conventions. This is in contrast to the type of director Truffaut and other critics at *Cahiers du cinéma* wanted to become – and, of course, did become in the 1960s: namely, Romantic artists, who work outside institutions, and whose expressive style requires the breaking of conventions.

As we saw above, one of the favoured methods of establishing the credentials of a director to be considered an *auteur* (and not merely a *metteur-en-scène* or a studio contract director) is to demonstrate a set of consistent themes or preoccupations, across a diversity of genres (e.g. similar or complementary motifs in Hawks's comedies, his Westerns and his action-adventures; the underlying unity of Minnelli's musicals and melodramas) or across films made for different studios (Hitchcock for Selznick and Universal; Preminger at first for Twentieth Century Fox and then as his own independent producer). A thematic analysis of a director's work thus always implies the presence of countervailing forces – most commonly those of producer and studio, occasionally that of genre – against which an *auteur*-director was deemed to have succeeded in imposing his signature and thereby remain true to himself and articulate his 'vision of the world'.

If we now apply the *auteur* argument to Polanski's *Chinatown*, we note that both the issues of thematic coherence and authorial identity are complicated by the fact that Polanski – born in Paris in 1933 – began his career in Poland in the 1960s where the (economic, ideological) constraints for a film-maker were quite different from those obtaining in a commercial, mainstream film industry. He subsequently made films in Britain before moving to Hollywood, which he left in 1976 for France, where he has been making most of his films since. In his career, therefore, the countervailing forces assumed to be operating in the Hollywood system, as well as the auteur's (stylistic, thematic) means by which to assert himself against them, are bound to be different from those assumed to have negatively or dialectically shaped the career of a Sam Fuller or Nicholas Ray. On the other hand, by the time he came to make *Chinatown*, Polanski had established a reputation as a highly distinctive director, with an offbeat approach even to conventional subjects as well as a strong existentialist undertow that closely affiliated him with various 'gothic', 'expressionist', 'film noir', or 'horror' genres in cinema history, all of which he often subverted by a strain of black humour and absurdist comedy. The strongest countervailing force in his case would be the change of language (from Polish to English to French) and the different conditions of production in the four countries in which he has directed. This makes his situation resemble that of 'independent' auteurs from a slightly older generation, like Orson Welles or Joseph Losey, who also moved in and out of several film industries.

But Polanski is also comparable to Hollywood directors of an apparently quite different generation, namely the expatriate or émigré directors of Hollywood in the 1930s and 1940s, such as Hitchcock, Fritz Lang, Billy Wilder, Max Ophuls, or Robert Siodmak. They, too, had either left their native country and its film industry to rebuild a career in Hollywood or been forced by political events to seek refuge in the United States. Adjusting more or less voluntarily and felicitously to the Hollywood production system, they were indeed contending with interfering producers (from the auteurist point of view) and a rigid studio system (from the European perspective). They also had to make certain genre conventions their own, by subverting or transforming them (Hitchcock transforming the woman's picture and the thriller; the directors from Germany giving the Weimar 'social picture' of the 1920s a new, more sombre inflection, as in the neo-expressionist *film noir* of the 1940s).

The trajectory of Polanski, however, does not finally fit into this mould either. On the one hand, one could claim that he was a political refugee from communist Poland, when the post-Stalinist thaw of the 1960s became once more the socialist permafrost of Poland's General Jaruselsky in the 1970s. On the other hand, Polanski's career move to Hollywood follows another pattern, that of the successful European director lured to Hollywood by an offer he could not refuse: in this he is more like Louis Malle, Jan Troll, Alan Parker, Philip Noyce, Ridley Scott, Paul Verhoeven, or Wolfgang Petersen – all of them directors whose talent Hollywood succeeded in 'buying in' from abroad. Polanski did become a refugee, in reverse direction, from Hollywood to Paris. He did not flee the US for political reasons, but jumped bail when facing a criminal conviction for statutory rape.

## 4.4. Deconstruction: theory

Is there such as thing as a theory and method in deconstructive criticism? After all, deconstructionists disparage all attempts to develop general, systematic theories with fixed doctrines and definable, repeatable methods, because they argue that texts cannot be mastered, for they are based upon paradoxes and aporias. Texts elude the grasp of theories, methods, and totalizing analyses that attempt to identify and determine once and for all a text's meaning, or themes. However, this failure to totalize opens up a different possibility: a 'negative hermeneutic' that focuses on details in a text that obscure or undo standard presuppositions concerning logical order, meaning, and intention. In film analysis, this involves focusing attention on non-narrative details that present in an oblique way a network of meanings that oppose, interfere with, or contradict narrative meanings.

Deconstruction is not, therefore, a theory but a strategy: a reading of texts with scrupulous attention to the point where discrepant or disruptive details are foregrounded. Deconstruction rigorously pursues marginal details or minor stylistic flourishes that escape rationality. It is not an arbitrary activity, for it has a specific procedure that can be identified and followed. But that procedure cannot simply be outlined as a three- or five-step process.

## 4.5. Deconstruction: method

As we point out in Chapter 1, the aim of theory is to provide guidance on how to establish general methodological principles to analyse texts. But this can lead, in Abraham Kaplan's words, to 'trained incapacity' (1964: 29). Our solution is to teach several theories, so that the film student can apply specific theories in appropriate contexts, rather than use the same theory in all contexts. The solution of deconstructionists is more radical. They argue that all general theoretical propositions block the activity of close reading because they create a tunnel vision effect, in which the analyst looks for and finds only what he or she wishes to see. Deconstruction involves 'looking at' the text again, focusing on elements that escaped the initial classification (in this instance, by thematic and auteurist analyses). Jonathan Culler notes:

> When one speaks of the structure of a literary work, one does so from a certain vantage point: one starts with notions of the meaning or effects of a poem and tries to identify the structures responsible for those effects. Possible configurations or patterns that make no contribution are rejected as irrelevant. That is to say, an intuitive understanding of the poem functions as the 'centre', governing the play of forms: it is both a starting point – what enables one to identify structures – and a limiting principle.
>
> (Culler 1975: 244)

How, then, can we make the anomalies, reversals, and asymmetries of Polanski as director-*auteur* enter into our considerations of the structure of *Chinatown* and the meaning-making inferences we wish to explore? This part of our chapter will suggest two distinct ways of 'deconstructing' auteurism and thematic criticism. The first might be called a 'poetics of production', and analyses the contending claims of authorship. In other words, it takes literally the countervailing forces against which an auteurist-thematic reading pitches itself. The second mode of deconstruction is that of a 'poetics of semiosis', where we shall look closely at certain surface elements and stylistic details of the film, examining them for their meaning-making potential, but without feeling the need to integrate them into a coherent whole. Rather, we shall allow them to disperse and to disseminate, thereby 'contaminating' and rendering unnecessary any pretensions to a single authorial meaning or authoritative interpretation with a claim to closure. In other words, the poetics of semiosis takes literally one of the unstated, implicit premises of auteurism and *mise-en-scène* criticism, namely its reliance on marginal details or minor stylistic flourishes to buttress the interpretation of an entire film. What was often chastised as an elitist or snobbish form of evaluative connoisseurship, because it reads films according to an additional layer of meaning, consisting of seemingly trivial and inconsequential aspects (leading to those 'delirious' or 'aberrant' reviews of a Michel Mourlet or Fereydoun Hoveda), can in this light be seen as merely the flip-side of the semiotic coin. For once one concentrates on the signifiers (the verbal, visual, and aural surface) of a film, their referentiality will always be multiple, sliding, unstable, excessive. The process of generating meaning (semiosis) from a film is in principle unlimited, unless and until the interpreter decides to terminate it, for instance, by applying the expressivist or commentative heuristics of *mise-en-scène* criticism, or by fixing on a set of meanings suggested by one or more of the universal schemata discussed above (section 4.1.3). To choose a 'perverse' reading, as the *Cahiers* critics did, is therefore simply to 'expose the device' of closure itself.

At the end of the chapter we shall be making reference to a number of film scholars (particularly David Rodowick, Tom Conley, and Kaja Silverman) who advocate, under different names and for different reasons, the return to poetological methods or hermeneutic traditions capable of generating such (unlimited) semiosis. Deconstruction itself, therefore, prevents us from translating 'theory' into 'method', other than by turning it back into a version of 'thematic' criticism – for instance, by identifying a number of moves or tropes, such as the evidence of puns, the strategy of subverted oppositions, the double negative which does not make a positive, or the verbal slippage which does not cancel a proposition so much as put it 'under erasure'. More important than such a list, however, is to grasp the underlying principle: that deconstructivist criticism more than any other mode allows the critic to start virtually *anywhere*, both within the text and by invoking external facts, beliefs, and myths, as long as the starting point helps to generate difference, in the sense of perceptible variation or discrepancy as well as in the sense of temporal delay or deferral. This we shall try to demonstrate in the subsequent section around the two kinds of poetics.

## 4.6. Deconstruction: analysis

### 4.6.1. The poetics of production

A first move in 'deconstructing' Polanksi as the *auteur* of *Chinatown* would be to assess the competing claims of the producer Robert Evans, the screenwriter Robert Towne, and the actors Jack Nicholson and John Huston, alongside Roman Polanski, to be considered the initiator, controlling force, decisive authority, or creative centre in the making (and subsequent success) of *Chinatown*. For instance, in a number of screenwriter's manuals as well as for screen-writing gurus such as Robert McKee (1999), Robert Towne's script for *Chinatown* has been held up as exemplary for the canonical story structure of classical Hollywood. Rarely if ever is the name Polanski mentioned when the solidity of the three-act structure, the subtleties of the introduction of the back-stories, and the sophistication of the double entendres in the dialogue are being praised. According to one commentator, seven out of ten screenwriting manuals of the last 20 years discuss *Chinatown*. A typical assessment, which ranks the director as merely the person who 'brings out the essence of the story', can be found in David Howard and Edward Mabley's *The Tools of Screenwriting* (1995: 177).

A not inconsiderable factor in the dense texture of the film is the performance but also the persona of director turned actor John Huston (playing the patriarch Noah Cross). At an earlier point in his career Huston had directed his own father, Walter Huston (in *Treasure of the Sierra Madre*), and his *Freud: The Secret Passion* can be read as a kind of anticipation of the different forms of authorial *mise-en-abîme* on display in *Chinatown* (see Wollen, in Bergstrom 1999). He also directed and played (the voice of) God and the part of Noah in *The Bible* (1966). Equally relevant is the allusion to John Huston as the director of the first of the modern '*film noir*' detective thrillers, *The Maltese Falcon* (to which the opening of *Chinatown* pays direct tribute), based on a book by one of the acknowledged masters of the hardboiled novel, Dashiell Hammett. In a film ostensibly about founding and maintaining a dynasty, John Huston is playing the patriarch, echoing the degree to which he himself is part of and has perpetuated a dynasty (directing films which star his daughter, Anjelica Huston). It makes *Chinatown* stand in more than one sense in an incestuous relationship with films like *The Maltese Falcon* and *The Big Sleep* (another film revolving around troubled father–daughter relationships, and frequently cited in *Chinatown*). The choice of actor for Noah Cross thus underlines an awareness not only of film history but of the peculiar in-joke self-reference (or deconstructive logic) of the 'New Hollywood' of which *Chinatown* became such a remarkable exemplar.

*Chinatown* was also a turning point in the career of its male star, Jack Nicholson, while his presence conversely proved decisive in giving the film 'crossover' appeal, i.e. winning a younger – as well as an art house – audience for what was in fact a mainstream commercial production. Nicholson came to (modest) prominence in *Easy Rider* and other small-scale 'New Hollywood' films, but after *Chinatown* he had enough box office clout to secure the backing for a sequel, *The Two Jakes* (1990), scripted by Robert Towne, produced by Evans, and directed not by Polanski but by Nicholson himself. While generally regarded as a worthy effort, the sequel does not enjoy either the critical reputation or cult status of *Chinatown*, thus retrospectively vindicating Polanski as the key ingredient in the 'success' of the 1974 collaboration. From another perspective, this collaboration was not successful for the participants, if we believe Andrew Sarris and others who have alluded to Polanski's rows with Faye Dunaway, the film's female star, his disagreements with Robert Towne over the ending, and also the strained relation with Robert Evans, who against Polanski's wishes decided to replace the original, harshly dissonant percussive music with a lusher, more 'romantic' jazz score (Wexman 1979: 91, quoting Sarris).

The thematics of the film could thus also be seen as the reflection of its own problematic coming-into-being. If one fastens on this network of uneven and competing power relations that went into the making of *Chinatown*, it is possible to read the film as not only 'about' a partly historical and partly fictional Los Angeles, in its 'heroic' phase of expansion (as also described in such well-documented histories of Los Angeles as Mike Davis's *City of Quartz*, and with Hollis Mulwray recalling the city planner Mulholland). In its story of corruption, of erotic and political power struggles, of deals and double-crossings, of incestuous genealogies and faked authenticities, *Chinatown* could be said to symbolically represent ('allegorize') aspects of 'New Hollywood' itself, as another generation takes over. The signifier 'Chinatown' would then stand for 'Tinseltown', as a place with a once glamorous but now murky past, poised to return and haunt the present. The pastiching of the formulas taken from the Hammett–Chandler detective fiction and the rewriting of classic *film noir* scenarios which *Chinatown* inaugurated (followed by other films of the early 1980s, such as *Body Heat* (Lawrence Kasdan, 1981) and *The Postman Always Rings Twice* (Bob Rafelson, 1981, also with Nicholson)) would then be ironically commented upon as 'incestuous' by the cynical Romantic and somewhat detached 'outsider' Polanski – thereby reaffirming his *auteur* status by being both 'inside' the film and commenting on it 'from outside'. In the manner of *auteur* criticism, we would attribute this particular form of self-deprecating reflexivity to him, rather than, say, to Robert Towne, whose screenplay for *Chinatown*, as we saw, has been canonized as 'classical', or to Robert Evans, who (apart from having himself been an actor in the 1950s, when among other roles he played the producer Irving Thalberg in *Man of a Thousand Faces*, 1957) went on to produce at Paramount a vast number of mainstream films of both *auteurs* and commercial directors, including *Marathon Man* (John Schlesinger), *Urban Cowboy* (James Bridges), *The Cotton Club* (Francis Ford Coppola), *Popeye* (Robert Altman), *Sliver* (Philip Noyce), and *Jade* (William Friedkin).

Depending on one's point of view, not least regarding these contests for authorship, *Chinatown* is either a cynical recycling of old movie clichés or a remarkable reinvention of the 'old Hollywood' as the 'New Hollywood', typified for some by giving previously underrated or dismissed B-movie genres or 1950s television series the blockbuster treatment of lush colour, top stars and special effects. The classic detective thriller was in black-and-white; what Polanski's art director Richard Sylbert has done is to use a very restricted palette of yellows to browns (from parched riverbed to dark panelled office). At the same time Polanski inverts (Hitchcock-fashion) the connotations of evil: murder and mayhem can now happen as much in bright daylight as at night-time. By furthermore reviving the charisma of a Hollywood veteran, featuring a female actress (Faye Dunaway) firmly associated with an early version of the empowered female (*Bonnie and Clyde*) and blending her with the eternally passive-aggressive *femme fatale* of the 1940s, while also launching a new male superstar, *Chinatown* bridges the generations in respect of the star system as well. Beginning in the mid-1970s, Hollywood once more came to international prominence and box office success, retooling itself and emerging from a 20-year slump (mid-1950s to mid-1970s) partly caused by television, but also accompanied by a realignment of film culture and film school training. *Chinatown*, while not quite such a self-consciously marketed blockbuster as Steven Spielberg's *Jaws* (1975), can nevertheless be seen as the 'prototype' of the planned remake which was to become so typical of Hollywood in the 1980s.

## 4.6.2. The poetics of (unlimited) semiosis

The second method, as indicated, tries to take literally the *mise-en-scène* critics' focus on marginal details of a film's style and surface signs. By extending their passion for the oblique and the overlooked to its logical conclusion, we are adopting a deconstructive approach to a reading of this film, valorizing aspects that may initially escape the spectator but which will nonetheless appear to follow a certain logic. Both David Rodowick and Tom Conley have developed a deconstructive approach to films, one that does not passively reproduce the dominant values indeterminately perpetuated through films. Rodowick argues for textual criticism that 'must be understood not as repeating what a text means, but as presenting the opportunity to construct positions from which it can always be read and understood in new and unforseen ways' (1991: 135). For Rodowick, then, critical reading becomes an act of creative intervention in which the reading encounters the text in a relation of difference, not identity.

Similarly, Conley develops a deconstructive approach to film by offering readings of the presence of alphabetical writing within narrative films. Following Derrida's critique of the subservience of writing to speech, Conley places the image on the side of spoken language against written language, and in so doing posits an essential difference between writing and filmic image. Conley's main aim is to trace the movement of difference between writing (film titles, shop and road signs, etc.) and the film images they appear in. He notes that these two channels of discourse result in:

> ... an activity – a pleasure – of analysis allowing spectators to rewrite and rework discourses of film into configurations that need not be determined by what is immediately before the eyes. Reworking of this order can lead, it is hoped, to creatively political acts of viewing. In this way, the literal aspect of film writing can engage methods of viewing that need not depend entirely upon narrative analysis.
>
> (1991: xxxi)

Conley wants to articulate and politicize the personal fantasies of each spectator when s/he subconsciously experiences the marginal (non-narrative) details within the filmic image.

Kaja Silverman has also pointed out that during the 1980s film theorists insistently analysed race, class, and gender in Hollywood cinema. The problem Silverman identifies with this approach is that films are reduced to their ideological master-codes, and the analysis is deemed to be complete when the film's class, race, and gender inequalities have been pointed out. While acknowledging the continuing importance of this work, Silverman finds that it ignores the individual's 'perversity and contradictions' (Hüser 1997: 12) and also subordinates the aesthetic to the political: 'We talk obsessively about "representations of women," "representations of blacks," "representations of queers," but we have forgotten that the issue here is precisely *representation*. ... art can help us transcend our ethical limits, limits that inhere precisely in our unconsciousness, and that it is via its aesthetic properties that it can do so' (pp. 7–8).

Perhaps these 'aesthetic properties' do not always broaden the meaning of the plot, or deepen the characters' psychology, but an awareness of the play of surface effects nonetheless amplifies the resonance the scenes have for the viewer: they 'thicken' the film's semantic texture and ignite surprising flashes of meaning that appear on the 'worked-over' (some would say 'overwrought' or 'baroque') body of a 'New Hollywood' studio product such as *Chinatown*. Finally, the tracing of such effects will lead us to consider, albeit briefly and by way of an open-ended conclusion, the vexing question – so often asked by incredulous students – whether meanings thus highlighted (or rather, these signifiers extrapolated by the critic as cues for meaning-making) are intended or merely accidental, fortuitous or fabricated by 'over-interpretation'.

As regards to 'method' or cast of mind, a deconstructive attention to surface both inherits the tools of *mise-en-scène* criticism (see Chapter 3) and is indebted to Roland Barthes, especially his later writings. Without going too deeply into the reasons behind Barthes's dissatisfaction with classical structuralism's binary oppositions and his coinage of the term 'third meaning' in the late 1960s, it is certainly from his influential essay (see Barthes 1977) that one can date the intensified impulse underlying the search for the uncoded or unsystematic elements in a photograph or other visual representations. For Barthes, 'third' or 'obtuse' meanings function outside the standard 'informational' (first, or denotational) and 'symbolic' (second, or connotational) meanings of conventional communication. In the examples from *Chinatown* that follow, the features we shall comment on are not strictly 'obtuse' in Barthes's sense, for they are almost all chosen in view either of their repetition or of the fact that they seem to be aligned in series and therefore form patterns of their own. They even contribute to the 'themes' and thus could be said to further instantiate, for instance, the commentative heuristics of *mise-en-scène* criticism. What we shall emphasize, however, are not merely the moments where the texture becomes 'thick', but also where referentiality somehow seems to be suspended, where the 'bottom drops out' of the film's phenomenal realism and perceptual verisimilitude, leaving the slippery surface and the sliding signifiers of potentially unlimited semiosis. This type of investigative detective story has also been called 'paranoia thriller'. As we shall see, *Chinatown* does exemplify several other characteristics of this sub-genre, and the film's narrative proceeds by revealing more and more layers of falsehood, deception and unreliable or duplicitous information. *Chinatown* shows its hero to be at once over-confident in his inferences and reckless in his repartees, but deplorably incapable of reading 'correctly' the clues he is given (see also Cawelti 1979: 566).

Many – though not all – of the sliding signifiers are verbal *and* visual. For instance, there is the semantic cluster around 'nose'. For much of the film, Jack Nicholson has to wear a bandage on his nose, as the result of a bloody encounter with the flick-knife of one of the villain's henchmen, who did not like him 'nosing around' and wanted to teach him a lesson. Apart from the rough poetic justice this punishment represents for a 'snooper' who professionally 'sticks his nose' into other people's business, made explicit in pointedly sexual jokes cracked by his colleagues at Jake's expense, the scene is memorable because the sadistic thug slitting the hero's nose is played by the director himself. A Hitchcockian auteurist touch, one might think, except that Hitchcock's personal appearances were never that interventionist in the narrative and at most metaphorically motivated (see Bellour 2000: 217–37). In *Chinatown*, however, Polanski's on-screen performance joins all the other filmic and extra-filmic contenders for (literal, narrative, diegetic) authority. Using his slight stature to advantage, he turns the brief cameo into a terrifying – and yet self-ironizing – portrait of a pocket-sized but potentially lethal psychopath. He also inverts a similar cameo, that of Jean-Luc Godard in his film *Le Mépris*, where Godard plays the 'assistant' to the (diegetic) director Fritz Lang, playing himself.

Another punning reference – this time visual – is built around 'glass'. It occurs in the sequence where Gittes follows Hollis Mulwray to the dam, where the sweet water is dumped into the sea. Tired of watching and waiting, Gittes lets a watch do the waiting, slipping one under the tyre of Mulwray's parked car, on the assumption that the watch glass will break when the car moves off, giving Gittes the length of time Mulwray spent at the water outlet. This information turns out to be a false trail, but the broken glass anticipates the broken eye-glasses that later in the film play an important part in leading Gittes to suspecting Noah Cross to have been actively involved in the murder of Mulwray, as it turns out a mistaken clue, but for the correct inference. The use of the watch as a prop is thus not only syntactically meaningful, in that it furthers the plot; it is also semantically relevant: the stopped watch figuratively predicts the stopping of Mulwray's life (the cultural associations of watch/heart; the etymological link glass/glasses). The scene illustrates well (typically highlighted by *mise-en-scène* criticism) how memorably, as well as insistently, narrative information or thematic knowledge is foreshadowed in classical cinema, as it circulates between the characters and objects on screen and the audience.

A more purely verbal slippage is associated with Noah Cross: he consistently mispronounces Jake Gittes' name, indicative of the low opinion he has of the detective, insultingly calling him 'Gits', which makes even 'Jake (fake) Gittes (git)' seem a derogatory parody of the virile names of other famous hard-boiled detectives: Sam Spade, Philip Marlowe, Lew Archer (Cawelti 1979: 565). On the more Freudian register of the (female) hysterical symptom, Evelyn Mulwray develops a stutter when she has to say a word beginning with 'f-', most notably when she mentions her 'father'. Her speech impediment is in turn echoed by a cultural speech impediment (the clichéd notion that the Chinese have difficulties pronouncing the 'r' sound) which functions like a Freudian slip when, as we shall see, the speaker, the Chinese gardener, gives away more than he knows or intends. Much of the film's referential material, such as settings, incidents, character and place names are in this fashion exploited for their 'semiotic' potential. They are treated as if they were literalized metaphors, to be punned on, or to engender double-speak and acoustic echo effects, all of which helps to weave the audiovisual surface into a network of enigmatic relationships, either contagiously spreading like a virus or tightly organized around the evil force at the centre. For the most potent sliding signifier focuses on 'the name of the father': Noah Cross.

While 'Noah' alludes to water via the biblical deluge, and to the Los Angeles' tycoon's ambiguous role in controlling its scarcity and abundance, the name 'Cross' reverberates through the film in a particularly insistent way, both literally and metaphorically. The 'Noah' cluster of associations holds the film together at a symbolic level around the water imagery and its connotations: salt water vs fresh water; the tide pool and the 'beginnings of life' (Hollis Mulwray) which Noah Cross has turned into a moral swamp, as opposed to tending it as an ornamental pond at the Mulwray residence. Water is a life-giving substance, but here it has been perverted and made paradoxical: not only is Mulwray's dead body found to have 'salt water in the lungs', as the pathologist dryly comments: 'in the middle of a drought, the water commissioner drowns – only in LA.' Earlier on, one of Gittes' associates can be heard off-screen saying that Mulwray 'must have water on his brain' while Gittes is fishing photographs out of a developing bath. He is then called to spy on Mulwray with his 'girlfriend', who are on a boat ride in Echo Park: 'more water,' as Gittes sarcastically (and superfluously) remarks. On a lighter note, the reference to moisture in the lungs becomes a running joke when applied to others: both police officer Lou Escobar and the pathologist at the city mortuary are suffering from coughs and colds they cannot shake.

It is the name 'Cross', however, that leads to the 'crucial' semantic knot: Noah Cross double-crosses his partner and son-in-law Hollis Mulwray, and then crosses him out, by having him killed when Mulwray begins to suspect foul play. If the cinephile might detect here a reference to the theme of crosses in Howard Hawks's gangster film *Scarface* from 1931, the contemporary viewer could associate the uncrossed gender lineage of Noah's inbreeding with the cross of the female chromosome, an idea prompted also by Noah Cross's genealogical references in his monologue to 'Mr Gits' about the tide-pools of primitive life and his desire to 'own the future'. Gittes himself introduces the verbal cue when, to a policeman taunting him, 'What happened to your nose? Somebody slam the bedroom window on it?' he aggressively replies: 'No, your wife got excited and crossed her legs a little too quick.'

In fact, Gittes might be said to borrow even more heavily from Noah Cross's arsenal of chiasmic gestures, when in the (San Fernando) Valley hall of records he asks the librarian for a ruler to 'read across', but in actual fact uses it vertically, to rip out the page, as if the ruler were the pair of scissors metaphorically alluded to in the 'crossed legs'. Soon thereafter, he cross-checks the names on the torn-out page of the land register with the obituaries in the newspaper, realizing that like the clues in a crossword puzzle, the names when brought together spell the massive fraud Noah Cross is perpetrating on the farmers. Scissors feature prominently on the sound-track. They can be heard snipping when Gittes is in the barber shop, where he has a violent disagreement with the mortgage broker; and the sound of garden shears form the background to Gittes' first visit to the Mulwray residence. As we shall see below, this by no means exhausts the semantics of the 'cross' in Noah Cross and *Chinatown*, but the examples give some idea of how a word or 'seme' can both focus and disperse themes across the body of a film.

## 4.6.3. Three exemplary scenes of the sliding signifier in *Chinatown*

We shall now examine three scenes in more detail. Two revolve around instances of purely verbal double entendres and puns, and the third is a combination of verbal punning and a sight-gag, rendered sombre by a more mythological reverberation, itself redolent with psychoanalytic symbolism.

The first scene concerns the segment where Gittes drives up to the Mulwray mansion for the first time. Altogether three times Gittes tries to enter a space associated with Mulwray's life, and three times he is both barred from entry and finds a way of circumventing the obstacle. Each time he obtains vital information that launches him on the next phase of his investigation, but he also gives his opponents an important advantage. The first obstacle is the secretary at the Department of Water and Power, the second is Khan, the Mulwray's Chinese butler, and in the third scene it is Lou Escobar at the dam who stops him with the revelation that Mulwray has drowned. Each location will be visited again by Gittes, with both an amplification and a reversal of the initial visit's results. In the scene under discussion, Gittes (as well as the spectator) is distracted from surveying the lush green lawn by a squelching sound off-screen that is finally revealed not to be off-screen at all, because its source is a Chinese chauffeur with a chamois leather washing Mrs Mulwray's maroon Packard. It gives us not only the graphic-acoustic presence of a surface – the glass pane of the car's rear window – but it also draws attention to the 'layeredness' of a representation: what is perceived as 'sideways' out of sight may also be 'behind' and out of sight. After finally being let in by the butler, Gittes finds himself on the lawn behind the residence, idly watching a Chinese gardener clearing what seem like weeds from an ornamental pond. In order to make conversation, the gardener is heard saying 'bad for the glass' while pointing at a withered patch of grass. Gittes, at first amused at the malapropism, steps closer to the pond, when his attention is caught by something gleaming just beneath the water's surface – a pair of glasses, as it turns out later. Before he has time to retrieve the object, he is interrupted by the arrival of Mrs Mulwray, who ushers him to one of the garden chairs and orders an iced tea for him and herself. Here the slippage grass/glass, inverting the earlier move from glass to grass, also shifts perception from the verbal to the visual, as the earlier had done from the visual to the aural. In each case, that which is displaced remains present and significant, even as it helps to distract and refocus Gittes' attention. This principle can usefully compared to what Jacques Derrida has termed 'under erasure', drawing attention to all those instances where terms or statements that are inverted, negated, or otherwise cancelled remain nonetheless present and active, indeed intensify their semiotic energy. In the case of 'bad for the glass', it is Gittes who has to repeat the phrase the next time he encounters the gardener, before the vital information is released, namely what it is that is bad for the grass (the fact that the ornamental pond contains salt water), and Gittes can finally come into possession of the 'glass' – when the gardener retrieves what Gittes assumes are Hollis Mulwray's glasses.

Once one's attention has been drawn to the principle of 'under erasure', its particular effects can be seen to inform much of the rest of the sequence – the discussion between Evelyn Mulwray and Gittes – as well as the peculiar logic of the plot, where the characters so often resort to 'covering up' in the form of doubling up. When Mrs Mulwray suddenly tells Gittes that she is prepared to drop the lawsuit for libel, she justifies it by saying: 'My husband seems to think you're an innocent man', to which Gittes replies: 'I've been accused of many things, but never of being innocent!' His cocky rejoinder puts under erasure the word 'innocent' in the sense of 'unaware', the more forcefully to draw attention to his present state of ignorance and future state of guilt. On another level, Evelyn Mulwray's gesture of 'dropping the lawsuit', then perjuring herself at the autopsy and subsequently paying him, in order to make her husband's surveillance seem her idea, and finally hiring him to find out who killed him, also conform to the peculiar logic of 'under erasure'. Each move is an act of cancellation and self-contradiction that merely aggravates the suspicion of her being implicated, accumulating the evidence Gittes thinks he has against her and preventing him from being of help. *Chinatown* literally features a scene of erasure, when Gittes – once more distracted by a sound – opens a door and sees two workmen scratching out Mulwray's name from his office at the Department of Water and Power, replacing it with that of his (corrupt) successor. But Derrida's notion of 'under erasure', apart from referring to a crossing out, where what is cancelled still remains visible, can also name a temporal doubling up. This, Derrida calls deferral: a delay and a difference, a notion which expands on Saussure's idea of difference, doubled in Derrida by repetition and temporal return. The principle is illustrated in another feature of the plot – we might call it the 'what goes around comes around' theme – which is the anxiety of several characters, and first expressed by Hollis Mulwray at the city council hearing, that they might be 'making the same mistake twice'. If 'under erasure' is implicit in Gittes' remark about his past in Chinatown, where he tried to protect someone from getting hurt and thereby made sure she got hurt, then his bungled action to protect Evelyn Mulrway results not only in getting her 'hurt', but in his truly 'making the same mistake twice'.

'Bad for the glass' revolves around a pair of glasses: not Hollis's pair, but those of Noah Cross – a man who wears bifocals. It is as if the film enjoins upon us a bifocal perspective, for if we want to understand what is going on, the sooner we learn to see through Noah Cross's eyes, the earlier we shall perceive the logic of the plot and focus on the salient features. In this respect, the scene seems to say, *Chinatown* as a whole is a 'grass'-film, as opposed to a 'glass'-film. It does not play on the classic articulation of the cinematic apparatus (with its emphasis on specular seduction) but on the rhizomatic, grass-like structure of endlessly proliferating shallow roots and surface branches.

The second scene is grouped around 'apple-core', as it first emerges when Gittes pursues Hollis Mulwray, and foreshadows the scene just prior to Gittes and Mrs Mulwray visiting the old people's home. As one of the many malapropisms, mispronunciations, and other verbal slips (such as the sign misspelt NO TREPASSING that opens the segment of Gittes' drive into the valley) that dot the film, it forms part of a pattern: 'apple-core' is the garbled sound Gittes' associate picks out from the violent conversation Noah Cross has with Hollis Mulwray prior to the latter's death. Only later do we learn that it refers to the Club/Ranch that serves Noah Cross as his operational base, the Albacore, the name of a type of tuna fish. But it is the (mistaken) association of 'apples' (in a scene that prominently features orange-groves: 'apples and oranges') which opens the semantically rich seam of associations.

It could be seen to draw attention to Mrs Mulwray's first name, Eve(lyn) who in a sense is 'tempting' an innocent Adam, as she enmeshes Gittes in events that lead him to eat from the tree of knowledge. But a more cross-hatched set of associations opens up when we note that one of the recently deceased in whose name the land is being bought is called 'Crabb', which is also the name of a type of apple (crab apples). And just in case we miss the reference, Gittes says – after perusing the list, and stopping at 'Crabb': 'how do you like them apples!' But 'crab' is, of course, also the name of a mollusc, and thus associated with sea and fish, which leads us to the literal meaning, the pennant in the flag, and the patchwork quilt the old ladies at the 'rest home' are making of 'Albacore'. Two distinct lines of associations therefore 'cross' and intersect around the proper name 'Crabb', in a film in which almost all proper names seem to have an additional layer of meaning.

The third scene concerns the furtive and hasty departure of Evelyn Mulwray after their brief lovemaking, interrupted by a telephone call. This Gittes has anticipated, and he slips out of the house while she dresses, in order to follow her. When Evelyn tends his nose-wound in the bathroom, Gittes notices a black speck in the green iris in one of Evelyn's eyes. She acknowledges it by calling it 'a slight flaw – a sort of birthmark'. In order to follow Evelyn, Gittes decides to kick in the red cover of one of her car's tail lights, so that it functions as the 'flaw' (not black this time, but white) that allows him to track her car in the dark, hoping to get to the heart of that other (tragic) 'flaw'. The chain of signifiers from flaw in the iris of her eye to the white tail light on the car also picks up the crushed watch-glass earlier on, which would now seem to anticipate not only the death of Mulwray but also the terrible gouging of Evelyn's eyes as the fatal bullet causes her to be impaled on the horn in the centre of her car's steering wheel.

This ending is already prepared for, in a minor register, by the 'black' (but actually red-blue) eye of Curly's wife, as punishment for her sexual transgression, whose pictures we see in the very opening of the film. In both cases, injury to the eye happens to a woman, when it should be the Oedipal male that is 'blinded', since it is the gouging of the eyes that he inflicts upon himself as punishment when he realizes that he has killed his father and slept with his mother. (For Oedipus themes, see Chapter 8.) As the bodily mark of incestuous guilt, it is visited in *Chinatown* on the daughter who is sacrificed to the patriarchal sexual transgression that goes unavenged, and in a very real sense is crossed out with Hollis's and Evelyn's deaths. The 'eye' of Sophoclean tragedy (Evelyn Mulwray) is in stark contrast to the 'nose' of Aristophanean comedy (Jake Gittes). While both are culturally conventional signs standing for sexual organs and whose damage symbolizes the threat of castration, their implications are typically asymmetrical. What begins as 'his' comic punishment ends in 'her' tragic death, while the obscene phallic power of the father is reinstated.

In selecting the three scenes above, we have deliberately not chosen the crucial and climactic one, which condenses the semiotic slippage with the genealogical-patriarchal slippage – that of the interrogation/slapping of Evelyn Mulwray by Jake at the denouement of the film. Note that Jake in his stupefied anger slaps Evelyn cross-wise, as if to mark her face with the 'Cross' of her maiden name, or to cross out the truth she is trying to tell him: 'She is my sister *and* my daughter' (while Gittes is still assuming that Catherine was Hollis Mulwray's mistress, and that it was Evelyn who was accessory to his death). He slaps Evelyn when she speaks the truth, possibly because, as she says, 'the truth is too tough for [him]'. She, on the other hand, is split between her fear of her father and her desire to protect her daughter. But she is also 'in denial' regarding the question whether her father 'raped' her, showing the full ambiguity of a daughter's position within the Oedipal/patriarchal law. Here *Chinatown* deepens the traditional thriller motif, according to which the *femme fatale* combines and condenses the duality of woman in the Hollywood film. As 'virgin' and 'whore', she is in both fantasmatic roles the projection of the younger male and thus the emblem – especially for the *film noir* hero – of the patriarch's obscene *jouissance*, in that he 'possesses' the woman in ways the hero never will.

The slippage of signifiers that the film practises so obsessively seems to have its roots, one could argue, in the traumatic slippage that lies at the heart of *Chinatown*. The signifiers daughter/sister are usually considered to be mutually exclusive when prefaced by the personal pronoun and naming the same person, yet here they have a single referent, 'Catherine'. It is as if the father–daughter incest was so 'unnatural' as to threaten even the order of language. The relation of sign to referent breaks down, 'causing' this deluge of duplicitous signs: yet another aspect of the general corruption, the political and climatic drought, that the perverse power of Noah Cross inflicts on the land.

## Conclusion

Yet even such a pursuit of the many rhizomatic networks and punning cross-references does not give one the feeling of 'catching' this slippery film. Nor is it easy to pin down its generic identity and temporal register. *Chinatown* performs the generic and symbolic codes of *film noir*, while also 'exposing' them: over-explicit, they return in a pastiche of the classical Oedipal narrative. The usually hidden incest motif is spelled out, inverted and displaced from son to father, and from mother to daughter. Similarly, the 'orientalist' themes or exotic motifs of a classic *film noir* like Orson Welles's *Lady from Shanghai* are here worked over as a 'multicultural' space, in the many enigmatic references to the chronotope 'Chinatown' (figured as a space and a place, as a time now and a time then). Race and gender (and, to a lesser extent, class) have surfaced from classical Hollywood's implicit or symptomatic meanings to become part of the film's explicit repertoire of thematizations. But 'Chinatown' is also the signifier for that more general crisis of referentiality –

the *mise-en-abîme* of levels of reality, and the turning inside out of what one assumed to be the case, a phenomenon, appropriately known in this case as 'Chinese boxes'.

A similar inversion and reversibility applies to the temporal register of 'now: then'. The period setting of the 1930s and the making of the film in the 1970s produces a 'nostalgia for the present' in Fredric Jameson's phrase (1992), suggesting that, as viewers, we are in time and out of it, incapable of making emotional sense of the present other than by framing it as a version of the past. But one can probably be more specific. *Chinatown* is a post-Watergate film, even though it is set in the 1930s. It re-imports the interpretations of *film noir* as they were formulated by French critics in the 1950s, and applies it to the 1974 topicality of Watergate (1973–74) – a traumatic story of ever-deepening circles of corruption – only to transpose a post-Watergate cynicism and political apathy back into the period where hard-boiled *film noir* world-weariness is supposed to have begun. The film (and its spectator) is thus split between two temporalities: the 'now' of the fiction, Los Angeles 1930s, and the 'now' of the film's making, Los Angeles 1974. We watch the socio-political events unfold with hindsight and the temporal irony this implies, but across the knowledge that the highest officials in the land are indeed capable of organizing vast conspiracies and masterminding elaborate cover-ups, while flouting the law and permitting blatant perversions of justice. From that knowledge the film derives its emotional verisimilitude, but to the time-shifting of genre and reference it also owes its effects of uncanny recognition. Insofar as the present is projected back into the period past, and the past is interpreted through the emotions and sensibility of the present, each fiction confirms the other, mutually sustaining a 'true (historical) lie'.

The paranoia genre of the early 1970s (*The Parallax View, Three Days of the Condor, All the President's Men*) is here used to put the detective on the trail of a plausible, i.e. an uncorroborated but historically not impossible conspiracy, which in turn motivates the elaborate play on 'cross' (anger and wrath) and double-cross (deception and cover-up). But 'cross' also because the structure of *Chinatown* is both linear (the unravelling of a mystery) and doubling up upon itself, because at the end Jake Gittes is not much wiser than he was at the beginning, and a good deal more vulnerable and exposed professionally: for him, Chinatown lies at the crossroads of his own murky career, to which he might be condemned to return, if his licence is indeed revoked, as Lou Escobar threatens, or if the undefeated Noah Cross takes revenge. At another level, as we saw, the film's themes (discussed in the first half of this chapter) have come to the post-classical surface texture of 'knowingness' (Robert Ray), 'allusionism' (Noël Carroll), and self-reference, making the very generic codes of the classical mode available for textual play. *Chinatown* 'knows' it is a *film noir* in the way no *film noir* of the 1940s and early 1950s could have known itself. Furthermore, it is a 'left-liberal' film in its emphasis on the Roosevelt portrait, undermined by the greed and self-interest of big business ('water and power'). With its fascination in the machinations of local politicians, and ecological issues, such as the water supply of a city like Los Angeles, it might also strike one as particularly 'European'.

In conclusion, the thematic readings with which we began and the deconstructive ones are not, strictly speaking, mutually exclusive. In one sense they complement each other, rather in the way that, in our chapter on the distinction between classical/post-classical Hollywood, *Die Hard* seemed to lend itself to an Aristotelian, Proppian, and Lévi-Straussian reading, while also 'responding' to a closer look at the surface elements and effects of its *mise en scène* of objects, its semantic texture and symbolic figurations. More generally, 'deconstructive' readings such as we have demonstrated them here may help us clarify why we feel we need to apply to contemporary Hollywood films such terms as 'postmodernity', 'intertextuality', 'intermediality', the 'uncanny', or '*mise en abîme*'. They do not, however, resolve which of these terms responds most pertinently to the 'symptoms' or features thus highlighted in the text, or indeed which features are symptoms and which are causes.

Our reading nonetheless makes a strong claim for textual analysis and close reading: if you like, for interpretation and against theory, for the specific case against generalization. We have not hesitated to impose a 'limit' on the unlimited semiosis: we have selected strands of the verbal–visual–aural fabric that had echoes in the explicit thematics, and have closed off further avenues when they did not seem (to us) to establish significant patterns. No doubt other interpretations are able (and indeed, judging by the proliferating literature on *Chinatown*, have already managed) to come up with other readings, either supplementing or maybe even contradicting those offered here. In this more general sense, deconstructive readings do undo thematic readings, in that the interpretive momentum is directed outwards, away from the single centre that Culler mentions, towards bifocal or multifocal perspectives. Deconstructive readings are centrifugal, in contrast to the centripetal energies mobilized in a thematic hermeneutic, aimed at establishing coherence *and* closure, coherence *as* closure. Does this answer the question whether we are 'over-interpreting'? Yes and no: yes, because the dispersal, the scattering, the chain reaction, and the contamination set up with the 'sliding signifiers' do not come to an end. With this, we also mean to signal that they exceed the control of any single individual, be s/he an actual person or a critical construct. The deconstruction of the *auteur* and the sliding signifiers are thus the recto and the verso of the same thing, in that both challenge an order not of fact, but of 'belief' – that in the *auteur* and the single source of meaning. No, it does not answer the question of 'over-interpretation' because it will remain a matter of temperament whether our procedure is perceived as arbitrary and perverse or as a token of the love of the text and of texture.

# 5 S/Z, the 'readerly' film, and video game logic (*The Fifth Element*)

## Introduction

During the 1960s in the humanities departments of many European (and later North American) universities, structuralism and semiotics offered a rich and innovative theoretical perspective on contemporary culture. During this time of ferment, however, structuralism and semiotics were also going through a transformation, which has usually been labelled a move towards *post-structuralism*. This shift can be traced by tracking the formulation and movement of ideas and concepts in the work of Roland Barthes. By the mid-1960s his structural and semiotic analysis of cultural media was at its peak. But during the next four years he began to challenge (under the influence of Jacques Derrida and Julia Kristeva) the rigid, scientific assumptions of structuralism and semiotics. In his 1970 book *S/Z* (translated into English in 1974: Barthes 1974) the results of the post-structural revolution can be clearly discerned. Barthes takes a short story by Balzac, 'Sarrasine', and breaks it up into 561 fragments in order to discern the way five types of code are 'braided' together in this story to create what Barthes calls a 'readerly' text (basically a text that positions the reader as the passive consumer of a pre-existing meaning). In the first half of this chapter we shall outline these five codes (the proairetic, the hermeneutic, the semic, the symbolic, and the referential) and identify them at work in the opening scene of Luc Besson's film *The Fifth Element* (1997), a European-financed blockbuster that attempts to imitate the Hollywood blockbuster formula.

In the second half of the chapter we shall place the film within a different context. The first half of this chapter looks backwards and places *The Fifth Element* within the context of the readerly text, as exemplified in nineteenth-century literature. Although *The Fifth Element* is a readerly text, as opposed to a 'writerly' text (basically a text in which the reader produces meanings), it contains more than simply the codes of the readerly text. The primary argument of the second half of this chapter is that the sequence of actions in the film (the proairetic code, in Barthes's terms) is not simply constructed in terms of an Aristotelian logic of linear causality, for at certain moments it switches to a 'digital narrative', as found in video games (and other electronic texts, and digital media in general). In the second half of this chapter we shall analyse the emergence of digital narrative in contemporary society, outline some of its main characteristics, and then analyse moments in *The Fifth Element* where the digital narrative structures the film's actions. We end by considering one of the problems with discussing a film's narrative as digital, a problem that revolves around the concept of 'interactivity'.

## 5.1. Theory: the five codes of S/Z

Roland Barthes opens *S/Z* by distinguishing structural analysis from textual analysis. 'Structural analysis' refers to an activity that equalizes all texts by reducing them to the same underlying universal system. This is the type of activity Barthes practised in the 1960s, culminating in his famous essay 'Introduction to the Structural Analysis of Narratives' (Barthes 1994: 95–135). The primary aim of structural analysis – practised not only by Barthes but also by other formalists and structuralists such as Vladimir Propp, Claude Lévi-Strauss, and A.J. Greimas – was to seek a universal narrative grammar. (Structural analysis is outlined in Chapter 2 above.) In the context of *S/Z*, 'textual analysis' refers to the *post*-structural activity that conceives the 'text' as a term that names a process or activity, rather than an object. From the perspective of post-structural theory, 'text' is no longer understood as a finished, inert object to be examined and dissected by the analyst (the structuralist conception of the text). Instead, the text is seen to be produced in the activity of reading. Moreover, the text's meaning is not produced in a uniform way (by tracing it back to the same underlying universal system, as the structuralists did). Instead, it is produced from the specific interaction of the text's multiple signifiers. A text's meaning is then produced by the multiple relations the text's signifiers enter into on the surface. However, the structuralists and post-structuralists also have a different conception of the term 'meaning': for the structuralists, meaning can be fixed, and is stable, for it can be anchored in the underlying universal system; for the post-structuralists, meaning is plural and transitory, for the text is a space where multiple and contradictory codes intersect and overlap at the same time. The post-structuralists also changed the meaning of the term 'interpretation', as Barthes explains:

> To interpret a text is not to give it a (more or less justified, more or less free) meaning, but on the contrary to appreciate what plural constitutes it. Let us first posit the image of a triumphant plural, unimpoverished by any constraint of representation (of imitation). In this ideal text, the networks are many and interact, without any one of them being able to surpass the rest; this text is a galaxy of signifiers, not a structure of signifieds; it has no beginning; it is reversible; we gain access to it by several entrances, none of which can be authoritatively declared to be the main one; the codes it mobilizes extend as far as the eye can reach, they are indeterminable (meaning here is never subject to a principle of determination, unless by throwing dice); the systems of meaning can take over this absolutely plural text, but their number is never closed, based as it is on the infinity of language.
>
> (Barthes 1974: 5–6)

Post-structuralists privilege modernist writers such as James Joyce and Lautréamont because they do not suppress the textual nature of the text, but foreground it (perhaps epitomized in Joyce's *Finnegans Wake*). Barthes calls these modernist texts 'writerly', and opposes them to classical 'readerly' texts. The defining characteristic of the writerly text for Barthes is that it makes the reader an active contributor to the text's meaning, rather than a mere consumer of a pre-existent meaning. The readerly text 'plunges the reader into idleness, whose only "work" is to accept or reject the text (reading becomes a referendum)' (Barthes 1974: 4). This is because a single meaning is privileged and overdetermined, offering little leeway for multiple meanings. The writerly text, by contrast, has plural meanings, and '[t]he more plural the text, the less it is written before I read it' (Barthes 1974: 10). However, Barthes also emphasizes that the distinction between readerly and writerly texts is not absolute. A readerly text also displays a limited amount of play – of ambiguity and connotation. A readerly text becomes (moderately) writerly through analysis, not only through reading, as is the case with the writerly text. To read *Finnegans Wake* is to experience the polysemic nature of the writerly text. But the writerly nature of Balzac's classically written (hence readerly) story 'Sarrasine' becomes evident by fragmenting the text, interrupting its flow by naming the codes at work in the resulting fragments.

However, Barthes only employs the distinction between readerly and writerly to print media – specifically, in terms of the distinction between classic realist texts (the readerly) and modernist reflexive texts (the writerly). From the context of electronic media such as hypertext, it is now possible to argue that Barthes uses the term 'writerly' in a metaphorical sense. When applied to hypertexts, the modernist label becomes irrelevant, although the reader as producer becomes a reality rather than a mere metaphor. (We shall explore this rereading of *S/Z* in section 5.4.)

The most notable – and notorious – aspect of *S/Z* is the five codes that Barthes identifies as he analyses the whole of Balzac's story 'Sarrasine'. These codes are: the proairetic, the hermeneutic, the semic, the symbolic, and the cultural/referential. We shall discuss each in turn.

The proairetic code, which refers to the sequence of actions in a narrative, is already developed (but simply called the 'level of actions') in Barthes's structural analysis. Structural analysis (beginning with Propp) produced an underlying grammar of narrative, the fundamental roles that characters play and the actions they perform. In his essay 'The Sequence of Actions' Barthes notes that this sequence of actions performed by characters creates the readability of a text, a coherent logic that creates the appearance of narrative rationality ('The Sequence of Actions', in Barthes 1994: 138). Barthes calls this the 'proairetic code' because proairesis is the Greek term used by Aristotle to name the planning of a course of action: '[proairesis names] the human faculty of deliberating in advance the result of an action, of *choosing* (this is its etymological meaning) between the two terms of an alternative the one which will be realized' (p. 139). The opening phrase of 'Sarrasine' – 'I was deep in one of those daydreams' – employs the proairetic code, namely, the narrator's action of daydreaming. In the rhetorical terms used in Chapter 1 above, the proairetic code structures the *dispositio*, or composition, of the narrative – its linear, temporal and irreversible order.

The hermeneutic code, like the proairetic code, also structures a text's linear, temporal, and irreversible order. It names 'all the units [in a text] whose function it is to articulate in various ways a question, its response, and the variety of chance events which can either formulate the question or delay its answer; or even, constitute an enigma and lead to its solution' (Barthes 1974: 17). More specifically, the hermeneutic code consists of several stages:

- a theme
- a formulation of the enigma
- a proposal
- several types of delay
- disclosure

The 'theme' names the subject or object of the hermeneutic code. The 'formulation' and 'proposal' work together to construct an enigma around the theme. The answer to these enigmas is inevitably delayed in order to maintain the reader's interest in the story by creating suspense and expectations. Barthes lists specific strategies of delay:

> ... the *snare* (a kind of deliberate evasion of the truth), the *equivocation* (a mixture of truth and snare which frequently, while focusing on the enigma, helps to thicken it), the *partial answer* (which only exacerbates the

expectation of the truth), the *suspended answer* (an aphasic stoppage of the discourse), and *jamming* (acknowledgment of insolubility).

(Barthes 1974: 75–6)

Finally, the formulated and proposed enigmas are disclosed, and others are established or, if there are no more enigmas to be resolved, then the story ends.

One of the primary enigmas in 'Sarrasine' is the identity of the old man seen at a party held by the Lanty family. The old man is therefore the 'theme' of the enigma. This enigma is formulated and proposed in the form of the question: Who is the old man? The Marquise de Rochefide, who is at the party, poses this enigma to the anonymous narrator, who knows the old man's identity and agrees to tell her. But, of course, he does not reveal the identity of the old man straightaway; he establishes a setting and narrates to the Marquise the story of the sculptor Sarrasine, particularly his sheltered upbringing, his education, and his visit to Italy, where he dramatically and fatefully falls in love with the beautiful Italian singer La Zambinella. Only towards the end of the story does the narrator divulge that La Zambinella is not a woman but a castrato, and that Sarrasine did not realize this either, which eventually leads to the latter's death. The narrator then reveals to the Marquise that the old 'man' is La Zambinella. The narrator's telling of the story is littered with delays, particularly equivocation (for much of the story the reader is under the impression that the old man may be the sculptor Sarrasine), while, within the story told, Sarrasine deliberately ignores hints and suggestions that La Zambinella may be a castrato (Barthes argues that Sarrasine continually snares himself).

The final three codes do not function to structure the text in the same way as the first two. Whereas the proairetic and hermeneutic codes structure the text into a broad linear flow (complete with delays and interruptions), the other codes constitute the details of the text – the objects, settings, character traits, common opinions, received ideas, special knowledge, and so on.

The seme is the code of connotation that confers upon the persons, places, and objects of a story an attribute, or associated meaning, which can be named in one word. In his analysis of 'Sarrasine' Barthes focuses on the semes that create character traits: 'If we set aside the semes of objects or atmospheres, actually rather rare (here [in 'Sarrasine'], at least), what is constant is that the seme is linked to an ideology of the person . . .: the person is no more than a collection of semes. Thus . . . [the character] Sarrasine is the sum, the point of convergence, of: *turbulence, artistic gift, independence, excess, femininity, ugliness, composite nature, impiety, love of whittling, will*, etc.)' (Barthes 1974: 191). Similarly, La Zambinella is described by means of the stereotypical semes of femininity (slender, delicate, beautiful); but, of course, the castrato is manipulating these semes to create the illusion of femininity. Within readerly texts, therefore, semes cluster around and attach themselves to characters, conferring upon them the illusion of a three-dimensional, well-rounded existence. That is, the readerly text creates the illusion that it is merely reproducing a pre-existing reality, whereas in fact it is constructing a fictional reality.

The symbolic code refers to the basic, general, abstract categories in which a culture or civilization organizes experience. A text can be read as a particular manifestation of these basic codes. The opening of 'Sarrasine' manifests several types of symbolic code, from the straightforward opposition between inside and outside (the narrator is seated in a window recess, and contrasts the cold night outside the window with the party taking place inside the Lanty mansion) to the more fundamental and general opposition between life and death (the old man symbolizes death, while the Marquise symbolizes life, especially when they are standing together at the party). Moreover, the enigma of the story 'Sarrasine' is based around the fundamental opposition between male and female, and the place of La Zambinella in that opposition. The symbolic code therefore operates at several levels of generality.

Finally, the cultural (or referential) code names the text's reference to common opinions, received ideas, and special knowledge: 'the numerous codes of knowledge or wisdom to which the text continually refers ... we shall call ... in a very general way cultural codes (even though, of course, all codes are cultural), or rather, since they afford the discourse a basis in scientific or moral authority, we shall call them reference codes' (Barthes 1974: 18). As a 'realist' readerly text, 'Sarrasine' makes numerous references to Parisian and Italian culture, art, social behaviour, and so on.

For Barthes, the whole of Balzac's story has been 'braided' together using these five codes. In untangling these codes, Barthes aims not to reconstitute them as a system, but simply to leave them unwound from one another: 'if we make no effort to structure each code, or the five codes among themselves, we do so deliberately, in order to assume the multivalence of the text, its partial reversibility. We are, in fact, concerned not to manifest a structure but to produce a structuration' (p. 20). However, it is common to group the codes (as we have already done) into those that construct (and are therefore tied to) the text's linear, temporal progression (the hermeneutic and the proairetic) and those that construct the thematic and referential details of the text (the semic, the cultural, and the symbolic). Furthermore, the proairetic and the hermeneutic are necessarily linked, in that the first structures the sequence of actions and the second creates enigmas and discloses information about those actions, and the characters that perform them.

## 5.2. Method: *S/Z* and film analysis

The first step in Barthes's post-structural analysis of the readerly text involves 'separating, in the manner of a minor earthquake, the blocks of signification of which reading grasps only the smooth surface, imperceptibly soldered by the movement of sentences, the flowing discourse of narration, the "naturalness" of ordinary language' (p. 13). Barthes goes on to call these blocks of signification 'lexias' and admits that 'this cutting up ... will be arbitrary in the extreme; it will imply no methodological responsibility' (Barthes 1974: 13). That is, Barthes does not limit his analysis by adhering to pre-existing units of language or meaning with which to divide the text. On many occasions in his analysis of 'Sarrasine', each lexia ends in the middle of a sentence. Nonetheless, the process of cutting up the text is governed by the need to observe the play of meaning on the text's surface: 'it will suffice that the lexia be the best possible space in which we can observe meanings ... all we require is that each lexia should have at most three or four meanings to be enumerated' (pp. 13–14). These meanings are of course the five codes. The second step in Barthes' post-structural analysis of the readerly text is therefore to identify and enumerate the codes at work in each lexia.

These two steps can apply to any text, not just written texts. As with readerly literature, the readerly film has a smooth surface which has been soldered together using the techniques of continuity editing, narration, and narrative structure. In cutting the film into fragments (we shall retain Barthes's term 'lexia' for convenience, since the invention of a new term for film is unnecessary and undesirable), we should not limit ourselves by only adhering to pre-existing units of film, such as the shot or the scene. The aim of such an analysis is not to reduce the film to an underlying system, but to 'interpret' it in Barthes's sense of the term: to remain on the film's surface and to unwind its network of braided codes.

For convenience, we shall indicate exactly how to identify the codes at work in a readerly film, and how to write up the analysis:

● The proairetic code simply designates actions, which Barthes abbreviates to ACT and represents in two steps: (1) the action is reduced to a static key word, a verb or noun; and (2) this key word is then expanded into a phrase and numbered, indicating the stage of the named action. For example, Sarrasine's journey from France to Italy is represented in lexias 197 to 200 (pp. 104–5). Each lexia represented a stage in the journey. Lexia 197 consists of the sentence 'Sarrasine left for Italy in 1758'. In terms of the proairetic code, Barthes analyses it as follows:

ACT. 'Journey': 1: to depart (for Italy).

'ACT' indicates that this lexia consists of the proairetic code; 'Journey' is the key word (in this instance a noun) indicating the generic action; '1: to depart (for Italy)' indicates the specific nature of that action (and its stage of progress).

The journey is completed in lexia 200, which reads (and begins mid-sentence):

> filled with desire to carve his name between Michelangelo's and M. Bouchardon's. Accordingly, at the beginning, he divided his time between studio tasks and examining the works of art in which Rome abounds.
>
> (Balzac, in Barthes 1974: 105)

Barthes analyses this lexia as 'ACT. "Journey": 4: to stay'. (It also relies on the referential code, as we shall see below.)

When analysing the proairetic code in a narrative film, identify the main generic action, the specific action being filmed, and the stage of that specific action. It is necessary to number the actions, for some will be articulated throughout the whole film, and numbering will assist in keeping track of them.

● The hermeneutic code (abbreviated to HER) names an enigma that the text establishes, holds in suspense (by means of snares, partial answers, suspended answers, and jamming), and then eventually discloses. The first enigma of the story 'Sarrasine' is the meaning of the title: what (or who) does it refer to? The second enigma is the source of the Lanty family's wealth, and the third is their origin (the conversations at the party centre around the second and third enigmas). A fourth enigma is gradually introduced as the party is under way – the identity of the mysterious old man who makes a sudden appearance. The old man is first mentioned in lexia 28:

> Observers, people who make it a point to know in what shop you buy your candlesticks, or who ask the amount of your rent when they find your apartment attractive, had noticed, now and then, in the midst of the Countess's [Countess de Lanty's] parties, concerts, balls, and routs, the appearance of a strange personage.
>
> (Balzac, in Barthes 1974: 41)

Barthes notes: 'Here a new enigma is proposed (a strange feeling) and thematized (a personnage) (HER. Enigma 4: theme and proposal)' (p. 41).

When analysing the hermeneutic code in a narrative film, identify the theme, formulation, and proposal of the enigmas; the delays in resolving those enigmas; and finally the disclosure of information that eventually resolves them. As with the proairetic code, it is also important to number the enigmas, for some will be articulated throughout the whole film, and numbering will assist in keeping track of them.

● The semic code (SEM) establishes specific connotative meanings in a text – that is, confers attributes upon settings (does the setting suggest the seme of wealth or poverty? etc.) and especially characters. When Sarrasine sees La Zambinella for the first time, the castrato is described (most notably in lexia 226) using the connotative signs, or semes, of femininity:

> The artist [Sarrasine] never wearied of admiring the inimitable grace with which the arms were attached to the torso, the marvelous roundness of the neck, the harmonious line drawn by the eyebrows, the nose, and the perfect oval of the face, the purity of its vivid contours and the effect of the thick, curved lashes which lined her heavy and voluptuous eyelids.
>
> (Balzac, in Barthes 1974: 113)

Barthes then simply labels this lexia 'SEM. Femininity (heavy curved lashes, voluptuous eyelids)' (p. 113).

When analysing the semic code in a narrative film, focus on the way in which settings and characters are established, for they are not (cannot be) presented in a neutral manner, but always according to a set of values (sometimes excessively, as in the case of La Zambinella). These values are the semes, which need to be indicated in one word (e.g. 'femininity' in the above example).

● The symbolic code (SYM) is the richest of all the codes. It operates on several levels of abstraction, because each culture or civilization organizes experience according to a multitude of basic, general, abstract categories, many of which relate to the semic code. One basic category that organizes experience is the opposition – or, as Barthes prefers, the antithesis – between inside and outside. In lexias 5–12 Balzac establishes an antithesis between the space outside the mansion and the space inside. Furthermore, the narrator is positioned on the boundary between these two spaces (he is sitting in a window recess):

> Thus, on my right, the dark and silent image of death; on my left, the seemly bacchanalias of life: here, cold nature, dull, in mourning; there, human beings enjoying themselves.
>
> (Balzac, in Barthes 1974: 25–6)

Barthes labels this lexia (number 12) 'SYM. Antithesis: AB: résumé' (p. 26). In previous lexias, the two terms of lexia 12, the outside (A) and the inside (B), were presented separately, with the narrator as mediator. In this lexia, they are presented together in summary form (hence Barthes's use of the term 'résumé').

Another more complex category of organization is the opposition between male and female. (Whereas 'femininity' or 'the female' by itself constitutes a seme, when placed in relation to 'masculinity' or 'the male' it constitutes an organizing principle, and becomes a symbolic code.) The description of La Zambinella quoted above imitates the patriarchal way of organizing sexual difference, in which women are set up as objects of the male gaze – a gaze based on voyeurism and fetishism (which are two structures in the male psyche that defend it against female sexuality). In the above example, Sarrasine's gaze fragments La Zambinella's body, and he evidently gains sexual pleasure simply by looking at La Zambinella (see lexias 241–5, pp. 117–18).

When analysing the symbolic code in a narrative film, abstract from it the most important basic categories of experience it employs. This will require skilled attention to the way the film's themes and symbols are structured and unified. This in turn is based on an ability to identify and isolate significant elements in the text, and to assign them a general function. To analyse the symbolic code is similar to developing a thematic reading of a film (see Chapter 4 above), since we need to make explicit and clarify the film's implicit meanings.

- The referential code (REF) is the most straightforward to identify, for one simply needs to note the type of knowledge the film is referring to. '[Referential/cultural codes] are references to a science or a body of knowledge; in drawing attention to them, we merely indicate the type of knowledge (physical, physiological, medical, psychological, literary, historical, etc.) referred to, without going so far as to construct (or reconstruct) the whole culture they express' (p. 20). Hence, Sarrasine's journey to Italy is completed in lexia 200 (quoted above), in which Michelangelo's name is mentioned, as well as that of Rome, as an artistic centre of the world. These are referential codes, and Barthes labels lexia 200 (in addition to the proairetic code) 'REF. History of Art' (p. 105).

When analysing the referential code in a narrative film, simply note the particular types of knowledge to which the film makes reference to authenticate and validate itself. In film the referential code is particularly strong, because the photographic image is based on the physical portrayal of actual settings and actors, which can easily be recognized. (See Chapter 7 for a discussion of the term 'physical portrayal'.)

## 5.3. Analysis: *S/Z* and *The Fifth Element*

Despite the importance and popularity of *S/Z* in post-structural literary theory, it has rarely been applied to films, with the exception of Julia Lesage's analysis (1986) of *Rules of the Game* (Jean Renoir, 1939). Raymond Bellour also refers to the proairetic code, the hermeneutic code, and especially the symbolic code in his analysis of *North by Northwest*, although Barthes's terms are simply integrated into Bellour's more widely focused textual analysis (see Bellour 2000: 86–7). However, Lesage presents an informal reading that offers a general (but useful) summary of the moments in *Rules of the Game* where the codes operate. She does not analyse the film in the step-by-step process of *S/Z*. In the following analysis we shall follow *The Fifth Element* as it unfolds, divide it up into pertinent lexia (according to the presence of and shifting relations between the codes), summarize each lexia, and then list and comment on the codes. We shall follow Barthes's practice of separating the list of codes by placing stars in front of each comment.

Plot summary. The film begins in a conventional manner, with a prologue set in Egypt in 1914, which serves an expositional function (it introduces us to the five elements and the threat to earth that will arrive in 300 years). The film then jumps forward 300 years. It singles out the main protagonist, Korben Dallas (played by Bruce Willis), his helpers, including father Cornelius (Ian Holm) and his assistant David, the antagonists – 'pure evil' (called 'Mr Shadow'), represented as a ball of fire in outer space that rushes towards earth, aided by Zorg (Gary Oldman) and the mangalores. The prized object is established early on – the four stones representing the four elements (earth, fire, water, air), and the fifth element, personified as 'the perfect woman', Leeloo (played by Milla Jovovich). The film also sets up a narrative conflict that needs to be resolved within a strict time limit: the evil ball of fire returns to earth every 5000 years to destroy everything. It can only be stopped by the four stones in combination with the fifth element. The protagonist is sent on a quest – to return the five elements to earth in order to save mankind – all within 48 hours. Meanwhile, the antagonists also attempt to obtain the stones. As expected, the protagonists win out. For this, Dallas receives the reward of consummating his love with the fifth element, the perfect woman. The moral of the film is transparent and banal: war and evil are bad, and can only be overcome through love.

Lexia (1): credit sequence. Every narrative film's credit sequence marks a transition from the non-fictional to the fictional realm. The non-fictional realm refers to the space occupied by the spectator (either the cinema auditorium or in front of the TV at home), and to the credits, which name the company that financed the film, plus the actors and technicians involved in the film's production. The image(s) behind the credits depicts the film's fictional space (the diegesis) which, in *The Fifth Element,* simply consists of rapidly moving objects entering from the top of the screen, travelling towards the spectator, and exiting at the bottom of the screen. The camera then pans up to reveal the source of these flying objects – a galaxy. The film's title is then superimposed over the galaxy. *REF. Finance company (Gaumont), director ('A film by Luc Besson'), actors and actresses (Bruce Willis, Gary Oldman, Ian Holm, Milla Jovovich, Chris Tucker, Luke Perry). The referential code also includes common knowledge about the four elements (earth, fire, water, air). **HER. Enigma 1: theme. The common knowledge about the four elements leads to the film's first enigma – what is the *fifth* element? ***SEM. Mystery. The electronic music score creates tension and mystery.

(2) After the film's title appears on screen, the credits continue, but this time over an image of the earth seen from space. An alien spacecraft enters screen right and moves towards the centre of the image, into earth's orbit. This is a typical (indeed, stereotypical) opening for a science fiction film. The electronic music heard in the film's opening continues, and is combined with distorted bass voices. In conjunction with the image of the earth, the music makes reference to *2001: A Space Odyssey* and to Ligeti's *Lux Aeterna*. *REF. Film technicians. Science fiction films (*2001*), and music (*Lux Aeterna*). **ACT. 'Journey': 1: to enter earth's orbit.

(3) The camera begins in space, complete with a shooting star (probably the alien spacecraft entering earth's atmosphere). The camera then pans rapidly down from space to earth, stopping on a very long shot of the desert with a large tomb in the background. A boy on a donkey walks into the image from screen right and moves towards the centre. Discordant strings are added over the rumbling electronic music, and tension is created through semitone notes. Ethnic Arabic reed music is also added, once the camera reaches the desert. A title is superimposed over the image: 'Egypt 1914'. *ACT. 'Journey': 2: to enter earth's atmosphere. 'Trek': 1: to travel through the desert. **REF. Egypt; World War 1 ('1914'). ***SEM. Menace (electronic music). Ethnicity (reed music). ****SYM. Antithesis 1: A: space. B: earth. This antithesis is mediated by the alien spacecraft entering earth's atmosphere. Antithesis 2: A: futuristic mode of travel (spacecraft). B: ancient mode of travel (donkey). Both the spacecraft and the boy on the donkey enter from screen right and move in the same direction. This formal parallelism highlights the differences between the mode of travel. Furthermore, the boy carries water (a symbol for life) whereas the alien spacecraft visits earth to take away the four stones and the fifth element, which protect life.

(4) The boy gets off his donkey, runs towards the entrance to the tomb, and leaves some water for the other boys sitting outside the tomb. Signs of Egypt (camels, Egyptian language, etc.) are clearly visible and audible. *ACT. 'Trek': 2: to arrive. **SEM. Ethnicity (modes of transport, language, clothes). ***SYM. Antithesis 3: A: outside. Antithesis 4: A: Middle East children.

(5) Inside the tomb, the boy stops and looks at two archaeologists. He then wakes up another boy (Aziz) who is meant to be providing light. The older

archaeologist (the professor) is standing by a wall interpreting hieroglyphics, and calls out to Aziz to provide more light. The younger archaeologist, Billy, repeats the professor's words, but without enthusiasm. *ACT. 'Trek': 3: to deliver water to the archaeologists. **SYM. Antithesis 3: B: inside. Antithesis 4: B: Western archaeologists. Antithesis 5: A: old. B: young (referring to the archaeologists at this stage). Antithesis 6: A: light. B: dark. ***REF. The psychology of the old (serious, self-important) and of the young (lack of interest, boredom).

(6) The professor begins to decipher the hieroglyphics (which predict a disaster every 5,000 years), and Billy makes notes, draws pictures, and responds in a half-interested manner. *ACT. 'Interpretation': 1: to decipher hieroglyphics. **SYM. Coded representation of disaster. ***REF. The psychology of the old and of the young.

(7) From nowhere, an old priest appears, takes the water from the boy, and sends him away. The priest then watches the archaeologists. *ACT. 'Trek': 3: to deliver water to the archaeologists (this action does not progress, but is simply transferred from the young boy to the old priest). **SYM. Antithesis 5: A: old. B: young (now referring to the Egyptians).

(8) The professor continues to decipher the hieroglyphics (of 'people gathering together the four elements of life – water, fire, earth, air – around a fifth one, a ... fifth ... element'). *ACT. 'Interpretation': 2: to continue deciphering the hieroglyphics. **SYM. Representation of the five elements. The professor slowly utters the film's title, therefore thematizing it within the film's diegesis. It is also symbolically represented as a hieroglyph (a person). ***HER. Enigma 1: thematization.

(9) Upon hearing the professor utter 'the fifth element' the priest decides to poison the water because the archaeologists know too much. *ACT. Kill: 1: to poison the archaeologists' water. The archaeologists know too much about the fifth element; hence it is established as a secret that must be concealed at any cost, even by a priest committing murder. The water, a symbol of life (and one of the four elements) becomes contaminated. **HER. Enigma 1: formulation of the enigma.

(10) The priest walks up to the two archaeologists and offers them water, while the professor offers part of his interpretation to the priest (the professor talks about good and evil, and a weapon against evil). The professor decides to throw the water away and drink a toast with grappa. Billy goes to fetch the bottle. *ACT. 'Trek': 4: to deliver the water. 'Kill': 2: thwarted attempt to poison. 'Interpretation': 3: to continue deciphering the hieroglyphics. **SYM. Antithesis 7: A: good. B: evil.

(11) The alien spacecraft, first seen in lexia 2, now lands next to the tomb, and slowly casts a shadow over everyone as it does so. The professor is completely oblivious to the aliens, and simply continues to interpret the

hieroglyphics. He demands light from Aziz, but receives it from the aliens. He then focuses on the figure of the fifth element ('This man, this perfect being, I know this is the key into it'). The aliens enter the tomb, kill the professor, and open the inner tomb containing the five elements. The priest knows the aliens, and is told that the stones are to be taken off the earth because of the coming war. *ACT. 'Journey': 3: to arrive on earth. 'Interpretation': 4: to decipher the fifth element symbol. **HER. Enigma 1: snare (due to his prejudices, the professor wrongly interprets the symbol of the fifth element as a 'perfect man'). ***REF. World War 1. ****SYM. Antithesis 6: A: light. B: dark. With the introduction of the aliens, the film brings into existence a complex web of antitheses (see Fig. 5.1). However, as the sequence progresses, the antitheses are regrouped. Antithesis 8: A: human. B: alien.

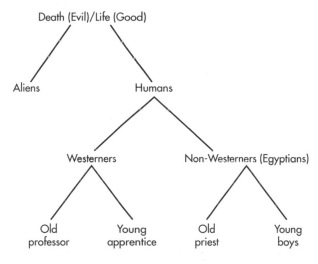

**Fig. 5.1.** The web of the symbolic code in the opening of *The Fifth Element*

   (12) Inside the inner tomb, four stones (symbolizing the four elements) are on display. In the centre is a sarcophagus containing the fifth element. The aliens remove them from the tomb. *ACT. 'Journey': 4: to retrieve the five elements. **SYM. The five elements are symbolized in three-dimensional form.

   (13) In response to the priest's plea that the earth is now defenceless against evil, the leader of the aliens remarks that 'when evil returns in 300 years, so shall we'. Perturbed by the aliens' presence and their killing of the professor, Billy pulls out his gun and threatens the leader of the aliens. The priest tries to

persuade him that the aliens are 'our' (the humans') friends, but only ends up 'alienating' himself (for Billy simply thinks that he is with the aliens). Billy slips and fires his gun. Although he doesn't harm anyone, the gunshots make the inner tomb close, with the leader of the aliens trapped inside (but not before he passes the key to the inner tomb to the priest). Throughout, ethnic reed music is heard, and combined with menacing electronic music. *ACT. 'Defence': 1: to shoot. 'Journey': 5: to exit the tomb. **SYM. Antithesis 9: A: life. B: evil. This lexia adds another – more general – layer to the web of antitheses represented above, between life (humans and aliens) and evil (death and destruction). Billy also groups the priest and aliens together, breaking the antithesis between alien and human. ***SEM. Ethnicity and danger.

(14) The spacecraft departs, and the priest vouches to safeguard the key. The soundtrack becomes louder; it combines ethnic music, vocal sounds, and a drum beat. *ACT. 'Journey' 6: to depart earth. 'Safeguard': 1: to protect the key to the inner tomb. **SEM. Ethnicity and danger.

(15) The scene ends with the camera focusing on a detail from the hieroglyphics, the symbol showing the moment when evil will return – when three planets are in eclipse. In the cut to the beginning of the next scene, the same three planets are represented in the exact configuration, except on a computer screen. The following shot, inside a spacecraft populated with humans, is overlaid with the title '300 years later'. *SYM. The time of evil's arrival is symbolized in hieroglyphics and a computer screen. **REF. Chronology: 300 years later (a temporal progression prefigured by the leader of the aliens).

The above analysis simply represents the first 11 minutes of the film. These 11 minutes clearly thematize and formulate the enigma around the fifth element, and set up a complex web of antitheses. Yet the enigma is not sustained throughout the whole film. It is resolved within 25 minutes of a two-hour movie (the fifth element is 'the perfect woman' – hence the professor's snare). Once the enigma is revealed, the main tension in the film comes from the imposition of a strict deadline: evil, represented as a ball of fire in space, heads towards earth and will destroy it in two days. A hero is established to save the earth, although obstacles are put in his way: the alien spacecraft returning the stones to earth is attacked; Zorg tries to possess the stones, etc. (The strategies of delay listed in the hermeneutic code can also be used to account for the delays in achieving the actions in the proairetic code.)

An analysis of the entire film in terms of Barthes's five codes would run into many pages. As an alternative, we shall attempt to analyse the whole film using a different strategy – by focusing on the film's narrative structure and its relation to digital narrative, as represented in video games.

# 5.4. Theory: video pleasure and narrative cinema

[V]ideo pleasure requires the player's total immersion in the electronic text, trust in the existence of a code imposed by invisible experts, and the self-affirming and empowering experience of its incremental mastery. Predicated on the ability to rapidly discriminate between circulating signs (some hostile, some neutral, and some friendly), and to appropriately respond to them, such a pleasurable mastery involves a skillful and rapid navigation in a chaotic electronic text, a navigation propelled by strategic violent moves administered digitally.

(Gottschalk 1995: 13)

Jerome Bruner reminds us that narrative is not a contingent, optional dimension of society, but is an essential, ecologically necessary structure with which individuals make sense of social complexity (Bruner 1991; 1992). In the process of structuring social experience, narrative necessarily reinvents itself in each epoch, offering a historically specific experience. Since the 1980s, new digital technologies have been interacting with cinema's nineteenth-century analogue technologies of optics, mechanics, and photochemistry. The most prominent mark of this interaction is the use of digital special effects in blockbuster movies. Although for the most part images are still produced photographically (exceptions being films such as *Toy Story*, *Antz*, and *A Bug's Life*), this photographic image is often supplemented by digital special effects. In Chapter 7 we write about the digitalized filmic image, focusing on the way the new technology has transformed cinema's analogue technology by modifying its form (e.g. the filmic image is no longer restricted to depicting profilmic events). Digital technology alters our relation to the image for this very reason, since what we see could have been generated on the computer, yet (in the case of invisible special effects at least) is conferred a photographic credibility.

In the remainder of this chapter we shall simply offer the beginnings of a discussion on the different structures of digital narrative, and the appearance of several of these structures in *The Fifth Element*. This digitization can be detected in the way film narrative has adopted the rules and strategies of video games. (The influence works both ways, of course, since many video games adopt the visual and aural aesthetics of science fiction movies.)

Before discussing the specifics of digital narrative and video games, we shall briefly refer to the work of George Landow on hypertext. It is primarily Landow who first realized that Barthes's *S/Z* – particularly his concept of the writerly – can be applied to hypertexts: 'In *S/Z*, Roland Barthes describes an ideal textuality that precisely matches that which in computing has come to be called hypertext – text composed of blocks of words (or images) linked electronically by multiple paths, chains, or trails in an open-ended, perpetually unfinished textuality described by the terms *link, node, network, web,* and *path*' (Landow 1997: 3). This ideal textuality is precisely the writerly text, a plural text 'unimpoverished by any constraint of representation (of imitation). In this ideal text, the networks are many and interact . . .' (Barthes 1974: 5). One of the radical possibilities offered by hypertext is that it allows the reader to interact with the text, to follow any of the numerous networks and links, and construct his or her own pathway through the information, unconstrained by the readerly text's strict linearity and predetermined meaning. Hypertexts, which incorporate interactivity, therefore embody the ideal of the writerly text, a text produced by the reader.

This raises a problem in analysing films as digital narratives: no matter how digital their narratives, films are not interactive. Yet digital narratives consist of numerous other structures, which we shall now outline. At the end of this chapter we shall return to the issue of narrative and interactivity.

## 5.5. Method: mastering the rules of the video game

Video games possess 'an excess of visual and aural stimuli' but also 'the promise of reliable rules' (Gottschalk 1995: 13). These rules, which are reliable in that they are systematic and unambiguous (for they are unencumbered by morality or compassion), constitute the video game's environment, or location, which is not restrained by the laws of the physical world. The game user can experience video pleasure primarily by attempting to master these rules, i.e. decipher the game's logic. Moreover, the desire to attain mastery makes video games addictive, which at times can lead to the user's total absorption into the game's rules and environment. This absorption in turn may alter the user's state of consciousness and lead to a momentary loss of self (see Fiske 1989: ch. 2).

Here we outline a number of the general structures used to construct these rules. When analysing digital narratives, attempt to identify several or all of these structures, since by themselves they do not define a narrative as digital. It is only when combined together that they begin to dominate a film's narrative structure. At present the list of structures is inductive, although it covers some of the most common rules to be found in video games, including:

- serialized repetition of actions (to accumulate points and master the rules)
- multiple levels of adventure
- space–time warps
- magical transformations and disguises

- immediate rewards and punishment (which act as feedback loops)
- pace
- interactivity

Video games are organized around the serialized repetition of actions for several reasons, including the accumulation of points and the opportunity to master the rules of the game. 'Once players have learned a set of skills,' writes Nicholas Luppa, 'they want to apply them in new situations. Elevating a game to other levels has long been a secret of good game design' (1998: 32). In other words, users are keen to refine their newly acquired competence in game play by applying and testing it in similar but more difficult environments.

Space–time warps represent an alternative way to reach another level. They are the video game's equivalent of the hypertext link, for they enable the player to be immediately transported to an alternative space (and time), leading to a sense of multiple fragmented spaces, with immediate transportation between them. Once the user has reached another level, his character on screen may be magically transformed into another character, or may don a disguise.

The user's accumulation of points acts as a feedback loop in the process of mastering the rules, since it represents a reward for good game play, and confers upon the user the sense that his competence is improving and the game is progressing. In similar fashion, the loss of points or a life acts as an immediate punishment for failing to master the rules. A repetition of this punishment leads to the user's premature death and an early end to the game. Serialized repetition therefore involves repeating the same stages of the game – usually at a faster pace, or moving up to another similar (but more difficult) level. According to Nicholas Luppa, pace is one of the most important features of video games: '[video games] require pacing and the beats that are being counted in that pacing are the beats between interactions'(1998: 34). The important point here is that the player controls the beats via interaction, which confers upon the player the feeling of control – the manipulation of a character in a usually hostile digital environment. Moreover, the interactions need to be immersive – that is, must focus the user's concentration, and must be multiple and varied. Interaction is also dependent on the interface design, which must be detailed, but also easy to use.

Video pleasure, created by a user's addiction to and immersion in a game, is therefore not simply a matter of a heightened stimulation generated by high-quality graphics, audio, and animation, but is also – and, I would argue, primarily – a function of these rules, of the user's success at mastering these rules. Of course, in discussing the popularity and pleasure of video games, we should not leave out their content and themes, which can in fact be summarized in one word – violence: 'The central organizing assumption of videology is unarguably that of violence. . . . The only relevant question posed by videology is not whether a particular situation calls for negotiation or violence but how efficiently can violence be administered' (Gottschalk 1995: 7). Moreover, the violent enemy to be destroyed is invariably coded as 'other'. The content of video games therefore perpetuates Western ideological myths, and playing games – especially by oneself – is said to lead to antisocial behaviour. Yet beyond these social concerns there are what Fiske calls important semiotic pleasures to be gained from video games (see Fiske 1989: ch. 2). Hopefully, the above discussion goes some way to outlining how that pleasure is generated.

## 5.6. Analysis: video game logic in *The Fifth Element*

Just as the filmic image is a hybrid between the photographic and the digital, the narrative in *The Fifth Element* is a hybrid between the classical (psychologically motivated cause–effect) narrative logic and digital (video game) logic. In the following we shall focus on those moments in the film when video logic becomes apparent.

What is significant about *The Fifth Element* is the way the banal story and its transparent moral are structured and conveyed to spectators. In his discussion of the film in his essay 'Infinite City' Nigel Floyd (1997) mentions the influence of graphic artists on the film's visual design. But what is more significant than this is the influence of the rules of video games on the way the film is structured.

It is easy to look at the content of the film and begin identifying the rules of video game logic metaphorically: for example, we could argue that the cityscape metaphorically represents the film's different levels of play, or that the scene where the mangalores shoot down the spaceship carrying the fifth element is a metaphorical representation of the game user's interactivity. However, we do not intend to read the film's content in such metaphorical terms. We are primarily interested in the way that content is literally organized according to video game logic.

The first half of the film sets up the characters, their relationship, and their aim – to obtain the four stones and save/destroy the earth. Korben is the primary protagonist, although he is aided by Cornelius, Leeloo, and 'the Federation'. Zorg is the main antagonist who works directly for 'Mr Shadow', and is initially aided by the mangalores, who later set out on their own quest to obtain the stones. There are a few video game moments in the first half of the film: for example, like a video game character, Leeloo is magically reconstructed/transformed (she gains another life); the mangalores seem to have 'won the game' early on by stealing the case of stones (the four elements) for Zorg; however, when Zorg opens the case, it is empty, which then initiates a serialized repetition of the action to capture the stones; as immediate punishment, Zorg blows up the mangalore leader (or allows him to blow himself up). The mangalores and Zorg have not mastered the rules of the game at this stage, and so they are punished (Zorg is empty-handed, the mangalore leader blows himself up).

Once the characters and their aim have been established, more prominent elements of video game logic become apparent. Approximately 50 minutes into the film, we find out that the stones are with the Diva on the paradise planet. This planet represents the film's next level of adventure, and the immediate aim is for the protagonists and antagonists to get on the crowded flight that goes to the next level. A competition to win two tickets to the planet is rigged by the Federation so that Dallas wins. Upon hearing this news on the radio, Cornelius and Leeloo visit Dallas at his apartment. Leeloo removes Dallas's name-tag from his door and puts it on the neighbour's door. Soon afterwards the police, acting under Zorg's instructions, attempt to arrest Dallas (Zorg has obviously found out as well that Dallas has two tickets to the planet). But because Leeloo put Dallas's name-tag on the neighbour's door, the neighbour is arrested. The mangalores in turn kidnap 'Dallas' from police custody. Soon afterwards, Cornelius steals the tickets from the real Dallas, goes to the airport and gives the tickets to his assistant David, and to Leeloo. David pretends to be Dallas, but Dallas turns up at the airport to take his rightful place. A mangalore then turns up at the airport and pretends to be Dallas. Significantly, he has changed his appearance, and looks like Dallas's neighbour. The mangalore has disguised himself – but as the wrong person! He fails to get onto the plane and has to run from the police (who presumably think he is Dallas). Then Zorg's helper turns up at the ticket desk and also pretends to be Dallas. The flight assistant, who by this time is becoming a little weary of this serialized repetition of action and disguises, prevents Zorg's helper from getting onto the plane. Upon hearing this news Zorg immediately punishes him by killing him. Meanwhile, Cornelius becomes a stowaway on the plane. The plane takes off, transporting Dallas, Leeloo (both disguised as tourists), and Cornelius at the speed of light to the next level of the game.

These scenes in the film are then dominated by the following rules of video game logic: serialized repetition, disguises, the attempt to move up to the next level, a feedback loop (in which unsuccessful characters are immediately eliminated and successful ones rewarded), and a space warp. However, once at this new level, we discover that the mangalores are there already (the leader, who blew himself up earlier, is now disguised as a waiter). Zorg also travels to the planet in his own ship. The same quest that took place on the previous level (locate the four stones) now takes place on the new level. How the mangalores get there, how the mangalore leader survived the explosion earlier in the film, why Zorg has Dallas arrested when Zorg can make his own way to the paradise planet, why Leeloo changes the name-tag on Dallas's door, and why there was such a fuss at the airport is only of concern to those who read the film in classical narrative terms. Within video game logic, the film makes sense. The game play on the first level is going to be repeated on the next level with essentially the same characters – except that now it is going to be played at a faster pace.

Only one narrative event takes place on the paradise planet – the protagonists retrieve the stones and return to earth (the film's final level). But this event is subordinated to the action sequences and to the Diva's singing. Furthermore, those unsuccessful at retrieving the stones are killed before the next level is played out.

Zorg suddenly turns up and steals the box from the Diva's room as she is singing. He plants a bomb, departs the planet, and opens the box to find it empty. This is a repetition of action performed earlier, when the mangalores delivered the (empty) box to Zorg. Zorg returns to the planet again, but this time is punished for his lack of success – although he switches off his own bomb, he is killed by a bomb left by the mangalores (which presumably kills all the mangalores as well).

The film ends in a conventional narrative manner – the formation of a heterosexual couple. But the ultimate objective of the narrative is not the transformation of characters, but survival – as is the case with video games. Character identification is achieved primarily by means of action – again, as in video games – rather than narrative development (there are few enigmas in the film once the identity of the fifth element is disclosed). Dallas does not so much develop as a character; he masters the rules of the game and proceeds to the next level, cashes in his points, and wins the ultimate prize – the perfect woman.

## 5.6.1. Spectacle, interactivity, and writerly texts

Story telling. It's not a game, it's an adventure. Every medium has its bias, the stories it cannot tell. ... We will want to tell the stories that demand interaction. But what does that mean? ... What is the story that can best be told with your meddling?

(Crockford, n.d.)

The main potential offered by digital media is that it introduces the dimension of interactivity to texts. In Barthes's terms, the text literally becomes writerly – in the sense that it is not completely written before the reader reads it, but is constructed by the reader. Yet what does interactivity add to narrative texts? And are the participant's choices merely fixed in advance by the computer software? One defining characteristic of narrative is that it has a predetermined structure based on specific outcomes. A participant's input can simply destroy that structure. The predetermined structure of narratives excludes the possibility of interactivity – that is, interactivity is incompatible with narrative structure. Narratives are therefore inherent readerly – it is narrative that makes a text readerly. This is why *The Fifth Element* employs all the video game rules listed above except interactivity.

One way to understand the opposition between narrative and interactivity is to think of narrative as spectacle. This may at first sound confusing, because film theorists from the 1970s onwards have opposed spectacle to narrative (most famously articulated by Laura Mulvey in 'Visual Pleasure and Narrative Cinema' and by Stephen Heath in 'Narrative Space', both to be found in Rosen 1986). Yet I am not referring to spectacle in this narrow sense. Instead, I am using the term more globally, in Guy Debord's sense of the 'society of the spectacle', a society (modern capitalism) in which direct experiences are replaced with represented experiences. Film is therefore a spectacle in this sense because it is a representation based on spatio-temporal displacement, which creates an irreducible distance between film and spectator. And it is this irreducible distance that minimizes interaction between film and spectator.

For a medium to become interactive (or writerly) requires it to go beyond spectacle (and narrative). Daniel Dayan and Elihu Katz (1985) distinguish 'spectacle' from 'ceremony' and 'festival'. In contrast to spectacle, ceremony and festival involve interaction, although to different degrees: festival involves a strong interaction between audience and the event they experience (as in carnivals), whereas ceremonies involve a measured interaction (reactions such as shouting and applause).[1] The recent emergence of interactivity as a cultural practice seems to suggest that we have gone beyond 'the society of the spectacle' – that is, beyond modern capitalism, towards what Fredric Jameson calls late or multinational capitalism. As an invention that emerged from modern capitalism, film is firmly rooted within the society of the spectacle. Interactive digital media, by contrast, need to be conceived along the lines of festivals and ceremonies – as writerly rather than readerly texts.

## Endnote

1    A film can become a festival in Dayan and Katz's sense of the term (as in screenings of *The Rocky Horror Picture Show*), and on occasions films are applauded (in which they momentarily become ceremonies), but these are exceptions to the norm.

# 6 Cognitive theories of narration (*Lost Highway*)

## Introduction

Martha Nochimson warns film critics and theorists that their linguistic and rational tools will miss or at least distort the specificity of David Lynch's films, which represent 'a level of non-rational energy on which all kinds of meaningful activity takes place' (Nochimson 1997: 6). Rather than suggest that Lynch has abandoned language and rationality, Nochimson argues that he places language and reason in the context of the subconscious, which has the effect of relativizing their 'imperialism'. Moreover, Lynch celebrates rather than distrusts the non-rational energy of the subconscious. He invites the spectator to 'suspend the desire for [rational] control by engaging in an empathetic relationship with a protagonist who, as a matter of survival, must learn to permit a channel to the subconscious in order to open the self to the universe' (Nochimson 1997: 11). For Lynch, the rationalist illusion of control and mastery creates a barrier to the real. In his films, Lynch unshackles himself from Western society's ultra-rational way of thinking, realizes that there is meaning beyond rationality, and tries to convey that our fear of letting go of rationality is simply a fear created by our prison-house of language.

Lynch uses the cinema to express non-rational energy in tangible form (visually and aurally). This energy is familiar to us all, but has been repressed in us by language, rationality, and education. This is one reason why Lynch's films seem to be nonsensical, but nonetheless evoke powerful feelings. It is easy to make nonsensical films that don't evoke any feelings at all, because they don't engage with the non-rational energy that Lynch evokes.

We can use the term 'uncanny' to describe the powerful feelings the non-rational energy evokes in us. This term designates a mood more than anything else – a mood created by uncertainty and confusion as the familiar world starts to become strange, and we begin to lose our bearings. Seemingly ordinary events – everything from a blazing fire in the fire place, traffic lights changing from red to green, the sound of the wind, to a drive along the road are rendered strange in Lynch's films. But Lynch does not simply present strange events; he also creates an uncanny feeling in the spectator. Spectators quite literally come out of his 1997 film *Lost Highway* feeling disoriented, since the film has challenged a number of the certainties we hold within the boundaries of our linguistic and rational world. Nonetheless, the strange world seems familiar at the same time – it is that realm of experience that language and rationality have made us repress. In this sense, Lynch's films are receptive to the subconscious, since they evoke a 'return from the repressed'.

Although Lynch's films are receptive to the non-rational energy of the subconscious, most spectators do not switch off their rational faculty when watching a film like *Lost Highway*, although this faculty does become challenged and has to work harder. Our aim in this chapter is to analyse *Lost Highway* in terms of its 'comprehensibility'. We do not aim to locate mysterious hidden meanings in the film, but want to understand how the film can be comprehended on the basic level of its story structure, and in terms of how the film's narration conveys that story to spectators. We shall attempt to demonstrate that the cognitive theory of narration David Bordwell pioneered in his book *Narration in the Fiction Film* (1985), and which Edward Branigan developed further in *Narrative Comprehension and Film* (1992), are ideally suited to analysing complex films such as *Lost Highway*. This is because cognitive theory constructs a model of the norms, principles, and conventions that explain how spectators routinely comprehend films. Cognitive theory can therefore highlight and account for the moments in a film where comprehension breaks down. Or, more positively, it can focus on the moments where the film goes beyond the spectator's routine and rational ('common sense') way of comprehending a film, and begin to determine how non-rational energy has influenced the film's structure and meaning.

## 6.1. Theory: *Narration in the Fiction Film*

In *Narration in the Fiction Film* David Bordwell develops a cognitive theory of film comprehension, which he explicitly opposes to a psychoanalytic theory of film. Psychoanalytic film theorists (whom we discuss in Chapters 8 and 9) define the experience of reality as not being delimited by the horizon of consciousness (or 'common sense'), but argue that it includes myth, ideology, and unconscious desires and fantasies. According to psychoanalysts, our consciousness is merely the tip or peak of our identity, most of which remains hidden and repressed. But for cognitive scientists, consciousness is not a mere superstructure, but the base, or basis, of identity. Following the cognitive scientists, Bordwell argues that film theorists should begin with cognitive explanations of filmic phenomena, and should move on to psychoanalytic explanations only if a cognitive account is found wanting: 'The theory I advance attends to the perceptual and cognitive aspects of film viewing. While I do not deny the usefulness of psychoanalytic approaches to the spectator, I see no reason to claim for the unconscious any activities which can be explained on other grounds' (Bordwell 1985: 30).[1]

The basic premise of Bordwell's theory is that narration is the central process that influences the way spectators understand a narrative film. Moreover, he argues that spectators do not simply absorb a finalized, pre-existing narrative, but must actively construct its meaning. Bordwell develops his theory within what is called the 'constructivist school' of cognitive psychology, which studies how perceivers 'make sense' of the world from inherently fragmentary and incomplete data and experiences. For example, we can only directly see three sides of a six-sided solid cube. But from this incomplete experience, we complete the cube by 'appending' the other three sides. Bordwell and other cognitive film theorists argue that film is like a six-sided cube in which spectators see at most only three sides on screen. The spectator has to complete the film by appending the other three sides, so to speak.

In Chapters 3 and 4 of *Narration in the Fiction Film* Bordwell outlines a cognitive theory of film that tries to explain how spectators complete a film's narrative, rendering it coherent. Spectators are not free rational agents who can simply 'fill in the gaps' in a film in any way they wish. Instead, intersubjective norms, principles, and conventions guide them. When watching a narrative film, spectators do not simply 'absorb' the data, because it is not complete in itself. Instead, they have to process this inherently incomplete data. And they process it using what cognitive psychologists call *schemata* – norms and principles in the mind that organize the incomplete data into coherent mental representations. Schemata are activated by 'cues' in the data. Bordwell notes that gaps in the data are the most evident cues, for they are simply the missing data that spectators need to fill in. For example, a cube 'suggests' its three hidden sides (the missing data) by a variety of cues, including the way the three visible sides are projected in space, the way the visible sides form edges, and so on. More accurately, the cube cues us to fill in the three hidden sides. This process of filling-in is called *hypothesis* or *inference generation*.

Narrative films cue spectators to generate inferences or hypotheses – but not just any inferences. When comprehending a narrative film, one schema in particular guides our hypotheses – the one that represents the canonical story format:

> Nearly all story-comprehension researchers agree that the most common template structure can be articulated as a 'canonical' story format,

something like this: introduction of setting and characters – explanation of a
state of affairs – complicating action – ensuing events – outcome – ending.

(Bordwell 1985: 35)

Moreover, comprehension of a narrative is made easier if it is organized
around a goal-oriented protagonist – a character who drives the narrative
forward towards his or her predefined goal.

Spectators do not, therefore, enter the cinema with a blank mind and
passively absorb the film's narrative. Just as each language-learner internalizes
the rules of his/her native language, so each film spectator internalizes a
schema, a template or set of norms and principles with which to comprehend
narrative films. In Western societies, spectators internalize a schema called the
canonical story format.

But exactly how does the narrative schema work? Bordwell notes that, when
spectators are presented with two events in a film, they employ the narrative
schema to attempt to link the events together - either spatially, temporally,
and/or causally. As the film progresses, spectators rearrange events,
disambiguate their relations and order, and in doing so, gradually construct a
story. Following the Russian formalists, Bordwell calls the resulting story the
fabula: 'the fabula embodies the action as a chronological, cause-and-effect
chain of events occurring within a given duration and spatial field' (Bordwell
1985: 49). Bordwell calls the actual order in which the fragments of the fabula
events are presented the plot, or syuzhet: 'The syuzhet (usually translated as
"plot") is the actual arrangement and presentation of the fabula in the film. It
is not the text in toto. It is a more abstract construct, the patterning of a story
as a blow-by-blow recounting of the film could render it' (p. 49).

The third element (after the fabula and syuzhet) that influences film
comprehension is style, which Bordwell simply defines as a film's 'systematic
use of cinematic devices' (p. 50). Bordwell defines narration as a combination
of syuzhet and style, which interact with the spectator's narrative schema in
constructing the fabula.

Bordwell emphasizes that the fabula is a mental representation, and that
spectators construct the fabula on the basis of cues in the syuzhet (and style)
interacting with the narrative schema. Moreover, he argues that the key to
comprehending a particular film is determined largely by the relation between
the fabula and the syuzhet – or, more specifically, by whether the syuzhet
facilitates or blocks the spectator's construction of the fabula.

Because the film's fabula is a mental representation the spectator constructs
during her ongoing experience of the film's syuzhet, the fabula is in a constant
state of change, due to the spectator's ongoing generation of new hypotheses,
strengthening of existing hypotheses, and abandonment of existing
hypotheses. Spectators may need to abandon hypotheses because they only

have a probable reality. Or they may generate several conflicting hypotheses on the basis of a few cues, and then reduce them as the syuzhet presents additional cues. Moreover, a film may deliberately lead spectators to generate incorrect hypotheses (the phenomenon of unreliable narration[2]), or the film may deliberately challenge the canonical story format: 'If the film does not correspond to the canonic story, the spectator must adjust his or her expectations and posit, however tentatively, new explanations for what is presented' (Bordwell 1985: 36). This is the case with *Lost Highway*.

## 6.2. Method

> The most analytically important variable is the set of formal correspondences between fabula and syuzhet. That is, to what extent does the unfolding syuzhet correspond to the logical, temporal, and spatial nature of the fabula we construct?
>
> (Bordwell 1985: 54)

The film analyst can extract a fairly rich methodology from Bordwell's cognitive theory of narration. Bordwell introduces a series of concepts to explain how narration works – that is, how syuzhet and style facilitate and hinder the spectator's construction of the fabula. These concepts include: various hypotheses the syuzhet encourages the spectator to generate; various gaps constructed by the syuzhet constructs; types of exposition employed by the syuzhet; tactics for delaying the release of fabula information; redundancy (the way some information is conveyed several times); and broad narrational strategies, such as knowledgeability, self-consciousness, and communicativeness.

A general principle is to look for cues in the film, including patterns, gaps, and the way the syuzhet is organized. More specifically, look for the way the canonical story format is cued or thwarted. Bordwell writes that: 'the schemata [particularly the narrative schema] need a firm foothold somewhere. The sequential nature of narrative makes the initial portions of the text crucial for the establishment of hypotheses' (Bordwell 1985: 38). Analysing the opening scenes of a film is therefore crucial to a cognitive analysis of narration.

Not all cues and hypotheses are the same. Bordwell identifies several types of hypothesis. You need to ask yourself: Is the film encouraging me to generate a curiosity hypothesis (that is, an hypothesis about past events) or a suspense hypothesis (is the film asking me to anticipate forthcoming events)? Is the hypothesis probable or improbable? Is it exclusive or non-exclusive? And at what level is the process of hypothesis generation taking place – a micro-level (moment by moment) or macro-level (large scale)?

Bordwell also identifies several types of gap (the most recognizable cue in the text). When analysing gaps, we need to ask: Are they temporary or permanent? Most are temporary – that is, resolved by the end of the film. Second, are they flaunted or suppressed? A gap is flaunted when the spectator is made aware that there is some information they need to know about the fabula, whereas a suppressed gap does not call attention to itself. Finally, are the gaps diffused or focused? A diffused gap is open ended, leading the spectator to generate a series of non-exclusive hypotheses, whereas a focused gap is clearly defined and leads the spectator to generate an exclusive hypothesis. A diffuse gap introduced at the beginning of a film can be gradually brought into focus as the film progresses.

The expositional moments in a film introduce pertinent background information about the settings, characters, and states of affairs. Exposition can be concentrated into a few scenes or, more rarely, diffused throughout the whole film. If concentrated, it may be preliminary (appearing at the beginning of the film) or delayed until the end (as in detective films). The syuzhet can also set up false leads, complications in the action, and subplots to delay fabula information. Or it may convey some information on several occasions (redundancy), to reinforce the importance of that information and ensure its effective communication. (This is why redundancy is a standard principle of classical narration.) We shall see that *Lost Highway* employs very little exposition. As the film unfolds, spectators gradually expect a delayed scene of concentrated exposition at the end. However, this explanation never arrives, which is one reason why the film is disorienting.

More generally, a film's syuzhet is constructed using broad narrational strategies, including knowledgeability, self-consciousness, and communicativeness. Under knowledgeability, Bordwell includes a syuzhet's range of knowledge and its depth. Is the knowledge limited to what one character knows about fabula events (restricted narration), or does it go beyond what any character knows (omniscient narration)? And is that knowledge deep (does it delve into the character's mental life)? Or does it remain on the surface (simply showing the characters' behaviour)? Second, a self-conscious narration displays a recognition that it is addressing an audience. Cues of self-consciousness include: characters looking into the camera, voiceovers addressing the spectator, and frontality of figure position. Third, the narration may withhold from the spectator some of the available information. For example, if the narration shows us the fabula through a character's eyes, is it willing to show us all the relevant information that character sees (in which case it is being highly communicative)? Or does the narration suddenly change perspective at a crucial moment, thus denying the spectator some important information (in which case it is less communicative)?

From these various principles we can begin to identify the film's internal norms – its specific syuzhet structure. We shall see that our experience of *Lost Highway* is strongly determined by a syuzhet consisting of flaunted focused gaps, as well as a radical challenge to the canonical story format.

## 6.3. Analysis

> Armed with the notion of different narrative principles and the concept of the syuzhet's distortion of fabula information, we can begin to account for the concrete narrational work of any film.
>
> (Bordwell 1985: 51)

The credit sequence of *Lost Highway* consists of a shot of a camera attached to the front of a car travelling very fast along a highway at night. The car's headlights illuminate the road. The credits appear from the middle of the screen, travel rapidly towards the camera, and pause momentarily (the letters appear to stick to the film screen) before disappearing 'behind' the camera and spectator.

In the opening scene we are introduced to Fred Madison (Bill Pullman) at home. Because of his frequent appearance in the opening scenes, we assume that Fred is the film's main protagonist. The scene opens with Fred sitting in the dark on the edge of his bed. He is smoking a cigarette and looking at himself in the mirror. The front-door intercom buzzes, and he hears the message 'Dick Laurent is dead'. He goes over to the window in another part of the house to look out, but he sees no one. As he heads towards the window we hear the off-screen sound of tyres screeching and a police siren.

We have seen Bordwell argue that a film's beginning is crucial because the spectator's hypotheses need to establish a foothold in the film early on. The intercom message leads the spectator to generate at least two hypotheses, focused around the questions: Who rang the bell? And, who is Dick Laurent? These two hypotheses are generated in response to the gaps in the fabula that the syuzhet has constructed. Firstly, knowledge about the fabula is severely limited. But this limitation is motivated because the narration is linked to Fred's level of awareness and experience of fabula events: the spectator sees and hears what Fred sees and hears. The knowledge is therefore deep and restricted, and the syuzhet is being communicative, because it gives the spectator access to this knowledge. (We shall see later in this chapter that Edward Branigan discusses character awareness and experience in terms of the concept of focalization.) The gaps in the fabula are, first, spatial. The restricted narration does not show us the identity of the person outside and does not show us the source of the off-screen sounds. This spatial gap in the fabula is evident to the spectator, and is therefore a flaunted (rather than a suppressed) gap. It is also a clearly delineated gap, and is therefore specific (rather than diffuse). Finally, it is temporary (rather than permanent) because it is eventually filled in at the end of the film. The hypothesis we generate about this spatial gap is a suspense, non-exclusive hypothesis operating at the film's macro-level. It is a suspense hypothesis because we assume the gap will be resolved in the future (so we anticipate the filling in of this gap at a later time in the film's unfolding); it is non-exclusive because it could have been anyone (we cannot generate a hypothesis suspecting a particular person); and it operates on the macro-level because it spans the entire film. The scale of probability/improbability usually refers to the hypotheses we generate. But in this case, the way the syuzhet fills in this gap at the end of the film is highly improbable. Although our hypotheses were non-exclusive, it is highly unlikely that any spectator would generate the hypothesis that Fred is *also* outside the house pressing his own doorbell!

The lack of information on Dick Laurent's identity is a temporary, flaunted, focused gap that leads the spectator to generate an exclusive curiosity hypothesis that operates on the macro-level (for his identity is not immediately resolved). In a more conventional film (one that follows the conventions of the canonical story format), the spectator's narrative schema would condition her to expect the next scene to contain exposition explaining who Dick Laurent is.

The screeching tyres and the police siren are not coded as prominent cues, and many spectators may not perceive them as cues, but as part of the film's 'reality effect' – that is, background noise that one may expect to hear, rather than a significant narrative event. In summary, the opening scene enables the narrative schema to gain a foothold in the film, since the spectator generates hypotheses in response to the gaps the syuzhet has constructed, and is anticipating events in future scenes.

The first scene ends on an establishing shot, a very long shot of the front of Fred's house in the early morning light. After a fade, the second scene begins by repeating this exterior establishing shot, except that this time it is night. Inside the house, we see Fred packing a saxophone into its case, and talking to Renee (Patricia Arquette), who wants to stay home and read rather than go to the club with him. This seemingly simple scene nonetheless keeps the spectator busy. It appears to follow the canonical story format by continuing to introduce the setting and characters, and by explaining a state of affairs. On the basis of the two exterior establishing shots (shown back to back), we generate the hypothesis that the film has now progressed from morning to evening of the same day. In other words, using our narrative schema, we establish a linear temporal relation between the two scenes. Second, information about Fred is conveyed indirectly: we assume he is a musician, and we find out from his talk with Renee that the two of them are married (Renee: 'I like to laugh, Fred.' Fred: 'That's why I married you.') The deadpan way the two characters interact, plus the sparse dialogue, may suggest that the marriage is at a stalemate, to the point where Fred's sax-playing bores Renee, and she invents improbable reasons for wanting to stay home (she does not appear to be the type of person who will spend her evenings at home reading).

In contrast to the end of scene 1, scene 2 ends abruptly, as we cut from the quiet interior of the Madisons' house to an image of the exterior of the Luna lounge and the very loud sound of sax music. This sudden break from scene 2 jolts the spectator, not only because of the contrast in sound and image, but also because there is no reference to the two gaps in scene 1. Fred does not mention the message he received on the intercom, and therefore we are no closer to finding out who the messenger was, or who Dick Laurent is. Reference to these cues would have strengthened the causal relationship between scenes 1 and 2. As it is, the two scenes are linked more tenuously – visually (the visual repetition of the establishing shot), and linearly (the progression from day to night), rather than causally. The syuzhet is marked by a lack of redundancy between scenes.

In scene 3 Fred is shown playing his sax and phoning his wife during an intermission. But no one answers the phone at home; the house appears empty. In scene 4 Fred returns home to find his wife asleep in bed. These two scenes introduce a discrepancy between Renee's words and actions. In combination with the way Fred and Renee interact in scene 2, the discrepancy enables the spectator to group these actions together and call them a complicating action, the next stage of the canonical story format. The complicating action can be called 'unhappy marriage', with the probability of infidelity on Renee's part. The spectator's hypothesis of infidelity is a near-exclusive hypothesis – one with only a few alternatives – and is generated on the basis of Renee's absence from the house in scene 3 (a flaunted, focused gap in the film's fabula). The infidelity hypothesis is the most probable, but because the narration is restricted to Fred's perspective, the spectator does not gain any more information than Fred possesses in order to confirm or disconfirm this hypothesis.

Scene 5, the next morning. Renee picks up the newspaper outside, and discovers a videotape on the steps, with no addresser, addressee, or message. After watching the tape, which shows the outside of their house plus a closer shot of the front door, the Madisons are understandably perplexed, and Renee generates the weak, improbable hypothesis that an estate agent may have made the tape. This scene again presents another flaunted, focused gap in the fabula (which can be formulated into the following question: Who made the tape?), and its only link to the previous scenes is a continuity of characters and settings. There is no narrative continuity between this scene and the film's previous scenes. But the narration does seem to establish an internal norm, whereby it selects very specific portions of the fabula to show – namely, actions and events performed early in the morning or late at night.

Scene 6. Renee and Fred in bed at night (the film therefore continues to follow the internal norm of only showing actions performed in the morning or at night). We see several of Fred's memory images – of him at the Luna lounge playing his sax, and seeing Renee at the club leave with another man (we later find out that he is Andy). Fred and Renee then make love, and afterwards Fred recounts a dream he had the previous night. We then cut to several of the dream images: Fred looking around the house at night, hearing Renee call out to him, and a shot of Renee in bed being frightened by a rapidly approaching, off-screen agent. The spectator shares this agent's vision as he approaches Renee, but we do not see who it is. Renee looks into the camera and screams (her look into the camera makes the narration mildly self-conscious). Fred is then shown waking up, and looking at Renee. But another face is superimposed upon her (we later find out that it belongs to the 'mystery man').

In this scene the narration continues to be restricted and deep, and seems communicative, as we gain access to Fred's memory and dream images. But the status of the memory images is ambiguous. To make sense of these images, we can generate the probable hypothesis that they refer to a fabula event that took place before the film begins, and that Fred is generating these images to fill in the gap in scene 3. We can paraphrase these images in the following way: 'Last night Renee was probably with the guy who accompanied her to the Luna lounge on a previous occasion.'

The dream images are also ambiguous. Above we noted that the narration in this scene is restricted and deep, and *appears* to be communicative. But a close analysis of later scenes in the film makes the film analyst realize that the narration in this scene is in fact being very uncommunicative, although its uncommunicative status is disguised. At this stage in the film, we are used to a communicative narration, with flaunted gaps. But in the dream sequence, we (or, at least, the film analyst) retrospectively realize that the narration contains suppressed gaps and is uncommunicative. This is why later scenes in the film jolt us.

Furthermore, Fred does not question Renee about her whereabouts the previous evening (although in the script he does[3]). He only mentions the dream he had the previous night. Therefore, the link between this scene and previous scenes is only temporal, rather than causal (although the memory images of the club do at least refer us back to the location of scene 3). Due to this lack of causal cues, the spectator tries to generate weak hypotheses to connect the mystery narrative (who is Dick Laurent?) to the romance narrative (perhaps the guy in the club is Dick Laurent, etc.).

Other events in this scene are even more vague. As Renee and Fred make love, the screen suddenly turns white for a moment (a white fade) and the action is slowed down. Although these make the narration self-conscious (both devices challenge the conventions of standard speed and black fades), it is unclear what these devices are meant to cue, other than the director's intervention (thereby defining the *mise en scène* as mannerist; see Chapter 3). Furthermore, the moment in which Fred wakes up and sees the mystery man's face superimposed upon Renee's face still constitute part of Fred's dream he had the previous evening. In other words, the scene ends inside Fred's dream; the narration does not return to the image of Fred in bed narrating the dream. But one thing at least is clear from this scene: Renee and Fred make love dispassionately, which strengthens the hypothesis that their marriage is in crisis.

Scene 7: the following morning. Renee finds another videotape on the steps. But this one shows more than the previous tape by filming inside the house, and ending on Fred and Renee asleep in bed. Renee then calls the police. The second videotape adds to the 'complicating action' chunk of the by now strained canonical story format.

In scene 8, two detectives watch the second videotape, and look around the house for possible signs of a break-in. Information is planted in the dialogue to facilitate the spectator's hypothesis-generating process. Fred tells the detectives he hates video cameras, because he likes to remember things his own way, not necessarily the way they happen. Many critics who reviewed *Lost Highway* saw this line as a nodal point on which to focus the previous scenes, as a key to the film's meaning – namely, many of the narration's twists can be motivated psychologically, as Fred's distorted view of events. The spectator also has the opportunity to test out this reading of the film in the next scene.

Scene 9: party at Andy's house, late at night. (Andy was shown previously in Fred's memory images – in scene 6 – of Renee and Andy leaving the Luna lounge while Fred plays his sax.) The canonical story format is challenged, and begins to break down in this scene. In the previous scene, Fred and Renee did not talk about going to a party at Andy's house. If they had done so, it would have strengthened the causal relation between the scenes. More radically, Fred is shown drinking two whiskies and then talking to 'the mystery man' (Robert Blake), whose face we have already seen superimposed over Renee's face in Fred's dream (recounted in scene 6). The mystery man says to Fred that they have met before (although Fred does not remember), and then defies Newtonian space–time physics by suggesting that he is in Fred's house at that very moment (that is, is in two places at once). The mystery man 'confirms' this by persuading Fred to phone his home, where indeed the mystery man also answers! In terms of their meeting before, we tend to side with the mystery man; first because of the comment Fred made in scene 8 (he likes to remember things his own way, not necessarily the way they happened); and second, because the mystery man appeared in Fred's recounted dream in scene 6 (his face is superimposed over Renee's face).

Challenging one of the fundamental background assumptions of the canonical story format (a character cannot be in two places at once) begins to open up inferential possibilities, as we have to try to explain or motivate this fundamental discrepancy in the film's fabula. Is Fred simply delusional, and are we sharing his delusions? This assumes that the suyzhet continues to be highly communicative by conveying Fred's deep experiences.

When Fred asks Andy who the mystery man is, he responds that he is a friend of Dick Laurent, to which Fred replies: 'Dick Laurent is dead, isn't he?' Troubled by this news, Andy protests that Dick Laurent can't be dead. (He also says to Fred, 'I didn't think you knew Dick', which is an odd thing to say immediately after telling Fred that the mystery man is a friend of Dick Laurent.) The mention of Dick Laurent's name finally brings into sharper focus one of the gaps opened up in scene 1. Through its linear progression from scene to scene, the suyzhet is now finally beginning to refer back to gaps in previous scenes.

Scene 10: Fred and Renee in the car on the way back from Andy's party. Renee describes how she met Andy ('I met him at this place called Moke's . . . We became friends . . . He told me about a job . . .'.) This is one of the few fragments of exposition the spectator has received from the suyzhet, which means that it is impossible to slot it into a context and make more sense of it. Instead, it remains a fragment of exposition. But from Fred's reaction we understand that he dislikes Andy, possibly because he thinks Renee is having an affair with him.

Scene 11. At home, Fred checks around the house. He switches off the alarm, hears the telephone ring (but doesn't answer it), and he and Renee then prepare for bed. The events that follow refer back to Fred's recounted dream in scene 6. What is extraordinary is that parts of Fred's dream are now repeated and 'played out' as non-dream events. As Fred wanders around the house, we hear Renee call out Fred's name in exactly the same way she did in the dream. In a few images we also see Fred moving around the house in the same way he did in his dream. In the bathroom, he looks intensely at himself in the mirror. He then walks towards the camera, blocking our view entirely (a self-conscious moment of narration). In the next shot, the camera is positioned outside a door.

This scene challenges the canonical story format further, since it distorts the notion of linear progression (unless we read the dream as a premonition). At the end of the scene, the suyzhet is also uncommunicative, because it creates a gap in the fabula as the camera is positioned outside a closed door. But on the basis of a shot in Fred's dream – of an unseen agent attacking Renee in bed, together with the hypothesis that Renee is having an affair – we can generate a near-exclusive, probable hypothesis that Fred is attacking Renee.

This hypothesis is confirmed in scene 12. Fred finds a third videotape on the doorstep, plays it, and sees, in addition to the initial footage on the second tape, a series of shots depicting him murdering and dismembering Renee. He acknowledges the video camera filming him, by looking directly into it (making the narration self-conscious). But for Fred watching the tape, the images are horrifying, and in desperation he calls out to Renee. He is suddenly punched in the face by one of the detectives who visited the house in scene 8. There is a flaunted ellipsis in the fabula at this moment in the film, as Fred is now being questioned about Renee's murder (scene 13). The syuzhet is both communicative and uncommunicative, since it shows us (via the video camera images) Fred murdering Renee, but it is uncommunicative in supplying information about who recorded the videotapes, who Dick Laurent is, the mystery man's ability to be in two places at once, and the identity between Fred's recounted dream and Renee's murder the following evening. More generally, the film is marked by a lack of synchronization between its fabula and unfolding syuzhet.

Retrospectively, we can now re-evaluate the film so far as a detective film, which Bordwell (1985: 64) defines as having the following characteristics: a crime (cause of crime, commission of crime, concealment of crime, discovery of crime) and investigation (beginning of investigation, phases of investigation, elucidation of crime). We can characterize the film as enacting a crime, with emphasis on its concealment and discovery, with a very condensed investigation (at this stage consisting of identification of criminal and consequences of identification). We hypothesize that Fred is the causal agent, motivated by jealousy, who carried out the murder soon after Andy's party.

The policeman throws his punch directly at the camera, suggesting the syuzhet's continued alignment with Fred. It also makes the narration self-conscious, not only because the action is directed at the camera, but also because it reminds a cine-literate spectator of similar moments in Hitchcock's films – most notably, *Strangers on a Train* and *North by Northwest*, where punches are similarly directed at the camera. In another Hitchcockian moment, Fred's trial is not shown, but is reduced to the voiceover of the judge pronouncing sentence, as Fred is led to his cell. This goes beyond Hitchcock's rapid depiction of Margot Wendice's trial in *Dial M for Murder*. (In *Lost Highway*, a scene taking place in the courtroom is in the script, but has been omitted from the final cut.)

There follows a quick series of scenes (sometimes consisting of three or four shots) as Fred is taken to his cell (scene 14), which is intercut with video images of Renee's murder (coded as Fred's memory images). Scene 15 continues with this theme, as Fred tries to figure out what is happening to him. In scene 16 he collapses in the prison courtyard, complaining of a headache. In scene 17 the prison doctor forces him to swallow some sleeping pills, and in scene 18, he has a vision of an exploding cabin in the desert, although the explosion is shown backwards (making the narration self-conscious). The mystery man then comes out of and goes back into the cabin. The iconography reminds the cine-literate spectator of the exploding beach house at the end of *Kiss Me Deadly* (Robert Aldrich, 1955) – a film that also begins with a shot from a camera attached to the front of a car travelling very fast along a highway at night. During these scenes in the prison, it becomes evident that Fred is not a rational, goal-driven agent who causally motivates narrative events, since he is unable to remember or explain his actions. But his state of mind motivates the lack of synchronization between the fabula and syuzhet.

The events in the second half of scene 18 and in the following scenes completely defy and undermine the canonical story format. Scene 18 ends on the following shots:

- Fred's cell; there is a sudden flash of bright light, and light bulb in his cell goes dim (perhaps representing the effects of an electrocution on the rest of the prison);
- the highway at night, repeating the image of the credit sequence; but this time, the car stops in front of a young man (whom we later find out is Pete Dayton);
- cut in closer to Pete, with a superimposed shot of his girlfriend, Sheila, and Pete's parents; Sheila is screaming Pete's name;
- big close-up of Pete's eyes, superimposed over an image of the light in Fred's prison cell;
- Fred frantically rocking from side to side in his prison cell, screaming and covered in blood (this image seems to be strongly influenced by Francis Bacon's portraits, to the extent that it can be read as a filmic equivalent to Bacon's still images);
- shot of the prison ceiling; the camera pans down to Fred;
- cut to an image of what looks like an open wound, and the camera moves towards it.

Working along the lines of a surreal logic, the syuzhet presents a series of fragmented fabula events, which retrospectively we infer signifies Fred's transformation into Pete. (The version of this event in the script is more explicit about the transformation.)

Scenes 19–25 depict a prison guard discovering Pete in Fred's cell, Pete's identification, his release, and his home and work life. It is as if the film has 'started again' or, more accurately, we seem to be watching the second half of another film, because the syuzhet has identified Pete as the film's main protagonist, and has introduced a new setting and additional characters. This sudden jolt in the film's fabula is caused by the fact that the previous protagonist, to whom we were given privileged access, and from whom the camera rarely departed, has suddenly and inextricably disappeared from the fabula.

This jolt is far more radical than superficially similar scenes in other films – such as the murder in *Psycho* of Marion Crane, the film's primary protagonist up to that point. In *Psycho*, the transfer from Marion to Norman takes place within a stable fabula. In *Lost Highway*, the fabula has been severely disrupted, creating a flaunted but diffuse permanent gap that is never filled in. But to attempt to fill in this gap, the spectator needs to generate the two mutually exclusive hypotheses: Is Pete the same person as Fred? That is, are two actors playing the same character? Or are the two actors playing two different characters? However, the syuzhet does not contain sufficient cues to enable us to choose one hypothesis over the other.

After the spectacular transfer of agency from Fred to Pete, we start to question the communicative status of the syuzhet. It seems to hide more than it shows. As we continue to watch the film unfold, the unresolved issues remain, because the film does not address or even acknowledge them – that is, until scene 24, when Pete's girlfriend, Sheila, mentions to Pete that he has been acting strangely since 'the events' of the previous evening. Also, the syuzhet continues to follow the internal norm establish at the beginning of the film – to depict events taking place early in the morning or late at night. In scene 25 Pete returns to work (as a mechanic), and in scene 26 he repairs the car of a gangster, Mr Eddy. The scene ends with Mr Eddy driving away from the garage where Pete works, and two cops who are following Pete identify Mr Eddy as Dick Laurent. One of the gaps presented in the fabula at the beginning of the film (who is Dick Laurent?) is now brought into clearer focus, although it raises another question: Why is Mr Eddy also called Dick Laurent? From this moment onwards, the suyzhet makes additional and more frequent references to the first part of the film, enabling the spectator to focus other gaps and refine hypotheses.

At the beginning of scene 27, Pete looks at himself in the mirror in the same way as Fred looked at himself just before he murdered Renee. But in this part of the film, Pete takes Sheila out on a date.

Scene 28. At work the following morning, Pete hears sax music on the radio – identical to the music Fred played at the Luna lounge. The music distresses Pete, and he switches it off. A few moments later, he meets Mr Eddy's girlfriend, Alice, played by Patricia Arquette, who also played Fred's wife, Renee. But, as Renee, Arquette looked vampish; as Alice, she conforms to the stereotype of the blonde femme fatale. Hypotheses we generated when Fred transformed into Pete recur here, but inverted. Now we need to ask: Are Renee and Alice the same character in disguise (because they are played by the same actress)? Or is Patricia Arquette playing two characters?

Scenes 29–32 depict the affair that Pete develops with Alice. In scene 33, after Alice has had to break off a date with Pete, we see Pete in his room, experiencing hallucinations and hearing strange sounds. The syuzhet is restricted, deep, and communicative because the spectator directly shares these experiences (the camera goes out of focus, we see Pete's hallucinations of Alice, and so on). In scene 34 Pete decides to go and see Sheila, and in scene 35, Pete's parents talk to him. They know what happened to him, but refuse to tell him everything. They tell him that he came home with Sheila and 'a man', but say no more. This scene is interrupted by a montage sequence repeating the shot, in scene 18, of Pete's parents and Sheila screaming, although this time it is not superimposed over an image of Pete. This is followed by a shot of the open wound, and a video image of Renee's mutilated body. These shots are coded as Pete's memory images, whereas previously they were coded as Fred's.

In following scenes, Mr Eddy threatens Pete, and Alice devises a plan whereby she and Pete will rob Andy and run away together. In scene 39 Alice tells Pete how she met Mr Eddy. She uses the same line that Renee used to describe to Fred (scene 10) how she met Andy ('I met him at this place called Moke's . . . We became friends . . . He told me about a job . . .'.)

Scene 40. Pete breaks up with Sheila, and then takes a phone call from Mr Eddy–Dick Laurent and the mystery man (confirming Andy's comment in scene 9 that the mystery man is a friend of Dick Laurent). When the mystery man talks to Pete, he uses the same phrases as he did in scene 9, when speaking to Fred at Andy's party ('We've met before, haven't we?' etc.). He then indirectly threatens Pete.

In scene 41, Pete carries out Alice's plan to rob Andy, but in the process Andy is killed. Pete finds at Andy's house a photo of Mr Eddy, Renee, Alice, and Andy standing together. Pete asks Alice 'Are both of them you?', echoing a hypothesis the spectator generates when first seeing Alice in scene 29. Pete then goes upstairs to clean up, but the corridor in Andy's house looks like a hotel corridor. Furthermore, we see flashes of light in the corridor, as we did in Fred's prison cell.

In scene 42 Pete and Alice drive to the desert to sell Andy's valuables to the mystery man at his cabin. Shots of the highway at night, and the shot of the burning cabin are repeated. In scene 43, Alice and Pete make love in the desert. Alice then goes inside the cabin, and Pete gets up. However, he has now inexplicably transformed back into Fred. But before we have time to adjust to Fred's sudden return to the fabula, the syuzhet presents a series of unusual shots and scenes. Fred looks into his car and sees the mystery man inside, staring back. We then hear the mystery man's voice off-screen, and he suddenly appears in the entrance of his cabin. He then goes inside the cabin in the same way he did in Fred's memory image in scene 18. Fred enters the cabin where he sees the mystery man, but no Alice. Fred asks him where Alice is, and he replies that her name is Renee. Despite the photograph in Andy's apartment, Renee and Alice may be the same person (although this still does not explain her disappearance after entering the cabin). The mystery man then confronts Fred about his name, and begins to film him using a video camera. As Fred runs out of the cabin into his car, several of the shots are from the mystery man's perspective filmed through the video camera, and the resulting images are the same as the three tapes sent to the Madison's home. We can now fill in one of the gaps generated in the first part of the film, for we have conclusive evidence that the mystery man made the videotapes. Moreover, the hypotheses about the relation between Alice and Renee, and Fred and Pete, are brought into focus, but they are not resolved, for the 'solutions' the syuzhet present are highly improbable.

Scene 44. Fred drives along the highway, and shots of the highway at night are repeated. Scene 45 takes place at the Lost Highway motel. Fred wanders along the corridors in the same way Pete did in Andy's house. Fred enters an empty room, while Renee and Dick Laurent make love in another room. Another gap in the fabula is filled in, as we realize that Renee is having an affair with Dick Laurent, not Andy. (Andy therefore presents the spectator with a false lead.) In scene 46, Renee leaves the hotel and Fred knocks out Dick Laurent, watched by the mystery man. In scene 47 Fred takes Laurent to the desert where he kills him, with the help of the mystery man. In fact, the mystery man suddenly appears just at the right moment, to hand Fred a knife. The mystery man then shoots Laurent, but a few moments later he suddenly disappears, leaving Fred with the gun in his hand.

In an attempt to make sense of what is happening in these scenes, we can return to the opening scenes, when we generated the hypothesis that Renee may be having an affair. We now see that Fred has followed her to the Lost Highway motel, and discovers that she is having an affair with Dick Laurent, whom Fred subsequently kills. The mystery man and Alice now seem to be figments of Fred's imagination. However, if we accept this, then it generates more questions and additional gaps in the syuzhet, such as: Who made the three video tapes?

Scene 48. The police are at Andy's house. The two detectives who questioned Fred look at the photo – but she is missing, strengthening the hypothesis that Alice is a figment of Fred's imagination. The two detectives realize that Pete's prints are all over the place, so they head towards Fred's house. For this scene, then, the film has 'flipped back' to the Pete side of the fabula, but has erased Alice from it. The police have generated the hypothesis that Pete/Fred has murdered Andy, possibly because Fred thought that Andy was having an affair with Renee. In terms of the film's fabula, perhaps Fred followed Renee to Andy's place first, killed Andy, and then followed her to the

Lost Highway motel, where he subsequently kills Dick Laurent. At some point in the fabula, he also kills Renee. (Obviously, in this reconstruction of fabula events, he does not kill her after going to Andy's party, because Andy is already dead.)

Scene 49. Outside Fred's house. Fred has just returned from the desert, and presses the intercom and leaves the message 'Dick Laurent is dead.' The two cops then turn up, and give chase. Scene 50: the film ends with the police chasing Fred as he continues to drive along the highway at night. He appears to undergo another transformation, but we are left with an image of the highway at night.

The gap opened up in scene 1 is now filled – it is Fred who rings his own doorbell and who leaves the message that Laurent is dead! The off-screen sounds of screeching tyres and the police siren are similarly repeated, but now as on-screen sounds. The final scenes fill in most of the gaps the syuzhet has generated, but they do not lead to a resolution, because the 'answers' they present pose additional questions since they are improbable answers.

From this cognitive reading of *Lost Highway*, we can discern several irresolvable ambiguities and inconsistencies. First, concerning character stability: in scene 9, at Andy's party, the mystery man is in two places at once. Fred is also in two places at once: in scene 1, he is inside his own house receiving the message on the intercom that 'Dick Laurent is dead' and in scene 49, which returns to scene 1, he is outside his house delivering the message. Other instabilities of character include Fred's transformation into Pete at the end of scene 18, and his transformation back again in scene 43; in scene 12 it appears that Renee is murdered, but in scene 28 she seems to return to the film's fabula. The spectator needs to ask whether Fred and Pete are the same character played by two different actors, or whether they are different characters. Are Renee and Alice two different characters played by the same actress, or the same character in disguise? And why is Mr Eddy also called Dick Laurent? Other irresolvable ambiguities include: in scene 6, in Fred's dream images, he sees the mystery man's face superimposed over Renee's face; but in scene 9, when the mystery man introduces himself, Fred cannot remember meeting him before. Scene 35 repeats the video images of Renee's murder, and a shot of the open wound; when they first appeared in scenes 15 and 18 (respectively) , they were coded as Fred's memories, but now they are coded as Pete's memories. Furthermore, the photo in Andy's apartment is shown in scene 41 and repeated in scene 48, but Alice is missing when the photo is shown again. Finally, there are ambiguities concerning the linear, temporal ordering of events: the events in scene 6 (Fred's recounted dream) are repeated (as non-dream events) in scene 11; and Fred's visions in scene 18, of an the exploding cabin from which the mystery man appears and disappears, are repeated in scenes 42 and 43, although they are not coded as Fred's visions.

But how can Fred's dreams and visions so accurately predict forthcoming events – unless those events have already happened? This suggests that the narrative of *Lost Highway* is organized like a loop – or better, a Möbius strip – rather than linearly. If this is the case, then scene 18, in Fred's prison cell, represents the twist in the Möbius strip, the twist where the topside is transferred to the underside. Scenes 1 and 49 are the moments where the two edges of the strip are connected together, with Fred represented outside his house on one side, and inside the house on the other. Moreover, to travel around the entire length of the strip, one needs to go around it twice – first on one side (from the intercom message to Fred's transformation in his cell), then on the other side (from Pete being released from prison to his transformation back into Fred), before we are returned to the moment where the two sides are joined (Fred conveying the intercom message to himself). The metaphor of the Möbius strip appears to accurately represent the structure of *Lost Highway*.

It is important to remember when discussing such ambiguous moments that our aim is not to disambiguate them, for this is a reductionist move that attempts to explain them away. Instead, we should attempt to explain how the ambiguities are produced, and what effects they achieve. These scenes contain either too few cues, or too many cues that contradict one another; or there are too many flaunted and suppressed gaps; or maybe the cue is a permanent gap. All these cues may lead the spectator to generate non-exclusive, diffuse hypotheses that are not brought into focus, or are 'resolved' in an improbable manner. Lynch's films are open to analysis as long as we do not try to reduce these ambiguous moments to a rational logic, but recognize that a non-rational but meaningful energy governs them. *Lost Highway* also prevents spectators from automatically applying schemata to it, since it goes beyond the common-sense, rational logic embedded in these schemata; instead, spectators become aware of the schemata's conventions, and work hard to apply them in new and unforeseen ways (spectators unwilling to do this stop watching the film).

## 6.4. Theory: *Narrative Comprehension and Film*

David Bordwell's *Narration in the Fiction Film* pioneered the cognitive theory of film, which flourished in the 1990s with books such as Joseph Anderson's *The Reality of Illusion* (1996), Edward Branigan's *Narrative Comprehension and Film* (1992), Gregory Currie's *Image and Mind* (1995), Torben Grodal's *Moving Pictures* (1997), Carl Plantinga and Greg Smith's (eds) *Passionate Views* (1999), Murray Smith's *Engaging Characters* (1995) and Ed Tan's *Emotion and the Structure of Narrative Film* (1996). These authors acknowledge the originality of Bordwell's book, and then proceed to refine the ideas articulated there, either by exploring underdeveloped areas (the role of emotions in cognition, how genres determine comprehension, the different levels on which spectators engage characters, the role of imagination and intentionality in comprehending fiction films), or re-establish cognitive film theory on a deeper foundation (such as ecology, biology, or neuroscience).

One frequent criticism emerges from these authors: Bordwell is an 'atheistic' narratologist because he does not recognize the role of an external 'master of ceremonies' controlling the events in the fabula. In other words, he does not posit the existence of external narrative agents (external to the fabula). He asks: 'must we go beyond the process of narration to locate an entity which is its source?' (Bordwell 1985: 61–2) and answers: 'To give every film a narrator or implied author is to indulge in an anthropomorphic fiction. ... [This strategy takes] the process of narration to be grounded in the classic communication diagram: a message is passed from sender to receiver' (p. 62). In place of this communication model, Bordwell argues that narration 'presupposes a perceiver, but not any sender, of a message' (p. 62). Branigan's cognitive model of narration presupposes both a sender and receiver of a film – in fact several senders and receivers.

Branigan draws upon concepts from cognitive science, narratology, and linguistics to develop his theory of film narrative and narration – more specifically, a theory of a story world's space, time, causality, of point of view, levels of narration, the relation between subjective and objective narration, and the relation between fiction and narrative. We shall not give a complete overview of Branigan's theory, but will instead focus on its most fundamental concepts and unique methodology. Like Bordwell, Branigan employs the concept of schema to explain the role of narrative in organizing the spectator's experience of a film. Moreover, Branigan does not represent the narrative schema as a linear list, as Bordwell does when writing about the canonical story format. Instead, Branigan develops a more open and dynamic model, one organized as a hexagon with the main narrative actions (exposition, complicating action, and so on) represented at the points of the hexagon, and linked together by connecting lines (Branigan 1992: 17). This model captures the complexity of narrative more than a linear model because it describes the recursive nature of narrative: 'Narrative is a recursive organization of data; that is, its components may be embedded successively at various micro- and macro-levels of action' (p. 18). The narration conveys these narrative events to spectators, and the uniqueness of Branigan's theory and methodology lies in the complex model of narration he develops in Chapters 3 and 4 of *Narrative Comprehension and Film*.

While chapter 3 outlines disparities and hierarchies of knowledge conveyed by film narration (concepts that are similar to Bordwell's concepts of the range, depth, and communicativeness of the narration), it is in chapter 4 that he develops a systematic theory and methodology of film narration. This theory is based on eight levels of narration, with a 'sender' and 'receiver' on each level (see diagram on p. 87 of *Narrative Comprehension and Film*). Branigan remains neutral on the controversial issue of whether we can describe narration as a form of communication (p. 107–10), but it is clear that he goes beyond Bordwell by theorizing the role of narrators in films.

Branigan defines narration as 'the overall regulation and distribution of knowledge which determines how and when the spectator acquires knowledge [of narrative events]' (Branigan 1992: 76). Whereas to study narrative is to find out *what* happens in a film, to study narration is to find out *how* spectators acquire knowledge of the narrative. The film agent is a crucial component in this process of knowledge acquisition.

For Branigan, a theory of film agents requires a fundamental distinction between historical authors, implied authors, narrators, characters, and focalizers. For the purposes of this section, we shall only focus on the latter three, since they are the most relevant in terms of methodology and textual analysis. Spectators comprehend characters as agents who exist on the level of narrative; the character is therefore an agent who directly experiences narrative events and who acts and is acted upon in the narrative world. A character whose experiences of the narrative world are then conveyed to spectators become focalizers. Narrators, on the other hand, do not exist in the narrative; they exist outside it on the level of narration. This means they have the ability to influence the shape and direction of the narrative.

One of the most important contributions Branigan makes to the study of film narration is his rigorous theory of focalization in film:

> Focalization (reflection) involves a character neither speaking (narrating, reporting, communicating) nor acting (focusing, focused by), but rather actually experiencing something through seeing or hearing it. Focalization also extends to more complex experiencing of objects: thinking, remembering, interpreting, wondering, fearing, believing, desiring, understanding, feeling guilt.
>
> (p. 101)

Branigan therefore distinguishes two types of focalization, each representing a different level of a character's experiences: external focalization, which represents a character's visual and aural awareness of narrative events (the spectator sees what the character sees, but not from the character's position in the narrative; the spectator shares the character's attention, rather than their experience); and internal focalization, which represents a character's private and subjective experiences, ranging from simple perception (optical vantage point) to deeper thoughts (dreams, hallucinations, memories).

The narrator is the third agent in film. For Branigan, a narrator by definition does not exist in the narrative world, but on the level of narration. The narrator is an omniscient 'master of ceremonies' who does not see anything from a perspective within the narrative. Although the narrator is absent from the narrative, its presence is felt on the level of narration. For example, elements of the film that spectators cannot attribute to characters attest to the narrator's existence, including unmotivated camera movements (not motivated by the movement of characters or objects), inter-titles, and foreshadowing effects. (In classical *mise en scène*, shot changes are usually motivated by character movement, character glances off-screen, or by off-screen sounds and voices.) If a character in the narrative does not motivate a technique, then the spectator attributes it to the external narrator. Classical narration is defined by its attempt to conceal the narrator's presence from the spectator, whereas modernist narration continually reveals the narrator's presence (by means of unmotivated cuts, camera movements, and so on).

To avoid confusion, we should note that a character can become a narrator in the narrative world, where we see the character narrating the events in the form of flashbacks (as in films such as *Double Indemnity* or *Sunset Boulevard*). But these character-narrators are still characters, and a narrator external to the narrative still narrates the film.

Finally, Branigan emphasizes that these film agents and the levels at which they operate are not immanent in the film, but constitute part of the spectator's narrative schema: 'Such concepts as "narrator," "character," and "implied author" (and perhaps even "camera") are then merely convenient labels used by the spectator in marking epistemological boundaries, or disparities, within an ensemble of knowledge; or rather, the labels become convenient in responding to narrative' (Branigan 1992: 85). We can go so far as to say that what exists on the movie screen is simply changing patterns of light and shade, from which the spectator then generates hypotheses to construct the film's fabula, including characters. It may sound strange to say that a character is simply a hypothesis generated by the spectator from a series of cues in the film, because characters seem so permanent. But as we have already seen, in *Lost Highway* the characters are not permanent, which prevents spectators from automatically applying their 'character' schema, making them aware of the schema's conventions.

From this brief outline, it should be evident that Branigan's theory of narration is more subtle than Bordwell's because Branigan makes more and finer distinctions. Moreover, Branigan does not use the same terminology as Bordwell. Branigan talks about 'diegesis' and 'narrative', rather than 'fabula' (although the terms are not equivalent); and 'levels of narration' rather than 'syuzhet' and 'cues', a difference that marks a fundamental philosophical difference between Bordwell and Branigan. 'The notion of levels of narration' Branigan writes, 'provides a way of escaping a simple structuralism as well as a strict empiricism, because comprehension is not made to depend upon a few basic surface units, or "cues," which may be endlessly combined in strings through addition and subtraction' (p. 112). For Branigan, schemata do not simply prime spectators to spot cues on the surface of a text. More fundamentally, they act as a cognitive frame or guiding procedure that enables the spectator to transform data and create perceptual boundaries. The basic information is present in the data, but spectators need to shape, transform, and segment it. A spectator can completely transform a 'text' by perceiving it on a different level. Moreover, the levels of narration that Branigan outlines are not mutually exclusive; spectators can interpret the data in the film on several levels simultaneously; in terms of agents of narration, the data, when interpreted as a shot, can be attributed to several agents at once. This philosophical principle should become clearer in the following two sections.

## 6.5. Method

From Branigan's theory of agents and levels of narration in chapter 4 of *Narrative Comprehension and Film* we can construct a typology of four types of shot:

1.  objective shots (not focused around the consciousness of any character within the film's diegesis [the film's narrative world]; instead, it is a shot motivated by an agent outside the film's diegesis – the narrator);
2.  externally focalized shots (shots focused, or focalized around a character's awareness of diegetic events, such as over the shoulder shots; they do not represent the character's experience, but their awareness);
3.  internally focalized shots (surface) – represent a character's visual experience of diegetic events, as in point of view (POV) shots (that is, optical POV shots; when we call a shot a POV shot in the following analysis, we mean an internally focalized shot (surface));
4.  internally focalized shots (depth) – represent a character's internal events, such as dreams and hallucinations.

From this typology, the analyst is able to label and identify any shot in a narrative film in terms of the agents who control it and the level(s) on which it operates.

## 6.6. Analysis

For the purposes of this section I shall limit myself to the first half of the film, concentrating on the distinctive characteristic of Branigan's theory and methodology – the various agents and levels of narration he outlines. The focus of the following analysis is therefore: What narrative agent (if any) motivates the selected images? And: What level of narration can they best be described as operating upon?

After the Madison's view the first video that has been sent to them (scene 5), the film cuts to the hallway leading up to the Madisons' bedroom. This hallway is draped by a distinctive red curtain (a characteristic feature of Lynch's films). What is the status of this shot? Is it simply a transitional shot between scenes? It seems to be a non-focalized shot – that is, a shot not controlled by any narrative agent in the film's diegesis, but controlled by an agent outside the diegesis – the narrator.

In scene 6 Fred's recounted dream consists of the following shots, which also raise intriguing questions in terms of agency and levels:

- We see Fred walking around the house and hear Renee calling out to him; we also hear Fred's voice-over recounting the dream. All of the recounted dream shots are therefore internally focalized (depth) shots (type 4).
- Image of fire (with exaggerated sound, rendering the fire uncanny). (Because this shot is part of the dream, it belongs to type 4; but within the dream, it is non-focalized (type 1).)
- Fred and voice of Renee.
- A puff of smoke rises from the stairway (as with the red curtain, smoke is another characteristic symbol in Lynch's films). This shot is coded as Fred's POV shot. In other words, within his recounted dream (level 4) we have a POV shot (level 3).
- Fred in hallway (there is an ellipsis, since he have moved location between cuts).
- Hallway. Again, this is a POV shot.
- Fred.
- Hallway and red curtain, and bedroom (coded as Fred's POV).

Here we have a repetition of the red curtain, but this time it is coded as Fred's POV. Whereas previously the shot could be read as a transitional shot, which means that it is non-focalized (objective, or belonging to the narrator), here Fred has now appropriated this image, as it is focalized around his vision *and* is part of his recounted dream.

With Fred still recounting or narrating the dream in voice over, the camera quickly moves towards Renee, and she screams. Fred then 'wakes up' – but this seems to be part of the dream. (This is the conclusion we reached in the 'Bordwellian' analysis of this scene.) In Branigan's terms, is this image of Fred waking up an internally focalized (depth) image (i.e. part of the recounted dream), or has Fred stopped recounting the dream? There are insufficient (or conflicting) data in the image to enable us to decide one way or the other. The voice-over has ended, and the film has returned to Fred and Renee in bed, the place where Fred began narrating the dream. This suggests that Fred has stopped narrating the dream. However, there is no continuity between this shot of Renee and Fred in bed with the shot of Fred beginning to narrate the dream. This is discontinuous because both of them are now asleep, and Fred is waking from the dream. He then sees the mystery man's face imposed over Renee's face. This means that he is not only narrating the dream to Renee but is also telling her that he woke up and did not recognize her. The film is inherently ambiguous about which description is correct. Furthermore, there are no other cues in the film indicating that Fred stops narrating the dream. If the second description is correct, it means that the dream remains open-ended – we don't know when and where it ends.

The second video (first shown in scene 7) also deserves closer scrutiny. As Renee and Fred watch the second video, Renee turns to Fred and calls his name. Fred looks at the TV screen. Cut to a shot of the hallway. This is a complex shot to describe. First, it is Fred's POV shot as represented in his dream. But another narrative agent has also appropriated it – this time the agent who has made the video (the mystery man). But as Fred watches this shot on screen, it becomes his POV shot again. He is therefore watching his POV shot within his dream, now being manifest in reality via the video. There are multiple layers of agency attached to this shot (as there are with many shots; however, here the presence of the various agents becomes apparent). Perhaps part of Fred's fear is that he feels someone has got inside his head and is now reproducing his dream on video. Cut to a close-up of Fred's eyes, and then cut back to the video image, now showing the red curtain, a shot used twice before, but this time it is attributable to the mystery man (or the mystery man appropriates it from Fred, who appropriated it from the narrator). The video then shows Renee and Fred in bed.

When Fred comments in the next scene that he does not own a video camera because he prefers to remember events his own way, not necessarily the way they happened, this comment seems (as we saw in the Bordwellian analysis of this scene) to be a nodal point on which to focus the previous scenes. Yet by looking at the previous scenes more closely, through the lens of Branigan's theory, we come to realize that the video images appropriate Fred's POV shots. In other words, there is no conflict between what Fred sees and remembers and what we see on video; yet Fred's comment serves to distinguish video images from his experience.

Later we can attribute the video images to the mystery man. The fluctuating attribution of agency to these shots gives us textual evidence to link the mystery man to Fred. Furthermore, we argued that the shot of the red curtain, when it is first seen, is a non-focalized shot (i.e. is attributable to the narrator); on its second appearance, Fred has appropriated it; on the third occasion, the mystery man appropriates it. We can use this description to link narrator to

Fred and the mystery man, and perhaps go even further and link the narrator with the historical director, Lynch. It is easy to make wild assertions (or hypotheses) about the relation between Fred, the mystery man, the narrator, and Lynch; what we need is textual evidence to support these hypotheses, so that we can attach or ground these assertions in the film itself.

In scene 11, Fred in the house after Andy's party, the shot of the red curtain is repeated for the fourth time, which could be the POV shot of an unseen agent, who then seems to confront Fred. Could it be the mystery man with his video camera recording what's going to happen in the house? (If so, then do we identify the narrator's–Lynch's camera with the mystery man's video camera?) Otherwise, it could be a non-focalized shot. Preparations for bed. Fred then looks at himself in the mirror in the same way he looked at the camera a moment ago. Renee then calls out, in the same way she did in Fred's dream. We then have a shot of the living room with two shadows (are they replacing the image of the blazing fire in Fred's dream?). Is this the mystery man following Fred with his video camera, ready to record what's going to happen next? Instead of finding out what happens next, the spectator is positioned outside a door. We then cut to the next morning, where Fred picks up the third videotape, which fills in the ellipsis of the previous scene. The dream can also be added to fill in this ellipsis, since we see Fred approaching Renee as she sleeps in bed.

This reanalysis of key scenes and shots from the first half of *Lost Highway* only begins to demonstrate Branigan's theory of agents and levels of film narration. But from this short analysis, its ability to make more and finer distinctions than Bordwell's theory make it a powerful tool, particularly in analysing moments of ambiguity, in more detail and with more subtlety. The spectator's hypotheses can be formulated more clearly, and exclusive hypotheses can be related to one another more precisely (by linking each to a particular agent and level of narration). Whereas Bordwell's theory offers a methodology that reads a film as a linear or horizontal string of cues that spectators try to identify, Branigan develops a methodology that reads a film both horizontally *and* vertically, which enables the analyst to recognize the complexity of a individual shot or scene. A notable example from *Lost Highway* is the shot of the hallway in the second video, which Fred is watching. Branigan's method of analysis not only revealed the complexity of this shot, but also supplied the tools to analyse it in detail.

## Endnotes

1   Noël Carroll similarly argues that: 'where we have a convincing cognitivist account, there is no point whatsoever in looking any further for a psychoanalytic account. ... For a psychoanalytic theory to reenter the debate, it must be

demonstrated that there is something about the data of which cognitivist (or organic) explanations can give no adequate account' (Carroll 1996b: 65). In this polemical statement, Carroll shifts the burden of proof to the psychoanalytic film theorists: they must explain why they use psychoanalysis as the starting point to theorize filmic phenomena.

2    See Bordwell (1985: 60–61) and Buckland (1995).

3    See Lynch and Gifford (1997: 11–12). At breakfast, Fred questions Renee (who is reading a book), after they have looked at the first videotape. This scene has been deleted and replaced with the single shot of the red curtain.

# 7 Realism in the photographic and digital image (*Jurassic Park* and *The Lost World*)

## Introduction

We currently see before our very eyes in contemporary Hollywood cinema a composite – a composite of the optical (or photographic) and the digital (or post-photographic) image. What is the ontological status (or 'mode of being') of this composite, that is, what is the status of its 'realism'? We shall attempt to untangle this complex issue in this chapter by reviewing the work of André Bazin, because he successfully identified the complex facets, aesthetics, and styles of realism in the cinema. We shall then apply Bazin to Spielberg's two films *Jurassic Park* (1993) and *The Lost World* (1997), focusing on their conformity to the aesthetics and style of realism as defined by Bazin. However, Bazin's theory only relates to the photographically produced image – that is, images based on optics, mechanics, and photochemistry. In the second half of this chapter we shall therefore update Bazin with the philosophy of modal logic – particularly its theory of possibility and possible worlds – to analyse the digital images in Spielberg's two films. We shall focus on the ontological status of the digitally produced dinosaurs – for they are not, of course, produced by means of optics, mechanics, and photochemistry, and so they cannot easily be analysed within the framework of Bazin's theory of realism without creating a paradox. By employing the philosophy of possible worlds we hope to overcome this paradox.

## 7.1. Theory: André Bazin on realism

In this section we shall consider Bazin's overlapping contributions to film history and film theory: specifically, his dialectical history of film (in which he identifies four stages of film's development); his identification of three styles of film-making (montage, editing (or *découpage*), and deep focus cinematography); and his identification of three facets of realism (ontological, dramatic, and perceptual).

## 7.1.1. The history of film style

Conventional film histories (such as Rotha 1930; Jacobs 1939; Sadoul 1949) chronicle technical achievements, and establish a canon of classic films from various national cinemas that manifest these achievements. In addition, a number of historians and film theorists interpret these technical achievements within a modernist framework, and valorize films that seem to them to exploit film's 'essential', or 'distinctive' aesthetic qualities.

These conventional film histories are organized according to a linear, organic model of birth–growth–maturity–decline. They propose that cinema's inherent capabilities as an artistic means of expression is to be found, not in its recording capacity, but in its formal innovations such as cross-cutting, high and low camera angles, scene dissection, and montage sequences. They viewed early cinema, based on the tableau format, as primitive – as naïve, simple, and unsophisticated. And they considered innovations in the early part of the twentieth century (breaking the tableau into shots, maintaining screen direction across cuts, and so on) to be moments of growth, which led to a stage of maturity in the 1920s where, they believed, cinema completed its stylistic development. Conventional film history is therefore constructed around the assumptions of linearity and essentialism, for these are the underlying principles of pioneer film-makers progressively searching for film's inherent capabilities which, when exploited, transform cinema into an art.

Conventional film historians and classical film theorists such as Rudolf Arnheim (1957) established an inverse relationship between recording capacity and art, for they assumed that cinema could only become a distinct art form by working against its photographic recording capacity. Conventional film history is therefore a history that perceives the growth of cinema in terms of its gradual marginalization of its recording capacity in favour of formal techniques that identify film as a distinct means of artistic expression. The coming of sound led to the decline of cinema, it is argued, because it emphasizes cinema's recording capacity. They believed that this decline was further exacerbated by the development in the late 1930s of deep-focus and long-take cinematography because these techniques return cinema to its primitive stage of development.

André Bazin questioned and contested this conventional history and theory of film. He accepted some of its premises – its essentialism – but challenged its linearity, and its definition of what is essentially filmic. For Bazin, film's inherent capabilities, or essence, is precisely its recording capacity, which he finds fully realized in the sound-track, and in long take and deep-focus techniques of the late 1930s and 1940s. Bazin replaced the modernist ontology of the day with a realist ontology.

In 'The Evolution of the Language of the Cinema', Bazin wrote a brief history of cinema up to 1950 and divided it, not only into silent film and sound film but, more crucially, into 'those directors who put their faith in the image and those who put their faith in reality' (1967b: 24). With this criterion in place, Bazin identified four stages in film's historical development:

1. Silent film's faith in the image, in which the formal (or 'plastic') dimensions of the image, plus montage, are exploited. The emphasis of this style of film-making is to be expressionistic, to impose symbolic and metaphorical meanings onto the content of the image, rather than faithfully reproducing the meaning of the content or maintaining spatial-temporal unity. Bazin mentioned parallel montage, accelerated montage, and Eisenstein's montage of attractions as typical formal devices of silent film's faith in the image.

2. Silent film's faith in reality, in which film's recording capacity is exploited: 'the image is evaluated not according to what it adds to reality but what it reveals of it' (p. 28). Although faith in the image is the dominant trend in silent cinema, Bazin argued that this second trend (represented by Stroheim, Murnau, and Flaherty) is just as important. By identifying these two opposing trends, Bazin challenged the linearity of conventional film history.

3. Development of editing (*découpage*) in sound film (1930-39): Bazin argued that the coming of sound (plus new story matter) created a synthesis between the two opposing styles in silent film-making. In particular, he emphasized the shift in silent film's faith in the image towards realism: 'It is understandable, as a matter of fact, that the sound image, far less flexible than the visual image, would carry montage in the direction of realism, increasingly eliminating both plastic expressionism and the symbolic relation between images' (p. 33). In place of silent film's reliance on montage, Bazin argued that sound film relies on editing, or *découpage*. The difference is that editing (unlike montage) is analytic, dramatic, and descriptive, that is, analyses and describes the filmed event according to its inner dramatic logic. Unlike montage, editing does not attempt to impose expressionistic meanings or distort the logic or spatio-temporal unity of an event; it serves simply to alter emphasis and viewpoint: '[In an edited scene,] changes of point of view provided by the camera would add nothing. They would present the reality a little more

forcefully, first by allowing a better view and then by putting the emphasis where it belongs' (p. 32). In other words, the editing is subordinated to 'the geography of the action or the shifting emphasis of dramatic interest' (p. 24). Moreover, silent film's faith in reality also changed, because one of the dominant characteristics of these edited sound shots is that they were usually in shallow focus.

4. Development of deep focus cinematography (or depth of field) in sound film (1940–50): deep focus cinematography stages several planes of action and keeps them all in focus in the same shot. For this reason, deep focus is usually combined with the long take and/or camera movement. Bazin argued that deep focus is not a passive recording of events, nor simply a return to silent film's faith in reality (as a number of conventional film historians such as George Sadoul argued). Instead, for Bazin, 'depth of field is . . . a dialectical step forward in the history of film language' (p. 35). By this he means that deep focus does not simply represent a linear development in film style, but is a synthesis of stages 2 and 3 of film history: in other words, deep focus *integrates* or *combines* editing into the unified space and time of the single shot. Bazin identified this new trend with Renoir, Wyler, Welles, and the Italian neorealists. In relation to Welles, he argued:

> Far from being . . . a return to the 'static shot' employed in the early days of cinema by Méliès, Zecca and Feuillade, or else some rediscovery of filmed theatre, Welles' sequence shot is a decisive stage in the evolution of film language, which after having passed through the montage of the silent period and the *découpage* of the talkies, is now tending to revert to the static shot, but by a dialectical progress which incorporates all the discoveries of *découpage* into he realism of the sequence shot.
>
> (Bazin 1991: 81–2)

From this dialectical history of film, Bazin established a typography of three styles of film-making: (1) montage (and the plastics of the image); (2) editing (*découpage*); and (3) deep focus. We shall return to this typology in section 7.2.

## 7.1.2. Three facets of realism

Bazin favours the techniques of deep focus and the long take because they maintain cinema's 'essential' or 'distinctive' characteristic, its realism, inherited from the photographic image's indexical link with reality, whereas montage breaks this indexical link (while *découpage* is a compromise between montage and deep focus). More specifically, Bazin identifies three facets of realism in the cinema: (1) an ontological realism; (2) a dramatic realism; and (3) a psychological realism (Bazin 1991: 80).

Ontological realism restores to the object and the decor their existential density, the weight of their presence. This is achieved by means of the photographic image's automatic, mechanical recording capacity, which takes a mold in light of reality: 'One might consider photography . . . as a molding, the taking of an impression, by the manipulation of light' (Bazin 1967a: 12). The photographic image does not diminish the ontological status of the events photographed because its recording capacity transfers reality to the image. We shall explore this type of realism in the following section (7.1.3).

Dramatic realism is achieved in the deep-focus, long-take shot because it refuses to separate several planes of action – the actor from the decor, the foreground from the background – since it respects the spatio-temporal unity of the scene.

Finally, the long-take, deep-focus shot achieves psychological realism by bringing the spectator back to the real conditions of perception, a perception that is never completely predetermined:

> (1) . . . depth of focus brings the spectator into a relation with the image closer to that which he enjoys with reality. Therefore it is correct to say that, independently of the contents of the image, its structure is more realistic;
>
> (2) [depth of focus] implies, consequently, both a more active mental attitude on the part of the spectator and a more positive contribution on his part to the action in progress. . . .
>
> (3) From the two preceding propositions, which belong to the realm of psychology, there follows a third which may be described as metaphysical. . . . montage by its very nature rules out ambiguity.
>
> (Bazin 1967b: 35–6)

Bazin immediately adds, however, that 'depth of focus reintroduced ambiguity into the structure of the image if not of necessity – Wyler's films are never ambiguous – at least as a possibility' (p. 36). Bazin's favourite example is depth of focus in *Citizen Kane*: '*Citizen Kane* is unthinkable shot in any other way than in depth. The uncertainty in which we find ourselves as the spiritual key or the interpretation we should put on the film is built into the very design of the image' (p. 36). In other words, the film's style imitates the film's theme.

## 7.1.3. Ontology and physical portrayal

Bazin's adherence to realism is clearly manifest in his famous essay 'Ontology of the Photographic Image' (Bazin 1967a). The essence of cinema for Bazin lies in its photographic capability, which mechanically (i.e. directly and automatically) records the light reflected from reality (i.e. the pro-filmic events, or subject matter in front of the camera) and fixes it on film. The light itself, rather than the human hand and mind, directly causes the formation of the photographic image. For Bazin, this automatic registration process results in an objective and impartial image of reality, for the image is identical to the reality that caused it (at least in terms of the light they reflect):

> In spite of any objections our critical spirit may offer, we are forced to accept as real the existence of the object reproduced, actually re-presented, set before us, that is to say, in time and space. Photography enjoys a certain advantage in virtue of this transference of reality from the thing to the reproduction.
>
> (Bazin 1967a: 13–14)

In sum, cinema is realistic because the photographic image produces an indexical imprint of reality: 'The photograph as such and the object in itself share a common being, after the fashion of a fingerprint' (p. 15).

As an aside, we need to note that the photograph can be viewed within two different ontological frameworks: 'essentialist realism' and 'phenomenalist naturalism'. Bazin's ontology of the photographic image is limited to 'phenomenalist naturalism', in which the photograph reproduces the singularity and contingency of the surface appearances of reality. By contrast, some photographs, such as Muybridge's multiple photographs and Marey's chronophotographs, represent more than the eye can see. That is, they decentre the eye, or improve upon it. They therefore conform to 'essentialist realism', since they represent dimensions of reality (the stages of a horse's gallop, for example) that the eye cannot see.

Bazin's definition of realism exclusively in terms of film's indexical imprint of reality aligns him to what Monroe Beardsley (1958: ch. 6) calls physical portrayal – to film's recording or documentation of the reality in front of the camera. This may work well for a theory of documentary film, but creates a problem when applied to fiction films. Documentaries are physical portrayals, epitomized in direct cinema, or what Bill Nichols calls observational documentary: 'An observational mode of representation allowed the film maker to record unobtrusively what people did when they were not explicitly addressing the camera . . . . But the observational mode limited the filmmaker to the present moment and required a disciplined detachment from the events themselves' (1989: 33). Practitioners of direct or observational cinema suggest that they transcribe truth and reality on screen – that is, record it directly. Like Bazin, they base their argument on the fact that film and camera record events mechanically and automatically.

But *all* movie cameras record events automatically by means of optics, mechanics, and photochemistry. When we watch *Citizen Kane*, we see the actor/director Orson Welles on a RKO set in 1940. The film is first and foremost a document about what a group of actors and technicians did in a studio on a certain day. The camera mechanically and automatically records

Welles in front of the camera, just as Frederick Wiseman – and other observational documentary film-makers – films what is in front of his camera.

The difference between *Citizen Kane* and observational documentaries is that *Citizen Kane* (as with all fiction films) attempts to negate or go beyond its direct, automatic, mechanical recording of reality, whereas observational documentaries emphasize the camera's direct recording of reality. To this end, they reduce a number of the fiction film's stages of film-making – the script, professional actors, sets, studio lighting, and staged, rehearsed events. In other words, fiction films negate their physical portrayal of reality in favour of presenting a fictional world. Yet, as Noël Carroll points out, Bazin focuses on physical portrayal even when writing about fiction films:

> Bazin's conception of photography ... seems to say that what is important about any photographic image – whether in a fictional context or otherwise – is what it re-presents, that is, documents. Yet what is literally re-presented or documented in a photographic fiction may be irrelevant to what the fiction represents. That is, when confronted with fiction, Bazin's theory implies strange results by ontologically misplacing, so to speak, the focus of our attention.
>
> (Carroll 1988a: 148)

In Beardsley's terms, fiction films can more readily be thought of as depictions or nominal portrayals. In fiction films, the photographic image is simply a means to an end. Depictions and nominal portrayals separate the photographic image from the reality that caused it. When we think of a photographic image as a depiction, we focus on it as a member of a class (the photograph of a particular person such as Orson Welles – the photograph as physical portrayal – also depicts the general term 'man'). A nominal portrayal 'represents a *particular* object, person, place, or event different from the one that gave rise to the image' (Carroll 1988a: 151). In this sense, in *Citizen Kane* Orson Welles nominally portrays Charles Foster Kane. More generally, Carroll writes that 'nominal portrayal is the basis of all fiction film' (p. 151). This is because the spectator needs to go beyond the particular physical portrayal and perceive or infer a particular fictional character.

Why, then, does Bazin focus obsessively on physical portrayal, even when discussing fiction films? He states his reasons in 'Ontology of the Photographic Image' (1967a): from the beginnings of civilization, humanity has attempted to cheat death. The ancient Egyptians attempted to preserve the human body through mummification. But it is only through the invention of photography, Bazin argues, that this desire is realized, for the photographic camera captures, freezes, and embalms reality, for the first time in the history of civilization.

## 7.1.4. Beyond Bazin: discursive theories of the 'impression of reality'

Contemporary film theorists replaced the notion of 'photographic realism' with the concept of the 'impression of reality', of which the work of Jean-Louis Baudry (1986), Daniel Dayan (1976), Stephen Heath (1981: 76–112), Colin MacCabe (1986), and Jean-Pierre Oudart (1990) is representative. Moreover, each develops his theory on a different level: Baudry on the level of the apparatus; Oudart, Dayan, and Heath on the level of the filmic text; and MacCabe within the filmic text. Here we shall briefly consider Heath's account of the theory of suture, and MacCabe's theory of realism, for comparison with Bazin.

Suture designates a process whereby the spectator is continually positioned and repositioned in an 'imaginary', as opposed to 'symbolic', relation to the image. (These terms are defined and discussed in Chapter 8.) Positioned in an imaginary relation to the image, the spectator enjoys a sense of mastery and pleasure, since he gains the impression of being an all-perceiving eye (analogous to the child at the mirror phase). The result of this imaginary positioning is that the spectator perceives the space of the image as unified and harmonious. For Heath, this position of imaginary plenitude and spatial unity constitutes the cinema's impression of reality. Realism is not, therefore, based on the image's relation to pro-filmic reality (as it is for Bazin), but on the cinema's ability to conceal from the spectator the symbolic dimension of the image (the image as signifier, as representing lack). Inevitably, the symbolic dimension of the image becomes apparent to the spectator when this illusion of all-seeingness is broken – most notably, when attention is drawn to off-screen space. The spectator's perception of spatial unity and harmony in the image is similarly broken. But a cut to this off-screen space realigns the spectator to an imaginary relation to the image (i.e. sutures the spectator back into the film), and restores to the image the sense of unity and harmony – at least until the symbolic dimension of the image becomes noticeable to the spectator once more. According to this theory, realism is nothing more than an effect of the successful positioning of the spectator into an imaginary relation to the image, a position which creates a sense that the film's space and diegesis is unified and harmonious.

In his theory of the realist narrative novel, Colin MacCabe set up a distinction between the discourse of characters (object language) and the discourse of the narrator (metalanguage). MacCabe establishes a hierarchy between object language and metalanguage, for the purpose of the metalanguage is to frame and fix the meaning of the object language. He then transposes this hierarchy to the cinema, and argues that in the classical realist film the discourse of characters is framed by the narrator. In other words, the narrator is privileged over the characters, and fixes the meaning and truth of what the characters do or say. MacCabe ascribes this hierarchy to classical realist texts because, he argues, 'classical realism ... involves the homogenization of different discourses by their relation to one dominant discourse – assured of its domination by the security and transparency of the image' (1986: 183).

## 7.2. Method

One of the practical consequences of Bazin's stylistic history of film is that we can identify which of the 'holy trinity' of film style a contemporary film alludes to, or quotes. Is the film's style dominated by the techniques of deep focus (with or without the long take), editing (*découpage*), and/or montage?

The identifying characteristics of deep focus are the following:

- The shot is dominated by multiple planes of action, all in focus, and is usually combined with long takes (shots of long duration) and camera movements; all of these techniques respect the unity of dramatic space and time, and decrease the need for montage or editing (since the long take, deep-focus shot incorporates editing in its structure).

The identifying characteristics of editing:

- It involves breaking the same space and action into fragments, showing each plane of action separately, and linking them via rules of continuity editing. For Bazin, editing is analytic, dramatic and descriptive, for it analyses and describes the dramatic events in a certain order and closeness but does not, Bazin believes, add meaning to those events, or deform their inner logic, as montage does. In the long take aesthetic, editing is used simply to link shots together; it does not function (as in editing) to analyse a unified space.

The identifying characteristics of montage:

- Like editing, montage involves the juxtaposition of shots, but for a different purpose: 'the creation of a sense or meaning not objectively contained in the images themselves but derived exclusively from their juxtaposition' (Bazin 1967b: 25). Montage does not attempt to create a unified space and time, but instead juxtaposes heterogeneous objects and events for the purpose of creating abstract, symbolic, or metaphorical meanings. Sergei Eisenstein used the term 'association' to name the symbolic meanings created by montage sequences. For Eisenstein, from the montage of two or more shots is created a chain of associations that do not exist in any of the individual shots. As an example, we shall look at a celebrated scene in Eisenstein's *Battleship Potemkin* (1925). After the Cossacks have massacred the people on the Odessa steps (the famous sequence) the response is that the *Potemkin* battleship fires on the headquarters of the military. This is followed by three shots of stone lions at the Alupka palace in the Crimea. The first shot depicts a lion lying down, the second depicts a lion seated, and the third a lion standing. The three shots of the lions create a montage unit. In terms of the content of each separate image, we simply have: a stone lion sleeping, a stone lion sitting, and a stone lion standing. Three concrete objects juxtaposed together. But what does it mean, and what effect does it create? First, due to the framing of the three separate lions, Eisenstein creates the impression that *the same* stone lion has moved from its sleeping position and has stood up. In terms of these three shots by themselves, Eisenstein has already created an abstract meaning that does not exist in each individual shot. The shots of the stone lions (the raw material), when taken in isolation, merely offer a representation of each lion. No shot shows a stone lion going through the motions of standing up – such an action is impossible anyway. But the juxtaposition of the shots creates the impression or the illusion of a stone lion being woken up. Eisenstein creates this impression purely and exclusively through the juxtaposition of the shots – montage. Above and beyond this illusionistic effect, this montage sequence can also mean – when viewed in the context of the previous scenes – that the Russian people (symbolized by the lion) are rising up against their oppressors.

Finally, in terms of discursive theories of the 'impression of reality', suture is a general process that, its adherents argued, operates on all levels of a film, although Oudart and Dayan in particular over-privileged the shot–reverse shot pattern of editing. In terms of MacCabe's hierarchy between object language and metalanguage, and the dominance of the latter (i.e. the discourse of the narrator) over the former (the discourse of characters), the narrator manifests his presence in various ways – by means of the camera, editing, or *mise en scène*. Sometimes the narrator is represented in the film and helps to fix the meaning of the characters' actions (as we shall see below, in a brief analysis of *The Truman Show*).

## 7.3. Analysis

Brian Henderson has noted that 'it has become a commonplace that modern film-makers fall between Eisenstein and Bazin, that they combine editing techniques and long takes in various, distinctive styles' (1976: 426). Henderson argues that in *One Plus One*, Godard 'erects a montage construction upon a series of long takes – in the aggregate a montage is created, though all of its ingredients, all the local areas of the film, are long takes' (p. 427).

But many other (and more popular) directors also combine the techniques of the long take and deep focus, editing, and montage. We shall analyse scenes from Spielberg's *Jurassic Park* and *The Lost World* in a moment. Bazin analyses an example from the film *Where No Vultures Fly* (Harry Watt, 1951) in a long footnote to his essay 'The Virtues and Limitations of Montage' (1967c). The primary aim of the example is to demonstrate the authenticity and realism 'inherent' in a shot that combines several planes of action. The film is about a young family who set up a game reserve in South Africa. In the scene discussed by Bazin, the young son of the family picks up a lion cub in the bush and takes it home. The lioness detects the child's scent and begins to follow him. The lioness and the child with the cub are filmed separately, and the shots are simply edited together. But as the child reaches home, the director abandons his montage of separate shots that has kept the protagonists apart and gives us instead parents, child, and lioness all in the same full shot. 'This single frame', writes Bazin, in 'which trickery is out of the question gives immediate and retroactive authenticity to the very banal montage that preceded it' (p. 49). In this particular example, the realism of the shot for Bazin is a matter of spatial unity, in which the child and the lioness clearly occupy the same diegetic space (more accurately, the shot conforms to dramatic realism). Indeed, Bazin concludes his footnote by writing: 'Realism here resides in the homogeneity of space' (p. 50). More specifically, the realism resides in the fact that this homogeneity of space is created optically.

Spielberg does not conform to one style of film-making identified above (montage, editing, or deep-focus), although he prefers editing. Nonetheless, he frequently constructs scenes using both editing and long takes, and occasionally deep-focus shots as well. The opening scene of *Jurassic Park* is typical. It begins with editing: the first six shots, which last a total of 33 seconds, are systematically organized into a shot–reverse shot pattern. Park wardens look off-screen and are intercut with shots of a crate containing a raptor. Shot 7 is the scene's establishing shot, and lasts 27 seconds. It contains extensive camera movement, a change in camera height, and intermittent moments of deep focus, particularly at the beginning, with lights in the extreme foreground, park wardens in the foreground and middle ground, and the crate in the background. Shot 9 is also a deep-focus shot with camera movement, although it lasts only six seconds. It consists of park wardens in the foreground and background, and the head game warden, Muldoon, in the middle ground. (In addition to the deep focus, the shot looks all the more 'Wellesian' because of the low camera angle.) The camera then tracks right to reveal the crate. In shots 1–6 the wardens and the crate are set in opposition via editing. In shot 7 they are united via deep focus in the same shot, and in shot 9 they are linked consecutively in the same shot via camera movement.

Another scene constructed using a mixture of editing, long takes, and deep focus takes place in Grant and Sattler's caravan during their dig in Montana. Hammond has flown in via helicopter and enters the caravan. He is followed by Grant, and then by Sattler. When Sattler enters (marking the beginning of the 50-second long take), Hammond is in the background (and there is additional space behind him), Grant is in the middle ground, and Sattler is in the foreground. Grant changes places with Sattler, as he introduces her to Hammond. All three characters then occupy the middle ground, before the shot ends and a conventional shot–reverse shot pattern begins.

The scene in the lab, where the tour group witnesses the birth of a raptor, also mixes aesthetic styles. The scene begins with a 44-second establishing shot, consisting of extensive camera movement, including the camera tracking back, which continually introduces new foreground space that creates a deep focus shot. This shot begins with a computer image of DNA and ends on the dinosaur eggs (the end result of that DNA). When the camera stops moving, the raptor eggs occupy the foreground, while six characters are carefully composed in the middle ground and background. The remainder of the scene is constructed using continuity editing, and consists of 22 additional shots lasting a total of 167 seconds. However, two of these shots qualify as moderately deep-focus: low-angle shots with five members of the group crouched around the hatching raptor egg. A robotic arm occupies the immediate foreground, the five characters occupy the foreground and middle ground, and background detail and movement is clearly visible.

One final sequence from *Jurassic Park* stands out in terms of its visual style: the scene towards the end of the film where Tim and Lex are chased by two raptors in the kitchen. In the opening establishing shot, the camera is placed at the back of the large kitchen, facing the entrance. Tim and Lex enter the kitchen (they are in very long shot, due to their distance from the camera) and run towards the camera, ending up in medium shot in the foreground with the door in the background (although it is not sharply in focus). The next action consists of one of the raptors looking through the window of the kitchen door. But rather than exploit the depth of this opening shot – or, more accurately, its unity of space – Spielberg decides to cut to a close-up of the window, and we see a raptor peering into the kitchen. There follows four shots in shot–reverse shot pattern, before a return to the deep establishing shot. After the two raptors open the kitchen door, the camera tracks from them in the background to the children hiding in the foreground. The raptors and children appear in the same shot, although not together; they are shown consecutively via camera movement, which maintains spatial unity but does not present the different planes simultaneously. Simultaneity is achieved in the shot in which one of the raptors sniffs the air. Initially, the raptor is shown on its own, in the background. But as the shot progresses, the camera tracks left to show the children hiding in the foreground, while maintaining the raptor in the background. Although the shot has considerable depth, and unites foreground and background, the focus shifts as the camera tracks left. As this sequence progresses, the simultaneous presentation of the foreground and background (occupied by children and raptors respectively) in the same shot increases, which increases the tension, suspense, and – most crucially for us here – dramatic realism of the sequence. This sequence has been skilfully choreographed to maximize the play between the foreground and background.

*The Lost World* contains similar scenes that mix styles. Shot 2 of the opening scene is a 52-second long take with extensive camera movement and moderate use of deep focus. The shot begins with the camera panning down from the sky to a beach. It then tracks right and stops when a yacht comes into view in the background. A crewman enters screen right in the middle ground carrying a bottle of champagne, and the camera tracks left to follow his movement. Almost immediately another crewman carrying a bottle of champagne enters screen right, this time in close-up in the foreground (only the bottle and his hands are visible). Therefore, within a few seconds several planes have been introduced, although they are not shown simultaneously, and are filmed using selective focus rather than deep focus. The camera continues to track left, covering the ground it tracked at the beginning of the shot, but this time it reveals a family on the beach. The remainder of the scene is constructed using editing.

A more obvious use of deep focus, combined with long take, occurs when Ian Malcolm visits Hammond at his home. While waiting in the hallway talking to Tim and Lex, Hammond's nephew, Peter Ludlow, enters. As he signs documents in the foreground, Malcolm, Tim, and Lex are shown in the background (and there is considerable space behind them as well). Malcolm then walks into the middle ground to talk to Ludlow, and in the background the children prepare to leave. As well as consisting of genuine deep focus and long take (of 73 seconds), the shot is positioned at a low angle, which reveals the ceiling.

In the scene in the large warehouse where Malcolm's team prepares its hasty departure, Spielberg employs another long take with carefully orchestrated planes of action. Shot 2 of this scene begins by tracking left, revealing the equipment in the extreme foreground and background, with Malcolm and Eddie in the middle ground, walking towards the entrance of the warehouse. When Ian and Eddie reach the entrance, they (and the camera) stop. Through the entrance we see Nick van Owen's van, in very long shot, reversing up into the warehouse. When he gets out of the van, he is in long shot, and the camera begins to track right again, to focus on the back doors of his van. He opens them, takes out two cases, walks towards the camera, and places them off screen on a table just below the camera. Van Owen is now in medium close up. The entire shot lasts 35 seconds.

One final shot worth mentioning appears when Ludlow's team arrives on Isla Sorna. Malcolm's team is positioned high on a ledge overlooking the wide open plane below, where Ludlow's team are catching dinosaurs. A 9 second deep focus tracking shot shows Malcolm's team in the foreground and Ludlow's in the extreme background.

Before moving on to the digital image, we shall briefly use Colin MacCabe's theory of realism to analyse contemporary films. This theory is particularly useful for highlighting the way the narrator in *The Truman Show* (Peter Weir, 1997) is depicted in the film's diegesis, and how he fixes the meaning of the characters. The actions and speech of Truman (as well as other characters), is framed and given meaning by the head of the TV channel, Christof. The spectator is placed in an omniscient position in relation to Truman (i.e. we occupy the place of the metalanguage, the framing discourse). We know that Truman's life is only a TV soap opera, but Truman doesn't know this. His knowledge is limited to what happens within the TV show, whereas the spectator is placed with Christof, who frames Truman's actions and speech. Christof also frames the actions and speech of other characters, who of course are also in on the illusion. At one point we see Truman's closest friend talkng to him, and we then cut to Christof feeding the lines to Truman's friend. Here the hierarchy between object language and metalanguage is clearly apparent.

But in other recent films we are placed with 'Truman', as it were. For example, in David Fincher's *The Game* (1997) we are always positioned within the game with Nicholas van Orton (played by Michael Douglas). He and the spectator do not know where the boundaries of the game end. In *The Truman Show*, by contrast, the spectator clearly experiences this boundary, and the film is about Truman becoming aware of this boundary, of quite literally coming up against the boundary of his world.

*Lost Highway*, analysed in Chapter 6, resembles *The Game* to the extent that the spectator is never privileged by a narrator or a metalanguage into knowing what is happening. But *Lost Highway* is more extreme because it has no stable character or narrator to centre the action and events (the film has characters and narrators, but they have a fluctuating identity). In MacCabe's now dated terminology, *Lost Highway* conforms to his definition of the subversive film, in which the narrative does not contain a unified metalanguage: '[in the subversive film] the narrative is not privileged in any way with regard to characters' discourses. The narrative does not produce for us the knowledge with which we can judge the truth of those discourses' (MacCabe 1985: 48).

Despite – or perhaps because of – his commitment to physical portrayal,

Bazin's theory of realism in the cinema is appropriate to our analysis of realism in the digital image. We shall therefore pursue his theory in the context of digital images.

## 7.4. Theory: digital images and modal logic

We shall now pursue and extend Bazin's theory of realism in the photographic image by considering the status of realism in the post-photographic (or digital) image. The question we want to focus on is: Can we explain the impact and popularity of *Jurassic Park* and *The Lost World* in terms of their 'realism' or, more specifically, their innovative digital effects that create photo-realistic and credible images of unobservable, nonexistent dinosaurs? To answer this question, we need to focus on the difference between the photographic and the digital image, and then introduce the modal theory of possible worlds as a way of explaining the realism of the previously non-observable dinosaurs.

The photograph, as a physical portrayal, is dependent upon the presence of a pre-existing real object, whose appearance is automatically reproduced by means of optics, mechanics, and photochemisty (or electronics, in the case of video). The photographic image is therefore indexically bound to the actual world. The photographic is an analogue of the real. However, the digital (or post-photographic) image is not determined or limited to the actual world in the same way. Whereas the photographic image is an analogue of the pre-existing real objects whose appearance it reproduces automatically, the digital image is produced by numerical digital codes, each of which is then realized on screen as a pixel, or point of light. The continuous lines, masses, and contours of the analogue are divided up into discontinuous, discrete fragments of information, or pixels, on a monitor. Lucia Santella Braga points out:

> Each pixel corresponds to numerical values that enable the computer to assign it a precise position in the two dimensional space of the screen, within a generally Cartesian co-ordinate system. To those coordinates are added chromatic coordinates. The numerical values [the digital code] transform each fragment into an entirely discontinuous and quantified element, distinct from the other elements, over which full control is exercised.
>
> (1997: 125)

The crucial phrase here is 'over which full control is exercised'. The 'film-maker' has the potential to transform each pixel into an entirely different value, for each pixel is defined in terms of a numerical matrix that can be modified and transformed by a mathematical algorithm. 'The result', writes Braga, 'is that the numerical image is under perpetual metamorphosis, oscillating between the image that is actualized on the screen and the virtual image or infinite set of potential images that can be calculated by the computer' (p. 126).

Practitioners of the special effects industry distinguish between invisible and visible special effects. Invisible special effects, which constitute up to 90 per cent of the work of the special effects industry, simulate events in the actual world that are too expensive or inconvenient to produce, such as the waves in James Cameron's *Titanic*. As their name implies, invisible special effects are not meant to be noticed (as special effects) by film spectators. Visible special effects, on the other hand, simulate events that are impossible in the actual world (but which are possible in an alternative world), such as the dinosaurs in *Jurassic Park* and *The Lost World*. The crucial aesthetic point in relation to the digital special effects in these two films in particular is that, while clearly visible, these effects attempt to hide behind an iconic appearance (or photographic credibility); that is, they are visible special effects masquerading as invisible effects. What we mean is that the digital images in *Jurassic Park* and *The Lost World* combine the aesthetics of both visible and invisible special effects, since they have the potential to replicate the realism and illusionism of the photographic image by conferring photographic credibility upon objects that do not exist in the actual world. What this implies is that, while the digital images of the dinosaurs are not produced optically, which means they are not real, observable events in the real world, they nonetheless create the impression that they are produced optically and that, therefore, the dinosaurs are pre-existing referents simply being photographed.

From this discussion we can begin to determine the motivation for the digital special effects in Spielberg's *Jurassic Park* and *The Lost World*: namely, to simulate the actuality of dinosaurs living in the present day. This actuality is of course an illusion – or, more accurately, what Richard Allen calls a sensory deception,[1] which shows dinosaurs inhabiting a world that otherwise looks like the actual world. In accordance with Allen's term, we see something that does not exist, but this doesn't necessarily lead us to believe that it actually exists. Of course, such deceptions have been created before by optically printing two separately filmed events onto the same strip of film. The result is a composite or layered image. In theory, this optically produced composite fabricates a spatio-temporal unity, giving the impression that the two separate events are taking place at the same diegetic space and time. The first event may be of live actions, and the second event may consist of stop-motion animation. However, the optical and photochemical equipment used in this process has inherent limitations that cannot be disguised – such as loss of resolution, grain, and hard-edge matt lines. Therefore, although optical composites can always give the impression that the two separate events occupy the same screen space, they eventually fall short in convincing the increasingly sophisticated spectator that the separate events occupy the same diegesis. Digital compositing equipment does not have the technical limitations inherent in optical printers, and so it can create a seamless blend of live action and animation, leading to the deception that the composited events do occupy the same diegesis.

In *Jurassic Park* and *The Lost World*, this deception is heightened even further in the moments when the digital dinosaurs and live action characters interact. In these shots, George Lucas's special effects company, Industrial Light and Magic (ILM), has created a seamless fusion of live action and computer-generated dinosaurs. (Of course, the Stan Winston studio also created live action puppet dinosaurs, but these have a pro-filmic reality beyond the film's capacity to generate a sensory deception.) Such a seamless fusion and interaction greatly contributes to the realism of these films. We can even argue that (however paradoxical it may sound), the shots showing the humans and digital dinosaurs interacting are the digital equivalent of the long takes and deep-focus shots praised by André Bazin for their spatial density and surplus of realism, in opposition to the synthetic and unrealistic effects created by montage.

But we cannot apply Bazin 'straight', of course. His realist ontology of the cinema, restricted to physical portrayal by means of optics, mechanics, and photochemistry, needs to be expanded to include the portrayal of 'possible worlds' in digital images. As we have already seen, the digital special effects in films such as *Jurassic Park* and *The Lost World* attempt to combine the aesthetics of both visible and invisible digital special effects – to repeat what we said above, they have the potential to replicate the realism and illusionism of the photographic image by conferring photographic credibility upon objects that do not exist in the actual world. In other words, digital special effects simulate realism and illusionism as theorized by Bazin and Heath (and the other film theorists mentioned above), whereas in other films visible special effects by themselves are used to create totally synthetic, futuristic worlds. For the moment, we are only concerned with the digital image's simulation of realism and illusionism and, more particularly, in the way spectators react to this simulation. Rather than referring, as one might expect, to Jean Baudrillard's theory of the simulacrum, we shall instead use the theory of possible worlds, because it will enable us to go some way towards explaining the ontology of the digital image.

The theory of possible worlds challenges the philosophy of logical positivism. For logical positivists, the actual world is all there is, and non-actual objects or possible states of affairs are meaningless because they do not correspond to immediate experience. It was only with the rise of modal logic (the study of possibility and necessity) that analytic philosophers broadened their horizons to analyse the possible as well as the actual.

Modal logic studies the range of possible – that is, non-actual – states of affairs that emerge from an actual state of affairs. For a number of philosophers (most notably David Lewis; see Lewis 1979), possible worlds have the same ontological status as the actual world. However, we do not subscribe to this extreme view here, but to a theory of possible worlds called conceptualism, which is represented in possible world literature most forcefully by the philosopher Nicholas Rescher (see Rescher 1969; 1975; 1979). Conceptualism offers a more modest view of possible worlds than a modal realist view. These possible states of affairs have a different ontological status, or mode of being, from the actual state of affairs. Rescher argues that possible worlds are constructs of language and the mind, whereas modal realists such as David Lewis argue that possible worlds are independent of language and the mind.

The following passage clearly and straightforwardly outlines Rescher's mind-dependent, conceptualist approach to possible worlds:

> . . . exactly what can the existential status of the possible-but-unrealized state of affairs be? Clearly – *ex hypothesi* – the state of affairs or things at issue does not exist as such: only *actual* things or states of affairs can unqualifiedly be said to exist, not those that are possible but unrealized. By definition, only the *actual* will ever exist in the world, never the unactualized possible. For the world does not have two existential compartments, one including the actual and another that includes the unactual. Of course, unactualized possibilities can be conceived, entertained, hypothesized, assumed, and so on. That is to say, they can, in a way, exist – or 'subsist' if one prefers – not, of course, unqualifiedly in themselves, but in a *relativized* manner, as the objects of certain intellectual processes. But it goes without saying that if their ontological footing is to rest on this basis, then they are clearly mind-dependent.
>
> (Rescher 1979: 168)

Possible worlds are mind-dependent because they cannot be located in nature, only in the thought processes and language of humans. And possible world-conceptualism does not lead to idealism because it can clearly distinguish between actual objects and states of affairs, which are independent of the mind, and possible worlds, which are inherently mind-dependent.

This is where the link between digital images and possible world theory emerges: the digital image is not bound or limited to the actual world in the same way as the optical image. At first glance it therefore seems that both the digital image and possible worlds have a similar ontological status: both articulate non-actual possibilities – that is, abstract, hypothetical states of affairs, whose ontological status is different from that of the actual world.

The power in the presentation of a possible world is increased when it is actualized on the movie screen with the aid of digital special effects, which create the perceptual illusion that the possible world is actual. The images of the dinosaurs are not produced optically, which means that they are not observable pro-filmic events physically portrayed using the nineteenth-century technologies of optics, mechanics, and photochemistry. This means that a digital image of a dinosaur cannot be compared and contrasted with its pro-filmic model or referent, because its referent does not exist in the real world. (This is a crucial issue, since it is impossible to verify that the dinosaurs have been faithfully 'reproduced', particularly in terms of skin colour, the sounds they make, and their movement; we simply cannot compare them to real dinosaurs in this respect.) The dinosaurs therefore exist in a conceptual possible world, and this conceptual possible world is being realized on screen via digital technology. The possible world cannot be realized via optical technology, because there is nothing for the optical technology to record (or physically portray). Moreover – and crucially – the digital special effects attempt to create the illusion that the images of dinosaurs are caused by pro-filmic referents (i.e. real, observable dinosaurs) – that is, that the dinosaurs are physically portrayed by means of optics, mechanics, and photochemistry. More generally, the possible world inhabited with dinosaurs is presented as if it were mind-independent – that is, the dinosaurs exist in the real world and have simply been recorded by the optical camera. And it is this illusion that seems to explain why Spielberg's *Jurassic Park* and *The Lost World*, inhabited by photo-realistic digital dinosaurs, have proved to be so popular.

## 7.5. Method

What methods can we extract from this theory of the digital image? Primarily we can indicate how the three facets of realism identified by Bazin, plus the contemporary film theorists' 'impression of reality', are created in the composited (photographic and digital) image. We can begin by identifying four elements:

1.  Interaction. Notice the way the digital dinosaurs and live action/real backgrounds are depicted interacting within a single shot. Interaction helps to create realism in the digital image, for the effects maintain (or create) the illusion of spatial and diegetic unity. This is analogous to Bazin's concept of dramatic realism, found in his discussion of spatial unity in the shot from *Where No Vultures Fly* and other films – most notably deep-focus shots in Welles's films, which create realism by means of the overlap of different planes of action. In digital images, the simulation of this overlap between digital and optical areas creates the illusion that they are seamlessly linked. Interaction also creates psychological realism, in that the spectator's gaze

can freely move from the digital dinosaurs to the photographic background and live action characters.

2.  Camera movement. Focus on the way camera movement is used in the composite mode, since camera movement poses special problems. Initially, it was impossible to use camera movement when compositing live action with special effects or animation. But ILM was able to overcome this fundamental principle of compositing in their breakthough film *Who Framed Roger Rabbit?* (Robert Zemeckis, 1988). This film created a seamless fusion of cel animation and live action while using extensive camera movement:

> The commandment of locking down cameras [i.e. keeping them stationary] for effects photography was particularly strict in filming and compositing live action and animated elements. *Who Framed Roger Rabbit?* would not only break the mold and have a lively camera tracking both live actors and animated cartoon characters, it would be up to ILM to see that the twain would met – to create through optical alchemy a world where humans and cartoons could live together.
>
> (Vaz 1996: 123)

In previous attempts to combine live action and cel animation, the live action had to be filmed using a stationary camera to provide the animators with fixed reference points around which to integrate the animation. But this resulted in a static composite in which the live action and animation, although occupying the same screen space, did not fabricate the impression of interacting with one another in the same diegesis. With *Who Framed Roger Rabbit?*, ILM created a more believable composite partly by means of camera movement which gave the impression that the camera is equally following the live action and cartoons, resulting in the illusion that they are occupying the same diegesis. Camera movement in the composite mode therefore creates both ontological realism and dramatic realism: first, the digital dinosaurs are made to seem as though they exist as pro-filmic referents in the diegesis, that is, that they have the same weight and density as the photographic background and live action characters; and second (and consequentially), they are seamlessly integrated into the photographic background.

3.  Motion blur. The composite mode has also developed a digital effect that reinforces the impression that digital and analogue events take place in the same unified space and diegesis: the illusion that spectators are watching movement. This effect is the motion blur. In live-action shots, when people and objects move, they become blurred. However, when objects are moved via stop-motion animation, they are not blurred;

instead, the animated model simply consists of quick, hard movements. As each frame is exposed, it photographs a still model. Before the next frame is exposed, the model is moved very slightly. The next frame then records the result of that motion, but it does not photograph the motion itself. The result is that the model is always pin sharp, however fast it is meant to be moving. But in producing motion in Spielberg's digital dinosaurs, motion blur is added to the image. In the composites, the live-action characters have optical blur when they move, and the digital dinosaurs have digital blur when they move. This strengthens the illusion that the humans and dinosaurs occupy the same diegesis (creating ontological and dramatic realism).

4.  Heath's discussion of the impression of reality – in which this impression is created by suturing the spectator into an imaginary relation to the image, producing the impression that the image's space is unified and harmonious – is also applicable to the new digital technology, since it conceals the symbolic mechanisms from the spectator more seamlessly than optical technology, thus suturing the spectator into an imaginary relation to the image.

## 7.6. Analysis

In the digital images of Spielberg's dinosaur films, trickery is of course employed to bring together in the same full shot humans and dinosaurs. The first sighting of the digitally created dinosaurs in *Jurassic Park* is significant in this respect. Approximately 20 minutes into the film, Grant (Sam Neil) and Sattler (Laura Dern) are given a tour of the park, where they see the dinosaurs roaming around. But the dinosaurs do not simply 'appear' in the film; instead, they are depicted through a strongly orchestrated POV sequence. The jeep transporting Grant and Sattler is brought to a sudden halt. In the back, Grant looks off-screen right and the camera dollies in on his face. The camera cuts to a new position as he then jumps out of his seat, takes off his hat and sunglasses, maintaining his face full-frame. But instead of cutting to what he sees, the camera instead cuts to Sattler, sitting in the front seat of the jeep looking at a large leaf. Two additional shots then depict Grant's hand as he forcefully turns her head away from the leaf and towards off-screen space. She similarly jumps out of her seat, mouth agape, and takes off her sunglasses. Only then do we cut to this off-screen space – of a brachiosaurus. Furthermore, Grant and Sattler appear in the shot, which therefore only represents their awareness, rather than their actual point of view. Or, in Edward Branigan's terms (outlined in Chapter 6 above), the shot is externally (rather than internally) focalized around the collective gaze of Grant and

Sattler, since they are present in the shot of the brachiosaurus. Dramatic and ontological realism are created by means of interaction and camera movement (as well as sound). The brachiosaurus is moving, and the camera pans to follow its movement. In other words, the camera movement is 'motivated' by the movement of the brachiosaurus, giving the impression that it is a pre-existent object in the diegesis that the camera is physically portraying. This impression is increased with the presence of the humans in the foreground, interacting – or at least overlapping with and reacting to – the brachiosaurus in the background. The brachiosaurus also interacts with its environment. It is depicted eating the branches of a tree, and when it moves the camera shakes slightly, and the sound of each footstep is clearly audible (which confers ontological realism upon the brachiosaurus). Finally, the light on the humans, the landscape, and the brachiosaurus is the same (the light in the photographic environment has been simulated in the creation of the digital dinosaur).

In *The Lost World*, the interaction and camera movement have been improved considerably. In the film's opening, we see the little girl on the beach feeding a piece of beef to a compsognathus. The interaction is quite subtle, as the slice of beef passes from the girl's hand to the creature's mouth (although it is significant to note that her hand partly conceals the interaction). Furthermore, the camera height is governed by the compsognathus (the camera is lowered), and a match on action cut is also effected when the compsognathus moves! That is, as it jumps towards the little girl, there is a cut to another camera angle while the compy performs its jump. Another subtle technique that increases dramatic realism in particular occurs when Malcolm's team looks for Sarah on Isla Sorna. A herd of stegosauruses passes both behind and in front of the team, creating a stronger interaction of the planes than was seen in *Jurassic Park*. But the strongest interaction of planes takes place when the second team, headed by Peter Ludlow, invades the island and chases the dinosaurs. The interaction far exceeds the simple overlap of planes seen earlier in *The Lost World* and in *Jurassic Park*, for it includes strong three-dimensional interaction, epitomized by a motor cyclist weaving through the legs of a running brachiosaurus, closely followed by the camera. It seems that the purpose of this interaction is motivated not by any story logic, but by the simple need to demonstrate the virtuosity of the digital technology that created such an interaction. And this is the primary difference between *Jurassic Park* and *The Lost World*: it is not a matter of 50 per cent more dinosaurs in the second film, but a more complex series of composited interactions between the live action and computer-generated dinosaurs.

Numerous shots of other interactions between humans and dinosaurs populate both *Jurassic Park* and *The Lost World*. What this means is that ILM has created a seamless composite of both the digital and analogue image in the same shot – that is, it layers, combines, and merges the digital and the analogue into a single coherent image, resulting in a unified diegetic space. The films that ILM worked on during the 1990s (not only Spielberg's dinosaur films, but also *Hook, Terminator 2, Death Becomes Her,* and *Dragonheart*) constitute an authentic composite cinema, or a mixed-media cinema.

# Conclusion

The traditional techniques for fabricating cinematic realism and illusionism – spatial and diegetic unity created by means of the long take plus deep focus, the reproduction of motion, together with high-resolution detail, and image compositing created via photochemical optical printing – have been mimicked and improved with digital technology. And so it appears that the cinema in the age of the digital has remained the same. It would seem paradoxical to suggest that digital realism is more real than photographic realism, because in fact the 'new and improved' digital realism offers just another – a more recent – cultural *vraisemblance*. We simply need to remind ourselves of the way the miniatures in Albert E. Smith and J. Stuart Blackton's *The Battle of Santiago Bay* (1899) or the stop-motion animation in the original *The Lost World* (1925) were viewed as realistic by their contemporary audiences. The fact that both films were shot photographically is not the whole story: in *The Battle of Santiago Bay*, it is the sense of scale – or the loss of actual scale created through the use of close-up photography – that fabricated the sense of realism, whereas in *The Lost World* (1925) it was the animation of the dinosaurs by means of stop-motion. Both techniques (loss of actual scale and stop-motion) fabricated a sense of realism because they had not at that point been reduced to a convention, a cultural *vraisemblance*. To carry this argument into the digital realm, we can say that, at the present time, digital special effects have yet to be reduced to a convention.

Can we seriously be arguing that the fabrication of realism in the digital image is 'business as usual'? The cinema in the digital age, we want to suggest, has remained the same, but is also utterly different. To take the idea of cultural *vraisemblance* to its logical conclusion is to end up believing in 'absolute relativism' – that everything is relative to everything else. The truth of the matter is that there is a progression of realism from the 1925 version of *The Lost World* to the 1997 version. That progression can be measured. For example, we said above that the realism in the 1925 version of *The Lost World* lies in its use of the then new technique of stop-motion animation. The problem with this technique is that it does not produce motion blur. The absence or presence of motion blur in an image is quantifiable (it can be observed and measured), and its presence in Spielberg's dinosaur films creates a more authentic realism than the realism created via stop-motion. Moreover, the interactions between digital dinosaurs and live action, created by means of digital compositing, is more credible than interactions created by means of optical compositing, because of the inherent limitations of the optical and photochemical equipment (loss of resolution and increase in grain when making optical copies of prints, hard-edge matt lines, etc.). Again, these inherent limitations and the resulting decrease in image quality can be quantified and measured. In Heath's terms these inherent limitations, which constitute the symbolic dimension of the image, are visible to the spectator; they therefore break his imaginary relation to the image. As a final example of a quantifiable difference between the photographic and the digital image, we simply need to refer back to what we said above about stationary cameras. The lack of camera movement in optical composites gave the resulting film a static look. But in the digital image, with the help of three-dimensional animation packages such as SoftImage, these optical limitations are overcome, allowing the camera to move about.[2]

However much we may wish to reduce the realism of the digital image to just another cultural *vraisemblance*, we need to take note of these technical advancements and determine their ontological, epistemological, and aesthetic potential. The composite nature of today's filmic image (photographic and digital) has utterly transformed the spectator's relation to the cinema. With the aid of digital technology, film-makers can fabricate a believable photo-realistic effect without being limited to the physical imprints left by profilmic events. As Dennis Muren, senior visual effects supervisor at ILM, observed with reference to *Jurassic Park*: 'The viewers will see something they have never seen before: dinosaurs that look as if they are actually in the shot. This is not the usual effects trickery, this is another level of experience' (Vaz 1996: 214).

## Endnotes

1   The term 'sensory deception' was coined by Richard Allen, who distinguishes it from 'epistemic deception': 'Most illusions are deceptive in two respects: They deceive the senses, and they lead us to make false inferences. We *see* something that does not really exist, and *believe* that it does exist. These two kinds of deception are distinguishable, however. We may experience a sensory illusion without being deceived into believing that what we see is real. The definition of illusion as deception must be modified. An illusion is something that deceives or is liable to deceive the spectator, but the deception need not be of the epistemic kind. Sensory deception does not entail epistemic deception' (Allen 1995: 98).

2   'The various software breakthroughs, building on the advances pioneered during *Death Becomes Her*, would allow for unprecendented freedom in the digital

compositing of CG [computer graphic] creations and live-action film. For the first time in ILM's history all restrictions on camera movement in background plates were removed, thanks to such tools as SoftImage, which allowed CG artists to create 3-D match-moves for any live-action plate and weave those shots with complex and hand-held camera moves' (Vaz 1996: 221).

# 8 Oedipal narratives and the post-Oedipal (*Back to the Future*)

## Introduction: Freud, Lacan, and Žižek: back to the future of symptomatic readings?

This chapter begins by interpreting a Hollywood film from the 1980s within the framework of the Freudian model of psychoanalysis (which is based on concepts such as the unconscious and repression, the Oedipus complex and the primal scene, primary process thinking and dream-work). It then considers the relevance to film studies of Lacanian psychoanalysis, which is centred on the relation between the imaginary, the symbolic, and the real in the formation of human subjectivity (and is based on concepts such as the mirror phase, the phallus, castration anxiety, fetishism, and the look). Rather than simply reproduce Freudian and Lacanian theory, we aim to highlight their fundamental concepts, explain them in straightforward language, and test their applicability in the context of a single film.

Other key psychoanalytic concepts relevant to this analysis are those that name inter- and intrasubjective processes, such as 'resistance' and 'transference', which are rarely discussed in film studies. They figure here in a partly metaphoric way to describe the relation between the critic and (the construction of) his object of analysis. For instance, we shall assume that a film offers resistance to analysis and that some sort of transference is likely to happen between theory and analysis. The former may manifest itself by the film already anticipating all the interpretive moves in the shape of explicit clues. The latter may be an all-too-perfect match between the theory and the analysis, with analysis merely mirroring theory and thereby 'colluding' with it. To take account of this process, the second part of the chapter considers more broadly the difference between making implicit meaning explicit and the dynamics that operates when implicit meaning becomes 'symptomatic'. In the final part, in a further turn of the screw, the work of the 'New

Lacanians'(notably Slavoj Žižek) is introduced, whose mode of film analysis not only 'symptomatizes' other symptomatic readings, but does so from a perspective which outlines the contours of a post-Oedipal, post-patriarchal society. A special kind of 'case history' of the present is being attempted by Žižek, supported by scanning a wide variety of cultural texts and sociopolitical events among which mainstream movies feature prominently.

We have chosen the popular sci-fi comedy – family adventure *Back to the Future* (Robert Zemeckis, 1985, screenplay by Zemeckis and Bob Gale) in order to examine the range of Freudian and post-Freudian concepts, as they might be useful in film interpretation and close analysis.

## 8.1. Freud and Lacan: theory

What is a classic Freudian reading? Although psychoanalysis has always been controversial and in recent years has been subject to devastating critiques, it continues to command support in the humanities, and especially among literary scholars and film analysts. This is partly because, in many respects, psychoanalysis is in the mainstream tradition of Western hermeneutics, reaching back to biblical exegesis and Renaissance humanism. The most unacceptable part of psychoanalysis for contemporary psychology and the cognitive sciences is the idea of the unconscious, i.e. the existence of a psychic entity inaccessible to introspection, voluntary recollection or conscious reasoning, and yet crucial in determining our actions, motives, and desires. What Freud claimed to have achieved was a 'Copernican revolution': decentring identity from consciousness and relocating it in the unconscious. In doing so, he pioneered a number of concepts and techniques whereby a specially trained expert ('the analyst') can have access to the unconscious. To Freud, the unconscious was the result of repression, the 'burying' of experiences or psychic events too painful or threatening to the subject's survival and wellbeing to remain conscious.

The so-called royal road to the unconscious were dreams, which Freud sought to decipher via interpretation. He argued that their form and manifest content are the result of dream-work. Dream-work in Freud, is constituted by a number of formal operations, such as condensation and displacement, and secondary elaboration: all in the service of a dynamic structure of wish-fulfilling fantasy. Operating even in the case of nightmares, the purpose of dreams is to protect sleep, and help resolve problems we are not able to cope with in waking life. Apart from dreams, the unconscious manifests itself also in slips of the tongue ('Freudian slips'), in bodily symptoms, and in other, physiologically hard to explain signs of bodily or mental dysfunction, such as lapses of memory or hallucinations.

Why assume that a film has an unconscious? According to Freud, the unconscious follows the pleasure principle (dreams are a form of wish-fulfilment), and dreaming is vital to our fantasy life. Insofar as films deal with fantasies, they could be considered analogous to dreams and qualify as manifestations of the unconscious. Yet much of Lacanian film theory was dedicated to establishing a different relation between desire, the drives, the screen, and the cinematic apparatus, in which the unconscious is the effect of certain incompatibilities and misalignments activated by the cinematic situation but not confined to it. Moreover, mainstream films are also narratives whose purpose, according to one prominent school of narratology, is to propose 'imaginary resolutions to real contradictions' (see Chapter 2 above, on *Die Hard*), where 'imaginary' could be understood as involving unconscious fantasy scenarios.

But are we talking about the film-maker's unconscious, the spectator's unconscious or would we wish to endow the filmic text with an 'unconscious' – if, for instance, we assume it to be 'authorless' – and ascribe to it the status of a collective product of a given society and period? In more anthropological terms, does it make sense to see a film as 'cultural text' whereby a society talks about itself to itself, and would this justify us speaking of it as having a textual 'unconscious'?

All these hypotheses and premises have been put forward, at one time or another, more or less convincingly. For our purposes, we shall ignore the ramifications of these issues – well explored in the literature – and settle for the notion that a film has an unconscious, here understood in the Lacanian sense of the effects of contradictory textual traces and incompatible significations noted by the analyst. This unconscious, therefore, is not hidden, but on the surface; it does not only point to classic symptoms and disorders, but also manifests itself in 'coincidences', so-called parapraxes (*fehlleistungen*) and slips of the tongue (what Freud called the 'psychopathology of everyday life'). As to the actual 'existence' of such an unconscious we adopt a robustly pragmatic stance: does the assumption of its presence 'work' in practice? Does a Freudian and Lacanian approach to a given film bring something new into view and foreground otherwise overlooked features? And finally, how does such added information clarify our response to, or render more complex our understanding of, a film?

# 8.2. Freud and Lacan: method

## 8.2.1. Freud

We shall restrict ourselves to a relatively limited number of Freudian themes or tropes, foremost among them the so-called Oedipus complex and – with respect to mainstream films – the Oedipal trajectory of the narrative.

- The Oedipus complex as understood in film studies basically asserts that most mainstream films are stories of the formation of normative identities, and that certain genres, notably the Western, the thriller, and science fiction, are often stories of (male) cultural initiation, answering the question: What does it mean to be/come a man? Most narratives can therefore be generalized or reduced to the 'founding' narrative, the male hero's transformation into a man. The first step in analysing a film narrative as Oedipal is to determine how the main male character channels his sexual desire away from his mother or mother figure (the pre-Oedipal realm of incestuous desire, in which he is in direct competition with his father) towards a 'mother substitute' (in which he becomes like his father). Raymond Bellour argues that the whole of *North by Northwest* (Hitchcock, 1959) enacts in its narrative trajectory the formation of a masculine identity – Roger Thornhill's acceptance of his separation from his mother and the fixing of his desire on a substitute woman (Eve Kendall), which leads to the formation of the heterosexual couple (Bellour 2000: 77–105).
- A second point often made by psychoanalytic critics, and following on from the Oedipal trajectory, concerns the gender relation of mainstream cinema. The classical Hollywood narrative, both in its story-line and in the complication it generates, seeks to translate the asymmetry that exists between male and female into a hierarchy. By remarking or un-marking the terms involved in this hierarchy, the films naturalize (i.e. make seem inevitable) the formation of the heterosexual couple, to the exclusion of any other social or emotional bond. The therapeutic function of mainstream Hollywood cinema would be to give play to fantasies of deviancy, disruption, and otherness, before channelling them in such a way as to affirm a single final goal: the establishment and maintenance of a nuclear family, under conditions of bourgeois ideology, capitalism, and patriarchy. The role of women in Oedipal narratives is therefore structural: they are placed as potential objects of the male hero's desire. The second step in analysing a film narrative as Oedipal would be to establish the role women are assigned in relation to the male hero. Teresa de Lauretis writes: 'The work of narrative, then, is a mapping of differences, and specifically, first and foremost, of sexual difference into each text. . . . to say that narrative is the production of Oedipus is to say that each reader – male or female – is constrained and defined within the two positions of a sexual difference thus conceived: male-hero-human, on the side of the subject; and female-obstacle-boundary, on the other'

(de Lauretis 1984: 122). In *North by Northwest* the narrative goes through a series of stages that test Eve Kendall, to ensure that she is suitable object of desire for the hero, Roger Thornhill. Only when the narrative establishes that she is a safe bet – that she is really a bored middle-class woman who wants to be married, rather than a duplicitous manipulating woman – is she ready to be saved by Thornhill and married off to him.

- A third aspect of Freudian analysis concerns the formal (linguistic) and figurative (visual) aspects of a film, where critics have sought to demonstrate the effects of processes analogous to those of Freud's dream-work (e.g. condensation and displacement, metaphor and metonymy, symbolic blockage). This type of analysis is not limited to narrative structure, but refers to the design, composition, and material texture of film images and sequences, often called *mise en scène* (see Chapter 3). More particularly, it tries to identify the *primary rhetoric* or driving force that shape a films. In carrying out this type of analysis, the film scholar argues that the rhetorical structure of a film is motivated or governed by unconscious or repressed desires. Thierry Kuntzel, for example, has argued that classical narrative films follow the logic of dreams and the processes of Freud's dream-work (1978; 1980; see also Chapter 2 above).
- A more indirect appeal to Freud is made in the so-called 'symptomatic readings', which probe a film text for its ambivalences and hidden depths, for its gaps and fissures, for its ruptures and contradictions. As indicated, we shall be looking at this aspect separately, when we come to characterize typically Lacanian readings and their consequences for film studies.

A Freudian interpretation therefore seems to be, in the first instance, a variation of a thematic reading, for it reduces a film's narrative to one implicit theme. However, the Oedipal theme is not so much implicit as repressed and unconscious, because it represents the unsayable, the ultimate taboo of society – the incest taboo. In film seminars focused on psychoanalytic interpretation, the very mention of the son's incestuous desire for his mother, and the symbolic punishment of castration that threatens him, typically arouses the suspicion and scepticism of many film students. One reason is because discussing films in terms of incest and castration stretches credibility. The psychoanalyst can reply that students are simply reacting against their primal, repressed incestuous desires or threats of castration. That is, they are in denial when they reject incest and castration as legitimate concepts with which to analyse works of the imagination. In return, the sceptic can reply that the psychoanalytic interpretation is in bad faith, since it mistakenly attributes false beliefs to the sceptic. Such repartee is a symptom of the vicious circle, in which it seems impossible to escape conflicting interpretations and adjudicate on a higher ground. Our pragmatic approach tries to substitute for this vicious circle a 'hermeneutic circle', in which the results of an interpretation can legitimate the procedures that have led to its formulation.

An additional criticism that can be levelled at psychoanalytic interpretation is that it is too reductive. Indeed, it is more reductive than thematic criticism, for it boils all film narratives down to the same 'universal' structure – to Oedipus. Psychoanalytic film critics begin to see Oedipus everywhere.

## 8.2.2. Lacan

Jacques Lacan is one of the most radical of Freud's interpreters. He returned to Freud's work and subjected it to a linguistic/semiotic/structuralist reading, in an attempt to make explicit Freud's 'message'. This message concerns the formation of an individual's subjectivity rather than his (ego-)identity, and particularly the role played in that formation by a speaker's position in language (which, according to Lacan, 'speaks me', even though I may think that 'I am speaking'). 'Identity' would be the illusion of autonomous agency and self-coherence, while 'subjectivity' names the contradictory structures and processes that make the effect of identity possible. Lacan theorized the dynamics of subject formation on two levels – the level of the imaginary and the level of the symbolic. In the 1970s and 1980s film scholars used these two concepts to argue that the uncanny manner in which a film engages or seems to address the spectator, even though s/he is absent from the film, is proof of the presence of the self-alienating instance Lacan called 'the other'. This 'other' is endowed 'with the power to transform or sustain categories of subjectivity' (Rodowick 1991: 6). Watching a film gives us a strange sense of empowerment, the illusion of being in control of the events, when in fact it is some other - apparently absent - cause, that controls us.

- The imaginary. Lacan uses this term to designate *the formation of an individual's sense of self-coherence and identity by means of images* – or, more specifically, by means of the individual's perception of its body in a mirror image. The young child first conceives of itself as a unified entity by perceiving its body image in a mirror, and then identifying with (i.e. internalizing or assimilating) that image. The mirror image therefore provides the young infant with a unified sense of itself. This sense of self (what psychoanalysts call 'the ego') is imaginary not only in Lacan's sense that it derives from images, but also because the individual's sense of self is an illusory, fictional unity. It is a sense of self that derives from the outside, from 'the other'. Christian Metz (1982) and Jean-Louis Baudry (1986) argued that this process of ego formation is re-enacted every time we go to the cinema (in Rodowick's words, the cinema is so seductive, because it [transforms or] sustains categories of subjectivity, by re-enactment and repetition). The cinema screen is posited to act as a mirror for the self, with the exception that the spectator identifies first with the look of the camera (primary identification) and second with characters on screen (secondary identification), rather than with a literal self image (Metz 1982: 42-57). The concept of the imaginary presents an optical-visual theory of identity formation, or at least the formation of the ego, the latter an essential part, according to Freud, of a human being's sense of being in the world and of possessing self-worth.

• The symbolic. The formation of the ego in the realm of images (the imaginary) is, however, only the first stage of identity formation. The second stage is the realm of the symbolic, a term Lacan uses to designate *the formation of a sexual identity by means of experiencing the Oedipal conflict*, as well as by having to come to terms with other symbolic codes, such as the acquisition of language. Again, our sense of sexual identity derives from outside, but this time Lacan designates the outside as 'the Other', or the law of the father. Moreover, as with the realm of the imaginary, the symbolic involves the individual assimilating, enacting or internalizing Oedipus/the Other/the law of the father. But the symbolic does not enrich the formation of the ego; instead it forms the unconscious. It is here that Lacan's different idea of the unconscious becomes crucial. Rather than denoting a neuropsychological concept that indicates an area of the mind housing primitive instincts or individual repressed memories, the Lacanian unconscious names the Other, the laws of language and society that control each individual. These the individual can never master or even be aware of: they remote-control and master-mind our self-presence, reminding us of our status as 'subjects'. We can only discern the influence of the Other/the unconscious in symptoms located in our behaviour, our dreams, and our speech (we discuss symptoms below). Moreover, in the symbolic the look becomes the gaze. Whereas the look can be mastered (in fact, it is a narcissistic look, hence its mastery is always self-mastery), the symbolic gaze, like all symbolic codes, can never be mastered. The gaze may be in the field of the visual, but need not be, because it is fundamentally discursive and not optical: 'Semiotics, not optics, is the science that enlightens for us the structure of the visual domain' (Copjec 1994: 34).

## 8.3. Freud and Lacan: analysis

### 8.3.1. Freud and Oedipus

Our chosen film, *Back to the Future*, fairly readily lends itself to a Freudian reading. The story is centred on Marty McFly, a small-town middle-America teenager in trouble at home and in school. A budding pop musician, he hangs out with Doc Brown, a scatterbrained inventor, but also Marty's friend and mentor. Near midnight on the day the story is set, Doc Brown expects Marty at the Twin Pines Mall, to demonstrate his latest invention, a time-machine in the shape of a plutonium-powered DeLorean car. After successfully 'teleporting' Doc's dog Einstein for 60 seconds, Doc gets shot by Libyan terrorists, from whom he stole their stolen Plutonium, but Marty manages to escape in the DeLorean, which accidentally transports him 'back' to his home town in 1955. There he arrives just in time – after a series of adventures, mishaps, and near-misses – to bring about the meeting of his parents and thus ensure his own and his brother and sister's (continuing) existence.

*Back to the Future* is a comic version of the well-known time-travel paradox, or time loop. Assuming you can travel back in time, so the paradox goes, what happens if you murder your own grandfather and thereby prevent yourself from being born? How can you travel back in time and not affect the future, which has already happened? Marty's story dramatizes this paradox, when he realizes that his escape from the Libyans has indeed taken him back in time, but not displaced him in space. One of his first encounters is with his future father, George, in 1955 a shy and bullied schoolboy, and his mother, Lorraine, an outwardly prim but sexually precocious teenager who promptly falls in love with Marty. His task, as he soon realizes, is to deflect these amorous and incestuous attentions away from himself and toward his future father, and to steer his father, too timid and immature to make advances on his own initiative, in the direction of female conquest. His dilemma is how to act decisively without seeming to act, and how to 'bring about' something that has already been accomplished.

The film thus thematizes an Oedipus complex, but in inverted form. Instead of the usual story of initiation involving good and bad fathers or punishing authority figures, flanked by an alluring but dangerous female (standing for the sexualized mother image), Marty encounters a weak father figure and his mother's desire for him, rather than his desire for her. Thanks to the time-travel device, Marty realizes that at the 'origins' of his troubles in life is a paternal instance who is no authority figure (and unlikely to become a father). The 'normal' Oedipal incest taboo of symbolically killing the father and sleeping with his mother is here, dream-like, turned into its opposite, with Marty strenuously rejecting the advances of Lorraine and equally strenuously trying to turn George into a 'man'. What makes this subterfuge of the plot necessary is not only the 'dream logic', where repression and primary process inversion are the signs of a censored wish-fulfilling fantasy. The 'dream/transport/time-travel' theme is itself a response to the fact that there is a problem in the present of 1985. There, Marty's father is a singularly inept, bullied, and immature individual, unsuitable as a paternal authority, too weak to even rebel against, but fit only to pity and despise. George lets himself be sadistically manipulated by his supervisor, Biff, he still eats breakfast cereal like a baby, and uncontrollably laughs at television reruns of *The Honeymooners*. His mother, on the other hand, is an untidy, overweight housewife, who drinks her breakfast out of a vodka bottle and puritanically tries to prevent her children from having friends of the other sex. Appalled by this dysfunctional family (his siblings are almost equally unappealing, and his mother's brother is in jail), Marty prefers the company of Doc Brown, the archetypal mad scientist, who is surrounded by clocks, but whose social skills and civic virtues also leave much to be desired. Marty's options for male role models are a choice of evils: between his father and Doc Brown, the choice is between two kinds of immaturity and self-indulgence; between his father and Strickland, the schoolmaster, the choice is between a born loser and a discipline-obsessed authoritarian.

The film develops a curious set of symmetric–asymmetric analogies between the two: both do not seem to grow old in the 30-year interval, but while Strickland, as Marty notes, seems to have been born bald and stayed that way, Doc Brown has too much unruly hair. One can also note that Strickland's strict timekeeping is parodied in Doc's collection of clocks, while his father's disgusting breakfast habits are anticipated in the mess of dog food and burnt toast Marty finds in Doc's Heath Robinson mechanized home. Marty's major anxiety is being a loser like his father (a prediction made by Strickland and seemingly born out by his rejection at a school audition), but he is unwilling to emulate the asocial (Doc Brown) or follow the anti-social (Biff) authority figure. The only 'sight for sore eyes' is his girlfriend, Jennifer, but their 'night under the stars' is threatened by the fact that Biff has wrecked George McFly's car which Marty had been hoping to borrow for the weekend. While she is the Oedipal 'substitute' for his mother, their kiss or consummation is several times interrupted and remains deferred even at the end. *Back to the Future* presents an initial situation, in which the 'normal' Oedipal trajectory has been doubly blocked, making the purpose of the narrative evident: to restore 'proper', i.e. heterosexual, Oedipal identity.

For this solution, the time-machine with which Doc Brown has fitted the DeLorean offers itself as the suitably paradoxical vehicle. Time travel becomes the (generically motivated) means for restaging the Oedipus complex as a 'deferred action' which is also a therapeutic anticipation. By travelling to the circumstances preceding his own birth, Marty both realizes the incest fantasy at the heart of Oedipus and engineers what in Freudian terminology is called the 'primal scene', the fantasy of witnessing the moment of one's own conception, i.e. the act of parental lovemaking. Finding himself back in 1955 allows Marty, in other words, to use his hindsight knowledge not to change history, but to make (his) history possible. He is able to repair a lack – his father's masculinity – and he is able to forewarn Doc Brown about the deadly assault of the Libyans with their missile-launching VW camper. In order to accomplish this, Marty has to substitute for his father several times. He is literally the 'fall guy' in the 'peeping tom' episode, where he gets run over by his future (grand-)father (a graphic submission to symbolic 'castration'), the prelude to becoming the object of Lorraine's desire. He repeatedly has to fight, defeat, or humiliate Biff, tormentor of his father and rival suitor (near-rapist) of his mother.

When Marty finally returns to the present and wakes up the next morning, his parents have turned into a sleek suburban couple. His mother is trim and beautiful, his father is about to become the successful author of science fiction novels, and his brother is wearing a suit to his upscale office job. To top it all, a brand-new four-wheel drive is in the garage, ready to take Marty and Jennifer on their night under the stars. In other words, having posed the problem of Oedipus in terms of a lack of a credible father figure, the film makes out of the time travel episode a comic nightmare that is the perfect wish-fulfilling fantasy. Now that he has 'ordinary' parents, we are meant to infer, Marty can face up to the Oedipal challenge. He can emerge as a fully constituted male (i.e. in the terms of the story: summon the courage to send his demo tape to the record company) and proceed with the heterosexual bond, eventually founding his own family.

## 8.3.2. Lacanian analysis

We can see how the basic elements of the Oedipus complex and its 'normal' resolution are present in the film, suitably rearranged. But we can also see that what is usually latent and hidden is here made explicit, indeed at once over-explicit and negated through the humour of situation comedy. It should make us alert to the resistance of the film to analysis – signalled by its 'knowingness' about psychoanalysis – and make us wary of the possible transference occurring between the analyst and the theorist, the latter using the film merely to corroborate a theoretical paradigm. A Lacanian analysis is helpful here: rather than insist on the Oedipal trajectory in its Freudian version (or apply Lévi-Strauss's and Propp's model of narrative lack and its restitution/resolution), Lacan's concept of identity does not, as we saw, imply a stable ego. Identity is nothing other than a play of shifting identifications: no identity without identifications, so to speak, and no identifications without anxiety and loss. The identifications are self-alienated and based on miscognition, and they concern something at once more fundamental and more fundamentally divided than identity, namely the conditions of human subjectivity. Thus resistance as knowingness, too, is only another version of anxiety, just as transference is only another manifestation of shifting identifications in a perpetually open field of identity formation.

According to Lacan, we mis-cognize ourselves as autonomous beings across a set of imaginary identifications and representations. The confirmation in the mother's look and in our reflected body image anticipates successful motor coordination and forms a (narcissistic) ideal ego, whose slave we will be for the rest of our lives. *Back to the Future* shows its anxious 'knowingness' even with regard to the mirror phase in its use of the photograph that Marty carries with him into the past, where he and his siblings can be seen to 'fade' in direct proportion to the unlikeliness of George McFly meeting/mating with Lorraine. But in true Freudian fashion, Marty's frantic self-scrutiny is double-edged: might his look not express the repressed wish of the narcissistic child that his brother and sister had never been born?

Other aspects of Zemeckis' and Gale's 'knowingness' in relation to film studies and psycho-semiotics are their references to voyeurism and their apparent awareness of the film-studies discussion around the concept of 'suture' (the way the act of looking represented in a film can 'stitch' the plot into the seamless narration of a self-consistent, realistic 'world'; see also Chapter 7). Voyeurism is thematized as a meta-theoretical issue in the scene where Marty watches George watch his mother. This sequence is a textbook illustration of the structure of the look, as it has been classically formulated by Laura Mulvey in her argument of the gender divide inherent in the act of looking (Mulvey 1989), where the male looks and the female is 'to-be-looked-at'. Wrapping himself around the phallic branch of a tree to steady himself as he watches Lorraine undress through binoculars (or ocular erection), George is observed by a disgusted Marty. Yet the very fact that George becomes a watcher watched makes him lose his grip on the tree, and he has to be rescued from a fatal fall by Marty, who sacrifices himself for his future father in the first of several filial substitutions. This one leads directly to his meeting his mother in place of his father.

The process of 'suture' is illustrated in the scene where Marty watches himself escape from the Libyans. In narrative terms, it is used to disguise the overlap of two temporalities, which succeeds by virtue of the ocular suture of the POV look. Marty is 'returning early' from 1955, in order to warn Doc Brown of the Libyans, but he arrives on the scene too late and can merely watch (from a safe distance) the original assault. Marty's act of looking and our sharing his point of view here makes us overlook the impossible fact of two time-worlds seemingly coexisting and therefore of two Martys existing simultaneously: the one who gets away from the Libyans and the one who watches the getaway. The scene might also be described as a typically Lacanian moment, because the look as optical point of view here substitutes, fetish-like, for the gaze of the Other, inscribed in the scene, as if to ensure that the subject 'Marty' survives his own disappearance (and symbolic death). The time-travel paradox could thus be reinterpreted in the light of these at once excessive and insufficient looks, where Marty's desire to assure his own procreation is a transformation of the Freudian primal scene into the register of spectacle and the look. What makes time-travel necessary is Marty's need to see himself seeing, a form of secondary narcissism that arises from the desire to assume the position of the gaze. In other words, he tries to gain control over the very economy of looking and being looked at, in an attempt to get at the gaze 'behind' the look.

## 8.3.3. Symptomatic readings

On one level, the emphasis on looking and its Lacanian elaborations allow us to redefine the plot's overall purpose. No longer aimed at ensuring stable Oedipal identity, *Back to the Future*'s narrative economy of repetitions and variations would serve to ward off 'castration anxiety' (if we describe it in Freudian terms), and to bridge the gap between the look and the gaze (if we use a Lacanian vocabulary). Either way, the film knows that the attempt must necessarily fail, for not even the 'happy ending' can assure a 'proper' submission to the patriarchal law and the restitution of its validity. In the face of the problem it poses so insistently, namely the absence of a credible symbolic (i.e. paternal authority under the universal law of castration), the 'formation of the couple' remains perfunctory. In the comic-grotesque picture of suburban bliss, social respectability, and imminent/instant celebrity that concludes Marty's story, too much remains unresolved, which may explain why there has to be a sequel, as announced by the return of Doc Brown in the final moments of the film.

The jarring notes in the family sitcom resolution, however, also offer an opportunity to ask what it is that the film covers up, and perhaps to recast its knowingness as a resistance, which requires a different hermeneutic strategy. In one sense, what psychoanalytic film analysis is trying to do is to give mainstream Hollywood movies a *symptomatic reading*. It wants to make these films speak about things they do not actually say explicitly as we watch their narratives unfolding, but which are nonetheless there, encoded in another language, the figurative and formal language of 'symptoms'. Psychoanalytic interpretation can be understood as a 'hermeneutics of suspicion', for it looks for hidden, repressed, or disguised meanings underlying the literal meaning of texts. Moreover, the 'hermeneutics of suspicion' assumes that the hidden meaning is essential to the film – it is the film's structuring absence or blind spot around which the system turns. Only the symptoms of that absent structure are visible. Symptoms require maieutic or interpretive processes to make their meaning apparent.

In another sense, psychoanalytic film theory might be blind to political or historical contradictions. If *Back to the Future* with its knowingness seems to frustrate a symptomatic reading, because it displays its symptoms so openly and names them psychoanalytically, this may itself be a form of defence and disavowal. But as the moments of excess – both comic and horrific – indicate, *Back to the Future* has other symptoms as well. These include odd coincidences and repetitions with slight differences; 'funny' incidents that are also dark and ominous; the presence of monstrous figures, such as Biff and the Libyans; Marty's own aggression and cruelty alongside his shame and embarrassment; the recurrence of certain actions and motifs; the presence of unsuspected patterns with respect to certain cultural or ethnic themes. Thus, too much symmetry and patterning may make further symptomatic interpretations necessary.

More broadly, when reading a film symptomatically, one assumes three things:

- that despite a film's clear, classical narrative (within the codes of verisimilitude applicable to a sci-fi fantasy and a family comedy) there is the secondary elaboration of another meaning;
- that the film puts up a certain resistance to this reading: that it tries to hide and disguise its darker sides, e.g. by being a 'comedy' or by deploying the stereotypical clichés of a genre;
- that the film's 'unconscious' refers neither to the author nor the spectator, but to the text, as a certain configuration of contradictory or 'overdetermined' cultural and film-historical signifiers, arranged in ways that can be read in a non-narrative, atemporal way as a kind of 'score' or 'symptomatology'. This has sometimes been called the 'allegorical' mode of reading 'realist' texts, both in literature and in films, and has been made popular by scholars such as Walter Benjamin in his *Arcades Project* (Benjamin (1999) and Fredric Jameson (1981)). As argued earlier, such an allegorical unconscious is not something hidden in the deep structure of the text, which the critic somehow excavates, but is itself an effect of the surface of the text, the vanishing point of any interpretative strategy. It is the *result* of a reading rather than its premise and precondition, and thus an instance of the hermeneutic circle trying to break the vicious circle.

Symptomatic readings have been crucial in the development of a certain form of cultural analysis. In particular, feminist concerns, issues of ideology, class and patriarchy, and more recently, issues of race and sexual preference have been articulated almost exclusively across the assumptions of such repressed meanings brought to the surface by 'allegorical' readings. In the case of *Back to the Future* these can highlight, for instance, the issue of politics and ideology. A good example might be the essay by Fred Pfeil comparing and (unflatteringly) contrasting *Back to the Future* with Terry

Gilliam's *Brazil* (Pfeil 1990: 227–42). Pfeil gives a lucid and perceptive introduction to several of the themes that also concern us here: for instance, he notes that *Back to the Future* has a classical double-plot structure of adventure and romance. He also highlights the reason for Marty having to travel in time, namely to be able to enter the Oedipal symbolic of his society, by having a credible father. In this roundabout way Marty attains the self-confidence that is held up (to ridicule and yet re-affirmed?) by the film as the (Benjamin Franklin) ideal of the American male: 'You can achieve anything if you set your mind to it'.

Pfeil also hints at the regime of repetition, and the mirroring function of certain characters when he remarks that the small-town bullies become the Libyan terrorists. In effect, Biff and his gang and the Libyan terrorists are doubles of each other in several respects. Both give chase in cars, both are dangerous, and both are outwitted by McFly in a home-made bricolage vehicle (skateboard/DeLorean), which causes theirs to crash into a derisory obstacle (the manure truck, the photo-booth). These parallels are, of course, clearly crafted by the screenwriters and therefore are in themselves not symptomatic but explicit meanings. Pfeil's main purpose is to delineate a meaning that the film itself does not seem to acknowledge, and which identifies its ideological project: a collusion with Reaganite politics of cynicism and nostalgia, indicated by the coexistence of Doc Brown's jibes against Ronald Reagan in 1955 (one of whose B-westerns, *Cattle Queen of Montana*, is shown in Hill Valley's only cinema) with the conservative agenda of rewriting the past in order to both justify and prolong the status quo: 'at the apex of the Reagan eighties ... we might well suspect that the film's construction of such a contradictory position, along with its attendant double pleasure of seeing-with-approval/seeing-through [the yuppie family as a put-up job], is a key component of its enormous success' (Pfeil 1990: 232). Pfeil contrasts the 'reactionary' plot of *Back to the Future* (reactionary in his view because following the standard pattern of Oedipal identity and libidinal renunciation, while not believing in either) with the 'progressive' plot of *Brazil* (progressive because although similar in respect of time travel – in both films, the hero tries to fix a mistake in the past so that things can change in the present – the latter is self-reflexive, dystopic and its anti-hero is cruelly punished and betrayed). Pfeil's essay is an excellent example of a symptomatic reading, but, as we shall see, it is possible to come to a quite different 'political' interpretation from his, on the basis of a very similar analysis of *Back to the Future*'s key scenes.

There have, however, been fierce critiques of symptomatic readings in general (by e.g. David Bordwell and Noël Carroll), arguing that there is no need to resort to a hermeneutics of suspicion for most issues that might be of interest to a film scholar, and that such readings are vitiated by the analyst's political agenda, like an adolescent distrusting his elders and authority figures on principle. For example, Noël Carroll argues that film theorists should *begin* with cognitive explanations of filmic phenomena, and should move on to psychoanalytic explanations only if cognitivism is found wanting: 'where we have a convincing cognitivist account, there is no point whatsoever in looking any further for a psychoanalytic account. ... For a psychoanalytic theory to re-enter the debate, it must be demonstrated that there is something about the data of which cognitivist (or organic) explanations can give no adequate account' (Carroll 1996b: 65; see also Bordwell 1985: 30). In this polemical statement Carroll shifts the burden of proof to the psychoanalytic film theorists, as they must explain why they use psychoanalysis as the starting point to theorize filmic phenomena. However, Carroll fails to recognize that psychoanalytic film theorists start from the unconscious because it is here that they locate the problematic core of identity, including that of the cognitivist, whose 'positivist' assertions are in denial of their own contradictory point of enunication or speaking position (see Žižek 2001).

In the case of Pfeil's reading, someone hostile to his conclusions while still sympathetic to the hermeneutics of suspicion might well ask: Why should the comic-realist version of the time travel problem in *Back to the Future* be reactionary and the more comic-absurdist treatment of the same issue by Gilliam in *Brazil* be progressive? By calling the latter self-referential, Pfeil applies a 'modernist' schema to his readings, in order to escape 'postmodern' relativism and cynicism. Yet there are ways of conducting readings which might not be called symptomatic, but which fulfil a similar purpose – to make the text speak about its own 'unconscious' or contradictory meaning-effects – that do not run into the same problems. Rather than use a hermeneutics of suspicion, we could for instance turn to a problem-solving routine. Instead of asking what the problem is that the character needs to resolve (the Freudian Oedipal option), or what the problem is that the director wants to solve (the modernist, self-reflexive option), we could ask: What is the problem to which the film thinks it is the answer (the 'cultural studies' and 'social text' option)? In this respect, Pfeil could be accused of not pushing his own reading nearly far enough. For him, time-travel seems inherently reactionary, because it is committed to leaving things 'exactly as we find them', underwriting the conformism of rewriting the past in the light of the future as the best of all possible worlds.

What Pfeil does not discuss is why time-travel should be necessary, or why rewriting should become such a political issue. If we ask which is the problem that time-travel is asked to 'resolve' (for instance, so that 'life can go on'), then another hermeneutic presumption would connect time-travel to a particular sense of history and of causality. For the film to think that the time-travel paradox can settle it, the problem must be located in history and, more specifically, in American history. Once primed in this direction, one might ask: what does the film have to say about race, and how does the issue of masculinity – Marty's entry into the symbolic – interact or intersect with the race issue, so prominent in recent discussions of America's historical identity? We shall be offering an argument that links the theme of damaged masculinity with that of race, and show how one discourse can substitute for the other, superimpose itself on the other, and indeed offer an 'imaginary solution' to the other. In this reading, the fact that the Oedipal trajectory is both inverted and foregrounded illustrates how it can serve as the 'mechanism' that allows another 'symptom' to both appear and disappear, and why time-travel can serve not only as a code of disturbed temporality but also as the (grammatical) mode of the hypothetical ('what if') and the optative ('if only').

The scene we want to focus on is the one where Marty is at the 'Enchantment under the Sea' dance and has to go on stage to play the guitar, because the band's lead guitarist has injured his hand while trying to help Marty get out of the trunk of his car, into which Biff's buddies had bundled him. More anxious about how to make sure he is being fathered than afraid of Biff, Marty hits on the idea of playing a Chuck Berry number, 'Johnny B Goode', slyly realizing that neither the audience nor the band had heard of this rock'n'roll classic. In fact, while Marty is playing, the injured lead guitarist, who happens to be Marvin Berry, picks up the phone to talk to his cousin Chuck, so that Chuck Berry can hear Marty's rendition of 'Johnny B Goode' and with it 'the sound' that Chuck 'has been looking for'.

As Marvin thrusts the phone at the camera, representing the space where the music is coming from, we cut to the stage, where one cannot but notice that Marty is also doing Chuck Berry's famous 'duck-walk' stage act. While we hear what Chuck Berry hears (via the phone), we also see (indeed, 'recognize') what Berry does not see (since he is miles away), allowing us, the spectators, along with Marty, to stay one step ahead in the game. But consider what is going on: at the height of Marty's plight about making his father into a man, so he can make a son, another substitution occurs, at once an inversion of and a parallel to the patrilineal passage of the main plot. Something passes between the father of rock'n'roll and a son who – in the present of the 1980s – plays a particularly 'white' suburban rock, that of Huey Lewis (another piece of knowingness, in that the teacher who turns Marty down at the audition is played by Lewis). So for Marty to be 'teaching' rock'n'roll to one of the black fathers of rock would be sweet revenge on both his white fathers. However, the film is more careful and circuitous, in that the scene introduces another modality: the 'son' *remembers rock'n'roll* which, however, perfectly matches the symbolic father's *anticipation of rock'n'roll* ('the sound you've been looking for'). In other words, Marty is able to assume Chuck Berry's patrimony, which is nothing less than the body language, the music culture, and with it much of the male ideal that was to define the essential features of American masculinity for the second half of the twentieth century – but only on condition that he doesn't become aware of it, i.e. that the 'true' or historical origins of this masculinity remain disguised and unacknowledged.

In other words, it would seem that covering the fictional-generic reason (Doc Brown's flux capacitor) and the Oedipal reason (making his parents meet) for Marty McFly's time-travel is a historical ideological reason, different from that given by Pfeil in his political critique. It is at once specifically American and deeply implicated in questions of race and otherness, for Marty's mission would now be to 'redeem' and 'reclaim' (black) rock'n'roll for the white all-American male, by fathering (or 'inventing') it a second time, in a gesture of appropriation narratively disguised as a double last-minute rescue: he saves the honour of the band, being the stand-in for the injured Marvin, and he makes his father take his mother home from the dance (and thus bond as a future nuclear family).

The perfect formal match of the temporal categories 'remembering' and 'anticipation' hides thus an equally perfect mismatch, perfect because inverting an ethical relationship (the debt owed by white masculinity to black culture), while at the same time repressing a history (the history of race). To this extent, the scene could serve as the very example of the formation of a trauma, insofar as trauma always requires two events, one apparently neutral, which nonetheless, by virtue of some isomorphic or parallel aspect of the experience, serves to activate the originary, repressed occurrence. The question therefore arises: What could be the event to which the repeated, 'inverted' invention of rock'n'roll corresponds, in order for the two to map themselves onto each other, and what could be the feature they have in common? To answer this we need to radicalize our notion of the 'symptomatic' reading and turn to the New Lacanians, who offer a different analysis of the symptom and of trauma.

## 8.4. Žižek and the New Lacanians: theory

Although not a 'school', the New Lacanians are said to comprise Slavoj Žižek, Joan Copjec and Juliet Flower-MacCannell. They are, broadly speaking, united by a new concern with what has been called the 'ethics' of psychoanalysis and its contemporary political ramifications. According to James Mellard, the New Lacanians emphasize Lacan's late notions of drive, *jouissance*, and the real at the expense of his early concepts of desire, the imaginary, and the symbolic; most are more interested in cultural studies and elements of popular culture than in literature [or film] alone; most construe the universe as ironic, tragic, or perversely paradoxical (so that everything contains its opposite); and because most color culture and its artifacts in dark tones, they are fascinated by film noir and related forms and themes.

(Mellard 1998: 395)

For our purposes, we might say that the New Lacanians supplant/supplement the earlier focus of (feminist) film-scholars on 'desire' and 'lack' (Mulvey 1975; Doane 1987) or the look and the gaze (Mulvey 1975; Silverman 1992) with other Lacanian notions, such as that of the drives, the symptom/ synthome distinction (which Lacan sees as fundamental to an understanding of sexual difference), and deferred action ('why a letter always arrives at its destination', Žižek 1992: 154). Their political concerns – the 'ethics' of psychoanalysis – revolve around democracy and totalitarianism, universality and multi-culturalism. Joan Copjec, for instance, is in this respect critical of Foucault and the type of gender politics (as well as the film theory) based on his writings (Copjec 1994; see also Chapter 9 below for a discussion of Foucault and film studies).

Instead of concentrating on the imaginary and the symbolic, when assessing the film experience in relation to a spectator (the 'subject'), the New Lacanians focus on the imaginary and the real. This shift is a double one: it tries to free film studies from its obsession with vision, illusion, and representation, especially as elaborated around sexual difference, and it tries to repoliticize the cinema, by tracking the various permutations of the symbolic order under capitalist globalization. The imaginary–real axis becomes the key relation that most accurately maps the spectatorial dynamics of (post-classical) Hollywood, many of whose films can be interpreted as red alerts to the vicissitudes of (postmodern) subjectivity in the realm of the social. This social realm the New Lacanians would typify as authoritarian-without-authority (i.e. without the traditional legitimacy of the symbolic, as manifest, for instance, in the 'submission to the law of castration' typical of patriarchy and bourgeois ideology). This new form of lawlessness within the law, Žižek calls the tyranny of the 'enjoying superego' (Žižek 1999).

The third concern of the New Lacanians is the study of the relationship between temporality and subjectivity. Exploring and extending a concept first introduced by Freud (*Nachträglichkeit*), they bring the idea of 'deferred action' to bear on a number of issues relevant to film studies – and to *Back to the Future*, our film under consideration – such as time-travel, non-linear narrative, post-gender identity, trauma, and symptom formation.

## 8.5. Žižek and the New Lacanians: method

Although Slavoj Žižek has over the past ten years published some 20 books (many dealing with film examples, and some devoted to studies of individual directors, such as Hitchcock, Lynch, Kieslowski: (1992; 2000), it is not easy to distil from his writings a transferable or transportable methodology. On the other hand, so distinctive is his approach, so recognizable is his style of argument, and so typical are the examples he chooses that one can (as Stephen Heath has done) speak of a 'Žižek film' (Heath 1999: 36).

- One repeated theme in the work of the New Lacanians is the notion that fantasy is not in opposition to reality but that which secures and anchors our sense of everyday reality. Indeed, it is fantasy which makes reality's brute facticity (the Real) meaningful and liveable.
- When looking at a film, we should try and identify the obsessional element, that which at first glance appears to be merely one feature or detail among others, but which sticks out or doesn't belong: this is the symptom (or 'traumatic kernel'), and it at once sustains, suspends, and subverts the apparent meaning or logic of an event.
- Among characters in films, Žižek distinguishes between *desire-creatures* and *drive-creatures*, the latter typified by a kind of relentless, unstoppable momentum, which powerfully pushes events in the direction of apparently senseless repetition but which speak of the energies that all living organisms mobilize toward their own self-annihilation. This momentum is Lacan's version of the Freudian death-drive, and as we shall see, it can help us understand the repeated interactions, but also the symbolic function of the pair 'protagonist–antagonist' in *Back to the Future*.
- Žižek has also interrogated the type of causal nexus advanced by a narrative. He often looks for points where the linear flow doubles up upon itself or forms a kind of inside out loop, a Möbius strip that points to a temporality of deferred action. Across this *Nachträglichkeit* another logic of desire manifests itself, in which all narratives necessarily unfold themselves from their end, hinting at a 'return of the repressed' coming from the future, not the past.
- The New Lacanians, finally, regard cultural productions as inherently political. They insist on the paradox of human agency, where an absolute rupture exists between the 'ethical' act of the individual subject and social authority, while at another level, the law and fantasy are not opposed (as so much radical thinking posits) but collusive and interdependent.

# 8.6. Žižek and the New Lacanians: analysis
## 8.6.1. Shame and humiliation

If we now once more look at *Back to the Future*, there are a number of features that might attract the attention of the New Lacanians. Foremost among them would be the figure of Biff. The curious relationship between him and Marty is that of antagonist and double, which explains Marty's over-identification with Biff and his role as Marty's nemesis. In more specifically Žižekian terms, what defines the relationship are, on the one hand, shame and humiliation and, on the other, 'obscene enjoyment', the tyranny of the superego. Both are traumatic, and thus bring us back to the issue raised above: what could be the event for which the fantasy of Marty 'inventing' rock'n'roll seems to be the cover or 'screen memory'?

The incident that springs to mind in *Back to the Future* would be the scene where Marty returns home after being first reprimanded and then disqualified at school, to watch a totalled car being towed to the parental home and witness Biff, the driver, berating George, the owner, for not having told him that the car had 'a blind spot' which, according to Biff, 'caused' the accident. Marty, himself unjustly disgraced, becomes witness to the spectacle of the father's humiliation, an impotent bystander in an act of public shaming, which, as Žižek once remarked when commenting on Serb atrocities in Bosnia, is like the rape of a daughter in the presence of the father, intended to destroy both family loyalty and the social bond. Ludicrous though the scene of the father's humiliation in *Back to the Future* appears, it is evidently intended by the film-makers as crucial, since it occurs twice: with exactly the same words being exchanged to round off the sadistic ritual, Biff bullies George at the diner in 1955, almost as soon as Marty meets him. However, whereas in 1955 George is told by Wilson, the diner's black waiter, to stand up for himself, in 1985 Marty's reaction, after Biff has left, is quite different. In response to his father's excuses, Marty lays into his father, berating him in terms that are not only similar but structurally identical to Biff's accusations, in that he, too, blames his father for what George, not Biff, has done to him, Marty, by ruining his weekend with Jennifer.

Humiliation is thus the key trope that defines the relation between George and Biff in *Back to the Future*. Here, too, time-travel ensures that the roles are reversed, and at the end, after Marty has woken up to his reformed family, it is McFly senior who patronizes Biff to the point of humiliating him. Waxing George's BMW, Biff has become a recognizable racial stereotype, the 'boy', familiar from classical Hollywood movies, often played by 'Stepin Fetchit'. Biff is the shoe-shining, shimmying black, who is lazy and up to no good, but funny and always ready to jump to attention, as Biff in fact does when he is 'caught out' telling a fib about the second coat of polish.

As if to underline the importance of this Stepin Fetchit figure for the transfer of paternity that the film needs to enact, he also figures in the 1955 past as the floor-sweeping waiter who enters the picture by intervening at precisely the moment Marty McFly recognizes his future father in horror and is too stunned to answer the latter's question: 'and who are you?' Luckily, Marty also 'recognizes' the black waiter as Goldie Wilson, and can confidently tell him that one day (Goldie) will be the mayor of Hill Valley. Thus not only appropriates rock'n'roll but claims the civil rights movement as well, since we already saw Goldie Wilson's election van in the opening scene, campaigning for a second term of office.

The trauma at the heart of the film, it would seem, is not so much – or not only – the inadequacy of this particular specimen of fatherhood which is George McFly, but the very idea of paternity and masculinity in relation to white American middle-class culture, which – as the film so carefully and in many ways so candidly demonstrates – must pass via the trauma of race if it is to find a stable identity inside the terms of a symbolic order. *Back to the Future* does not achieve stable identity for its protagonist, since the film keeps gyrating between these master–slave, father–son reversals, without finally inscribing 'blackness' into its cast of castrating and castrated figures, other than by a 'black and white minstrel' dissimulation. The reason for this is that race is connected with shame and humiliation, but true to the dream logic of reversals that drives the narrative, this humiliation in the film attaches itself to the white protagonists, as if to cover for the shame that white America does not/did not feel about centuries of humiliating its black population. It is here that the parallel between Biff and the Libyans provides a crucial link.

### 8.6.2. The foreign policy of victimhood

Humiliation before the eyes of the 'son' is also at issue in the scene where the Libyan terrorists gun down Doc Brown, while Marty helplessly looks on – in fact, as we saw, while two Martys helplessly look on. Given the nationality of the assailants, it is not difficult to think of the scene as a metaphor for any number of the then still recent political humiliations of the US: Kennedy at the Bay of Pigs, Lyndon B. Johnson in Vietnam, Richard Nixon's impeachment, Jimmy Carter's Iran hostage crisis, Ronald Reagan's unsuccessful showdown with Colonel Qaddafi – all, in a sense, presidents appearing as impaired or humiliated fathers. Critics such as Pfeil speaking of the film's sympathy with 'Reaganite revisionism' might consider what *Back to the Future*'s rewriting of America's postwar/Cold War history thinks it ought to accomplish: to mitigate the memory of national disgrace several times over. Doc Brown double-crossing the Libyans who stole the plutonium (here an energy source used as 'car fuel') can even be read as a symbolic revenge for the oil crisis, instigated by the Arab countries after their own perceived humiliation by Israel and its Western supporters. When Doc reappears at the end, the DeLorean not only takes off like a jet fighter-plane. It is powered by banana skins and recycled beer-bottles, indicating the sci-fi wish that America might become energy self-sufficient.

The apparently irrelevant and defamatory introduction of Libyans into the plot thus signals a chain of associations that do in fact have a bearing on the political and ethical dimension of the narrative. They stand for what Žižek would call 'the big Other', the instance (here, America's always threatening enemies, the forces of Reagan's 'evil empire') in whose inscrutable and omnipresent gaze the subject constitutes his desire (here, the national pride of self-evident supremacy and superpower status). The Libyans, with their makeshift rocket-launcher VW camper, symbolize the derisory but dangerous enemies that stand in the way of America's perfect self-image, whose 'foreign policy' combats terrorism and supports freedom fighters. The logic follows what Žižek has called 'the dialectic of the victim' in America's international interventions: the ethnic or national 'other' is tolerated as long as he behaves like a victim, i.e. is too poor, suffering, or incapacitated to manifest an agenda of his own. Once the other does manifest aspirations, he ceases to enjoy victim status and is declared a terrorist, since to the racial supremacist, Žižek argues, 'the desire of the other is intolerable': yesterday's victim is today's terrorist. Yet once the desire of the other can be manipulated to coincide with that of the United States, the relation changes once more, and today's terrorists may become tomorrow's freedom fighters, as in Reagan's adoption of the Nicaraguan 'Contras' as freedom-fighters even to the point of making secret deals with a 'terrorist' state (Iran), in order to support them illicitly with arms (the 'Iran–Contra' affair).

There are several points one might wish to make about this reading of *Back to the Future*. First, it is fairly unusual, at least until the late 1980s, for a mainstream Hollywood film, with a perfectly traditional agenda – to chart the rites of passage to adulthood for a young white male along the Oedipal path of incest and parricide – to resort so explicitly to race as the field of symbolizations, from which the moves intended to stabilize subjectivity and secure identity it then draws. To believe the film, this recourse to race has to do with the disturbances and confusions surrounding the figure of the father, since the weak, absent, or inadequate father becomes by the 1980s – the decade that saw the 'revival' of Hollywood – almost the founding condition of contemporary American action and adventure films (from Spielberg's *ET* to *The Last Action Hero*). In *Back to the Future* (as in many other films of the 1990s, notably *Pulp Fiction*) the signifiers of black culture function as fetishes, as libidinally invested invocations of otherness. It might be useful to examine whether such films therapeutically 'work through' this trauma or, by contrast, are – deconstructively and thus deliberately – 'putting on' the mask of race in order to support a masculinity no longer secured by the white Oedipal father. In other films, the play with race is doubled by a political discourse worrying about America's status as a superpower at the end of the bipolar world order of the Cold War (*Independence Day, Mars Attacks!*), but only *Back to the Future* probes a trauma.

### 8.6.3. The symptom: does it sustain or subvert the system?

Second, a question thus arises about what in the film functions as the symptom around which either a deconstructive or a therapeutic reading can organize itself. What is the element, in other words, that sustains the 'reality' of the film, its verisimilitude as a fiction? In classical Hollywood it is often said that gender sustains the film (i.e. women as objects to be traded between men, or as objects to be possessed by the look underpin the narrative functioning), but that this mechanism of gender imbalance is present without being problematized/thematized. Feminist symptomatic readings have therefore focused on both demonstrating and deconstructing the mechanism in question, even arguing that women are the 'trouble' that is necessary for the classical text to function at all. As already briefly discussed above, and taken up once more in Chapter 9, earlier feminist theory tended to imply that so perfect was the ideological operation of the classical film that it made the gender asymmetry 'invisible' or hidden. However, there was one genre that attracted feminist film theorists, as well as Lacanians, because it seemed to be hysterical in relation to femininity, highlighting it as excessive. This genre was *film noir*, where it is the *femme fatale* that marks the excess inherent in the (male) classical text, while underscoring that its disruptive power is irrecuperable.

Such an assumption, however, also redefines the traditional (Freudian) notion of woman as unknowable, and Lacan's formula of woman as the 'symptom' of man (see Žižek 1992: 31–67). Gender trouble can now be seen as the element that (still) sustains the film as a classical text, but it also subverts its perfect ideological functioning, by keeping suspended the resolution between the two ways of reading the figure of the *femme fatale*. At once necessary and excessive, the *femme fatale* is the reason why, to the New Lacanians, *film noir* already announces the slow agony of classical patriarchy. Paradoxically and parodistically symbolized in the underworld boss, corrupt politician, or drug baron, the father figure is readable as the embodiment of excess and superego lawlessness, not least thanks to the pastiche versions and cross-generic revivals of *film noir* in the 1980s and 1990s. According to Žižek, this figure represents the paternal authority not subject to castration, the obscenely 'enjoying' father. Outside the law and yet executing the law, he invariably counts among his possessions the *femme fatale*, keeping the hero in thrall but also leading him to (self-)destruction. We have already come across a particularly over-explicit version of such 'superego enjoyment' in *Chinatown*'s Noah Cross (see Chapter 4), who 'owns' Mrs Mulwray, the film's *femme fatale*, several times over. Yet one could equally well cite *Pulp Fiction*'s Marcellus Wallace, over-explicit as a traumatic figure of transgression and excess, in that he is black and can call one of his henchman 'my white nigger', while also owning Mia, his white wife. She, in turn, is 'playing at' being a *femme fatale* as well as being positioned as such by Vince (notably in the initial discussion with Jules as to whether a foot massage for the boss's wife is a transgression or a transaction).

Compared to these films, *Back to the Future* would seem to be classical, rather than post-classical, in that gender sustains the narrative but does not subvert it. The women are shown to be perfect specimen of male Oedipal identity formation: the flirtatious/prim division of Lorraine is played out, in order to be followed by the integrated, totally passive 'I love you/I wait for you' Jennifer, unproblematically passed from her Daddy to Marty. What is missing, in other words, is the subversive presence of a *femme fatale* and her power to sustain ambiguity. But given that the film is so explicit about the hero's Oedipal fixation and incest fantasies, the symptom, it is safe to assume, has shifted, as has the enjoying superego, now also located elsewhere.

### 8.6.4. The regime of the brothers

This brings us to our third point: what sort of strategy is a Hollywood film following when appearing to make race the discursive site of a symptom, naming it, while at the same time risking subversion of its own ideological project? Here another aspect of the political analysis of the post-Oedipal society put forward by the New Lacanians might prove helpful: the idea, taken from Freud's later metapsychological writings, notably *Totem and Taboo*, that with the 'death' of the totemic father social power reconstitutes itself around the 'regime of the brother' (Flower-MacCannell 1995), held together by mutual implication in crime, bonded through acts of violence, and sustained by rituals of humiliation.

In *Back to the Future* such a 'regime of the brother' is in fact present in the form of the 'small-town bullies' headed by Biff, who now emerges as the film's key 'symptomatic' figure. Appearing at one level as one of the excessive or unacceptable authority figures Marty faces, and on another, as a dramatic 'device' to provide the obstacles for the hero to overcome, Biff in fact sustains and suspends the narrative's emplotment of 'normal' Oedipal identity. Marty and Biff exemplify the distinction, alluded to above, between desire-creatures and drive creatures: desire creatures live under the threat of castration (for them desire is a function of lack, and lack can be 'filled' by a fetish-formation, i.e. a substitute, such as Jennifer for Lorraine). Drive creatures, on the other hand, are not subject to desire: they go on regardless, they are unstoppable, unkillable, because they embody the death drive. Such a creature is Robocop before he has paternal memories, or the shape-shifting Terminator II; in the case of *Back to the Future* it is Biff, because he is effectively undefeatable. However many times Marty beats him, outwits him or trips him up, he will always come back to haunt, torment, and aggress. In this sense Biff not only sustains and suspends but also subverts the Oedipal trajectory of the film.

As a drive creature, opposed to Marty, a desire creature driven by anxiety and lack, Biff is a permanent threat to the symbolic order. But Marty and Biff are also alter egos, or as Žižek might phrase it – Biff is Marty 'giving in to his desire'. We already noted how Marty berates his father in exactly the way that Biff does, in the matter of the smashed-up car. But we can now assign another meaning to the 'blind spot': it represents the Big Other's demands on George, which can never be met, and which both Biff and Marty appropriate, giving them full power over George's guilty conscience. Likewise, in respect to Marty's repressed and censored incest feelings, it is Biff who stands in for him, or rather they both occupy the blind spot of Lorraine's disavowal of her sexuality. In the scene of the 'petting' in the car, for instance, where Biff takes the place of Marty as Lorraine's sexual partner, before he is socked by George, there's a showdown that was actually planned for Marty. If we see Biff as Marty's double, then Biff merely 'acts out' what Marty is repressing. If we see Biff as a drive creature, then we note that there is a drive-side to Marty's desire-identity, indicating the road not taken by Marty – as indeed by the film's overt narrative – apparently opting for the reinstatement of 'traditional' Oedipal identity and patriarchal structures of the symbolic (i.e. 'accepting castration'). Biff points to the other possibility of the fatherless society, if Marty had instead become part of the unruly post-Oedipal force, a member – or, more likely, the leader – of a 'gang'. The film indicates its knowledge about this road in a curious detail. When Marty returns from 1955 to 1985, his home-town seems to have changed: it is a dirty place, litter everywhere; a drunk or homeless man sleeps on a bench, and a general feel of urban ghetto dilapidation hangs improbably about the place. The cinema is no longer advertising whatever would be the 1985 version of *Cattle Queen of Montana*, but has become a porn house, showing *Orgy American Style* – suggestive in itself, but apparently the title of a well-known exploitation movie featuring gang rapes and street mayhem.

There are a number of New Hollywood films of the 1990s, from *Goodfellows*, *The Usual Suspects*, and *Things to Do in Denver When You're Dead* to *Casino* and *Fight Club* that dramatize the post-totemic rule of the brothers, under the sign of the absent big Other, or of the big Other as the obscenely 'enjoying' father. Significantly at the end of *Back to the Future*,

Marty's options are still open, because the final kiss does not seal the submission under the Oedipal law – it is interrupted by Doc Brown, who has uncovered further 'trouble' ahead.

### 8.6.5. Time-travel and the superego's demand

Whatever this trouble is in the sequel (and it seems a fair bet that Biff will have a role to play in it), our analysis has uncovered a complex network of relations that ties paternity and masculinity in this film not so much to gender (as is traditionally the case in classical Hollywood) but to race and international politics, centred on shame and humiliation, of which the reverse side, according to the New Lacanians, is the 'obscene enjoyment' of the superego.

What distinguishes *Back to the Future*, furthermore, is that few Hollywood films from the 1980s get as close to hinting at a truth about the nature of American race relations, namely that it is centred on rituals of humiliation, which is its way of suggesting – albeit in the form of the symptom – that some sort of debt may have to be acknowledged. While in one sense *Back to the Future* could be seen as covertly making use of race, in order to shore up a very traditional all-white American masculinity, in another sense the film speaks of a difficult debt and even guilt. Explicitly, Marty manages to become a man by enlisting race in order to improve the father-image that allows him to become adult. His emancipation and empowerment seems purchased not only at the price of rewriting history (especially the history of American popular culture) but also at the price of once more stereotyping black Americans with the very same gesture that begins to acknowledge their place in this American history. Such would be the case if this rewriting and stereotyping of race were not taking place around the figure of Biff, incoherently but symptomatically placed at different discursive sites: fairy-tale villainy, white supremacist racism, 'international terrorism', black-and-white minstrelsy, and finally black gangland brotherhood.

Such a reading of Biff as the 'symptom' of Marty redefines the symptom as synthome, as the coded message in which the subject receives, but does not recognize, the truth about his own desire. Hill Valley with *Orgy American Style* playing highlights a significant dimension of half-acknowledged awareness of superego enjoyment, and thus also of guilt and responsibility regarding white America's more troubling impact on the world and on part of its own citizens. What do the New Lacanians and the 'ethics of psychoanalysis' have say about such guilt? If Biff's appearance and actions function as both the truth and the mask of America's bad conscience, he does not so much fulfil the structural place of the superego as mark the place where its effects can be registered – in the absence of the symbolic order. Žižek has argued that the more one pays tribute to the superego, the more tribute it extorts. Not only that: following the call of the superego makes you feel guilty, but the more you follow it, the more you feel you have betrayed yourself and thus you feel even more guilt. According to Žižek, this dilemma forms a perfect vicious circle, what he calls 'the ethics of guilt', to be distinguished from the traditional workings of the symbolic order, which in fact it replaces:

> The parental figure who is simply 'repressive' in the mode of symbolic authority tells a child: 'You must go to grandma's birthday party and behave nicely, even if you are bored to death – I don't care whether you want to, just do it!' The superego figure, in contrast, says to the child: 'Although you know how much grandma would like to see you, you should go to her party only if you really want to – if you don't, you should stay at home'. The trick performed by the superego is to seem to offer the child a free choice, when, as every child knows, he is not being given any choice at all. Worse than that, he is being given an order and told to smile at the same time. Not only: 'You must visit your grandma, whatever you feel,' but: 'You must visit your grandma, and you must be glad to do it!' The superego orders you to enjoy doing what you have to do. 'You can do your duty, because you must do it' is how Kant formulated the categorical imperative. The superego inverts the Kantian 'You can, because you must' in a different way, turning it into 'You must, because you can'.

> (Žižek 1999)

In *Back to the Future*, it is in the first instance the slogan 'You can achieve anything if you put your mind to it' that could be seen as a command from the superego: the impossible demand made on the American psyche by the existence of the American dream. But it is precisely insofar as the film puts this slogan under erasure that it opens itself up to that darker superego negatively outlined by Biff. Faced with the conundrum represented by George (absent paternal law) and Biff ('terrorist' response to this absence), Marty begins to realize that America's 'can do' optimism is no longer an option – that his future is blocked until and unless he goes back to where the (postwar) American dream was arguably first dreamt, the 1950s middle America of the emerging suburbs – Hill Valley, in other words. Marty's time-travel, instead of being a Reaganite apologia for keeping things the way they are and rewriting the past in the image of the present, is in fact almost the exact reverse. It is an attempt to make use of the time-travel paradox – i.e. that you can go back to the past, on condition that you change as little as possible and yet make the big difference – in order for him to fashion from it a new 'ethics', that of 'deferred action', which says: your mode of agency, now that you can travel back in time, is to will and accept what has happened, which is to say, to take responsibility for it.

To recapitulate the two modes of how to interpret the travel and the time-loop paradox with respect to Hollywood: one is to say that history is only a discourse or a set of representations which we can make or fake, rewrite and alter (the airbrushed photograph or the digital images, as in *Zelig* or *Forrest Gump* – though in both films matters are a bit more complicated than that). The other way is to say that since we cannot change anything in the past, we might as well learn to love that which we don't like about our past (for instance our parents, all that which has made us what we are, or black popular culture, all that which has made us want what we now imagine we are).

It is along the latter line of reasoning that Žižek might place time-travel: he effectively says, 'Accepting what you cannot change is the essence of the Kantian notion of freedom: do as if you were morally free to choose the right action (for the common good).' It is also where John Rawls's notion of 'justice' meets Jean-Jacques Rousseau's idea of 'freedom': if you want to do what you ought to do, then you are free. For Žižek this has become contaminated and perverted by the command of the superego: 'Enjoy' (an 'ethical' reworking of Marcuse's ideas on consumerism, once consumption becomes the basis of capitalist economic growth and social reproduction. Leisure is now serious business, and having fun is a civic duty).

*Back to the Future* itself fulfils a (utopian) wish, in order to assuage a historical guilt: to undo a historical wrong about race and politics. It uses the genre of sci-fi and time-travel, and refigures individual agency and responsibility. If we now look briefly at some of the other films mentioned in the beginning of this chapter, we can recognize similar constellations, often enough articulated also around race and masculinity (*Pulp Fiction*), the failing symbolic order and the obscene enjoyment of the Father (as in *Twelve Monkeys* and *Brazil*), or the need to travel in time in order to assure yourself of your own identity, i.e. to 'accept' castration (which now appears in the guise of the inevitability of the past itself) in *Total Recall* and *Twelve Monkeys*.

## Conclusion

Contrary to the critiques of Freud, Lacan, and symptomatic readings as an illegitimate, logically flawed or ideologically driven partisan modes of interpretation, we have tried to show how the New Lacanians formulate a different form of cultural critique and cultural analysis, when it comes to conducting a 'history of the present'. There is indeed an ideological agenda: that our Western, liberal-democratic societies are not healthy, and that the many technicist, political, futurological discourses of freedom, unlimited growth and possibility, of human rights and the new world order actually mask a pervasive 'sickness', which can best be located in the new 'postmodern' subjectivities, and tracked via the various social texts, of which mainstream popular blockbuster movies are one significant manifestation. However, in the process of this diagnosis, the very notion of the 'symptom' has undergone a major change in meaning, and with it, the fundamental assumption of psychoanalysis, namely that of an unconscious, somehow hidden beneath or behind consciousness.

Žižek posits the necessity of the 'symptom' as the condition of the subject to be able to live social reality at all. Politically, he argues that liberalism, love of freedom, or the hype of virtual reality are so many signs of a new authoritarianism (the obscene Father/superego, the Big Other reinvested with 'enjoyment') whom we are more and more exposed to: The new authoritarianism which lacks authority. In a sense, Žižek picks up the old Hegelian dialectic, according to which the more we think we are free, the more we are in chains (Kojeve–Sartre–Althusser: the dialectic of freedom and necessity). In which case, Žižek wears his 'Lacan' as a kind of disguise (a madcap-jester gesture, rather like the persona of Hitchcock, his favourite director), in order to 'pass' as postmodern. To politicize psychoanalysis and give it a new ethical dimension, Kant is reread after deconstruction, and Hegel after Freud. For if Lacan argued that Freud added the unconscious to Hegelian philosophy, then Žižek, in the guise of the New Lacanian, gives a Hegelian reinterpretation of the role of the unconscious.

Strange as it may seem, the New Hollywood, according to Žižek, is Lacanian, insofar as it struggles to reinvent a tragic view of life at the very moment when the experience economy of unlimited fun reigns supreme. While American technological supremacy is unchallenged, and biogenetics has reached a new stage of 'can do' pragmatism, the artefacts of the US dream machine quiver with anxiety about history, suggesting that without a symbolic order, without Oedipal identity and an ego, America is lost to the Real and the Superego. It can be seen as a very 'conservative' message. Yet insofar as they seem impelled to invent a new ethical imperative out of postmodern subjectivity and post-colonial identity, films such as *Back to the Future* are remarkably alert to the 'perversely paradoxical' travels and travails enjoined upon those who have to dream the past in order to remember the future.

# 9 Feminism, Foucault, and Deleuze (*The Silence of the Lambs*)

## Introduction

Critics of psychoanalysis and psychosemiotics in film studies may well argue that 'apparatus theory' separates the eye as vision from the I of grammar and speech; that it divides the eye as mind from the eye as body, and that it cuts the eye of perception off from the other organs of embodied sensation. These objections could be summarized by saying that the emphasis on specular or ocular perception in classical film theory and Lacanian film analysis has systematically ignored the importance of the spectator's body as a continuous perceptual surface and an organizing principle of spatial and temporal orientation. When theorizing the film experience, in other words, psychoanalytic film studies treat the spectator–screen relationship as if it were based on a perceptual 'illusion' (by suggesting that objects which move on the screen are really there), which in turn assumes that vision is always transitive, i.e. a matter of 'seeing something', when it could just as well be aspect seeing, or 'seeing-as' (Wittgenstein). At the same time, apparatus theory unwittingly reinforces (bourgeois) ideology's disembodied, decontextualized, dematerialized version of watching movies, while also critiquing (with its call for 'anti-illusionism') mainstream cinema for producing such alienated forms of human experience. The change in emphasis implicit in apparatus theory from Freud to Lacan, from narrative emplotment (the Oedipal trajectory of structuralist analysis) to the dynamics of intersubjectivity (where viewer-identity is suspended and deferred in the mirror-stage) can only, according to such a line of argument, perpetuate this impoverished or indeed erroneous idea of cinematic spectatorship. Even the New Lacanians, whose shift of attention from the (optical) look to the (discursive) gaze, from the Imaginary/Symbolic to the Real, and from image to the sound-and-image field elaborates a different understanding of the interplay of perception, cognition, and sensation, could be charged with not having mitigated this state of affairs but merely – or needlessly – complicated it.

These and similar constructions of the cinema as psychic, perceptual, or projective illusion have been the point of attack of cognitivists and analytical philosophers, who question the notion that in the cinema one is dealing with either illusion/simulation or with alienation/reification. They argue that the perception, recognition, and apprehension of objects, people, or places in the moving image need involve neither deception nor suspension of disbelief (Carroll 1988b: 89ff.). Apprehension and comprehension in the cinema call upon the same cognitive faculties and perceptual activities as ordinary seeing and knowing: 'The theory that [moving] pictures are cognitive or epistemic illusions ... has been thoroughly debunked and can be laid to rest' (Allen 1997: 78–9.)

Yet many film scholars not persuaded by the debunking efforts of cognitivists but equally dissatisfied with psychoanalytic or Marxist accounts have in recent years turned to the French philosopher Gilles Deleuze and his two cinema books (*The Movement Image*, 1986, and *The Time Image*, 1989) when looking for an alternative conceptualization of the film experience as an embodied, spatio-temporal event. Deleuze is not a film theorist in the commonly accepted sense. As has often been pointed out, he theorizes *with* rather than *about* the cinema (Stam 2000: 258; Pisters 2001: 17). What seems to have drawn him to the cinema is the relation of bodies, matter, and perception, seen as a traditional philosophical problem, and in the twentieth century most vigorously explored by phenomenology. Although it is Henri Bergson's *Matter and Memory* (1991) that he cites for such key concepts of his cinema books as the crystal image, rather than Husserl or Merleau-Ponty, Deleuze is as much a philosopher of being, becoming, and time as they are. Where he is innovative is that for him the moving image (and thus the cinema) is the most philosophically rich instance of the inseparability of matter, temporality, and consciousness, which in his view is as decisively indicative of our modernity as, say, binoculars or the *camera obscura* were for Cartesian philosophy. According to Deleuze, the problem with traditional film theory is twofold:

● First, it conceives of the cinema as (static, photographic) images that move, rather than as movement-images and time-images. These for Deleuze are not bound to a specific material support (whether retinal, photographic, or digital) but are realities in their own right, part of the energies, the flux and intensities that embed thought and the material world in what might be called the 'supermedium' of multi-layered durations and coextensive temporalities (Deleuze's 'sheets of time').

● The second problem Deleuze has with film theory is that it tries to model moving images and their time-based articulations on literary narrative and the language analogy (as was the case with the structuralist semiotics of Christian Metz), thereby either ignoring or misconstruing that which is distinctive about cinema, namely the kinetic modulations of movement and the potential infinity of images, their rhythms and plasticity. The cinema experience for Deleuze is an unmediated and enveloping reality, at once actual and virtual, at once mental, somatic, and physiological, made up of 'optical sound situations' rather than visual perceptions, a succession of open events rather than culturally or linguistically coded representations.

However one judges the arguments Deleuze offers for considering the cinema as an experience in which matter thinks and thinking matters – there are many for whom his lyrical-metaphoric discourse is 'a mere curiosity' – it is easy to see why his work has attracted scholars who are either trying to think about the cinema experience differently or are concerned with theorizing post-photographic imaging modes and 'virtual reality'.

To make these rather large questions a little less unwieldy, this chapter will begin by reviewing the transformations and internal developments of the psychoanalytic approach to film and the cinematic apparatus, as it became reflexive in respect to gender and sexual preference (under the names of feminist film theory/gender theory/queer theory), often by turning away from both Freud and Lacan, and towards Foucault and Deleuze, in search of a politically equally responsible theory of embodied perception. Thus, the problematics of gender will be the main reason why this chapter also takes a detour via Foucault and queer theory, in order to finally see how valuable Deleuze might be for such a film analysis. In the second part, therefore, both theorists will help us to indicate how, starting from the notion of bodily boundaries, gender, and embodied perception, film analysis might take on board the shifts of interests and assumptions signalled generally by the move from psychoanalysis to anti-psychoanalysis in film studies and cultural theory.

As our film example we have chosen *The Silence of the Lambs* (1991; directed by Jonathan Demme, screenplay by Ted Tally, after the novel by Thomas Harris). The choice is motivated not least because the film proved both controversial and popular with critics working on gender and sexual preference but – to our knowledge – has not yet been exposed to a Deleuzian reading. *The Silence of the Lambs* gave rise to a major debate among feminists, and between feminists and gay rights activists. At issue was its 'sexual politics', revolving in large part around the significance of the central character, Clarice Starling, played by Jodie Foster. Put very briefly, the film created contradictory reception positions: some women's groups thought of it as exploitative and sexist, others – more positively – detected a feminist horror film, with a strong, active female character who slays the monster. The ones accusing Demme of sexism merely saw the classic male fantasy of the woman put at risk by men and then sadistically punished for taking these risks. Gay activists, on the other hand, perceived *The Silence of the Lambs* as homophobic because it pathologizes homosexuality, notably in the figure of James Gumb (or 'Buffalo Bill'), the serial killer and transvestite/trans-gender psychopath. Ironically, the third central character, Hannibal Lecter, did not divide opinion anywhere near as much. Thanks to an astonishing performance by Anthony Hopkins, 'Hannibal the Cannibal' was recognized as an unusual kind of monster in the horror film: superhumanly intelligent, attractively seductive, amiably lethal. His ancestors are perhaps better known from decadent literature (and maybe even surrealism): the dandy-aesthete-connoisseur, for whom murder is a fine art. In the subsequent decade, it was this character that has enjoyed a folk-hero media afterlife and has become an instantly appreciated icon. As will be seen, it is partly around Hannibal Lecter that our reading will change gear and paradigm, and not only because he obliged some critics to ponder the divide between the monstrous and the human, being caught by the film between their feelings about two kinds of monster: the visible evil of Buffalo Bill's gender-and-body horror, and the invisible and almost unthinkable evil of Hannibal Lecter's mind-and-brain horror.

## 9.1. Feminism and film: theory

While the psychoanalytic film theory of Christian Metz, Jean-Louis Baudry, and Stephen Heath had initially concentrated on questions of 'primary identification', on the 'reality-effect' and 'subject construction' as the conditions of the classical Hollywood cinema's legibility and textual coherence, feminist film theory began with the realization that this classical cinema was also a system of visual representation implicated and complicit in maintaining sexual difference, i.e. the uneven distribution of power between men and women: 'In this debate [about sexuality and representation], the cinematic image is taken as both the model of and term for a process of representation through which sexual difference is constructed and maintained' (Rose 1986: 199). At least since Laura Mulvey's essay 'Visual Pleasure and Narrative Cinema' (1975), feminist film theory concentrated on deconstructing the terms of this complicity, eventually focusing on the question why female spectators can take pleasure in watching movies at all, given their sexist ideological import.

This is not just a matter of story material or role modelling. What Mulvey implied about the functioning of narrative and spectacle in classical cinema was that the subject addressed by the Hollywood text is gendered and male by virtue not only of the dominant forms of visual pleasure – voyeurism and fetishism, traditionally analysed as male perversions – but also by the close formal convergence of narrative progress (the desire to see and to know) with the filmic process itself as exemplified in the workings of the cinematic apparatus or 'dispositif' (see Rosen 1986). As Mary Ann Doane put it, reviewing the debate some ten years later: 'With respect to a narrativization of the woman, the apparatus strains; but the transformation of the woman into spectacle is easy. Through her forced affinity with the iconic, imagistic aspects of cinema, the woman is constituted as a resistance or impedance to narrativization' (Doane 1987: 5–6). The conditions of female spectatorship in narrative cinema are therefore either submission to the regime of the gaze, the perversion of a perversion so to speak, or involve taking pleasure in the subject effects of a sexual identity not her own: 'Confronted with the classical Hollywood text with a male address, the female spectator has basically two modes of entry: a narcissistic identification with the female figure as spectacle, and a "transvestite" identification with the active male hero in his mastery' (Doane 1987: 9). The very concept of female spectatorship thus names a theoretical impossibility, and in practice produces 'a mixed sexual body, . . . a hermaphrodite'. While the institution cinema has always courted women as an audience, its textual system works to deprive the woman 'of a gaze . . . of subjectivity and repeatedly [transforms her] into the object of a masculine scopophilic desire' (p. 2).

We can see how this might be immediately relevant to *The Silence of the Lambs*, and not only to the relationship between the female heroine and female audiences, but as a description of the identity-confusion of one of the characters, namely Buffalo Bill, as if he was the very embodiment of the dilemma of Doane's (and Mulvey's) female film spectator.

## 9.2. Feminism and film: method

What is a feminist reading of a classical/post-classical Hollywood film? The most widely imitated model is that inaugurated by Mulvey's 1975 essay 'Visual Pleasure and Narrative Cinema' (also in Mulvey 1989: 14–26). This complex and polemical piece has often been reproduced, and in the process also been reduced to a checklist of psychoanalytic concepts, such as fetishism, voyeurism, castration anxiety, phallus, and disavowal. Generations of undergraduate and graduate essays have winnowed her argument down to such core statements as 'the gaze is male' (or: 'the man looks, women are to be looked at'), 'sadism demands a story', 'desire is lack'. These were applied to the canon of classical films as well as to more recent mainstream cinema (though it is now also common to find post-classical films being used to critique Mulvey's assumptions). For the subtler narratological and ideological implications of Mulvey's arguments around cinema and sexual difference, there are abundant commentaries published on the topic. Those interested in 'doing' a feminist film analysis may nonetheless – depending on the particular theoretical framework chosen – wish to consider the paradigmatic moves listed below, or look out for common points of critique, when discussing the representation of women in the classical Hollywood text:

- the role model thesis: negative/positive stereotyping (Rosen 1973; Haskell 1973);
- the repression thesis: women generate a contradiction that the text seeks to repress (Cook and Johnston 1988);
- the disturbance thesis: woman is 'trouble' in the system, generating the core dynamics of the male-centred narrative trajectory;
- the containment thesis: classical film needs the woman-as-trouble to function at all, but then has to 'contain' her in order to come to an ideologically acceptable closure (Bellour 2000; Heath 1981);
- the excess/lack thesis: melodrama (Mulvey 1989: 39–44), woman's film (Doane 1987).

Some of the chief points of criticism of Mulvey can also be itemized:

- Her argument is heterosexist (Doane and Bergstrom 1990).
- She (initially at least) makes no room for lesbian identification.
- She devalorizes masochism as an 'originary' subject position of the cinematic experience (Studlar 1988).
- Finally, she posits the ideological construction of gendered identity as a successful, hegemonic activity, whereas it is possible to argue that patriarchal identity-formation via the cinema is only partly successful; hence her theory might be seen as actually assisting ideology in its attempt to construct, via popular culture, gendered identities (see also the quotation from David Rodowick in Chapter 8 above).

In the wake of the intense engagement with Mulvey's theses there have been many exemplary feminist analyses of individual films: those of Mary Ann Doane (1987), Teresa de Lauretis (1984), Kaja Silverman (1988), Barbara Klinger (1994), or Tania Modleski (1988) come to mind.

## 9.3. Analysis: a feminist reading of *The Silence of the Lambs*

In several respects, *The Silence of the Lambs* lends itself to an analysis within the categories of the 'classical' or canonical story format: the screenplay shows a clear three-act division, with introduction and coda (the first act ends with Clarice's discovery at the Baltimore warehouse; the second with the trick offer made to Hannibal by the FBI; and the third with the showdown in Buffalo Bill's house); the narrative moves are based on repetition/resolution (the successive encounters between Clarice and Hannibal Lecter, the introduction of past, present, and future victims of Buffalo Bill); the character constellations play permutations on triadic relationships (Clarice Starling–Hannibal Lecter–Buffalo Bill), with overt mirroring and more covert echoes linking the characters. A Proppian analysis would similarly reveal the layeredness of the actants' functions around injunctions (rules and their infringement), senders, envoys and antagonists, magic objects, helpers and villains. The film also has a deadline structure to 'contain' the narrative and steer it in a linear direction, which even leads to the (albeit unconsummated) formation of a (heterosexual) couple, once the threat to traditional categories of sexual difference (in the person of Buffalo Bill) is eliminated. In its dynamics of suspense and spectator involvement, *The Silence of the Lambs* is also quite classical: powered by a detection plot, the action moves inexorably towards a final cathartic showdown and finishes with the heroine's victory, followed by a coda, in which closure is neatly balanced by the possibility of an opening towards a sequel (an indication of the film's post-classical 'knowingness', but also of its cleverly perverse negotiation of a traditional if not 'reactionary' version of heterosexuality).

The story concerns a young policewoman at an FBI training academy who is given the assignment to befriend a very dangerous criminal, Hannibal Lecter, a former psychiatrist, now imprisoned for multiple murder and cannibalism, but who may be able to help the police identify a serial killer on the loose who murders young women and then skins them. Clarice Starling becomes deeper and deeper involved in the world of Hannibal Lecter, who helps her but extracts his own price, by psychoanalyzing her and penetrating her personal psychic secret, the trauma of the lambs, whom she tried but failed to rescue as a young girl, and the obscure link this incident may have with the death of her father, the nonexistence of a mother, and her escape from a (sexually abusive) guardian-uncle. Guided by Lecter, she eventually tracks down the serial killer and, in a gruesomely protracted showdown, is able to kill him. The film ends with Clarice's graduation ceremony at the police academy, and a phone call from Lecter, who managed to escape and is now once more at large, somewhere in the Caribbean, 'rewarding' her by promising to desist from any further unwanted attention.

*The Silence of the Lambs* is interesting for feminist film theory because it makes the site of gender/sexuality the explicit focus for questioning the relation between seeing and knowing. Buffalo Bill's victims are strangely overwritten texts: he cuts shapes out of their skins and leaves an insect in their throats, so that detection becomes not only the usual inventory of clues as to time, place, or cause of death, but immediately a matter of interpreting and 'reading' the body (of the victim) in order to read the mind (of the murderer). But so horrific are these bodies, so overpowering the marks of violence inflicted upon them, that close examination, proximity of vision, and detailed observation become almost impossible. In one memorable scene in a funeral parlour, where Clarice has to overcome this ocular revulsion as well as the stench of decomposition, in order to train her sights at the most minute detail, such as glitter nail polish and triple ear-piercings, she is herself the object of the gaze: before the autopsy, a serried row of policemen and detectives stand around observing her observing, and during the autopsy, her boss Crawford continues to observe her. Already in the credit sequence, when entering a lift on her way to her superior, Jodie Foster's size and femininity is contrasted with the tall males surrounding her at the FBI academy, an emphasis on body- and gender-based difference that is repeated several times over. In another scene, when interviewing Hannibal Lecter she strains to scrutinize his face, but due to the lighting in his cell and the perspex pane that separates them, it is he who seems to be observing her, from behind her back, trying to observe him. This shot of mirror-like superimposition is often featured in the film's publicity material, suggesting the ubiquitous gaze of Hannibal Lecter enveloping Clarice. In the final showdown, it is Buffalo Bill who, equipped with night-vision goggles, can see Clarice groping her way through his pitch-dark lair, unaware that he is watching her, and we with him, complicit in this sadistic spectacle that makes a mockery of her having a loaded gun but not the sight to aim it. Thus, while in one sense Clarice is in possession of the traditionally male look of scrutiny and detection, this look is frequently undermined as a symbol of mastery and the possession/position of knowledge.

Another point of interest for feminist film criticism is the question of gender and genre, notably feminist readings of the thriller/slasher/horror film. At one extreme, *The Silence of the Lambs* can be regarded as a classical thriller film in the Hitchcock mode, following on from *Psycho* and *The Birds*, revived and radicalized in films such as Brian de Palma's *Dressed to Kill* or John Carpenter's *Halloween*: a female heroine is being asked or forced to play detective, to enter dangerous territory, which exposes her extreme vulnerability as spectacle. The gendered architecture made up of looking and being looked at, which after Mulvey is said to determine spectator–screen relations (both on-screen and between screen and audience) is here redefined with respect to what constitutes a horror film for women: knowing one is observed without seeing (cf. Williams 1984). As indicated, feminist critics of *The Silence of the Lambs* were split between arguing that the woman's look functioned partly as it does in Hitchcock – for the sadistic pleasure of the male – but partly also as a signifier of the empowered female: Clarice/Foster not only embodies a positive (female) role model, showing courage and determination, she is also a woman operating in an all-male world as a 'professional'. Demme's film, along with those of Wes Craven, Tobe Hooper, and other contemporary horror films made by male directors, would then be 'deconstructing' the Hitchcock slasher/horror film, by opening it up to the ambiguities of female visual pleasure and to a more complex play of cross-gender identifications. One model for such readings is provided by Carol Clover and her analyses of what is at stake for female spectators (1992): 'Clover believes that in slasher movies identification seems to alter during the course of the picture from sympathizing with the killer to identifying with the woman-hero. Clover also argues that the (apparently male) monster is usually characterized as bisexual while the woman-hero is not simply a "woman." She is often "unfeminine," even tracking the killer into "his underground labyrinth"' (Staiger 1993: 147). In fact, Clover also argues that the female heroine or 'final girl' is often a stand-in for the adolescent male, allowing identification and projection to fasten on a 'safe' substitute, in order to explore homoerotic desires.

Another type of reading might invoke Barbara Creed's theory about the modern horror film. She argues that the ambiguous gender of the monster and the attraction/repulsion which the genre holds for female spectators symbolizes the 'monstrous feminine', the 'phallic mother', and the female subject position of 'abjection' vis-à-vis the primary, abandoned love-object (Creed 1986; 1993). The absent mother in Clarice's life seems to 'return' in all these bloated, disfigured, or lacerated female bodies she is called upon to inspect and to investigate.

Finally, a more mythological interpretation of Clarice Starling would point to her as a kind of latter-day Ariadne, who tracks down two kinds of man-beasts, two incarnations of the Minotaur – that of the bisexual Buffalo Bill in his dungeon, or earthworks labyrinth, and Hannibal Lecter as the master at the centre of a mental labyrinth (Jim Hoberman, cited in Staiger 1993: 150). There are, of course, other mythological echoes, relating to the Judeo-Christian iconographic traditions that could be identified and even given explicitly readings: Salome and the severed head of St John the Baptist, for instance, or the role of the sacrificial lamb in the Christian Easter mythology, probably adapted from pagan rituals of redemption and renewal.

In these generic, metapsychological, and mythological readings, the film challenges classical feminist film theory in that female spectatorship and heterosexuality no longer line up as mutually sustaining categories. For instance, the reason Hannibal Lecter's sexuality remains unmarked is that he is so severely heterosexual (the way he 'defends' Clarice Starling's honour in prison against the lewd Midge, his next-door cellmate). At the other extreme, Buffalo Bill puts the binary system of sexual difference into crisis, in the way he explicitly and compulsively restages the Lacanian mirror phase, which leaves the question of sexual identity disturbingly unresolved for spectators of either gender. The knowing reference to the mirror as unstable conferral of identity highlights Buffalo Bill's confusion as to his own gender, but the invitation 'Fuck me' which he narcissistically addresses to his own mirror image is also typical of the post-classical text taunting the spectator, who now has to decide whether this is a man speaking to his own female psyche, a woman 'trapped' in a male body perversely self-fashioned in a woman's dress, a gay addressing another man, or a transsexual idealizing his self-image as the object of another's desire, regardless of gender.

By staging these possibilities, and simultaneously suspending them, *The Silence of the Lambs* also became the occasion for feminists to examine some of the limits of the constructivist argument around female masquerade and the performativity of gender, once essentialist positions have been deconstructed. On the other hand, the film leaves space for the motif of cross-dressing traditional gender roles also to transfer itself metaphorically to another character: as already suggested, Clarice herself can be read – even before Jodie Foster was 'outed' as a lesbian – as a trans-gender figure in relation to the traditionally male occupations of police work, homicide investigation, and the detection of criminal pathology.

When filtering the film through the issues of (classical) feminist film studies, one's reading of *The Silence of the Lambs* is centred on Clarice and her 'problem'. This would be how to 'make it' in a man's world, when the markers of sexual difference and gender identity have come under pressure intersubjectively, through the pathology of figures like Buffalo Bill and, socially, by the improved career opportunities open to college-educated women. In addition, the film excessively elaborates its Oedipal initiation story, though this time centred on a female, occupying the structural position of the male: surrounded by overpoweringly present good father figures that turn out to be bad (Crawford/Chilton) and bad father figures that are also good (Hannibal Lecter), Clarice has to cope with the violent death of her biological father, a policeman shot on duty, and the trauma of real or imagined childhood abuse. However, once attention shifts to Buffalo Bill, who in spite of being a serial killer of young women is also a figure of pity (in his desperate desire to change his gender) and of provocation (besides being a misfit, he is clearly a rebel, surrounded by the paraphernalia of a heavy metal rocker, a psychedelic drop-out, and a deranged Vietnam veteran), one may wonder whether his attacks on women are not, symbolically speaking, a form of cross-dressing: as a transsexual, he literalizes male anxieties about sexual identity in the wake of 'feminism'. For given his unconventional identifications and object choices, and a verbal–visual discourse that splits him between stereotypically homosexual behaviour and Lecter's prevarication around identifying him as either transsexual or transvestite ('he's tried a lot of things, I suspect'), Buffalo Bill undermines traditional notions of phallic masculinity more effectively than he threatens the cultural codes of femininity, which he copies with his needlework and travesties in his dress.

We can now understand more clearly why *The Silence of the Lambs* divided the activist gender community. The film offers entry-points to several kinds of transgressive, non-normative fantasies of negotiating gendered identity, on either side of sexual difference and on both sides of the law, but for all that no less troubling: Buffalo Bills kills his women not for sexual gratification but in order to dress himself in their skin, and Clarice kills Buffalo Bill in self-defence as an officer of the law, but not without thereby also re-establishing the dividing lines of gender roles and sexual difference that she herself is challenging. If feminists thought the film progressive and empowering, where gays saw homophobic and criminalizing portrayals of sexual 'deviance', does this mean that their positions were symmetrically related – around the implicit 'norm' of heterosexuality? Such a stance would remind us of the objections voiced against Mulvey's purported 'heterosexism' underlying her feminist position. It would seem that the boycotts and protests against *The Silence of the Lambs* were also indicative of a rift in the 'rainbow coalition' of gender, obliging feminists, lesbians, and gays to discover that they had divergent interests and stakes when it came to the identity politics of cinematic representation.

Arguing along similar lines when reviewing the debate on women's right to pornography (rather than *The Silence of the Lambs*), Stephen Heath has pointed out the fallacy of what he calls 'equal opportunity subject positions' (Heath 1999: 37–8), meaning thereby the notion that each group has a right to its own sexual fantasy material, without this impinging on the self-image or social recognition of other groups. Citing Slavoj Žižek, Heath notes that fantasy scenarios are at once highly specific and intimately connected with one's sense of reality, since it is fantasy which 'anchors' social reality. But if, as Žižek claims, one has to have a fantasy (a 'symptom') in order to function at all in everyday reality and not be overwhelmed by the Real, then it follows that one does not have a choice in one's fantasies, be they violent, racist, or sexist. The split between feminists and gays around the reception of *The Silence of the Lambs* would thus be inherent in the politics of representation, rather than a contingent feature of the ideological construction of this particular film. A parallel argument has been made by Judith Halberstam, from a more 'postmodern' perspective:

> I resist the temptation to submit Demme's film to a feminist analysis that would identify the danger of showing mass audiences an aestheticized version of the serial killing of women. I resist the temptation to brand the

film as homophobic because gender confusion becomes the guilty secret of the madman in the basement. I resist indeed the readings that want to puncture the surface and enter the misogynist and homophobic unconscious of Buffalo Bill, Hannibal the Cannibal and Clarice Starling. . . . Gender trouble is not the movie's secret, it is a confession that both Starling and Buffalo Bill are all too willing to make. . . . It seems to me that *The Silence of the Lambs* emphasizes that we are at a peculiar time in history, a time when it is becoming impossible to tell the difference between prejudice and its representations, between, then, homophobia and the representations of homophobia.

(Halberstam 1991: 40–41)

Both the fallacy indicated by Heath and the impossibility pointed out by Halberstam would suggest that we may have reached a deadlock in our interpretation, and that a move to another conceptual level is needed if we are to resolve it. One may have to deconstruct the key idea of feminist film theory, namely that the cinematic image is a gendered representation, as well as a central tenet of cultural studies, which sees filmic texts as sites of contested 'representations' (mostly of class, race, and sexual orientation). At the same time, the deadlock implies a theoretical move from 'sexual difference' to 'gender': 'every society has a sex/gender system – a set of arrangements by which the biological raw material of human sex and procreation is shaped by human, social intervention, and satisfied in a conventional manner, no matter how bizarre some of the conventions may be' (Gayle Rubin, in Reiter 1974: 165). Put differently, one could say that while gender, being culturally constructed, needs to be 'articulated' (or 'performed'), sex needs to be 'shown' (on the body as physiological absence/presence of, for instance, breasts, penis), implying that while sex is of the order of sight and the specular (involving the psychoanalytic paradigms of fetishism and disavowal, voyeurism and castration anxiety), gender belongs to the register of the discursive and the performative, and thus necessitates a different kind of 'sexual politics' (see Butler 1989, and also Rubin's notion of the 'theatricalization' of a sexual practice as distinct from the role this practice might play in identity politics). An emphasis on gender, one might say, once more underlines that tendency in film studies which sees the various 'regimes of visibility' in crisis, in that gender challenges the visually confirmed self-evidence of sexual identity.

To sum up our feminist reading so far, and linking it to our previous chapter, we might say that whereas Robert Zemeckis's *Back to the Future* showed an unworkable patriarchal order from the perspective of the adolescent male, Demme's *The Silence of the Lambs* shows the unworkable patriarchal order from the perspective of the young professional female.

Instead of the failing father or the incompetent/impotent fathers confronting Marty McFly, Clarice Starling encounters in her FBI bosses and Hannibal Lecter a succession of potent and powerfully destructive/abusive super-fathers, dangling crucial clues and rewards in front of her, while seeming to own the outcome in advance. Yet there is, as in *Back to the Future*, also an almost textbook knowingness about the elements of identity formation that need to be lined up, in order to work out the (still heavily – or happily) Oedipal trajectory of Clarice's initiation as a professional 'special agent'. Nonetheless, if the 'problem' in the two films is similar, the 'solutions' are different: this time it does not involve sci-fi gadgets and time-travel, but a special kind of body horror, where the boundaries of inside and outside, of skin and flesh, of seeing and knowing, of bodies and minds are transgressed and traversed. But this merely underscores another ironic twist that all along lay in store for our psychoanalytic-feminist reading: the horror at the heart of the film is not Buffalo Bill's 'severe criminal pathology' or sexual perversion, but psychoanalysis itself, in the figure of Hannibal Lecter, whose patient Buffalo Bill once was. Lecter penetrates Clarice's mind and gets under her skin in ways that turn out to be as brutal and almost as much of a violation of her personhood as Buffalo Bill's violation of the young women's bodies in order to get (at) their skins.

As such, *The Silence of the Lambs* once more raises the question, discussed also in the previous chapter: What does the (film) analyst do when the theory s/he wishes to apply in order to position a film critically is not just openly on display, but stands accused of the ultimate evil? The dilemma leads her to look for another type of interpretation, preferably anti-psychoanalytic: this, then, is the point where one would to turn to Michel Foucault, to find there a different account of vision, a political reading of sexuality and the body, and a deconstruction of the power relationships inherent in the discourse of psychoanalysis. Foucault's critique takes us to Deleuze, where questions of the visible and the knowable, of the look and 'body politics' receive further redefinition, while also introducing a set of new concepts.

## 9.4. Foucault and Deleuze: theory

Michel Foucault and Gilles Deleuze are thinkers in the tradition of Friedrich Nietzsche. This means that they are critical of the Enlightenment project of the progress of pure reason, of truth and moral self-improvement. These values and ideals were regarded by Nietzsche as the ruses of the 'will to power', as rationalizations of a particular class, race, religion, or gender, in the struggle to arrogate dominance over others. Thinkers in the Nietzschean mould are sceptics, especially with regards to epistemology, i.e. the claims of philosophy to be able to establish the foundations of universally valid knowledge or 'truth'. Foucault and Deleuze are also sometimes known as anti-humanists, because they regard 'man' to be a recent 'invention', dating from post-Renaissance humanism, in which a particular version of individualism began to reign supreme. Humanism manifests its supremacy by drawing various strict lines of division and exclusion: mind vs body, reason vs madness, male vs female, subject vs object, observer vs observed. Our two philosophers are intent on breaking down, opening up and re-organizing these binaries. Both Foucault and Deleuze are thus in some sense concerned with new classification systems, new taxonomies, and they salute each other as 'topographers' or 'cartographers'. Where Foucault regards himself self-consciously as an 'archaeologist' and a 'genealogist', Deleuze, for instance, called his cinema books neither a theory nor a history, but a 'natural history' of the cinema, as if he was arranging specimens, or defining class, type, and genus (1997: 46). Both are profoundly 'spatial' philosophers, even if their spatiality is often directed towards analysing multiple temporalities.

### 9.4.1. Foucault

More specifically, Foucault has presented a trenchant critique of the association of light and vision with reason and truth in what he calls 'the classical age' (roughly from Descartes to Hegel, or from the Sun King to Napoleon). While this critique is elaborated around three great discursive formations – the 'invention of madness', the 'birth of the clinic', and the 'history of sexuality' – each of which goes well beyond the problematics of the cinema, Foucault's extrapolation and examination of the various 'scopic regimes' that according to him characterize modernity do, albeit implicitly, address issues also pertinent to film studies. In particular, his thematization of the 'panoptic gaze' (of which more below) has been widely taken up by film scholars and in visual culture studies.

Secondly, Foucault offered a critique of psychoanalysis, and in particular of Freud's theory of repression. For him the nexus power–prison–pleasure was central to the modern state, and therefore had to be redefined, if one was to engage in progressive politics at all. At the same time, it was important to understand why psychoanalysis emerged at a particular point in history, and what kinds of complicity might have favoured its official establishment (for instance, he notes the coincidence of Freud's treatment of the Oedipus complex with the criminalization of incest in Western societies). Foucault also remarked upon the reliance of psychoanalysis on speech and silence, and its alignment of therapy with (religious) confession, including the elevation of the doctor/therapist to a priest-like figure: 'It would be fairer to say that psychoanalysis doubled the absolute observation of the watcher with the endless monologue of the person watched – thus preserving the old asylum structure of non-reciprocal observation but balancing it, in a non-symmetrical reciprocity, by the new structure of language without response' (Foucault 1988: 250–1, cited in Jay 1993: 292). From it, Foucault concluded that Freud's method could not but assist the state, religion, and other discourses of power in maintaining the status quo and keeping the subject in thrall. Rather than safeguarding an 'interiority' inaccessible to control and discipline, the modern 'subject' (political as well as psychic) was the effect of the discourses that the different 'regimes' of power inscribed on 'the body' – an entity/category that neither Enlightenment philosophy nor bourgeois society, neither Marxism nor psychoanalysis had a place for other than as criminalized, medicalized, subordinate, or symptomatic. Again, taking his cue from Nietzsche, Foucault saw the body as having its own history, at once matrix for and site of the great discursive formations he described. Whether 'madness', 'sexuality', 'discipline', 'punishment', 'surveillance', or 'love and friendship' – in each case, the task was to restore to the human body the dignity and legibility denied to it by philosophy, theology, and psychoanalysis. Such a different appreciation of the body also appealed to post-feminist film theory and gender studies, and was to have an impact on the way the film experience began to be analysed.

Finally, Foucault was a forceful critic of normativity of any kind, and an advocate of transgressive action and limit-experiences. He has therefore been a valuable ally to be invoked by minority groups of very different kinds. His key insights regarding the questions of sexuality and gender can be found in his *History of Sexuality* and *The Birth of the Clinic*. In both works, Foucault thinks of sexuality in terms of the institutions that define it, and not in the first instance as bodies with specific sexual preferences. The latter are only of interest to him insofar as they are connected with and articulated through discourses, which via compulsive heterosexuality try to regulate bodies and identities across the flows of power and pleasure mobilized by these practices: 'Sex was, in Christian societies, that which had to be examined, watched over, confessed and transformed into discourse' (Foucault 1989: 138). As a homosexual who militated for gay rights, he has been a valuable figurehead in the struggle for recognition and redefinition of non-normative forms of masculinity; as a victim of AIDS he furthermore played an important part – beyond his death – in the various awareness-raising campaigns of the 1980s and 1990s. More recently, lesbian critics, too, have enlisted his anti-essentialist and non-normative positions for sophisticated arguments around same-sex identity formation and radically constructivist accounts of gender: '[Repetition] becomes the non-place of subversion, the possibility of a re-embodying of the subjectivating norm that can redirect its normativity. Consider the inversion of "woman" and "woman", depending on the staging and address of their performance, of "queer" and "queer", depending on pathologizing or contestatatory modes' (Butler 1997: 99–100).

Thus, if Freudian psychoanalysis (and the feminist film theory influenced by it) was concerned with *sexuality*, and was often (even if only by default) normatively heterosexual, then Foucault in our context is above all the theorist of *gender*, where gay and lesbian identities are not implicitly regarded under the aspects of deviancy or 'otherness', but as part of the overall dynamics of power and pleasure that link the individual to the social formation, to practice and to politics.

Adapting these concerns to the issues of film theory is not without its problems, and while Foucault has been enormously influential in the humanities across a broad front, there are few film theorists who would see themselves directly as his disciples. If anything, Foucault has had a more demonstrable effect on the rethinking of film history – with his notion of 'archaeology of knowledge', 'history as genealogy', and the 'archive', as well as his way of thinking about institutions and power – than on film theory. Nonetheless, as already indicated, there are a number of issues in film analysis where Foucault's insights are relevant. On one topic, for instance, which has taken up much space in previous chapters, namely the cultural 'crisis of masculinity', one might say that for Foucault, masculinity was not in crisis, or rather, only insofar as Oedipal, i.e. normatively heterosexual masculinity within bourgeois society and patriarchy has always been an untenable proposition. Several of Foucault's followers (e.g. Leo Bersani) have raised the question of phallic identity vs Oedipal identity, which in turn, has inspired film scholars such as Kaja Silverman and Steven Shaviro to apply these insights to specific films (Silverman 1992; Shaviro, 1994). The other, more broadly Foucaultian field of film analysis might be what is known as 'queer theory'.

## 9.4.2. Deleuze

Especially in the books co-authored with Felix Guattari, Deleuze has taken up much of the agenda of Foucault's project, notably his anti-Freudianism and his concern with the micro-politics of power, in view of promoting more open (i.e. non-family based) communities and an egalitarian, non-repressive society. Foucault once famously said that 'perhaps one day, this century will be known as Deleuzian' (Foucault 1977: 165), arguing that Deleuze

> causes us to reflect on matters that philosophy has neglected through centuries: the event (assimilated in a concept from which we vainly attempted to extract it in the form of a *fact*, verifying a proposition, of *actual experience*, a modality of the subject, of *concreteness*, the empirical content of history); and the phantasm (reduced in the name of reality and situated at

the extremity, the pathological pole of a normative sequence: perception-image-memory-illusion).

(Foucault 1977: 180)

Redistributing oppositions such as truth/illusion, fact/experience, history/pathology across such terms as 'event' and 'phantasm' may seem very tempting when thinking about the cinematic experience as a spatio-temporal event that can engage the viewer with heightened perceptual-sensory intensity. But before trying to do so, some broader considerations are in order. Like Foucault, Deleuze is an anti-foundational, post-structuralist thinker, which for those hostile to so-called 'Continental philosophy' merely connotes neo-Romantic anti-rationalism and a typically postmodern relativism. In fact, not that different from Anglo-American philosophy, Deleuze is against totalizing theories or systems (e.g. those of Hegel, Marx, Freud), and favours a piecemeal ('micro') approach to political as well as theoretical problems. Also not unlike analytic philosophers, Deleuze is anti-Saussurean (preferring the semiotics of Charles Sanders Peirce) and anti-psychoanalytic (though his theory of the brain might not find favour with cognitivists).

In line with most French thinkers of the past 50 years, Deleuze has had to come to terms with the political failure of socialism in general and May 1968 in particular. This is why some commentators have accused him (and Guattari) of having opted in their politics for a pre-Marxist version of anarcho-communism, with a utopian but also dangerous penchant for, on the one hand, a Maoist-style ultra-radicalism and, on the other, a primitive/tribal view of political economy, revolving around the gift and potlatch, around symbolic exchange and communitarian reciprocity, while violently opposed to market capitalism, representational democracy, and the institutionalization of laissez-faire liberalism (see Richard Barbrook, 'The Holy Fools', in Pisters 2001: 159–76).

If Deleuze, too, draws his basic thinking from Nietzsche, one could argue that it is from the affirmative 'gay science' side of Nietzsche that he takes his cue, rather than by embracing the relentlessly negative, acerbic critique of bourgeois society and Christian morality that appealed to Foucault.

Also unlike Foucault, Deleuze did pronounce on the cinema in two major books. These, as already mentioned, are primarily concerned with countering the linguistic-semiotic turn in film theory. They recast the phenomenological realism of the previous generation of French film scholars around André Bazin in a language of sensory immediacy and bodily perception. Deleuze also seeks to define a historical break between classical and modern cinema, by dividing the cinema between what he calls the movement-image and the time-image. Perhaps paradoxically, it seemed to us that only some of the concepts elaborated in the cinema books are relevant to the issues discussed in this chapter, while others we are introducing originate from Deleuze's more generally philosophical or literary texts.

Thus, thinking with Deleuze about cinema raises a delicate issue: which Deleuze are we talking about? Foucault, in the passage cited above, was reviewing *The Logic of Sense* (Deleuze 1990), but there is also the Deleuze of *Anti-Oedipus: Capitalism and Schizophrenia* (1985) and *A Thousand Plateaus* (1987) (both co-written with Felix Guattari), who develops challenging concepts that have been applied to the cinema, besides the two cinema books themselves (*The Movement Image* and *The Time Image*). Still others prefer Deleuze's writings on Foucault, Kafka, Proust, and Francis Bacon, or *The Fold: Leibniz and the Baroque* (Deleuze 1992) as a source for ideas about the cinema. For instance, *Anti-Oedipus: Capitalism and Schizophrenia* already in the title makes clear that Deleuze and Guattari's thinking is anti-psychoanalytical. There, they reject Lacan's notion of desire as lack, claiming that it is a move that colludes with the dominant bourgeois ideology in much the same way that Foucault accused Freud's theory of the Oedipus complex as extending the regime of confession and self-monitoring, instituted by the church and the bourgeois state.

Second, Deleuze has argued that, for his own film theory, the look (or gaze theory as it is sometimes called) is far less relevant than the almost constitutive place it occupies for psychoanalytic and feminist film theory:

> I'm not sure the notion of the look is absolutely necessary. The eye is already there in things, it's part of the image, the image's visibility. . . . The eye isn't the camera, it's the screen. As for the camera, with all its propositional functions, it's a sort of third eye, the mind's eye. You cite Hitchcock: he does, it is true, bring the viewer into the film. But that's nothing to do with the look. It's rather because he frames the action in a whole network of relations. . . . The frame for him is like a tapestry frame: it holds within it the network of relations, while the action is just a thread moving in and out of the network. What Hitchcock thus brings into the cinema, then, is the mental image . . . he goes beyond the action-image to something deeper, mental relations, a kind of vision.
>
> (Deleuze 1997: 54–5)

Third, unlike Foucault, Deleuze has said little explicitly about gender and sexuality. In fact, he seems to have avoided any direct engagement with the discussion around sexual difference, feminism, gay politics, or queer theory. But on some of the questions that stand behind these debates – 'seeing' (vision) vs 'saying' (discourse), biological vs constructivist identity, psyche vs body – Deleuze does hold decisive views and has developed strong concepts (mostly elaborated in *A Thousand Plateaus*, e.g. 'deterritorialization' and the 'body-without-organs', 'becoming . . . woman' and 'body, brain, thought', 'desiring machines', and the 'rhizome' i.e. non-hierarchical, multiform, reversible relations and connections with respect to 'identity politics'). These offer a rich conceptual vocabulary or network of metaphors with which to think about 'body matters' also in the cinema (see Pisters 2001).

Finally, Deleuze's idea of the 'fold' has been transferred from the Baroque to the cinema, in order to differentiate between classical and modern cinema (possibly including post-classical cinema as well). Defined as a paratactic series, as a permeable surface at once inside and out, or a fan-like proliferation of segments, the fold becomes a key feature of 'the event' as a mode appropriate for describing the contemporary cinematic experience.

# 9.5. Method: Foucault and Deleuze

## 9.5.1. Foucault

As indicated, Foucault has only rarely expressed himself on the cinema, mostly in relation to its uses and misuse as popular memory (Foucault, in Wilson 2000: 159–72, 181–5). But he did contribute at least one term that is frequently cited when deconstructing the cinematic apparatus: this is his reference to Jeremy Bentham's panopticon, an architectural ensemble that permits the surveillance of prisoners through vision and self-observation. This opens up two lines of 'application': one would be to treat the panopticon as an institution and a discourse, and the other is to see it as a sort of cinematic apparatus and a dispositif. In the first case, we would be looking further into the idea that institutions are, for Foucault, not so much buildings that house a bureaucracy with a history and a tradition, but something that reproduces itself in certain internalized practices and actively produces discourses. These discourses are the 'positive', generative manifestations of power, and thus 'penetrate' the individual in ways that are not visible. They cannot be simply 'resisted' or 'opposed', which is why classical political debate and struggle has to be replaced by a 'micro-politics'.

Foucault's work can therefore enable us to rethink and reanalyse the cinema using the following concepts:

● *Institution as discourse.* For something as both material and immaterial as the cinema, the notion of 'institution as discourse' is not without interest. It might give one an instrument for understanding the complex interaction in the cinema of economics and emotions, of film production as an industry and spectatorship/reception as a psychic and somatic event. At the same time, films – and especially genre films – often involve institutions-as-discourses in the fabric of the action: 'the police' for instance (in a detective film), or 'the military' (in a war film), or stereotypical figures that embody institutions/discourses, such as the sheriff in a Western, or the mad scientist in a sci-fi film. More recently, questions of race and ethnicity in the cinema have often been treated in a Foucaultian manner, across an analysis of the discursive regime of power/knowledge/pleasure.

- *Power and discipline.* As a structure that emphasizes 'being looked at' over 'looking', the panoptic gaze can be invoked to rethink the cinema as a *dispositif* of power and discipline, rather than as one that generates or inscribes sexual difference. For instance, as if responding to feminist film theory's distinction between narrative and spectacle, and their definition of woman in the cinema as a 'spectacle, to be looked at', Foucault once famously remarked: 'our society is not one of the spectacle but of surveillance ... We are neither in an amphitheatre, nor on the stage, but in the panoptic machine, invested by its effects of power, which we bring to ourselves, since we are part of its mechanism' (Foucault 1979: 217).

- *Planes of vision, scopic regimes, enfolding gazes.* When deconstructing vision and the look in a given film in Foucaultian terms, we would be looking not only for the gendered imbalance and asymmetry, but for the mutual implication of looks and speech, the possibly even more complex geometry of planes of vision, scopic regimes, enfolding gazes, and self-surveillance mechanisms than those proposed by feminist readings. Deleuze once described what he called Foucault's 'folds of vision' as 'an ontological visibility, forever twisting itself into a self-seeing entity, on to a different dimension from that of the gaze and its objects' (Deleuze, cited in Jay 1993: 398). In other words, the panoptic gaze of surveillance is, unlike that of spectacle (with its neat division and tidy hierarchy between seeing and being seen), both interiorized and external, both invested with someone looking and marking an empty space, both a model of malevolent visual discipline and of human conscience as 'self-surveillance' (see also quote from interview in Foucault 1981: 152–5).

- *Madness and pathology.* A special instance of vision and the gaze might be the question of madness and pathology. In Foucault, the history of madness points to different scopic regimes in history. As Martin Jay sums up this point: '*Madness and Civilization* showed the extent of Foucault's appreciation of the role of vision, or more precisely, specific visual regimes in constituting cultural categories. ... The modern category of insanity, Foucault contended, was predicated on the dissolution of the medieval and Renaissance unity of word and image, which liberated a multitude of images of madness and deprived them of any eschatological significance. As a result, madness became pure spectacle, a theatre of unreason' (Jay 1993: 390, citing Foucault 1988: 70). Such a conception could be usefully tested in the horror film, and the figure of the monster, or in the thriller genre, where the villain is often pathological – a psychopath, or emotionally unstable – and where suspense and drama revolve around the question: How can one tell what are the symptoms or traces of this pathology, and how different, finally, is such a character from us and our idea of normality?

- *Persecution.* Foucault's thinking on madness, medicine, and the clinic in Western societies since the Enlightenment profoundly affected his stance on gender matters, and homosexuality in particular as a practice that has been persecuted, prohibited, and minoritized: 'My problem is essentially the definition of the implicit systems in which we find ourselves prisoners; what I would like to grasp is the system of limits and exclusion which we practice without knowing it; I would like to make the cultural unconscious apparent' (Foucault 1989: 71).

- *Sensory, tactile, sonorous surface.* But perhaps more important for understanding the role of gender in relation to the cinema is that the sensory, tactile, sonorous surface and envelope of the screen/skin/body makes it possible to regard the film experience as something other than the Oedipalized identity machine. It is in this respect that same-sex love and homosexuality, that is, non-reproductive, socially 'useless' sexuality, might be regarded, beyond questions of 'representation' and 'role models', as an alternative metaphor for the cinema experience as an embodied event: 'Another thing to distrust is to relate the question of homosexuality to the problem of "Who am I?" and "What is the secret of my desire?" Perhaps it would be better to ask oneself, "What relations, through homosexuality, can be established, invented, multiplied and modulated?" The problem is not to discover in oneself the truth of sex, but rather to use sexuality henceforth to arrive at a multiplicity of relationships. And no doubt that's the real reason why homosexuality is not a form of desire but something desirable. Therefore we have to work at becoming homosexuals and not be obstinate in recognizing that we are' (Foucault 1989: 203–4).

The direction of this quotation, its emphasis on multiplicity, its reference to 'becoming' and on desire as separate from subjectivity all strike a very Deleuzian note, outlining a programme in some ways quite distinct from the Anglo-American project of gender politics in cultural studies.

## 9.5.2. Deleuze

More generally, with regard to Deleuze's method, his philosophy as a whole could be said to be designed to forestall what we have set ourselves as our goal: to distil from a body of theory a set of procedures that can be deployed in the day-to-day business of generating film analyses. 'While one can dialogue with

Deleuze, try to philosophize like Deleuze, or do with other philosophers something analogous to what Deleuze does with Bergson, it seems somewhat more problematic to "apply" Deleuze, to simply "translate" analysis into a Deleuzian language' (Stam 2000: 262).

Consequently, there have been precious few Deleuzian analyses of individual films, beyond adumbrating or extending those he himself has given in the cinema books, which often enough are non-systematic, aphoristic reformulations of the reviews and auteurist views of the *Cahiers du cinéma* critics from the 1950s and 1960s. In particular, apart from a few bold attempts (Buchanan 2000; Pisters 2001), examples of Deleuzian analyses of contemporary Hollywood films (especially when compared to Žižek's many New Lacanian analyses) are as yet hard to find. However, as we hope to show, a Deleuzian reading can produce new insights, without wholly travestying the ideas from which they derive. Of the concepts named above, we shall be selecting only a small number for special consideration, chosen in part in view of our film example, and partly because these seem to us fruitful, even though they may not come from the 'cinema books' (see above). However, we shall begin with one key concept that does come from the cinema books, namely the distinction between the 'movement image' (action, affection, perception image) and the 'time image' (recollection, crystal image), because of the question – often posed – whether post-classical American mainstream cinema can actually be fitted into Deleuze's schema, given that he hardly discusses Hollywood films from the 1970s or beyond, and that many of the most challenging films were made in the 1990s, i.e. after the publication of the cinema books. There is, furthermore, evidence to suggest that Deleuze himself would not have particularly cared for this new brand of cult, blockbuster, or genre films.

The seductive – but also unsettling – experience when encountering Deleuze's cinema books is that one all too easily loses one's bearings. Thrown in at the deep end of his thought, there is no outside leading to an inside, so that reading Deleuze is a wholly immersive experience. As such, it resembles nothing so much as a contemporary Hollywood spectacular, where the images and sounds surround one, where one is taken on as roller coaster ride, where the sheer somatic impact makes the pulse race before the mind has caught up. So violently does Deleuze discard the categories of conventional film analysis and disregard the niceties of reasoned argument that one either learns how to float on his prose or soon drowns in it. In other words, the most empathetic-mimetic relationship his books establish is with certain of the films he discusses, and with many he does not mention at all.

The concept we want to highlight first (although in the subsequent analysis it will appear at a later point) is the very general distinction which Deleuze makes in the history of the cinema, between the movement (or 'action') image and the time (or 'crystal') image. As explained above, it serves both as a chronological divide (roughly, before and after the Second World War) as well as an almost ontological divide (between two kinds of 'being' in the cinema), while, for the impatient reader, it may also signal a continental divide (between Hollywood and European cinema). What concerns us here is to decide which of his two broad types of image might apply to contemporary Hollywood movies, and there, we propose to highlight a line of argument he pursues at the end of his first cinema book, where Deleuze speaks of:

- *The crisis of the action image.* After identifying what we have been calling the classical Hollywood cinema with the movement (action–affection) image, and relating its dominance to the sensory–motor schema of goal orientation, purposive action, and a causal nexus between seeing, feeling, doing, Deleuze discovers in the late work of Hitchcock, but also in John Cassavetes or Robert Altman, a crisis in the action image: 'If one of Hitchcock's innovations was to implicate the spectator in the film, did not the characters themselves have to be capable of being assimilated to spectators? But then ... the mental image would be less a bringing to completion of the action-image, than a re-examination [of] the whole movement-image ... through the rupture of the sensory–motor links in a particular character' (Deleuze 1986: 205). This, as we shall see, applies rather well to one of the characters of *The Silence of the Lambs*, though, one would argue that this 'rupture' of which Deleuze speaks finds itself compensated in the contemporary American cinema by a kind of psychotic hyperactivity, in which the movement and action *come at* the characters, rather than *emanating from* them. The consequence are either what could be called the 'new thinking image' of characters being inside each others' minds, or the kind of hysterical action scenario where the natural world (*Twister*), a vehicle (*Speed*), or a creature-person (*Terminator*) are 'out of control' and the protagonists can only react, parry, or otherwise shield themselves from being attacked, assailed, or annihilated.

A concept frequently invoked by Deleuze (and Guattari), when trying to think beyond individualism, identity and traditional notions of personhood is the:

- *Body without organs (BwO).* 'A BwO is made in such a way that it can be occupied, populated only by intensities. Only intensities pass and circulate. Still, the BwO is not a scene, a place, or even a support upon which something comes to pass. It has nothing to do with fantasy, there is nothing to interpret. .... It is not space, nor is it in space; it is matter that occupies space to a given degree – to the degree corresponding to the intensities produced. It is non-stratified, unformed, intense matter, the matrix of intensity' (Deleuze and Guattari 1987: 153). When applied to the cinema, BwO can help resituate such perennial issues of film theory as 'identification' (i.e., the affective or cognitive link between the spectator and the protagonists) and the communication or relation (non-dramatized and non-verbalized, but thematized and intuited) that exists between characters in a film. BwO may also allow us to understand how in much contemporary cinema the dividing line between inside and out, but also the boundaries between bodies, have become difficult to draw, and in any case no longer refer to a (psychic) interiority and a (physical) externality, but to two sides of the same surface or extension.

In a universe such as Deleuze's which is in constant flux, and where identities are neither fixed nor intersubjectively determined, a character's mode of being is a permanent

- *Becoming* . . . But whereas a certain Heraclitean becoming would imply a constant movement in order to stay the same, for Deleuze the issue is more complex. Instead of being unique and individual, we are all bad or imperfect copies, simulacra or automata, so that our most ethical state of being in the world is neither 'being true to oneself' nor 'becoming the same', but a 'becoming-other', in which one's encounter with the world develops along different 'segmental lines' – hard line, molecular line, and line of flight – indicative of the difficulties of having such an encounter at all. In terms of contemporary cinema, one might immediately point to the prevalence of mutants, shape-shifters, cyborgs, or other man–machine combinations as indications of Deleuzian 'becoming-other' in the wake of new special effects technologies such as morphing. But this would be to short-change the concept and instrumentalize it. Nor does it directly correlate with the discussion in cultural studies on 'recognizing otherness' and post-colonial theory's contested territory of 'othering'. As we shall indicate below, when 'applying' the term to *The Silence of the Lambs*, Deleuze sees the process as at once physical and bodily, rather than metaphoric or semiotic, and it is political, violent, affecting minorities whose state of oppression, suffering, and abjection bars them from most other forms of action and communication.

A final concept from the Deleuze arsenal that might prove fruitful for film analysis addresses neither character interaction nor identity politics, but concerns the film experience considered as 'event'. This concept is that of

- *The fold.* For Deleuze, the opposite of the sensory–motor scheme of the action image is the 'purely optical and aural situation', in which perception itself is what happens and what constitutes the cinematic event. But as with certain cognitivists cited at the beginning of the chapter, this perception is less a (transitive) seeing of something, a specular structure separating subject from object, or a voyeuristic seeing/being seen. Rather, it is an enveloped perception, at once continuous and plural, active and passive, directional and surrounding. The semiotic interval and the presence/absence of illusionism find themselves replaced by the interstice, the recto and verso, the inverse and the obverse, in short: the fold. Thus, one crucial feature of the modern media event, which the cinema paradigmatically embodies, is that such an event only exists in order to be seen, while the spectators' sense of 'being there' already exhausts the event's meaning. In this sense, Deleuze's fold, as a structure of 'total visibility', joins Foucault's panoptic gaze as an alternative to the theories of the look/gaze as propounded by psychoanalytic film studies.

# 9.6. Analysis

## 9.6.1. A Foucault reading

In a Foucault-inspired reading of *The Silence of the Lambs*, a central place would be occupied by the FBI as an institution externally dedicated to law enforcement and internally to disciplining its members and recruits. What is interesting about the figure of Clarice in this context is that her Oedipal trajectory masks a more fundamental and more paradoxical journey, namely one that signifies Agent Starling's successes (killing Buffalo Bill, graduating from the FBI academy) as also her failures. She now finds herself inscribed in the official, male power–desire–domination machine, but – one may ask – at what cost to her personhood?

The reason why Clarice's triumph is also her failure is that, when gauged by this trajectory, she in fact undergoes a series of 'tests' which are not so much concerned with her individual suitability for the job as devised around the trope of 'professional' and 'woman'. This is to some extent also an 'initiation', but one that would be more accurately described as interpellation (the first word heard in the film is the call 'Starling!') and as a 'staging' of her femaleness (highlighting her as sexed, via body size and bodily manifestations): besides the voyeuristic/fetishist looked-at-ness that surrounds Agent Starling/Jodie Foster, the most startling thing is the extent to which other markers, mostly body-based and connoting 'femininity' are deployed: body fluids, body odours, swallowing, ingestion, excretion, secretion – all potentially coded as transgressive (Hannibal comments on her perfume, he makes her repeat Midge's words about her body odour, we see underarm perspiration on her sweat-shirt in the lift after her morning training session in the woods, Midge throws his semen at her, and we note the white smelling salts applied to her upper lip when inspecting the corpse).

The whole journey from being the object of the look (and exposed to male possessors of the look) to becoming herself possessor of the look, described above, could in fact be seen as a ruse, a lure: precisely the one that feminist critics found themselves caught up in. Consider the opening scene: the setting, the music, and the sound effects conjure up the atmosphere of a horror film with a hidden stalker lurking in the woods, but these turn out to be a 'false' set of anticipations because the stalker is a fellow FBI employee, calling her by her name to tell her she has to present herself to the chief of her section, where she is subsequently rewarded with an assignment. In other words, the 'trick' suspense has revealed another kind of truth: that she has been trapped by the promise of preferment, and that there is, at this level of interpellation, no different between a stalker and a messenger: either role suits her FBI boss, himself a test-and-surveillance machine.

Empowerment for a female, the film suggests, is an ambiguous gift: thanks to Foucault's concept of power, the empowered female (one side of the opposition of the feminist reception of the film) now emerges as both alienated from and constituted by her subjectivity. The contested reception of *The Silence of the Lambs* by different groups of feminists can thus be seen to be inscribed into the film from the beginning. For the trajectory that she actually undergoes is the transformation from a body-and-gender being, with various (and, as Lecter sadistically points out, still contradictory) class ambitions and personal histories, into an odourless, sexless bureaucratic 'agent'. In this sense, her body is the 'price' she has to pay for participating in the 'equal opportunity capitalism' of the corporate–military–forensic–criminal–justice complex which here is the FBI. Agent Starling/ Hannibal Lecter connect along the heterosexual axis, and their eyes communicate along perception as sensation, but even more so they are joined along the line of knowledge–power–confession as described by Foucault, and cited by him in his critique of the psychoanalytic paradigm.

In this perspective Hannibal Lecter becomes not the opponent but merely the 'excessive' embodiment or supplement of the incorporeality of this corporate system, doubled in the intrusiveness and ubiquity of the information society, supported by forensic science, psychiatry, and psycho-analysis. The FBI not only 'needs' Hannibal to help them solve a series of crimes in which he is obscurely implicated; rather, Hannibal is part of the FBI machinery, he and they work hand in hand. In a way, he is the 'obscene enjoyment' (as Žižek would say) of the system, the uncanny database intelligence of the modern administrative government, figured in a quasi-mythological but also palpably contemporary monster. If characters like Charles Foster Kane in *Citizen Kane* were the human face of capitalist America during the era of 'primitive accumulation', of the robber barons, the tycoons, and the press tsars, then Hannibal Lecter proves that today's corporate capitalism in collusion with the federal government no longer needs a 'human face' but a leather-faced grimace, attached to a 'super-brain', ubiquitously penetrating minds and feasting, gourmet-fashion, on human flesh and brain-matter.

By contrast, Buffalo Bill, the 'Gumb/dumb' character, would in this light attain a more positive reading. Indeterminate as far as sexual difference is concerned (and hence a source of contention in the reception of the film by gays), he becomes an 'authentic' figure precisely to the degree that he shows the contradictory workings of the 'history of sexuality' on his own body. But he also literalizes the invitation to self-improvement and 'self-storage' which contemporary society addresses to its subjects as consumers. Not only does Buffalo Bill contest all definitions of gender and elude its categorizations, his performativity of sexual allure can have a perversely liberating, even 'resisting' dimension, insofar as it executes one kind of logic of the system. If in the Lacanian paradigm mentioned above he seems to be comprehensible as a being caught within the Imaginary of the mirror-stage, and slave to the most alienated of self-images, in the Foucaultian paradigm Buffalo Bill becomes a subversive, because wholly dedicated, worker at the site of body- and self-commodification. By taking the system more seriously than it takes itself, he is in the vanguard of a particular form of consumption, that of self-expression turned 'self-fashioning', engaged in the permanent bricolage art of identity formation.

A body-artist and avant-gardist of constructed gender, Buffalo Bill and his makeover identity is reminiscent, because rendered parodic-pathological, of the periodic self-invention of pop performers and music-video icons such as Madonna, Prince, or Michael Jackson. The line between the criminal (the extreme embodiment of the system itself, which takes the system at its word) and the resister/contester of the system (Buffalo Bill as the one who refuses to have his body/self 'written' by the dominant binary divides) becomes a fine one indeed, and in a sense he is Agent Starling's double, his ethics of transgression the inverse of her law enforcement: the meticulous skin-and-needlework is testimony to his dedication and professionalism, which is why one could say that, unlike Clarice, his failure is in fact his triumph, making his death a heroic self-sacrifice, in that it vindicates his refusal of normative heterosexuality. Perhaps this is how one might explain his enigmatic gesture of tenderly stroking Clarice's hair before letting himself be killed, by a panicky Clarice firing in his general direction, after hearing the clicking of his gun's safety catch. What if the lamb that Clarice 'saves' is not Catherine Marshall, but Gumb/lamb, by granting him a sacrificial death and salvation?

Such a slightly perverse conclusion might already indicate the general direction that a Foucault reading could take. For instance, one might ask: in what 'discursive space' do these three protagonists come together? First of all, the institutional/discursive sites of the federal justice system, of medical and criminal pathology: who is mad and who is sane, where to draw the line? What do we make of figures such as Dr Chilton, who may not be criminally insane but who is certainly shown to be dangerously stupid? Foucault's point that madness in the pre-classical period had its own spaces within and at the margins of society – as in the Ship of Fools – and only in the classical period became the spectacle and 'theatre' of the asylum, marked off from the sane by framing, separating and encasing them in ways that accentuated their visibility while silencing their words, could be said to be held up for (post-classical) renegotiation in *The Silence of the Lambs*.

Then, there is the discursive space of the body, once we think of these bodies differently. The 'quid pro quo' trading of knowledge between Clarice and Lecter, heavily eroticized and pleasurable to both, opens up an exchange, a deal that puts Clarice level with Buffalo Bill regarding the secrets of their respective pathologies (childhood trauma/childhood abuse), but it also pits Clarice against Hannibal Lecter, because of the offer she makes him which turns out to have been a ruse for which he nearly falls ('"Anthrax Island" – nice touch, Clarice'). This cat-and-mouse game (not just a 'ping-pong game', as Klaus Theweleit calls it (1994: 37), because of the additional dimension that includes Buffalo Bill, who is intercut as the third player, with his own cat-and-moth game), enfolds the characters in a self-monitoring, self-surveillance system ('Look deep into yourself,' Hannibal mockingly and riddlingly tells Clarice), yet one that is not primarily based on vision.

More directly panoptic is the gaze relayed between the three men on the 'inside' – Dr Chilton, Crawford, Hannibal – and the(ir political masters) outside: Krendler, from the Justice Department, and Senator Marshall, going live on TV. What makes it different from the male gaze of feminist film theory is not only that its 'sexual difference' import is either directly thematized (by Lecter, for instance, regarding Crawford and others: 'Don't you feel eyes moving over your body, Clarice?') or not relevant (in the case of Chilton, Krendler, and Senator Marshall), but also that each of the characters is both looking and knowing him/herself observed, by the internalized gaze of the respective institution or their own self-scrutinizing ambition/conscience. They all, at a certain point, make a spectacle of themselves, in the knowledge that they are being watched: from Senator Marshall, pleading for her daughter in front of the national TV audience, to Hannibal Lecter, fully aware, of course, that his interviews/conversations with Clarice are being recorded and monitored.

On the other hand, the Foucaultian reading also reaches its limits, in that it does not adequately account for the eccentric position and personality of Hannibal Lecter, when mostly seeing him as part of the 'system'. The refusal embodied in his dandyism, but also in his excessive heterosexuality, would not be fully valorized, although there is a line of argument which would say that Hannibal is in fact a 'homosexual' who wears his verbal and social heterosexuality as a disguise, a mask and masquerade. It is here that Deleuze may offer a way forward, because neither sexual difference nor the gaze, panoptic or otherwise, are for him the most salient categories.

## 9.6.2. A Deleuze reading

There is, first of all, something very Deleuze–Guattarian about the world of *The Silence of The Lambs*: what is striking is the outrageously indecorous mingling of bodies and minds between the three central characters, the seeping, bleeding, and conflating of their discrete and otherwise contrasting psychic profiles. The way their particular somatic selves, kinetic traits, and peculiar intensities are taken apart, mixed up, and reassigned is a good example of what Deleuze and Guattari mean by 'de-territorializing', the movement away from established limits and boundaries, towards new or even archaic forms of psychic, as well as bodily organization.

Thus, a Deleuzian anti-psychoanalytic reading might start with one feature of Hannibal Lecter not yet commented upon here but crucial to the fascination emanating from this figure: his cannibalism, the fact that he eats his victims. His is a taboo-breaking figure of a special kind, in one sense disrespectful of the most fundamental and basic boundaries between bodies and within bodies, but in another sense an 'incorporator', whose strength and perspicacity comes precisely from his ability to redraw these boundaries between inside and outside. Quite clearly, the totemic behaviour of Buffalo Bill (dressing himself in his victims' skins like a suit of armour) and the atavistic-tribal power politics of Hannibal Lecter (eating people's livers, biting off their faces, or otherwise ingesting their body parts) are symmetrically related: their most fundamental body schemata are different from those of other mortals, and could be described more accurately in Deleuzian terms of the 'body-without-organs', as 'matter that occupies space ... to the degree corresponding to the intensities produced'. Especially Hannibal Lecter would probably have appealed to Deleuze's gnomic sense of humour, in that he pastiches by literalizing the 'body-without-organs', seeking radically to de-form in order to transform the power relations that make up the social bond, by exposing it to quite different yet no less 'actual' intensities and desires than those which normally regulates how people interact. Here the 'devouring eye' is no mere metaphor of love or covetous possessiveness, and the fundamental body schemata of container and contained are 'flattened' into sheets of skin, with only a recto and a verso, but no volume or depth.

The psychic violence and erotic desires usually domesticated in the family unit of 'Oedipus' and the incest prohibition are in these characters translated into a micro-schizo-politics of body and skin, and a materialist-immanent commerce of brain, thought, and flesh. Taken together with Clarice and the haunting image of the bleating lambs, the three protagonists come together under the primitive but sacred rituals of sacrifice and slaughter, emphasizing the fact that, in many respects, the film works with icons, with images readable only at the threshold where actions trace out emblematic designs and where – in Foucault's terms – the preclassical unity of word and image resurfaces with traumatic force.

From the 'body-without-organs' and the deterritorializations practised by Hannibal, it is easy to see how consistently the film is presenting us with partial objects and multiply articulated levels of existence, with 'altered states' and their successive stages. They can best be gathered together under the denominator 'metamorphosis', a process graphically represented in Buffalo Bill's trade mark of an exotic moth which he lodges in his victims' throats.

This motif (which, as we shall see, is much more pervasive than the term indicates) is perhaps the most directly Deleuzian aspect of the film, because it refers us to his concept of 'becoming', briefly described above, and extensively treated in Deleuze and Guattari's book on Franz Kafka, not only because Kafka's most famous story is called *Metamorphosis*, but because here was an individual whose many forms of marginalization made him take action. In his case, he developed a style of writing that was as physical, literal, referential as any mode of action can be, because it 'creates through the real without representing it': this would be the meaning of 'becoming' in Kafka, whose 'becoming-animal' or 'becoming-insect' was the most authentic encounter with the world.

Translating the Deleuzian paradigm into the character constellation of *The Silence of the Lambs*, the figure of Buffalo Bill would again not be identified with his mirror-image – as in the feminist-Lacanian reading – but with the moth, the cocoon, which he painstakingly feeds with honey. As one of the entomologists at the Smithsonian remarks: 'Somebody loved him.' He feeds the moth in order to help the butterfly/moth out of the cocoon, while at the same time he starves the women to 'help' them out of their skins. Feeding honey to a death's-head moth, fasting 'size 14' women, or feasting on human liver – with these bodily features the film introduces us (and initiates Clarice) to a different lifecycle, that of insects, perhaps, rather than humans. For Buffalo Bill's behaviour is only the most obvious example of what is going on in all the main characters, namely their perpetual transformation, depicted as an unfolding, a divesting and attiring, a transmutation and metamorphosis.

This, as indicated, Deleuze would call 'becoming ... animal, insect, woman'. It is signalled by repeated movements towards breaking out: of a skin, a carapace, a phantasm, or a cage. It has to do with flight and liberation: the moth as James Gumb's totem animal, but also Hannibal, crucifying and eviscerating the policeman, as if to graphically depict his own escape as an act of voiding a body and shedding a carapace at the same time, while Clarice tries to leave behind the phantasm of the lambs to clothe herself in the insignia of office, uniform and badge, investiture and diploma.

In order thus to reinterpret Hannibal Lecter, and indicate to what extent he is at the heart of the passive–active network that the film weaves around the trope of metamorphosis, we might quote Deleuze on a key distinction made in his cinema books, namely the shift from the movement image (or action image) to the time image (or crystal image):

> The cinema of action depicts sensory-motor situations: there are characters, in a certain situation, who act, perhaps very violently, according to how they perceive the situation. Actions are linked to perceptions and perceptions develop into actions. Now, suppose a character finds himself in a situation, however ordinary or extraordinary, that's beyond any possible action, or to which he can't react. It's too powerful, or too painful, too beautiful. The sensory-motor link is broken. He is no longer in a sensory-motor situation, but in a purely optical and aural situation.
>
> (Deleuze 1997: 51)

In this sense Hannibal Lecter, too, is a Deleuzian figure, now not so much in relation to 'becoming other' as insofar as he is 'brain' *and* 'screen', while his incarceration cuts the link with the sensorimotor scheme. We never quite see him eliminate Midge, nor learn exactly how he manages to escape his cage, hoist one policeman, and skin the other's face to put it on as a mask: crucial parts of the action are always missing, the film cuts from one temporal event to another, without the intermediary steps. The fact that he cannot move is the locus of his power and it is the power of making mental constructions, inferences – he elicits from Clarice her past and colonizes her future. While he seems to encourage the linear investigative drive, he actually deflects it, turns it inward, makes it mental. One could think of the immobility of a character from the 'classical cinema', such as Jeffries (James Stewart) in Hitchcock's *Rear Window*, who is normally read in Lacanian terms as the epitome of voyeurism, and contrast his confinement with that of Hannibal Lecter. The difference is striking, even though Lecter, too, expresses his desire for a 'view' ('Belvedere'). But his voyeurism is of an entirely different nature: once we see him as a brain, it is Lecter's cannibalism that becomes crucial, because it is in some sense proof of his ability to ingest a mental world, his facility to be 'inside' someone's mind in no time at all.

Early on in the film, just after he has explained to Clarice the nature of her assignment, Crawford says to her: 'Believe me, you don't want Hannibal Lecter inside your head.' This remark can be understood in a Foucaultian sense as warning her of the insinuating cannibalism of psychoanalysis and other technologies of discursive penetration. But since he only warns of what he knows will come to pass, Crawford's advice can also be seen as laying out the topology of the two characters' engagement with each other, also captured in a sentence of Deleuze, cited by Žižek: 'If you are caught up in another person's dream, you are lost' (Žižek 1994: 212). At the same time, Deleuze might well have agreed with Alphonse Bertillon, the founding father of criminology, when he said: 'One only sees that which one observes, and one observes only things which are in the mind' – a sentence that Thomas Harris, author of *The Silence of the Lambs*, used as his epigraph in *Red Dragon*, the first of the Hannibal Lecter novels.

But in another sense, this feeling of being inside someone else's head, dream, or fantasy is perhaps the most striking feature of contemporary mainstream cinema. Hollywood goes to enormous lengths to blur the distinction between 'subjective' and 'objective', often telling its stories as if they were taking place in a world diegetically independent from the characters within it, only then to reveal that – either wholly or in crucial respects – this world is one which depends on being seen, observed, sensed, or imagined by someone, or – more complicated still – only exists in the spaces of overlap between two characters' mutually intersecting fantasy or memory spaces (*The Truman Show, Nurse Betty, American Beauty, eXistenZ, The Matrix, Memento*). It brings us back to the nature of Deleuze's (and Guattari's) mode of thinking, which earlier on I called 'immersive'. One could also describe it – more polemically – as hermetically sealed against the 'outside', sustaining itself only by virtue of its own self-defined concepts and modes of thinking, which mutually refine but also confine each other in a seemingly seamless web or cloth or skin/skein that knows only extension and inversion, an enveloping undulation apparently without beginning or end.

This *mise-en-abîme* of mental worlds in the service of sustaining the impression of/immersion in a diegetic world which is also a mental universe is called by Deleuze 'the fold', and he connects it to seriality and series, to the manifold in Leibniz's thinking, and to the involuted successiveness of vistas without prospect known from the Baroque. For Deleuze, the fact that the characters seems to be constantly in each others' minds or trying to encase them in their worlds is a consequence of the 'sheets of time' into which human beings are always already enfolded.

'The fold' thus defines the nature of Deleuze's argumentative strategy which – with reference to the cinema – might be called a mimetic embrace of his subject, describing in what sense Deleuze does indeed think *with* the cinema rather than *about* it. For 'the fold' serves to redefine the nature of the cinematic fascination, or at least, that exerted by the contemporary (though not exclusively) Hollywood cinema – now examined and explained not through the psychoanalytic paradigm of absence, fetishism, and disavowal, nor through the cinematic apparatus and it structure of interpellation and suture, but rather, by trying to make Deleuze's notion of the fold productive in conjunction with his definition of the 'event', as described by Foucault in the quotation above, and allowing us to re-situate the problem with which we began: how to redefine and reinterpret the cinematic experience.

# Conclusion

What we have done in this chapter is to conduct our three readings of *The Silence of the Lambs* around each of the three main characters: for the feminist case, it is Clarice Starling and her 'problem' that occupies centre stage; in our Foucaultian analysis we gave a privileged place to Buffalo Bill as the pathologized target of state power and the 'victim' of abuse from childhood on, seeking violently as well as tenderly to transgender and trans-dress/gress an identity imposed on him by societal norms of strict gender separation. Finally, the third analysis thematized Hannibal Lecter, as the figure that appeared to us to embody some intriguingly Deleuzian concepts, such as the radical 'deterritorialization' of conventional body schemata in his special kind of 'cannibalism' that refuses to distinguish between brain, mind, and flesh. Each reading thereby necessarily realigns the other characters, ascribing to them different values or even inverting their ethical identities. At the same time, the general conceptual focus has remained constant, insofar as sexual difference and gender; the Lacanian look and the panoptic gaze; the crossing and recrossing of boundaries between bodies, sensations, and successive stages of a deployment/development have in each reading served as the argumentative thread and metaphoric quilting.

However, such a tripartite division has above all schematic-didactic value: it should not disguise another intended movement of the analysis, which was concerned with transitions or gradations not only of sexed, gazed-upon, and gendered bodies but of concepts:

- from sexual difference to notions of performed gender and the multiform encounters of mind, matter, and sensuous perception;
- from 'subject' and 'subjectivity' to 'body' (as a site of discourses, images, and intensities, rather than a sexed material entity) providing the theoretical fields of negotiating identities, identifications, and corporeal experience in the cinema;
- from thinking progress, initiation and closure, to thinking metamorphosis, repetition, seriality;
- from thinking narrative and trajectory (initiation) to 'event' and 'phantasm', i.e. to new taxonomies of the audiovisual situation of the cinematic experience.

It is our contention that the two approaches – feminist film theory's (broadly structuralist) gendering of apparatus theory, alongside the post-structuralist articulations of identity/subjectivity/body by Foucault and Deleuze, with respect to the question of sexuality and gender in the cinema – have yielded a number of insights and results. For instance, it made it possible to claim that film theory's successive use of Freud and Lacan, polemically critiqued by Foucault and Deleuze, has followed a certain internal logic, and is not merely the expression of an externally imposed change of intellectual paradigm, such as the often-invoked move in film theory from 'psycho-semiotics' to 'cultural studies'.

Instead of seeing these theories and the methods derived from them as incompatibly juxtaposed, we tried to trace their antagonisms along several lines of transformation and rupture around the notion of sexual difference (which underpinned the feminist concern with power and inequality), opening out into the notion of gender. The sex/gender problematic was thus extended at the theoretical level, in order that *The Silence of the Lambs* and its controversial reception could be analysed in a way that made the controversy comprehensible also within the text. We have thus offered a complementary reading to the deadlocks variously noted by Stephen Heath, Janet Staiger, and Judith Halberstam. More specifically, thanks to Foucualt and Deleuze, the nexus of power and personhood, of difference and opposition, but also of desire and pleasure could be seen as multiform and decentred, localized, and micropolitical, rather than as categorical and absolute, which is how it often appears in the binary and exclusionary articulations of militant practices and academic discourses. For Foucault and Deleuze, energies flow in either direction, sexuality is multi-layered, and affective connections can be established across apparently insuperable barriers and antagonistic concepts – those of good and evil, of male and female, of pleasure and horror.

The conflicting viewing positions have thus been resolved not by adopting an either/or, or both ... and stance, but by a kind of theoretical layering, appealing to a reconceptualization at another level, which allowed us to see this particular film (though the same would be true of many other contemporary films: apart from the ones already cited, David Fincher's *Se7en* and *Fight Club* come to mind) presenting us with different worlds, and several ways of conceiving their protagonists' and antagonists' identities. The key concept that permitted the shift is that of the body, or rather the move from 'subject' and 'subject position' to body, figured not only as the inseparability of consciousness, matter, brain, and flesh, but also as the non-antagonistic relation of inside and outside, of surface and extension, sexuality and gender. The body becomes not only a topographical 'site' for an inscription of the world and its different kinds of textuality. It also emerges as the locus of energies and intensities emanating from it and oscillating between spectator and screen. In respect of the film experience, the body is thus both foundational and constructed, an a priori given and the result of that which it is not – image, schema, representation.

# Conclusion

## What is interpretation and what is analysis?

This book has been trying to resituate what we think we are doing when studying individual films closely. We have asked what is close textual analysis and film interpretation in the university, and what is the difference between analysis and interpretation. In the introduction, we cited the assertion of David Bordwell that no link exists between theory and analysis. This may be true in the sense that a film analysis does not deductively flow from a theory, and that in many ways a theory and an analysis construct their objects differently, which is to say, they address different readers and different interests. Yet, by the same token, an analysis does not come without implicit assumptions; not only can these vary enormously, they can also be made explicit, and one traditional way of making assumptions explicit is to formulate them as a theory. One factor that therefore accounts for the variability is theory, which is to say the rendering explicit and coherent of the implicit assumptions made by film analysts. In this limited respect – but nonetheless on both historical and theoretical-pragmatic grounds – we disagree with Bordwell: film analysis has in the past given rise to theory (one thinks of André Bazin and his analysis of neo-realism), and film theory can render explicit the intuitive or hidden agendas of practical analysis (even if some of the most influential theories have in fact not operated in this manner: see below).

The preceding chapters have not tried to redress this imbalance. Rather, they have been more modest, both making apparent and rendering explicit how, depending on one's theoretical framework and the methods derived from it, an analysis will reveal different aspects of a film, or even leave room for interpreting the same features of a film differently.

This last point raises once more the question as to how one might best describe the difference between analysis and interpretation. It is a topic that has frequently been discussed in film studies, very often polemically: see Robert Stam's 'Textual Analysis' and 'Interpretation and its Discontents' (2000: 185–200). Yet it seems to us that what is involved in both analysis and interpretation can be defined quite generally. For Edward Branigan,

It is apparent that one aim of a global interpretation is to propose (new, non-diegetic) contexts in which a fiction may be seen *non*fictionally, that is, seen to have a connection to the ordinary world. Under an interpretation, a fiction may offer knowledge about the real world and may come to possess, if not a truth value, then at least relevance, significance, appropriateness, value, plausibility, rightness or realism.

(1993: 8)

Branigan offers this account in the context of assessing the basic premises underlying Bordwell's influential book on interpretation, *Making Meaning* (1989). Drawing on Monroe Beardsley, Branigan sees analysis and interpretation as two steps in what are for him four distinct but interlocking activities: description, analysis, interpretation, and evaluation. While *description* employs a 'nominative construction and can be empirically verified', *analysis* 'is concerned with problems of segmentation, with breaking something into component parts in order to discover how it works and creates effects'. *Interpretation*, in this scheme, 'makes a generalization . . . in an attempt to explain what wider contexts are appropriate for comprehending some aspect of a phenomenon.' 'Finally, an *evaluation* makes a normative judgement.' Here, analysis and interpretation are part of a hierarchy and of a sequence of moves, where interpretation (and evaluation) should ideally be preceded by analysis (and description), the latter establishing the empirical and formal grounds of the former.

If we were to summarize this schema, in order to highlight the difference between analysis and interpretation, we might say that analysis (like description) aims at a certain degree of objectivity, being deduced from a set of pre-given observable phenomena or formal procedures and rules. Interpretation (like evaluation), by contrast, necessarily makes room for the element of subjectivity, of personal experience or judgement: interpretation makes connections – at a certain level of abstraction – between statements that at first glance do not belong to the same cognitive or conceptual categories. Interpretation thus does not have as its aim the production of new knowledge, but the connection of existing knowledge in novel and (hopefully) illuminating ways. As Eugene Donato has put it, paraphrasing Michel Foucault:

Analysis and interpretation are . . . two modes [that] co-exist yet are fundamentally opposed to each other. If interpretation plays on the gap resulting from the interjection of the subject, analysis requires the elimination of that subject as a necessary prerequisite to the study of the formal properties which condition the unfolding of any particular type of discourse.

(1972: 97)

On the other hand, if – following Beardsley and Branigan – we consider analysis and interpretation to be on the same continuum of the activities of criticism, then we can say that analysis, for heuristic or procedural reasons, argues that the phenomena it describes are located 'out there' in the object (film, literary text, artwork), whereas interpretation sees itself more engaged in a kind of dialogue between object and subject, interpretans and interpreter, acknowledging the dimension of 'in here'. This latter view is not unconnected with the realization that many of the theories in the humanities, and thus the theories film scholars are likely to turn to or have internalized, are theories of interpretation or hermeneutics, whether one thinks of Freudian psychoanalysis or Lévi-Strauss's structuralism, of Marxist ideological critique or Derridean deconstruction. This suggests that 'interpretation' (as an activity, or indeed as an institution) is in fact the more general category, of which analysis is one particular practice or precondition, either legitimated through use – as in the phrase 'close textual analysis', derived from literary criticism – or emphasizing the reductionist thrust of such an activity, distilling from the plurality and diversity of instances some general rules and principles. It is in this sense that we can understand Bordwell's remark, which, because it subsumes analysis under interpretation, only apparently contradicts what we have just been asserting about the distinction between 'out there' and 'in here':

> Interpretation takes as its basic subject our perceptual, cognitive, and affective processes, but it does so in a roundabout way – by attributing their 'output' to the text 'out there'. To understand a film interpretively is to subsume it to our conceptual schemes, and thus to master them more fully, if only tacitly.
>
> (Bordwell 1989: 257)

This 'mastery' is perhaps a moot point here. We distinguish analysis – the mastery of certain schemes – from interpretation, by emphasizing the dialogical dimension, the two-way process, which by definition cannot be an act of 'mastery'. From interpretation we ask: What is it trying to do with the text, and also: What does the text do with the spectator, the interpreter? In other words, we see our study as constitutively context-dependent, an interchange, and we are not at all disturbed by the prospect that it proves the often-heard and only half-cynical phrase, 'Interpretation always finds what it is looking for'. We acknowledge the measure of truth contained in the sentence by conceding that the subjectivity of the analyst-interpreter shapes and to some extent determines the objectivity of his analysis.

Another point about 'mastery' worth mentioning is that analysis is always a question of authority, of power. It would be foolish to claim, insofar as we are talking about a practice mostly taking place in a pedagogical setting, that there is a level playing field concerning whose interpretation may carry the day and, therefore, what type of analysis is considered 'legitimate'. This not only applies to the relation between teacher and student, between the institution and those seeking access to or validation from the institution. It also applies to the relation between the text and its interpreter. One prevailing school of analysis (backed by a powerful theory) assumed that the film text determines the way it wants and needs to be read, and that for specific ideological but also formal and technological reasons, the (film) text 'positions' us as viewers and 'readers'. Whatever the merits or problems of this type of analysis, in the classroom situation it is generally we who do something to the text, even as we explain how the text positions us (the 'we' and 'us' in this sentence would appear not to refer to the same group of individuals).

This paradoxical power relationship is especially evident in one form of interpretation, which in some quarters has given the practice altogether a bad name: we are referring to the so-called 'hermeneutics of suspicion' (also discussed in Chapter 8). Briefly put, the text is presumed to be hiding its real intentions, namely to do something to us and 'position us', yet it is the interpretation that does something to the text, namely to make it say (against its will) what it is trying to hide. To its supporters, such a hermeneutics of suspicion has been a powerful defence against the rhetorical and ideological work of the text. To those critical of 'subject-position' theory, it seems as if its practitioners have succumbed to paranoia, obstinately and ingeniously elaborating a conspiracy theory, where in the name of 'critical discourse' and 'symptomatic readings' against the grain, films are subjected to third-degree interrogations, in show trials whose outcome is fixed in advance.

This is a somewhat exaggerated version of the polemics that has kept film studies lively and vigorous in recent years. It should not downplay the fact that behind the contested methodological and theoretical arguments there are genuine differences of opinion. These, perhaps, have less to do with the difference between analysis and interpretation, or even with interpretation as a worthwhile activity, and more with the changing status of film and the cinema as objects of scholarly enquiry. In its relatively brief history, film studies has run through a number of such status definitions, and seems once more in the midst of yet another change. After initially (i.e. from roughly the 1920s to the early 1960s) asking whether a film can be a work of art (and if so, whether it obeys classical rules or subscribes to a modernist aesthetic), film studies began in the mid-1960s, under the influence of semiotics and structuralism, to conceive of film as a text, picking up preoccupations with film language already present among Soviet film-makers, but also extending the language analogy to film as discourse, a notion owing its critical force to the theories of Marx, Freud, and Nietzsche.

However, the 1960s also saw the (brief) flourishing of an avant-garde for whom the cinema served as a model of the mind, and of a (more enduring) theory that regarded film as a 'philosophical toy' about perception, cognition, and consciousness. It is this status definition of the cinema as a conundrum for philosophy that in the 1980s and 1990s reinvigorated the discussion of film and philosophy on a broad front, stretching from cognitivist science and experimental psychology to phenomenology, analytic philosophy, epistemological scepticism, and Bergsonian vitalism. What these diverse strands have in common is the place they accord to the cinema as a type of experience – perceptual, cognitive, affective, material – prior to seeking to define its aesthetic, linguistic, ideological, or textual status. Whether this amounts to a shift of emphasis or a radically different departure remains to be seen. Our sense is that in the contest between film as text and film as experience, or film as discourse and film as event, one may want to take sides but need not be forced to choose. Rather, one should welcome the plurality, providing it keeps the film analyst reflexive about the respective theoretical assumptions and students are equipped with the relevant methodological skills to continue to conduct valid film analyses.

## Interpreting the paradigms of interpretation and analysis

These remarks should suffice to explain why in the preceding chapters we have both implicitly and explicitly assumed that contemporary American (Hollywood) movies are important to study, and why they are paradigmatic for the challenges facing film analysis in general.

More practically, we have been reviewing but also showing in action some of the particular, historically specific paradigms that have been applied to films, such as *mise-en-scène* criticism, thematic readings, and auteurist analysis. We called them paradigms in order to indicate their conceptual status, somewhere between a theory and a method of analysis, but nevertheless sufficiently established for us both to extrapolate from the practice the elements of a theory and, on the other hand, to specify some of the rules of this practice in terms of a method. Therefore, we might say that while in each of our chapters the outline of the theory is followed by the statement of a method, both are in fact indissolubly linked to a practice which in our model follows on from theory and method but which in another, historical as well as procedural sense has often preceded both. What, then, can we conclude from our exercise about the validity and claims of these different paradigms?

### Classical/post-classical (Chapter 2)

Contrary to the claims that, with regard to contemporary American cinema, it is 'business as usual', but also contrary to the claim that we must assume a radical break between classical cinema (that of the 1920s to the 1960s), and the mainstream Hollywood product of the past two decades, the chapter has tried to demonstrate that we are here dealing in many ways with a false opposition. The problem of the classical/postclassical is rather like a crystal: it occupies several dimensions and can be turned in different directions, each time revealing a configuration that marks both the differences and the similarities, both the continuities and the breaks. Our conclusion was that the post-classical, quite correctly, still contains the term 'classical', but that in relation to the classical it is both 'reflexive' and 'excessive', and therefore can neither be situated conceptually in a linear, progressive, chronological line nor pictured as a dialectical or directly antagonist relationship.

- *Die Hard* seemed to prove this point by being perfectly readable as a classically constructed Hollywood film. Yet what made it interesting and exciting was the often ingenious and always knowing way it actually staged and celebrated this carefully crafted classicism, by teasing (or irritating) its critics with sustained bouts of verbal, visual, and ideological transgressiveness.

## *Mise-en-scène* criticism, thematic criticism, auteurism (Chapters 3 and 4)

Contrary to V.F. Perkins's claim that *mise en scène* as a film-making practice is dead, recent film critics have found it worthwhile to apply this concept to contemporary cinema. Adrian Martin distinguishes classical, expressionist and mannerist *mise en scène*, and argues that Perkins is simply lamenting the death of classical *mise en scène* (although it has many adherents in contemporary film-making practice). The categories of expressionist, and mannerist *mise en scène* are added to cover new film-making practices. Also, critics like Jonathan Rosenbaum continue to review films using the concept, while Bordwell has developed his historical poetics out of *mise-en-scène* criticism (citing Arnheim and Bazin) and from art history. Looking at the examples we have chosen, we might say that:

- *The English Patient* in a sense simply reproduces classical narrative and self-consciously evokes and nostalgically celebrates classical *mise en scène*.
- *Chinatown*, by contrast, is a transformation of classical *film noir*, which stages its devices, but also breaks the rules in the process, refracting them across the history of *film noir*'s subsequent reception and interpretation.

What has emerged is that for traditional modes of analysis, narrative is absolutely crucial, however much *mise-en-scène* criticism and even thematic-auteurist criticism could and can afford to take the basic principles of cinematic narrative for granted. In each case the critical discourse either elaborates the narrative one or exists only in relation to and interchangeably with the principles of story construction as they have obtained in the fiction film in since the 1910s.

## Video game logic and cognitivist criticism (Chapters 5 and 6)

Perhaps the most incisive challenges to canonical story construction have come from the study of interactive narrative, and from the cognitivist approach to narration. It now seems at least theoretically conceivable that the conditions of filmic comprehension and of intelligibility can be established on a basis other than the classical narrative models introduced and examined in Chapter 2, and implicitly adhered to in Chapters 3 and 4, even where we tested them by their apparent opposite: post-classical cinema, statistical style analysis, and deconstructive criticism.

At the same time, it is self-evident in the case of video game logic, and implicit also in the case of cognitivism, that the shift of paradigm and the apparent sidelining of narrative as the key principle of meaning-making has paralleled certain technological changes, such as digitization, which are transforming the cinema as well as our ways of thinking about it. Although we would not wish to put forward an argument derived from technological determinism, it is reasonable to conclude that different media practices are partly responsible for putting the classical story structure under pressure. The new technologies (of post-photographic moving images) implement new modalities of sound and image recognition and perception, which we also wanted to consider in the form of case studies:

- Luc Besson's *The Fifth Element* must in this situation be regarded as a hybrid, since it places itself between classical narrative and digital narrative (as represented in video games). For all practical purposes, it still behaves like a mainstream Hollywood film, at the generic cusp of science fiction and fairy-tale fantasy. However, in its story development and in its mixture of genre elements, it allows itself also to be read within another mode, that of the multi-stranded, branching, or otherwise non-linear construction of the computer or video game, where characters are player-positions and have several lives, and where actions repeat themselves, often at another level of difficulty or in another diegetic world.

- David Lynch's *Lost Highway* develops, much more decisively than *The Fifth Element*, a radical break with classical narrative and *mise en scène*. In contrast to Besson (and also Spielberg: see below), Lynch does not use new technology to do so. In fact, he prides himself on sticking to conventional optical and sound technology in producing the effects in

*Lost Highway*: for instance, the sounds are still 'real' – i.e. the sounds of household objects such as fridges are slowed down and reversed in order to create an eerie background noise, as opposed to being synthetically created from digital sources.

## Digital realism (Chapter 7)

This chapter sets out to prove that new imaging technologies need not function deterministically: far from generating new story formats or implying a break with classical *mise en scène*, computer-generated effects can actually reinforce the classical modes. The chapter finds that the traditional theory of realism – as represented by André Bazin – continues to have relevance to the analysis of contemporary American film, where the 'new digital realism' of post-photographic images has at times vigorously revived the sort of sensory surface and deep-space realism once attributed to the unique properties of the celluloid image.

- In the case of Steven Spielberg's *Jurassic Park* and *The Lost World* one could say that both films do not so much follow canonical story structure as mimic it, along with implementing classical *mise en scène*, by citing photographic reality. One could even call this modality 'parody' because some of the special effects confront photographic realism with its own impossibility. But one could also think of Spielberg's special effects as 'kitsch', recalling the tendency in art and crafts to reproduce with the most modern technology the aesthetic effects and material properties of a previous technique or technology. This description fits Spielberg (along with many other contemporary directors) in the sense that they use new (digital) technology to reproduce the 'effects' (of photographic realism) and the 'products' (of studio and location shooting) that now belong to an earlier period and earlier stage of technology in the film industry. Here, a continuity is affirmed, but now in the performative mode of that continuity's self-conscious or self-effacing 'staging'.

## Psychoanalytic, post-psychoanalytic, and anti-psychoanalytic criticism (Chapters 8 and 9)

One of the recurring themes in almost all the chapters has been the element of 'knowingness', of 'irony' and 'pastiche' not only in the generic tone of the films but also in their manner of situating their stylistic and formal procedures. They are aware of their special status of 'coming after' the classical mode, reviving it, mimicking it, deconstructing it. But they are so self-assuredly aware of this place and status that they have, in some sense, also overcome it, finding themselves in another realm, another mode, another episteme, even if we have as yet no more than an intuition what this means for the future of the cinema, and even if we do not as yet have a name to mark the 'transitional', 'in-between', 'hybrid' or 'post' stage of the present practice.

This poses special problems to an interpretation committed to the psychoanalytic paradigm or which proceeds via the 'hermeneutic of suspicion', in that the films 'mirror' the analyst, giving little purchase to the gesture that seeks to wrest from them their secret or hidden meaning.

- In Robert Zemeckis's *Back to the Future* we are confronted with such a classically Oedipal plot that a Freudian analysis risks becoming a description rather than an interpretation. Even a Lacanian reading around the mirror phase finds itself pastiched in the plot's use of a fading photograph: by seemingly accommodating them, the film resists analysis within the framework of these models. Outlining within its arch-conventional family comedy format the contours of a post-Oedipal, post-patriarchal society, *Back to the Future* could be said to hint at a different psychosocial organization, repositioning ideals of masculinity and racial superiority, but taking from psychoanalysis not the idea of an unconscious, but such concepts as 'deferred action' and 'repetition compulsion'. Rather than referring to a possible logic of the subject, these achronological temporalities now stage the logic of the film industry, with its remakes, sequels, prequels, and revivals.

- *The Silence of the Lambs.* The crisis of critical purchase also applies to *The Silence of the Lambs*, notably with respect to its contradictory reception by feminists, gays, and gender activists. Focusing initially on feminist and queer readings of the film, and the deadlocks these types of analysis seem to generate, the chapter rereads the films' character-constellation in categories derived from two major anti-psychoanalytic thinkers, namely Foucault and Deleuze, and their theories of the body, in contrast to psychoanalysis' reliance on the concept of the subject. What is important, however, is that 'body', too, is not a positive entity, which interpretation could 'read' and critically position. In the cognitive and affective relation human beings maintain with their environment, which is to say, their capacity for experience (including the film experience), the body is both foundational and constructed, a fantasy formation and a material-physiological fact. It marks the limits of the film-as-experience, and returns us once more to the film-as-text, since only through some sort of segmentation and semiotization, that is, through analysis, can sensation become experience.

Analysis is, finally, a key term when studying movies and accounting for the film experience. Coming after description and preceding interpretation, it is engaged in a movement that is, so to speak, bidirectional – taking us from the visible, perceptual, sensory phenomena which is the film to the invisible structure(s) and process(es) that have generated those phenomena, and then leading us to a further visibility in another medium, that of language and verbal discourse, where these structures or patterns are rendered legible, intelligible, communicable, and therefore available to interpretation, which is to say, open to dialogue and debate.

In spite of this book seeming to adhere to a broadly semiotic or perhaps 'cognitive semiotic' project, the juxtaposition or interaction of different paradigms in the preceding chapters has reaffirmed our sense of a film as both a personal experience and an interpersonal event or encounter. As such, film analysis continues to require the skills of hermeneutics, of reading surfaces and textures, structures and schemata. Interpretation is what we do every day also with the sensory input we receive from the 'real world', just as interpretation is crucial to any interchange with other human beings, whether verbal or non-verbal. There can be no end to interpretation, and thus no end to the needs for acquiring the skills of analysis.

# References

Allen, Richard (1995), *Projecting Illusion: Film Spectatorship and the Impression of Reality* (Cambridge: Cambridge University Press).

———— (1997), 'Looking at motion pictures', in Richard Allen and Murray Smith (eds), *Film Theory and Philosophy* (Oxford: Clarendon Press): 76–94.

Altman, Rick (1980), 'Moving lips: cinema as ventriloquism', in R. Altman (ed.), *Sound and Cinema* (special issue, *Yale French Studies*, 60): 67–79.

Anderson, Joseph (1996), *The Reality of Illusion: An Ecological Approach to Cognitive Film Theory* (Carbondale: Southern Illinois University Press).

Anderson, Lindsay (1955), 'The last sequence of *On the Waterfront*', *Sight and Sound*, 24, 3: 127–30.

Arnheim, Rudolf (1957), *Film as Art* (Berkeley: University of California Press).

Barthes, Roland (1974), *S/Z*, trans. Richard Miller (New York: Hill and Wang).

———— (1977), 'The third meaning', in *Image, Music, Text*, trans. Stephen Heath (London: Fontana): 52–68.

———— (1994), *The Semiotic Challenge*, trans. Richard Howard (Berkeley: University of California Press).

Baudry, Jean-Louis (1986), 'Ideological effects of the basic cinematic apparatus', in Rosen (1986: 286–98).

Bazin, André (1967a), 'The ontology of the photographic image', in *What is Cinema?* (Berkeley: University of California Press): 9–16.

———— (1967b), 'The evolution of the language of the cinema', in *What is Cinema?* 23–40.

———— (1967c), 'The virtues and limitations of montage', in *What is Cinema?* 41–52.

———— (1991), *Orson Welles: A Critical View* (Los Angeles: Acrobat Books).

Beardsley, Monroe (1958), *Aesthetics: Problems in the Philosophy of Criticism* (New York: Harcourt, Brace & World).

Bellour, Raymond (2000), *The Analysis of Film*, ed. Constance Penley (Bloomington: Indiana University Press).

Bergson, Henri (1991), *Matter and Memory*, trans. N.M. Paul and W.S. Palmer (New York: Zone Books).

Benjamin, Walter (1999), *The Arcades Project*, trans. Howard Eiland and Kevin McLaughlin (New York: Belknap).

Bergstrom, Janet (ed., 1999), *Endless Night: Cinema and Psychoanalysis, Parallel Histories* (Berkeley: California University Press).

Bordwell, David (1969), 'Alfred Hitchcock's *Notorious*', *Film Heritage*, 4, 3: 6–10; 22.

——— (1985), *Narration in the Fiction Film* (London: Routledge).

——— (1989), *Making Meaning: Inference and Rhetoric in the Interpretation of Cinema* (Cambridge, Mass.: Harvard University Press).

——— (1997), *On the History of Film Style* (Cambridge, Mass.: Harvard University Press).

———, Janet Staiger, and Kristin Thompson (1985), *The Classical Hollywood Cinema: Film Style and Mode of Production to 1960* (London: Routledge).

Braga, Lucia Santaella (1997), 'The prephotographic, the photographic, and the postphotographic image', in Winfried Nöth (ed.), *Semiotics of the Media: State of the Art, Projects, and Perspectives* (Berlin: Mouton de Gruyter).

Branigan, Edward (1992), *Narrative Comprehension and Film* (New York: Routledge)

——— (1993), 'On the analysis of interpretative language', *Film Criticism*, 17: 2–3.

Bruner, Jerome (1991), 'The narrative construction of reality', *Critical Inquiry*, 18, 1: 1–21.

——— (1992), *Acts of Meaning* (Cambridge, Mass.: Harvard University Press).

Buchanan, Ian (2000), *Deleuzism: A Metacommentary* (Durham, NC: Duke University Press).

Buckland, Warren (ed.) (1995), *The Film Spectator: From Sign to Mind* (Amsterdam: Amsterdam University Press).

Butler, Judith (1989), *Gender Trouble* (London: Routledge).

——— (1997), *The Psychic Life of Power* (Stanford: Stanford University Press).

Camper, Fred (1976), '*Disputed Passage*', in Nichols (1976: 339–44).

Carroll, Noël (1988a), *Philosophical Problems of Classical Film Theory* (Princeton: Princeton University Press).

——— (1988b), *Mystifying Movies: Fads and Fallacies in Contemporary Film Theory* (New York: Columbia University Press).

——— (1996a), *Theorizing the Moving Image* (New York: Cambridge University Press).

——— (1996b), 'Prospects for film theory: a personal assessment', in David Bordwell and Noël Carroll (eds) *Post-Theory: Reconstructing Film Studies* (Madison: University of Wisconsin Press): 37–68.

Cawelti, John (1979), '*Chinatown* and generic transformations in recent American films', in G. Mast and M. Cohen (eds), *Film Theory and Criticism* (New York and Oxford: Oxford University Press): 559–79.

Clover, Carol (1992), *Men, Women and Chainsaws: Gender in the Modern Horror Film* (Princeton: Princeton University Press).

Colbert, Mary (1997), 'Beyond effects: an interview with John Seale', *Cinema Papers*, 115: 6–9, 44.

Conley, Tom (1991), *Film Hieroglyphs: Ruptures in Classical Cinema* (Minneapolis: University of Minnesota Press).

———— (1997), 'Evénement-cinéma', *Iris*, 23: 75–86.

Cook, Pam, and Claire Johnston (1988), 'The place of women in the cinema of Raoul Walsh', in Constance Penley (ed.), *Feminism and Film Theory* (London: Routledge).

Copjec, Joan (1994), *Read my Desire: Lacan against the Historicists* (Cambridge, Mass.: MIT Press).

Corbett, Edward P.J., and Connors, Robert J. (1999), *Classical Rhetoric for the Modern Student* (Oxford: Oxford University Press).

Creed, Barbara (1986), 'Horror and the monstrous feminine: an imaginary abjection', *Screen* 27, 1: 44–71.

———— (1993), *The Monstrous Feminine: Film, Feminism, Psychoanalysis* (London: Routledge).

Crockford, Douglas (n.d.), 'Quest into the unknown', http://www.communities.com/people/crock/ quest1.txt

Culler, Jonathan (1975), *Structuralist Poetics: Structuralism, Linguistics, and the Study of Literature* (Ithaca: Cornell University Press).

Currie, Gregory (1995), *Image and Mind: Film, Philosophy, and Cognitive Science* (Cambridge: Cambridge University Press).

Dayan, Daniel (1976), 'The tutor-code of classical cinema', in Nichols (1976: 438–51).

———— and Elihu Katz (1985), 'Electronic ceremonies: television performs a royal wedding', in Marshall Blonsky (ed.), *On Signs* (Baltimore: Johns Hopkins University Press): 16–32.

de Lauretis, Teresa (1984), *Alice Doesn't: Feminism, Semiotics, Cinema* (Bloomington: Indiana University Press).

Deleuze, Gilles (1986), *Cinema 1: The Movement Image* (London: Athlone Press).

———— (1989), *Cinema 2: The Time Image* (London: Athlone Press).

———— (1990), *The Logic of Sense* (New York: Columbia University Press).

———— (1992), *The Fold: Leibniz and the Baroque* (University of Minnesota Press).

———— (1997) *Negotiations, 1972–1990* (New York: Columbia University Press).

———— and Felix Guattari (1985), *Anti-Oedipus: Capitalism and Schizophrenia* (Minneapolis: University of Minnesota Press).

———— and Felix Guattari (1987), *A Thousand Plateaus: Capitalism and Schizophrenia* (Minneapolis: University of Minnesota Press).

Doane, Mary Ann (1987), *The Desire to Desire: The Woman's Film of the 1940s* (Bloomington: Indiana University Press).

───── and Janet Bergstrom (eds) (1990), 'The spectatrix', special issue of *Camera Obscura*: 20–21.

Donato, Eugene (1972), 'The two languages of criticism', in R. Macksay and E. Donato (eds), *The Structuralist Controversy* (Baltimore: Johns Hopkins University Press).

Elsaesser, Thomas (1987), 'Tales of sound and fury', in Christine Gledhill (ed.), *Home is Where the Heart is: Studies in Melodrama and the Woman's Film* (London: BFI).

Esquenazi, Jean-Pierre (1997), 'Films et sujets', *Iris*, 23: 129–45.

Farringdon, Jill (1996), *Analysing for Authorship: A Guide to the Cusum Technique* (Cardiff: University of Wales Press).

Fiske, John (1989), *Reading the Popular* (London: Routledge).

Flower-MacCannell, Juliet (1995), *The Regime of the Brother: After the Patriarchy* (New York: Routledge).

Floyd, Nigel (1997), 'Infinite city', *Sight and Sound*, 7, 6: 6–8.

Foster, Don (2001), *Author Unknown: On the Trail of Anonymous* (London: Macmillan).

Foucault, Michel (1977), *Language, Counter-Memory, Practice* (Ithaca: Cornell University Press).

───── (1979), *Discipline and Punish: The Birth of the Prison* (New York: Vintage Books).

───── (1981), *Power/Knowledge: Selected Interviews and Other Writings 1972–1977* (New York: Pantheon Books).

───── (1988), *Madness and Civilization: A History of Insanity in the Age of Reason* (New York: Vintage Books).

───── (1989), *Foucault Live* (New York: Semiotexte).

Gottschalk, Simon (1995), 'Videology: video-games as postmodern sites/sights of ideological reproduction', *Symbolic Interaction*, 18, 1.

Greimas, A.J. (1983), *Structural Semantics: An Attempt at a Method* (Lincoln: University of Nebraska Press).

Grodal, Torben (1997), *Moving Pictures: A New Theory of Film Genres, Feelings, and Cognition* (Oxford: Clarendon Press).

Halberstam, Judith (1991), 'Skin-flick: posthuman gender in Jonathan Demme's *The Silence of the Lambs*', *Camera Obscura*, 27: 37–53.

Haskell, Molly (1973), *From Reverence to Rape: The Treatment of Women in the Movies* (New York: Penguin Books).

Hauge, Michael (1988), *Writing Screenplays That Sell* (London: Elm Tree Books).

Heath, Stephen (1981), *Questions of Cinema* (London: Macmillan).

───── (1999), 'Cinema and psychoanalysis: parallel histories', in Bergstrom (1999).

Heath, Stephen (1975), 'Film and system: terms of analysis', *Screen*, 16, 1: 7–77; 16, 2: 91–113.

Henderson, Brian (1976), 'Toward a non-bourgeois camera style', in Nichols (1976: 422–38).

Hillier, Jim (ed.) (1985), *Cahiers du Cinéma. The 1950s: Neo-Realism, Hollywood, New Wave* (Cambridge, Mass.: Harvard University Press).

——— (ed.) (1986), *Cahiers du Cinéma. The 1960s: New Wave, New Cinema, Reevaluating Hollywood* (Cambridge, Mass.: Harvard University Press).

Howard, David, and Edward Mabley (1995), *The Tools of Screenwriting* (New York: St. Martins Press).

Hughes, Robert (1955), '*On the Waterfront*: a defence', *Sight and Sound*, 24, 4: 214–15.

Hüser, Rembert (1997), 'Crossing the *Threshold*: interview with Kaja Silverman', *Discourse*, 19, 3.

Jacobs, Lewis (1939), *The Rise of the American Film* (New York: Harcourt Brace).

Jameson, Fredric (1972), *The Prison House of Language* (Princeton: Princeton University Press).

——— (1981), *The Political Unconscious: Narrative as a Socially Symbolic Act* (Ithaca: Cornell University Press).

——— (1990), *Signatures of the Visible* (London: Routledge).

——— (1992), 'Nostalgia for the present', in Jane Gaines (ed.), *Classical Hollywood Narrative: The Paradigm Wars* (Durham, NC: Duke University Press): 253–73.

Jameson, Richard (1980), 'Style vs. "style"', *Film Comment*, Mar.–Apr.: 9–14.

Jay, Martin (1993), *Downcast Eyes: The Denigration of Vision in Twentieth Century French Thought* (Berkeley: University of California Press).

Kaplan, Abraham (1964), *Conduct of Inquiry: Methodology for Behavioral Science* (San Francisco: Chandler).

Kavanaugh, James (1980), '"Son of a bitch": feminism, humanism, and science in *Alien*', *October*, 13: 91–100.

Kenny, Anthony (1982), *The Computation of Style* (Oxford: Pergamon Press).

Kleinhans, Chuck (1976), 'New theory, new questions', *Jump Cut*, 12/13: 37–8.

Klinger, Barbara (1994), *Melodrama and Meaning: History, Culture, and the Films of Douglas Sirk* (Bloomington: Indiana University Press).

Kuntzel, Thierry (1978), 'The film work', *Enclitic*, 2, 1: 39–62.

——— (1980), 'The film work, 2', *Camera Obscura*, 5: 6–69.

Landow, George P. (1997), *Hypertext 2.0: The Convergence of Contemporary Critical Theory and Technology* (Baltimore: Johns Hopkins University Press).

Lesage, Julia (1986), '*S/Z* and *Rules of the Game*', in Nichols (1986: 476–500).

Le Sueur, Marc A. (1975), 'Film criticism and the mannerist alternative, or Pauline and Stanley and Richard and Agnes', *Journal of Popular Film*, 4, 4: 326–33.

Lévi-Strauss, Claude (1972), *Structural Anthropology* (London: Penguin).

Lewis, David (1979), 'Possible worlds', in Michael J. Loux (ed.), *The Possible and the Actual: Readings in the Metaphysics of Modality* (Ithaca and London: Cornell University Press, 1979): 182–9.

Luppa, Nicholas V. (1998), *Designing Interactive Digital Media* (Boston: Focal Press).

Lynch, David, and Barry Gifford (1997), *Lost Highway* (London: Faber and Faber).

MacCabe, Colin (1985), 'Realism and cinema: notes on some Brechtian theses', in *Theoretical Essays: Film, Linguistics, Literature* (Manchester: Manchester University Press): 33–57.

———— (1986), 'Theory and film: principles of realism and pleasure', in Philip Rosen (ed.), *Narrative, Apparatus, Ideology*: 179–97.

Martin, Adrian (1992), 'Mise en scène is dead, or the expressive, the excessive, the technical and the stylish', *Continuum*, 5, 2: 87–140.

McKee, Robert (1999), *Story* (New York: HarperCollins).

Mellard, James (1998), 'Lacan and the New Lacanians: Josephine Hart's *Damage*, Lacanian tragedy, and the ethics of *Jouissance*', *PMLA*, 113, 3.

Metz, Christian (1974), *Film Language: A Semiotics of the Cinema*, trans. Michael Taylor (New York: Oxford University Press).

———— (1982), *Psychoanalysis and Cinema: The Imaginary Signifier* (London: Macmillan).

Modleski, Tania (1988), *The Women Who Knew Too Much: Hitchcock and Feminist Theory* (London: Routledge).

Mulvey, Laura (1975), 'Visual pleasure and narrative cinema', *Screen* 16, 3: 6–18.

———— (1989), *Visual and Other Pleasures* (London: Macmillan).

Murch, Walter (1995), *In the Blink of an Eye: A Perspective on Film Editing* (Los Angeles: Silman James Press).

Nichols, Bill (1976) (ed.), *Movies and Methods: An Anthology* (Berkeley: University of California Press).

———— (1986), *Movies and Methods*, vol. ii (Berkeley: University of California Press).

———— (1989), *Representing Reality* (Bloomington: Indiana University Press).

Nizhny, Vladimir (1962), *Lessons with Eisenstein*, trans. and ed. by Ivor Montagu and Jay Leyda (New York: Hill and Wang).

Nochimson, Martha (1997), *The Passion of David Lynch: Wild at Heart in Hollywood* (Austin: University of Texas Press).

Oppenheimer, Jean (1997), 'Ministering to *The English Patient*', *American Cinematographer*, 78: 30–37.

Oudart, Jean-Pierre (1990), 'Cinema and suture', in Nick Browne (ed.), *Cahiers du Cinéma 1969–1972: The Politics of Representation* (Cambridge, Mass.: Harvard University Press): 45–57.

Perkins, Victor (1962), 'The British cinema', *Movie*, 1: 2–7.

—— (1972), *Film as Film: Understanding and Judging Movies* (Harmondsworth: Penguin Books).

—— *et al.* (1963), 'Movie differences', *Movie*, 8: 28–34.

Petric, Vlada (1982), 'From mise en scène to mise en shot: analysis of a sequence', *Quarterly Review of Film Studies*, 7, 3: 263–81.

Pfeil, Fred (1990), *Another Tale to Tell: Politics and Narrative in Postmodern Culture* (London: Verso).

—— (1993), 'From pillar to postmodern: race, class and gender in the male rampage film', *Socialist Review* 23, 2.

Pisters, Patricia (ed., 2001), *Micropolitics of Media Culture: Reading the Rhizomes of Deleuze and Guattari* (Amsterdam: Amsterdam University Press).

Plantinga, Carl, and Greg Smith (eds, 1999), *Passionate Views: Film, Cognition, and Emotion* (Baltimore: Johns Hopkins University Press).

Poague, Leland (1986), 'Links in a chain: *Psycho* and film classicism', in Marshall Deutelbaum and Leland Poague (eds), *A Hitchcock Reader* (Ames: Iowa State University Press).

Propp, Vladimir (1973), *Morphology of the Folktale* (Austin: University of Texas Press).

Reiter, Rayne R. (ed.) (1974), *Towards an Anthropology of Women* (New York: Monthly Review Press).

Rescher, Nicholas (1969), 'The concept of nonexistent possibles', in *Essays in Philosophical Analysis* (Pittsburgh: University of Pittsburgh Press).

—— (1975), *A Theory of Possibility* (Oxford: Blackwell).

—— (1979), 'The ontology of the possible', in Michael J. Loux (ed.), *The Possible and the Actual: Readings in the Metaphysics of Modality* (Ithaca and London: Cornell University Press): 166–81.

Rodowick, David (1991), *The Difficulty of Difference: Psychoanalysis, Sexual Difference, and Film Theory* (New York and London: Routledge).

Rose, Jacqueline (1986), 'The cinematic apparatus: problems in current theory', in *Sexuality in the Field of Vision* (London: Verso).

Rosen, Marjorie (1973), *Popcorn Venus: Women, Movies and the American Dream* (New York: Coward, McCann, and Geoghegan).

Rosen, Philip (ed., 1986), *Narrative, Apparatus, Ideology: A Film Theory Reader* (New York: Columbia University Press).

Rotha, Paul (1930), *The Film till Now* (London: Cape and Harrison).

Ryle, Gilbert (1949), *The Concept of Mind* (London: Hutchinson).

Sadoul, George (1949), *Histoire du cinéma mondial: des origines à nos jours* (Paris: Flammarion).

Salt, Barry (1974), 'The statistical style analysis of motion pictures', *Film Quarterly*, 28, 1: 13–22.

——— (1992), *Film Style and Technology: History and Analysis* (London: Starword).

Sarris, Andrew (1970), Review of *Rosemary's Baby, Confessions of a Cultist: On the Cinema, 1955–1969* (New York: Simon and Schuster): 373–6.

——— (1996), *The American Cinema: Directors and Directions* (New York: Da Capo).

Shaviro, Steven (1994), *The Cinematic Body* (Minneapolis: University of Minnesota Press).

Sigelman, Lee, and William Jacoby (1996), 'The not-so-simple art of imitation: pastiche, literary style, and Raymond Chandler', *Computers and the Humanities*, 30, 1: 11–28.

Silverman, Kaja (1988), *The Acoustic Mirror: The Female Voice in Psychoanalysis and Cinema* (Bloomington: Indiana University Press).

——— (1992), *Masculinity at the Margins* (London: Routledge).

Smith, Murray (1995), *Engaging Characters: Fiction, Emotion, and the Cinema* (Oxford: Clarendon Press).

Staiger, Janet (1992), *Interpreting Films: Studies in the Historical Reception of American Cinema* (Princeton: Princeton University Press).

——— (1993) 'Taboos and totems', in Jim Collins, Hilary Radner, and Ava Preacher Collins (eds), *Film Theory Goes to the Movies* (London: Routledge): 142–54.

Stam, Robert (1992), *Subversive Pleasures: Bakhtin, Cultural Criticism, and Film* (Baltimore: Johns Hopkins University Press).

——— (2000), *Film Theory: An Introduction* (Oxford: Blackwell).

Studlar, Gaylyn (1988), *In the Realm of Pleasure* (Urbana: University of Illinois Press).

Tan, Ed (1996), *Emotion and the Structure of Narrative Film: Film as an Emotion Machine* (Mahwah, NJ: Erlbaum).

Telotte, J.P., and John McCarty (1998), 'Roman Polanski', in Andrew Sarris (ed.), *St. James Film Directors Encyclopedia* (New York: St. James Press): 387–90.

Theweleit, Klaus (1994), 'Sirenengesang, Polizeisirenen', in A. Rost (ed.), *Bilder der Gewalt* (Frankfurt/M: Verlag der Autoren): 35–70.

Thompson, Kristin (1999), *Storytelling in the New Hollywood: Understanding Classical Narrative Technique* (Cambridge, Mass.: Harvard University Press).

Truffaut, François (1976), 'A certain tendency of the French cinema', in Nichols (1976: 224–37).

Vaz, Mark Cotta (1996), *Industrial Light and Magic: Into the Digital Realm* (London: Virgin Publishing).

Wexman, Virginia Wright (1979), 'Roman Polanski: critical survey', in Gretchen Bisplinghoff and Virginia Wright Wexman, *Roman Polanski: A Guide to References and Resources* (Boston: G.K. Hall): 7–12.

Williams, Linda (1984), 'When the woman looks', in M.A. Doane, P. Mellencamp, and L. Williams (eds), *Re-Vision: Essays in Feminist Film Criticism* (Frederick, Mass.: University Publications of America): 83–99.

Willis, Sharon (1997), 'Mutilated masculinities and their prostheses', in *High Contrast* (Durham, NC: Duke University Press): 27–59.

Wilson, David (ed.) (2000), *Cahiers du Cinéma, vol. iv, 1973–1978 : History, Ideology, Cultural Struggle* (London: Routledge).

Wollen, Peter (1982), *Readings and Writings: Semiotic Counter Strategies* (London: Verso).

Žižek, Slavoj (1992), *Enjoy your Symptom! Jacques Lacan in Hollywood and Out* (London: Routledge).

—— (1994), *Metastases of Enjoyment* (London: Verso).

—— (1999), 'You may!', *London Review of Books*, 21, 6 (18 March). Online at: http://www.lrb.co.uk/v21/n06/zize2106.htm

—— (2000), *The Art of the Ridiculous Sublime: On David Lynch's Lost Highway* (Washington: University of Washington Press).

—— (2001), *The Fright of Real Tears: Krzysztof Kieslowski Between Theory and Post-theory* (London: British Film Institute).

# Index

*48 hours* 62
*2001: A Space Odyssey* 157

*A Bug's Life* 161
*A Kind of Loving* 90
abstraction 2, 285
Aldrich, Robert 70
*Alien* 34
Allen, Richard 210
*All Quiet on the Western Front* 93
*All the President's Men* 143
Altman, Rick 14
Altman, Robert 85, 271
analysis viii, 1, 13–17, 23, 25, 27, 284–93
Anderson, Joseph 186
Anderson, Lindsay 120
*Antz* 161
*Apocalypse Now* 94
Aristotle 6, 7, 11, 26, 29, 30, 31, 33, 35, 39, 61, 84, 144, 147, 149
Arnheim, Rudolf 5, 8, 24, 196, 289
*auteur* 8, 18, 19, 24, 83, 86–7, 89, 91, 105, 117, 122, 126–8, 133, 144, 145, 288, 289

*Back to the Future* 18, 21, 66, Chapter 8 *passim*, 260, 261, 292
Bakhtin, Mikhail 29, 30, 64
Ballhaus, Michael 95
Barthes, Roland 43, 118, 121, 135, 147–55, 160, 166
*S/Z* 18, 19, 30, 121, Chapter 5 *passim*
*Battleship Potemkin* 204
Baudrillard, Jean 211
Baudry, Jean-Louis 202, 225, 252
Bazin, André 5, 7–8, 21, 24, 195–203, 204, 209, 211, 213, 265, 284, 289

Beardsley, Monroe 201–1, 285
Bellour, Raymond 17, 29, 35–6, 40–1, 42, 43, 46, 47, 50, 156, 223
Benjamin, Walter 232
Benveniste, Émile 15
Bergson, Henri 250, 270, 288
*Beyond Rangoon* 94
*Bible, The* 131
*Big Sleep, The* 17, 42, 53, 74, 132
*Birds, The* 40, 84, 256
*Bitter Moon* 123
*Blood and Sand* 93
*Body Heat,* 132
*Bonny and Clyde* 133
*Bostonians, The* 18
Bordwell, David 3, 7, 11, 15, 16, 17, 18, 20, 28, 29, 31, 35–6, 42, 43, 46, 58, 87, 88, 90, 92, 121, 122, 169–74, 180, 186, 187, 193, 233, 284, 285, 286, 289
Borzage, Frank 91
Braga, Lucia Santella 209
Branigan, Edward 15, 18, 20, 42, 43, 169, 174, 186, 187–90, 191, 193, 215, 284–5
*Brazil* 22, 64, 233, 234, 247
Brooks, Cleanth 16
Bruner, Jerome 161
Bukatman, Scott 28

*cahiers du cinéma* 29, 83, 85, 86, 126, 127, 130, 270
Cameron, Ian 88
Camper, Fred 82, 91–2
Carroll, Noël 14, 43, 84, 143, 193–4, 201, 233, 234
*Casino* 244

Cassavetes, John 271
*Caught* 108, 122
Chabrol, Claude 82, 83
*Chinatown* 18, 19, 66, Chapter 4 *passim*, 243, 289
Chomsky, Noam 15
*Citizen Kane* 100, 199, 200–1, 274
*City of Angels* 94
classical film theory 5, 7–8, 21, 24, 287
classical Hollywood 3, 8, 17, 18, Chapter 2 *passim*, 83, 122, 131, 144, 242, 271, 288–9
Clayton, Jack 90
Coen Brothers 85
cognitive film theory 3, 5, 9, 15, 18, 20, 25, 35, 54, Chapter 6 *passim*, 250, 272, 290
Colbert, Mary 94
colonialism 35, *see also* post-colonialism
coherence (Perkins) 84, 89, *see also* credibility
*Color of Money, The* 95
*Commando* 62
commentative heuristic 87–8, 89, 99, 123, 135
computer games, *see* video games
Conley, Tom 130, 134
Connors, Robert, and Edward Corbett 7, 11, 12, 25, 33
continuity editing, rules of 37, 42, 196, 203
*Conversation, The* 94
Copjec, Joan 236
Corrigan, Tim 28
*Cotton Club, The* 133
Craven, Wes 257
credibility (Perkins) 84, 85, 89, 101, 210, *see also* coherence
Creed, Barbara 257
*cul-de-sac* 123
Culler, Jonathan 121, 129, 144
Currie, Gregory 186

Day, Ernest 19
Dayan, Daniel 167, 202, 204

*Death and the Maiden* 123
*Death Becomes Her* 217, 218
Debord, Guy 167
deconstruction 18, 19, 35, 65, Chapter 4 *passim*, 242, 257, 286, 290
deep structure 66, 67–9
De Lauretis, Teresa 15, 223, 254
Deleuze, Gilles 18, 22, 250–1, 261–2, 264–7, 268, 269–73, 277–82, 292
  becoming, 22, 250, 272, 278
  body without organs, 22, 266, 271–2, 277–8
  deterritorialization, 22, 266, 277–8, 281
  the fold, 22, 266, 267, 272–3, 280–1
  movement (action) image, 22, 270–1, 272, 279
  time (crystal) image, 270–1, 279
Derrida, Jacques 139–40, 146, 286
*Dial M for Murder* 180
*Die Hard* 18, Chapter 2 *passim*, 144, 222, 298
*Die Hard 2* 28
*Die Hard with a Vengeance* 28
digital images 9, 10, 18, 21, 161, 195, 209–19, 290
disavowal 15
*Disputed Passage* 82, 91–2
*Diva* 64
Doane, Mary Ann 39, 253, 254
*Dog Day Afternoon* 34
Donato, Eugene 285
*Double Indemnity* 189
*Dragonheart*, 217
*Dressed to Kill* 256

*Easy Rider* 132
Ebert, Roger 44, 69, 72, 73
Eisenstein, Sergei 81, 102, 197, 203–4
emotion 3, 187
*English Patient, The* 11, 18, 19, Chapter 3 *passim*, 289
enunciation 15, 16
*ET* 241
Evans, Robert 131, 132

*eXistenZ* 20, 280
expressivist heuristic 87–8, 89, 91, 94, 101

*Falling Down* 57
Fellini, Frederico 87
feminist film theory 9–10, 11, 15, 18, 22, 26, 41, 251–61, 276, 281, 282, 292
Ferrara, Abel 85
fetishism 3, 10, 16, 22, 39, 155, 220, 243, 253, 273, 280
*Fifth Element, The* 18, 19, 20, Chapter 5 *passim*, 290
*Fight Club* 244, 282
film noir 38, 124, 126, 128, 131, 132, 142, 143, 144, 237, 242, 289
*First Blood* 43
Fiske, John 164
Flaherty, Robert 197
Flower-MacCannell, Juliet 236
Floyd, Nigel 164
focalization 15, 174, 188, 190, 191, 215
Ford, John 127
*Forrest Gump* 247
Foucault, Michel 18, 22, 251, 261–5, 266, 267–9, 273, 274, 276, 281–2, 285, 292
    institution as discourse 22, 267–8, 273, 275
    madness and pathology 22, 268
    persecution 22, 269
    planes of vision (scopic regimes, enfolding gazes) 22, 268
    power and discipline 22, 268, 274
    sensory, tactile, sonorous surface 22, 269, 274
*Frantic* 123
Freud, Sigmund 18, 21, 38, 47, 54, 220–6, 243, 247, 249, 251, 262, 263, 265, 282, 286, 287, 292
*Freud: The Secret Passion* 131
Fuller, Sam 128

*Game, The* 208
generalization 9, 19, 285
Genette, Gérard 16, 29, 43

*Ghost* 94
*Gigi* 40, 41
Godard, Jean-Luc 82, 83, 136, 204
*Godfather Part III, The* 94
*Golden Bowl, The* 19
*Goodfellows* 244
*Gorillas in the Mist* 94
Greimas, A.J. 26, 33–4, 40, 43, 49, 54–5, 147
Griffith, D.W. 36
Grodal, Torben 186
Guattari, Felix 264, 265, 266, 271, 277, 278, 280

Halberstam, Judith 259–60, 282
*Halloween* 256
*Hangover Square* 43
*Hannibal* 22
Hawks, Howard 36, 127, 137
Heath, Stephen 42–3, 56, 167, 202, 211, 215, 218, 238, 252, 259, 260, 282
heightened significance 84, 89, 96
Henderson, Brian 204–5
*High Noon* 46
Hinson, Hal 44, 45, 69
Hitchcock, Alfred 10, 36, 56, 58, 88, 127, 128, 136, 180, 238, 248, 256, 257, 271
Holt, Seth 91
*Hook* 217
Hooper, Tobe 105, 257
Hoveda, Fereydoun 130
*Howards End* 19
Howe, Desson 45, 62
Hughes, Robert 120
Huston, John 131
hypertext 161–2

idealization 2
*Independence Day* 242
interpretation, 16, 27, 284–93
    symptomatic 220–1, 231–6, 247, 287, 292
*Invasion of the Body Snatchers* (Siegel) 119

*Jade* 133
Jameson, Fredric 29, 34, 143, 167, 232
Jameson, William 93
*Jaws* 133
*Johnny Guitar* 84–5
Joly, Jacques 80
*Jurassic Park* 9, 10, 18, 21, 84, 109, 110,
    111–15, Chapter 7 *passim*, 291

Kaplan, Abraham 6, 129
Katz, Elihu 167
Kavanaugh, James 34
Kenny, Anthony 104–5
Kieslowski, Krzysztof 238
*Kiss Me Deadly* 181
Kleinhans, Chuck, vii, viii
Klinger, Barbara 254
*Knife in the Water* 123
'knowingness' (Robert Ray) 78–9, 122,
    143, 229–30, 231, 261, 291
Kristeva, Julia 146
Kuntzel, Thierry 43, 47, 75, 224

Lacan, Jacques, 18, 21, 22, 220–6, 230,
    236–7, 242, 247, 248, 249, 251, 266,
    282, 292, *see also* new Lacanians
*Lady from Shanghai* 142
Lakoff, George 15
Landow, George 161
Lang, Fritz 128, 136
*Last Action Hero, The* 241
Lesage, Julia 155–6
Le Sueur, Marx A. 83–4, 85, 86
*Lethal Weapon* 43, 54, 55, 62, 64
*Letter From an Unknown Woman* 107, 122
Lévi-Strauss, Claude 26, 30, 31, 32–3, 35,
    40, 43, 47, 144, 147, 229, 286
Lewis, David 212
*Lonedale Operator, The* 36, 40
Losey, Joseph 128
*Lost Highway* 9, 18, 20, 31, Chapter 6
    *passim*, 208, 290–1
*Lost World, The* (1925) 217
*Lost World: Jurassic Park, The* 18, 21,
    Chapter 7 *passim*, 291

Lucas, George 211
Luppa, Nicholas 163
Lynch, David 168–9, 193, 238

*M* 47
MacCabe, Colin 29, 56, 202, 204, 208
male body 66, 69–71
male rampage films (Pfeil) 43, 54, 64–5
Malle, Louis 128
*Maltese Falcon, The* 131, 132
Mamoulian, Rouben 93
*Man of a Thousand Faces* 133
Mann, Anthony 70
Mann, Michael 85
mannerism 18, *see also* mise–en–scène,
    mannerist
Mannoni, Octave 15
*Marathon Man* 133
*Marnie* 36
*Mars Attacks!* 242
Martin, Adrian 83–5, 88–9, 289
Marxism 10, 250, 263, 265, 286, 287
*Matrix, The* 20, 280
*Maurice* 19
McCarty, John 123
McGee, Robert 131
Mellard, James 236–7
*Memento* 20, 280
*Mépris, Le* 136
method viii, 4, 5–13, 17, 23, 288
*metteur en scène* 86, 89, 91, 93, 127
Metz, Christian 1, 15, 42, 43, 225, 251,
    252
Milestone, Lewis 93
Minnelli, Vincente 86, 127
*mise en abîme* 47, 49, 52, 131, 143, 144,
    280
*mise en scène* 18, 54, Chapter 3 *passim*,
    130, 133, 135, 144, 224, 288, 289,
    291
    classical 83–5, 89, 91, 94–5, 189,
        289
    expressionist 83, 85, 89, 289
    mannerist 83, 85–6, 88, 89, 91, 95,
        178, 289

*mise-en-scène* heuristics 88–90, *see also* commentative heuristic, expressivist heuristic
*mise en shot* 81, 102–3, 105
Modleski, Tania 15, 254
Morton, A.Q. 104
*Mosquito Coast, The* 93
*Most Dangerous Game, The* 43, 47
Mourlet, Michel 80, 130
*Movie* 82, 126
Mulvey, Laura 15, 167, 230, 252–4, 256, 259
Murch, Walter 19, 92–3, 94, 98
Murnau, F.W. 197
*My Beautiful Laundrette* 64

narration 16, 18, 20, 37–8, 64, Chapter 6 *passim*
  unreliable 172
narrative, 3, 4, 9, 11, 12, 14, 15, 16, 18, 19, 20, Chapter 2 *passim*, 149, 161, 164, 166–7, Chapter 6 *passim*, 232, 281, 289–90
  Oedipal, 21, 33, 38–9, 41, 46, 55, 61, 66, 68, 70, 141, 142, Chapter 8 *passim*, 249, 273, 292
  *see also* focalization narration
new film history 2, 23
new Lacanians 18, 21, 236–48, 249, 270
new media, 18, *see also* digital image, video games
Nochimson, Martha 168
Nichols, Bill 200
*North by Northwest* 41, 74, 156, 180, 223, 224
*Notorious* 88
Noyce, Philip 128
*Nurse Betty* 280

*On the Waterfront* 119–20
*One Plus One* 204
Ophuls, Max 107–8, 122, 128
Oudart, Jean-Pierre 202, 204

*Parallax View, The* 143

Paramount decree 61
Parker, Alan 128
*Party Girl* 91
*Passage to India* 19
Paul, William 90
Peirce, Charles Sanders 15, 265
Perkins, Victor 82, 83, 84, 85, 90–1, 101, 289
Peterson, Wolfgang 128
Petric, Vlada 81
Pfeil, Fred 54–5, 64–6, 70, 71, 77, 232–3, 234, 236, 240
*Pirates* 123
Plantinga, Carl 186
Poague, Leland 10
poetics of production 130, 131–3
poetics of semiosis 130, 133–42
Polanski, Roman 117, 122–4, 126, 130, 131, 133, 136
*Poltergeist* 105
*Popeye* 133
possible worlds 18, 21, 195, 211–13
post-colonialism 35, 66, 71–3, 272
*Postman Always Rings Twice, The* 132
post-modernism 35, 64, 65, 144, 259
post-structuralism 3, 9, 18, 19, 27, 35, 265, *see also* Barthes, Roland, *S/Z*
*Predator* 43, 62
Preminger, Otto 127
Propp, Vladimir 26, 29, 31, 33, 39, 43, 47, 49, 58, 144, 147, 149, 229, 255
*Psycho* 10, 182, 256
psychoanalytic film theory 3, 5, 9, 10, 15, 18, 22, 25, 27, 54, 169–70, Chapter 8 *passim*, 249–61, 273
pull focus 94, 98–9
*Pulp Fiction* 22, 76, 241, 243, 247

queer theory 22, 264, 292
Quine, W.V.O. viii

race 27, 35, 42, 64–5, 69–71, 232, 235–6, 239–40, 242, 245, 247, 268
*Rain Man* 94
Ray, Nicholas 128

realism, 36, Chapter 7 *passim*, 291
  ontological 198–201
  dramatic 198–9, 205, 213
  psychological 198–9
  *see also* credibility
*Rear Window* 42, 279
reception studies 2, 3, 10
Reisz, Karl 90
*Remains of the Day, The* 19
Renoir, Jean 89, 198
Rescher, Nicholas 212
rhetoric 6–13
  *actio* 7, 13
  *dispositio* 7, 11–12, 17–18, 23, 24, 149
  *elocutio* 7, 12–13, 23, 24
  *inventio* 6–11, 23–4
  *memoria* 7, 13
  topics 7–11
  tropes 12
Richardson, Tony 90
Rivette, Jacques 36, 82, 83
*Rocky Horror Picture Show* 167
Rodowick, David 130, 134, 225
*Room with a View* 19
*Ronde, La* 108
*Rosemary's Baby* 120–1, 123
Rosenbaum, Jonathan, 289
Rudolph, Alan 85
*Rules of the Game* 156
Russian formalism 29, 31, 35, 171
Ryle, Gilbert 5, 6, 23

Salt, Barry 43, 81, 103–4, 106–8, 110
Sarris, Andrew 120–1, 126–7, 132
Saussure, Ferdinand de 15
*Scarface* (Hawks) 137
Schatz, Thomas 28
Schlesinger, John 90
Scorsese, Martin 95
Scott, Ridley 128
Seale, John 19, 94–5, 101, 114
selective focus 94, 98–9, 100–1
semiotics
  film semiotics 5, 8, 15, 251, 265, 287, 293

semiotic square (Greimas) 26, 32–5, 40, 54–5, 64, 72
  *see also* Barthes, Roland
*Se7en* 22, 282
Shaviro, Steven 264
*Shining, The* 34
Shklovsky, Victor 31
*Silence of the Lambs, The* 18, 22, 66, Chapter 9 *passim*, 292
Silverman, Kaja 15, 130, 134, 254, 264
Siodmak, Robert 128
Sirk, Douglas 122
*Sliver* 133
Smith, Barbara 121
Smith, Greg 186
Smith, Murray 186
sound 14, 27, 29, 191, 196, 197, 290–1
spectacle 18, 26, 27, 29, 45, 62–3, 68, 77–8, 166–7
*Speed* 271
Spielberg, Steven 17, 21, 105, 115, 133, 195, 205, 241, 290, 291
Staiger, Janet 10, 17, 31, 58, 282
Stam, Robert 284
Sternberg, Josef von 86
statistical style analysis 18, 19, Chapter 3 *passim*, 290
*Strangers on a Train* 180
Stroheim, Eric von 197
structuralism 3, 9, Chapter 2 *passim*, 146, 147, 149, 189, 225, 249, 282, 286
style (definitions) 104, 171
stylometry, *see* statistical style analysis
*Sunset Boulevard* 189
surface structure 66, 67–9
surrealism 124
*Surviving Picasso* 19
*Suspicion* 56
suture 202, 230, 281
Sylbert, Richard 133

*Talented Mr Ripley, The* 19, 94
Tan, Ed 186

*Taste of Fear* 91
Taylor, John Russell 87
Telotte, J.P. 123
*Tenant, The* 123
*Terminator, The* 271
*Terminator 2* 217
Theatre of the Absurd 124
thematic criticism, 18, 19, Chapter 4
    *passim*, 224, 225, 288, 289
*Things to Do in Denver When You're
    Dead* 244
theory viii, 3, 4–5, 17, 23, 284, 288
Thompson, Kristin 17, 28, 31, 43, 58
Thomson, David 53
*Three Days of the Condor* 143
*Titanic* 210
Todorov, Tzvetan 51, 121
*Total Recall* 20, 22, 247
*Touch of Evil* 42
Towne, Robert 126, 131, 132
*Toy Story* 161
tradition of quality 86
'trained incapacity' (Kaplan) 6, 129
*Treasure of Sierra Madre* 131
Troll, Jan 128
Truffaut, François 82, 86, 127
*Truman Show, The* 204, 208, 280
Tsivian, Yuri 43
*Twelve Monkeys* 22, 247
*Twister* 271
*Two Jakes, The* 132

uncanny 168–9
*Urban Cowboy* 133

Verhoven, Paul 128
video games 18, 19–20, 63, 78, Chapter 5
    *passim*, 290–1
  rules of video game construction
    162–4
Vidor, King 86
voyeurism 3, 10, 15, 16, 22, 38, 155, 230,
    253, 273, 279

*We Live Again* 93
Welles, Orson 86, 89, 128, 198, 200
Wexman, Virginia Wright 124
*Where No Vultures Fly* 205, 213
*Who Framed Roger Rabbit?* 214
Wilder, Billy 128
Williams, Linda 15
Willis, Sharon 70–1
Wiseman, Frederick 201
*Witness* 94
*Wolf Trap, The* 88
Wollen, Peter 29
Wyler, William 89, 198, 199

*Young Mr Lincoln*, 29

*Zelig* 247
Žižek, Slavoj 18, 21, 221, 236–42, 245–8,
    259, 270, 274, 280